Contemporary Islam

Islamic interpretation is easily among the most controversial subjects in contemporary scholarship and social commentary. Both in the Islamic world and in the West, interpreting Islam has become a "cottage industry." The ranks of interpreters are incredibly diverse, including not only a wide range of Muslim scholars, activists and traditionalists, but also foreign policy experts, government officials, journalists and religious leaders. Everyone, it seems, has become a stakeholder in the future of Islam.

Starting with the assumption that the contentious pluralism of contemporary Islamic thought contains the hidden promise of a new and dynamic synthesis, *Contemporary Islam* explores the hermeneutical as well as practical bases for creative responses to some of the most crucial issues facing Muslims: political participation, democracy, human rights, terrorism, nonviolence, peacemaking and intercultural dialogue. By assembling the voices of a remarkably distinguished group of scholars, this volume provides a compelling model for bridging the gaps that plague Islamic interpreters – gaps between ideals and realities, between traditional and modern interpretive sciences, and between the "House of Islam" (dar al-Islam) and the Western political world.

Contemporary Islam provides a compelling case for renewal, and for the reassertion of Islamic dynamism within the current global context of human experience, making it essential reading for students and scholars with interests in Islam and politics.

Abdul Aziz Said is the senior ranking Professor of International Relations and also occupies the Mohammed Said Farsi Chair of Islamic Peace at American University (Washington, DC). His publications include: *Concepts of International Politics in Global Perspective* and *Peace and Conflict Resolution in Islam*.

Mohammed Abu-Nimer is a Professor of International Peace and Conflict Resolution Studies at American University (Washington, DC). Abu-Nimer has published many articles on the application of conflict resolution models in non-Western contexts. His latest publication is *Nonviolence and Peacebuilding in Islam: Theory and Practice*.

Meena Sharify-Funk is currently an Adjunct Lecturer on Islam at the University of Waterloo in Ontario, Canada. She has written and presented a number of articles and papers on women, Islam and the politics of interpretation. She also has co-edited the book, *Cultural Diversity and Islam*.

Contemporary Islam
Dynamic, not Static

Abdul Aziz Said,
Mohammed Abu-Nimer and
Meena Sharify-Funk

Routledge
Taylor & Francis Group
LONDON AND NEW YORK

First published 2006
by Routledge
2 Park Square, Milton Park, Abingdon, Oxon OX14 4RN

Simultaneously published in the USA and Canada
by Routledge
270 Madison Ave, New York, NY 10016

Routledge is an imprint of the Taylor & Francis Group

© 2006 Abdul Aziz Said, Mohammed Abu-Nimer, and Meena Sharify-Funk

Typeset in Garamond by
Taylor & Francis Books
Printed and bound in Great Britain by
Antony Rowe Ltd, Chippenham, Wiltshire

All rights reserved. No part of this book may be reprinted or reproduced or
utilised in any form or by any electronic, mechanical, or other means, now
known or hereafter invented, including photocopying and recording, or in any
information storage or retrieval system, without permission in writing from
the publishers.

British Library Cataloguing in Publication Data
A catalogue record for this book is available from the British Library

Library of Congress Cataloging in Publication Data
A catalog record for this book has been requested

ISBN10 0–415–77011–4   ISBN13 978–0–415–77011–8 (hbk)
ISBN10 0–415–77012–2   ISBN13 978–0–415–77012–5 (pbk)

Library
University of Texas
at San Antonio

For Mohammed Said Farsi and Hani Farsi: through their efforts they have helped to promote the study and understanding of Islamic values and traditions, and of Islamic contributions to the quest for global peace and human solidarity.

This book is also dedicated to the many seekers of knowledge who, by upholding the spirit of Alexandria, challenge all peoples to rethink boundaries and to connect with perennial human capacities for creative imagination and moral courage.

Contents

Biographies

Editors

Abdul Aziz Said is a Full Professor of International Relations at American University (Washington, DC) where he also occupies the Mohammed Said Farsi Chair of Islamic Peace and is the Director of the American University's Center for Global Peace. He is responsible for developing several educational, research, and outreach programs and is a frequent lecturer and participant in national and international dialogue and peace conferences, lecturing in more than one hundred universities in the United States and in all of the continents. Some of Said's books include: *Concepts of International Politics in Global Perspective*, *Peace and Conflict Resolution in Islam*, and *Cultural Diversity and Islam*.

Mohammed Abu-Nimer is an Associate Professor of International Peace and Conflict Resolution at American University's School of International Service (Washington, DC). Abu-Nimer has published many articles on the Israeli-Palestinian conflict, application of conflict resolution models in non-western context, and conflict resolution training models in journals and various edited books. His latest publications are *Reconciliation, Coexistence, and Justice: Theory and Practice* and *Nonviolence and Peacebuilding in Islam: Theory and Practice*.

Meena Sharify-Funk is currently an Adjunct Lecturer on Islam at the University of Waterloo in Ontario, Canada. She also has a PhD in International Relations from American University's School of International Service (Washington, DC), with areas of specialization in International Peace and Conflict Resolution, Islamic Studies and a particular focus on the status of women in the Islamic world. She has written and presented a number of articles and papers on women, Islam and the politics of interpretation, Islamic conceptions of peace and conflict resolution, and the role of cultural and religious factors in peacemaking and has co-edited the book, *Cultural Diversity and Islam*. She has also coordinated three international conferences: one at the Washington National Cathedral, entitled "Two Sacred Paths: Islam and Christianity, A Call for Understanding" (Fall 1998), one at American University in Washington, DC, entitled "Cultural Diversity and Islam" (Fall 1998), and another at the Library of Alexandria, Egypt, entitled, "Contemporary Islamic Synthesis" (Fall 2003).

Contributors

Zainah Anwar is the Executive Director of Sisters in Islam, an organization of professional Muslim women in Malaysia committed to promoting women's rights. She is also the director of the Asian-Pacific Resource and Research Center for Women. Anwar was formerly a member of the Human Rights Commission of Malaysia, Chief Programme Officer for the Political Division at the Commonwealth Secretariat in London, and a Senior Analyst at the Institute of Strategic and International Studies.

Mohammed Arkoun is Professor Emeritus of History of Islamic Thought at the Sorbonne Nouvelle (Paris III) in France. He has been Visiting Professor at numerous universities, including: Princeton, UCLA, Temple (Philadelphia), Amsterdam, and Louvain-La-Neuve (Belgium). A Berber from the mountainous region of Algeria, Arkoun has written extensively on Arabic and Islamic culture and thought, and has been published in various languages. Some of his publications include: *L'Humanisme Arabe au I'VE/Xe Siecle, Pour une Critique de la Raison Islamique, La Pensee Arabe, Rethinking Islam* (translated by Robert D. Lee) and *The Unthought in Contemporary Islamic Thought*.

Azyumardi Azra is currently the Rector and Professor of Islamic History at the Syarif Hidayatullah State Islamic University in Jakarta, Indonesia. He also is a founder and chief editor for *Studia Islamika*, an Indonesian journal of Islamic studies and is on the board of editors for *Journal of Qur'anic Studies*, SOAS in London. Azra has been a visiting professor at University of Philippines, Diliman, University of Malaya, and New York University. Additionally, he has given lectures and presented papers at various universities, conferences, seminars, and workshops worldwide on Islamic education, civil society, politics and theology.

Asma Barlas is an Associate Professor and Chair of the Department of Politics and former director of the Center for the Study of Culture, Race, and Ethnicity at Ithaca College, New York. She has a BA in English Literature and Philosophy and a MA in Journalism from Pakistan, and a MA and PhD in International Studies from the University of Denver in Colorado. Barlas was born in Pakistan, where she was one of the first women to be inducted into the Foreign Service. Her career was cut short, however, when General Zia ul Haq fired her for criticizing his military regime. She then joined an opposition paper, *The Muslim*, as assistant editor but was forced to leave the country for the US in 1983 where she later got political asylum. Barlas has received several fellowships and grants, including from the United Nations Department of Public Information, the American Association of University Women, and the American Institute of Pakistan Studies. Her most recent work has focused on how Muslims produce religious knowledge, especially patriarchal exegesis of the Qur'an. She has explored this theme in her book, *"Believing Women" in Islam: Unreading Patriarchal Interpretations of the Qur'an*, as well as in book chapters and journal articles published in the *Journal of Qur'anic Studies* and in *Macalester International*. She also has been invited to present her work at international conferences and venues in

Germany, Britain, Pakistan, and (via digital video) India. (A list of her writings can be found at http://www.ithaca.edu/faculty/abarlas/index.htm.)

Mustafa Ceric is the HE Grand Mufti Bosnia and Herzegovina. He received his doctorate degree at the University of Chicago, Department of Near Eastern Languages & Civilizations (NELC), in the field of Islamic Theology. He has been a visiting lecturer at many universities and Islamic Centers on various Islamic issues. Currently, he is involved in Muslim-Christian dialogue as a member of the Ad Hoc Steering Committee of the European Council of Religious Leaders for Improved Muslim-Christian Relations. Work for this committee and other dialogue initiatives helped earned him the 2003 UNESCO Félix Houphouët-Boigny Peace Prize.

Farid Esack is a South African Muslim theologian who studied in South Africa, Pakistan (Islamic Theology), the United Kingdom (Qur'anic Hermeneutics) and Germany (Biblical Hermeneutics). As a person committed to inter-religious solidarity for justice and peace and the struggle against apartheid, he played a leading role in the United Democratic Front, The Call of Islam, the Organization of People Against Sexism and the World Conference on Religion and Peace. Among others, he has written *But Moses went to Pharaoh, Qur'an, Liberation and Pluralism, On Being a Muslim*, and his most recent book, *A Short Introduction to the Qur'an*. Esack has also published widely on Islam, gender, liberation theology, inter-faith relations, religion and identity and Qur'anic hermeneutics. Formerly a National Commissioner on Gender Equality appointed by President Nelson Mandela, he has taught at the Universities of Amsterdam and Hamburg and more recently at Union Theological Seminary in New York and the College of William & Mary. Currently, Esack occupies the Besl Chair in Religion and Ethics at Xavier University in Cincinnati, Ohio.

Nadia Mahmoud Mostafa is an Associate Professor of International Relations and the Director of the Center for Political Research and Studies, Faculty of Economics and Political Science at the Cairo University. She also is the Supervisor for the Dialogue of Civilizations Program at Cairo University. Her areas of interest are international relations in Islam, from both epistemological and theoretical levels.

Serif Mardin is currently the Chair of Islamic studies at Sabanci University in Istanbul, Turkey, and was also the former Ibn Khaldun Chair of Islamic Studies at American University's School of International Service (Washington, DC). His papers and chapters appear in numerous journals and edited books. Mardin's books include *Religion and Social Change in Turkey, The Complete Works of Serif Mardin Vol. I–IV*, and *Cultural Transitions in the Middle East*.

Armando Salvatore received his PhD from the European University Institute in Florence, Italy, 1994. He is currently a Senior Research Fellow at the Institute of Social Sciences, Humboldt University, Berlin, where he is completing his Habilitation. His PhD dissertation was granted the 1994 Malcolm Kerr Dissertation Award in the Social Sciences of MESA (Middle East Studies Association of North America). He founded, in 2000, the Forum of Social Research. His primary interest lies in the analysis of the multiple links between religious, political-philosophical, and legal traditions, and notions of practical and public reason. He links this program in social theory with an empirical interest for how a variety of traditions enter into tension with and impact upon global modernity through the activities of social movements and civil associations. Urban Egypt, Palestine/Israel, and various regions of Western Europe are currently his main areas of investigation.

Chaiwat Satha-Anand is a Professor of Political Science at Thammasat University in Bangkok, Thailand. For over twenty years, he has been working in the field of peace research, focusing specifically on Islam and nonviolence. In the past, he has served as the Vice President of Academic Affairs at Thammasat University and President of the Social Science Association of Thailand. His most recent publications include *Islam e Nonviolenza* and *The Frontiers of Nonviolence.*

Recep Senturk is an Associate Professor of Sociology who holds a PhD from Columbia University, New York. He is currently the Chair of History of Science in the TDV Center for Islamic Studies (ISAM), Istanbul. His primary interest is in the sociology of human rights and sociology of knowledge. His works include: *Modernization and Social Science, Narrative Social Structure: Anatomy of Hadith Transmission Network,* and *New Sociologies of Religion.* He is currently working on a book, entitled *Sociology of Rights: Human Rights in Islam between Universal and Communal Perspectives.*

A. Reza Sheikholeslami holds the Soudavar Chair of Persian Studies at Oxford University and is a Professorial Fellow at Wadham College. He has received awards from the Social Science Research Council and has been a Fulbright Fellow. Trained as a political scientist in the United States, he taught at the Department of Political Science, University of Washington, and subsequently was affiliated with the Middle East Center of Harvard University. Sheikholeslami's publications include articles on class, state, religion, and revolution in Iran. His books include: *Political Economy of Saudi Arabia* and *The Structure of Central Authority in Qajar Iran.*

Acknowledgments

This edited volume would not have been possible without the continuous support and encouragement of many individuals. We are grateful to all of them. First and foremost, we offer our gratitude to all who participated in the international conference, "Contemporary Islamic Synthesis," including those who were not able to submit their papers. We would like to give special thanks to Ismail Serageldin, director of the New Library of Alexandria, Egypt, for hosting this timely gathering, and to his devoted staff, especially Khaled Khouessah, Hanan Abdelrazek, and Mona Elnashar. Thanks are also due to Betty Sitka of the American University Center for Global Peace, whose attentiveness to crucial logistical and administrative tasks helped to make the conference possible, and to Zen Hunter-Ishikawa and Jacqueline Lee, who assisted with implementation of the conference program. We also want to recognize Carrie Trybulec for her commitment, energy, and dedication to the American University's International Peace and Conflict Resolution Division and its many timely projects.

A debt of appreciation is also owed to His Royal Highness Prince Bandar bin Sultan bin Abdulaziz, former Ambassador of Saudi Arabia to the United States, and to Ambassador Ahmed Khattan, of the Royal Embassy of Saudi Arabia. Lastly, we would like to thank Nathan C. Funk for his many significant contributions to the planning and facilitation of the conference, and for his efforts to serve as a resource to the editors of this volume.

Introduction

Few contemporary topics are more controversial than Islamic interpretation. In the West as well as in the Muslim world, interpreting Islam has become a virtual "cottage industry." The ranks of interpreters are incredibly diverse, including terrorism experts, government policymakers, and journalists as well as religious studies scholars, political scientists, Muslim *'alims* and religious fundamentalists of varied confessional backgrounds. Though traditional religious leaders would not recognize many interpreters' views as authoritative, interest in how Islam is understood and practiced has expanded dramatically in recent years. Among Muslims as well as among non-Muslims, it seems that everyone has become a stakeholder in the future of Islam.

For most Westerners, tragic events such as 9/11 in Washington DC and New York City, 3/11 in Madrid, and 7/7 in London provide the context of relevance for interest in Islam. Why have a significant minority of Muslims accepted radical teachings? What are these teachings, and how can they be counteracted? Though many Muslims share these concerns about the misappropriation of Islamic symbolism, the stakes for believers are different, and higher. Committed Muslims cannot be interested in Islamic interpretation for instrumental reasons alone; they must also think seriously about issues of truthfulness and authenticity: How can Muslims remain true to the essential teachings of a 1400-year-old monotheistic tradition, while also enhancing their ability to engage the modern world and overcome experiences of marginalization and decline?

Whatever the context of our interest may be, there is one question that ought to precede all efforts to generalize about what Islam demands of those who adhere to it: *Whose* Islam? Just as there are many Christianities and Judaisms, so, too, are there many formulations of Islamic piety and politics that contend for the attention of Muslims, and that represent themselves as the only "authentic" perspective to those who do not declare themselves believers. Only clear recognition of Islam's internal diversity can prevent gross distortions of contemporary Islamic realities, and provide a basis for exploration of more profound questions about how precepts of faith are translated into historical practices.

Whether we approach the subject of Islamic interpretation from "within" or "without," accepting Islam's internal diversity is the absolutely vital point of departure for approaching crucial questions about how Muslims can cope with worldly

challenges constructively: What does it mean to be Muslim in the twentieth (CE)/
fifteenth (CE) century? What can contemporary Islamic interpretation offer in
response to issues such as political participation, democracy, human rights,
terrorism, nonviolence, peacemaking, and intercultural dialogue? How can individual Muslims – who cannot look to a unified church for authoritative guidance –
remain true to their individual responsibility for seeking the Muslim ideal? What
role can Muslims outside of the Muslim world (Muslims in the Western societies)
play in redefining the current discourse? What is the role of non-Muslims in discussions about the meaning of Islam? And perhaps most importantly, who is willing to
come to the table? Such questions can only be answered in an intelligent and responsible manner if we recognize that – precepts of unity notwithstanding – Muslims are
answering these questions in diverse ways. Among the many voices articulating
visions for the future of Islam, those who are as committed to dialogue as they are to
their own solutions merit special attention.

The Spirit of Alexandria

On October 4–5, 2003, a group of distinguished scholars of Islam gathered at the
newly renovated Library of Alexandria in Egypt to explore these questions and challenge conventional wisdom about Islam. United by their uniformly distinguished
credentials and by a common conviction that Islam demands a current progressive
outlook on politics and history, these scholars sought to contribute to the formulation of new narratives.

The choice of venue was symbolic: The largest and greatest Hellenistic city in the
ancient world, Alexandria has always been a cultural crossroads. Often a center of
political power as well as a destination of those driven by intellectual curiosity,
ancient Alexandria was a point of convergence for Greek, Roman, Jewish and Syrian
culture that drew scholars from throughout the ancient world. Scholars proclaimed
her Royal Library "a wonder to the world." Though warfare and political turmoil
resulted in the tragic loss of the original Library of Alexandria, Islamic and Western
civilizations are deeply indebted to the knowledge that was preserved and transmitted there. The modern rebirth of the Library of Alexandria represents not only a
retrospective effort to pay homage to Egypt's universal city, but also a prospective
affirmation of the best values that the library represented: openness, intellectual
dynamism, and unity of knowledge and civilization.

Conference attendees were energized by the experience of discussing Islamic
interpretation within this universal context – a context that affirmed Islam's many
centuries of conversation with diverse systems of knowledge from many different
cultures. Although the scholars' responses to these questions varied, their reflections
were informed by a shared assumption that the ideals of Islam are emergent rather
than static. Like other religions, Islam is not only an abstract set of theological
propositions, but also a historical dynamic that finds expression in the lived experiences and circumstances of people. Understanding the practical and existential
meaning of Islam, then, requires willingness to discover opportunities for creativity
amidst the tensions that give rise to acts of interpretation. What was authentically

Islamic hundreds of years ago may not convey the spirit of Islam in today's specific circumstances; each generation of Muslims has an obligation to engage in earnest dialogue to understand and implement the values of their faith. The conference discussion asserted the idea that Muslims are obligated to continuously reexamine and reevaluate the impact of their changing environment (sociopolitical, economic, cultural, etc.) on the ways in which every Muslim views and lives his/her ideal and real Islam. This condition is a necessary step in the process of addressing the current decay in any Muslim society.

By reflecting on Islam in such terms, the scholars assembled in Alexandria found themselves in direct contradiction to a great deal of Western as well as Muslim conventional wisdom, which posits a fundamental incompatibility between Islamic and Western values. In the present context of conflict and insecurity (as viewed by many policy-makers in Western countries), it is easy to mistake the dominant narrative of Western-Islamic relations – a narrative that is being recounted by Muslims and Americans alike – for the only narrative. According to this story of confrontation, Western societies and Muslim societies share few common values, and are entrapped by an intensifying "clash of civilizations" with deep historical roots. In this "us versus them" story of conflict, opposition between contrary civilizations can only be resolved through the political defeat and cultural assimilation of one civilization by the other.

In both America and the Muslim world, this story is repeated by those who argue that the most important lessons for dealing with contemporary problems are to be found in historical analogies to epic struggles against implacable foes. Muslim militants, for example, proclaim that there is no difference between US and Israeli predominance in the Middle East and Crusader occupation of the Eastern Mediterranean between the eleventh and thirteenth centuries. For their part, Western countries' pundits and members of the foreign policy community in Washington often invoke the "clash" thesis, usually before arriving at the conclusion that a World War II or Cold War analogy is more political: threats posed by extremist Islamic ideologies and terrorist networks demand responses such as those used to "roll back" fascism and communism. Whether told by Muslims or non-Muslims, especially by Americans and Europeans, however, such narratives of epic confrontation promote conflict escalation as the only viable strategic response to present difficulties.

As they challenged interpretations of Islamic values that posit irreconcilable conflict with the West, the scholars in Alexandria generally agreed that Islamic-Western relations have as much to do with politics as they do with cultural practices and religious interpretations. Many argued that Muslims share a significant cultural heritage with the West, and are capable of reconciling Islam with modernization and democratic values if given a chance by their political regimes and foreign forces to do so. Present difficulties in relations between Muslim and Western societies, they suggested, represent the tragic but not inescapable outcome of a complex historical process. Islam, as a set of theological beliefs, is capable of responding to the challenges of the modern world if given a chance to do so, especially by its gate-keepers. This is possible because Islamic civilization is not an "exceptional" case among world cultures, uniquely predisposed to conflict or resistant to democracy. The human common denominators that unite the Islamic historical experience with the historical experiences of other world cultures are far more significant than the differences, and the problems of Muslims may be understood in terms that are similar to those used to explain challenges of political, cultural, and economic development faced by other peoples.

There is undoubtedly a strong historical basis for this view. Islam and the West are joined by common roots within the Judeo-Christian and Hellenic cultural continuum. Classical Islamic civilization grew to maturity in the Fertile Crescent – the birthplace of Western civilization – and was constructed out of Arab, Biblicist, and Hellenic cultures. In Baghdad as well as in the distant cities of Muslim Spain, Islamic scholars often collaborated with Christians and Jews to translate, preserve, and enrich the legacy of classical Greek learning. Islamic civilization also cast a wider net by integrating Persian and Central Asian as well as Indian components within its cultural synthesis, becoming a bridge between East and West. Western thinkers such as Thomas Aquinas, Roger Bacon, and Maimonides found great merit in the thought of Muslim philosophers such as Averroes and Avicenna – even as their Muslim contemporaries were rejecting what would become integral ideas of the Western Renaissance. Copernicus read heliocentric planetary theories in Arabic, and even Dante Alighieri is believed to have gained inspiration from Muslim thinkers such as Muhyi'iddin Ibn al-'Arabi. More recently, Ralph Waldo Emerson as well as Johann Wolfgang von Goethe found much to admire in the writings of Shamsuddin Hafez, a Muslim poet of Shiraz, Iran.

Theological Doctrine and Historical Dynamic

The fact that so much has been integrated within Islamic cultures indicates that Islam is not only a theological doctrine, but also a historical dynamic. As a historical dynamic, Islam was often a quite inclusive enterprise, embodying a spirit of encounter with the other. Just as it is impossible to understand classical Islamic civilization without reference to the dynamic roles played by non-Muslim minorities, so too is it misleading to formulate an understanding of Western civilization that excludes the contributions of Islam.

As many contributors to this volume have emphasized, affirming the richness and dynamism of historical Islam can provide a basis for new and constantly emerging Islamic syntheses that acknowledge essential theological affirmations that have remained constant throughout history. For example, doctrines concerning the unity of God, the prophethood of Muhammad, and the special nature of the Qur'an as a definitive summation of Abrahamic monotheism. At the same time Muslims, while noting discontinuities and divergences, have reached conclusions about the political and cultural implications of these beliefs. As many scholarly accounts have demonstrated, the cultural openness of Islamic culture often surpassed that of Europe during the Middle Ages and the early modern period. In Andalusia, the centuries of Muslim rule between the arrival of Abd al-Rahman in 711 and the fall of Granada in 1492 generated remarkable artistic and scholastic achievements through a symbiosis of Islamic, Jewish, and Christian cultures, and provided the conduit through which Aristotelian philosophy returned to the European intellectual milieu. Though often criticized when compared with modern norms for political pluralism and citizenship rights, the *dhimmi* system of Muslim empires granted considerable cultural and religious rights to non-Muslim minorities.

Addressing diversity and pluralism has become a crucial aspect of most societies' attempts to adjust to the incredible changes (technological and sociocultural) that faced the world in the last century. Due to many factors, Muslim societies have struggled with great difficulties in constructively addressing these themes.

Among Muslims, puritanical tendencies compete with progressive and reformist trends supporting democratic change, as well as with more traditional patterns of faith and belief that have proven far more tolerant of religious and cultural diversity than is generally acknowledged. Ironically, those who claim to defend Islam by rejecting pluralism negate the "genius of Islamic civilization," which manifested greatness by harmonizing Islamic precepts with diverse intellectual and cultural influences.

Although Western scholars sometimes resort to a simplistic "good Muslim"/"bad Muslim" dichotomy, there is a growing literature that is providing useful guidance for distinguishing between "Islamic terrorism," a destructive and anti-pluralist reaction to perceived external threats, and Islam revivalism, a reformist (*islahi*) movement to revitalize the community from within. Where violent Islamic movements attribute the ills of Islamic civilization almost exclusively to foreign infiltration and internal diversity of opinion, Islamic revivalists accept responsibility for internal sources of malaise, and seek to adapt Islamic culture in ways that might help Muslims meet modern problems more effectively.

From this perspective, both the call for radical measures and the call for reforms in the Muslim world stems from deep feelings of powerlessness fostered by governmental corruption, autocracy, inequality, and subservience to foreign masters. The difference between the two groups is in their fundamental interpretation of the appropriate measures that should be used in addressing these problems. Reformists rely on values and sets of beliefs that give an equal space for the "other" to exist and live among Muslims, and assume internal responsibility regarding the dynamics and perpetuation of the policies of oppression and discrimination against the other in every Muslim society. The exclusivists play down the internal responsibility and place the blame on external forces, adopt conspiracy theory, and withdraw from the current world by declaring their intention to return to the fifth and sixth century Arab cultural practices disregarding at least a thousand years of Islamic civilization. Western actions that help to restore the sense of security by collaborating to correct shared problems and providing Muslims with a sense of political efficacy might inspire creative thought and action.

Identity without Identity Politics

While expressing generalized support for such conclusions, most of the scholars gathered in Alexandria also emphasized the importance of remaining mindful of

Islam's distinctiveness – a distinctiveness that can accommodate and live creatively with other cultures, particularly when relations are based on the principle of complementarity.

Creative coexistence, scholars affirmed, can only be achieved when prominent representatives of civilizations agree to renounce divisive and polarizing notions of cultural triumphalism. Triumphalism – the assertion by one culture of absolute superiority on all indices of progress and enlightenment – leads not only to hubris and destructive conflict, but also to a rejection of the most vital source of cultural dynamism: openness to what the "other" has to offer. No scope for learning remains; "foreign" cultures must be rejected and defeated. In contrast, a relationship between civilizations that accommodates and even values cultural differences provides an indispensable foundation for fostering mutual respect and enduring cooperation.

From this standpoint, the "clash of civilizations" reveals itself for what it really is: a "clash of symbols" in which complex belief systems are being reduced to politicized slogans and images in order to sustain certain hegemonic cultural and economic interests. Such symbols are also used to reject the Muslim or non-Muslim "other," and to impose conformity upon populations who may or may not accept "Muslim" or "certain Western ideologies" as an exclusivist identity.

The damage that this form of identity politics wreaks upon rich cultural traditions is convincing many in Muslim societies and Westerner societies that their current estrangement is unsustainable. Since September 11th, many in these societies have become increasingly distrustful not only of each other, but also of the more humanistic and life-affirming values within their traditions. Simultaneously, many in Western societies are finding that they cannot retain a fully "Western" way of life without peaceful relations with Muslims (insofar as the term "Western" is intended to evoke themes of democracy and human rights).

This realization is echoed by those in the Muslim world who seek to transcend the exclusivist traditional "reflect or reject" framework for relations with the non-Muslims (especially Western societies), and who are actively seeking opportunities to preserve the integrity of their own Islamic convictions about human dignity, tolerance, and inclusivity in matters of faith and belief.

Though stories of confrontation and rivalry inform us of tensions that do in fact exist; nonetheless, they neglect the common ground shared by Islamic and Western cultures. Acting on common interests and values, however, will require a new approach to dealing with differences, founded upon a vision that will enable people in such communities (Muslim and Western) to achieve fuller engagement across the boundaries of culture and religion.

The scholars assembled in Alexandria also felt strongly that peace between Islamic and Western cultures is possible, and that it does not depend on cultural uniformity. They also made strong arguments for moving beyond reactionary attitudes and symbolic positions, toward genuine mutual knowledge. Retreating from the challenges of active engagement, they suggested, only serves to strengthen the position of exclusivists and militant fundamentalists in both communities.

In the modern world, retreat to a cultural ghetto by any group, be it Muslim, Jewish, Christian, Buddhist, or Hindu, is not only a denial of the rich diversity of the contemporary cultural experience, but also a rejection of responsibility for future generations. Instead of retreating into deep subjectivity, we need to develop a process of communication capable of generating new insight. Such a process should involve active and open listening and a commitment to sustained dialogue. Thus creative mechanisms and channels of communication and interaction are needed to foster such relationships (instead of rushing to achieve immediate rewards, a quick end of conflict, or complete understanding). The new forms of interaction will seek to help each side understand how the other community expresses its basic concerns, while encouraging both sides to work together in the discovery and creation of shared meanings and priorities. This would challenge people in the Western and Muslim societies to better understand their own values and ideals as they learn to share them in new ways. Such forums should not be confined to theological dialogue but be applied to political, economic, social, and any form of interaction.

Because the present world affords no scope for authenticity in isolation or security through empire, Muslims and Westerners need to experience themselves "in relationship" rather than "out of relationship." Both sides must find meaning in the common tragedy of their estrangement as well as in the possibility of reconciliation. They must also reconsider their traditional ways of construing values in dichotomous terms – i.e., "individualism vs. community," "reason vs. passion," "science vs. faith," "materialism vs. spirituality," "efficiency vs. hospitality," "freedom to do vs. freedom to be." When cultures view these sets of values as polarities rather than as complementarities, they are more likely to find themselves locked into adversarial relationships with those who are perceived to have different priorities. Recognizing that seemingly opposed values can actually reinforce each other opens new possibilities both for intercultural relations and for full development of the human personality. In addition, the above set of values do not exist in a pure or totally polarized forms in any given Muslim or Western societies. Such values are distributed within and manifested in a range which allows more overlap between people in both Muslim and Western contexts. Thus through learning to view these cultural values in a dynamic, flexible, and complex rather than dichotomous way becomes a crucial awareness gained mainly through open and safe interaction between members of these societies. Violence and wars are excellent and fertile grounds for negating and preventing the emergence of such awareness.

An affirmative approach to relations between Islam and the West must underscore peace as a shared ideal of both civilizations, and draw attention to the ever-present possibility of choice. Muslims and Westerners share many similar ideals, and yet follow cultural traditions that formulate and apply these ideals in unique ways that are not fully commensurable. On the contrary, such ways are underlined by common basic human needs, such as security, recognition of identity, growth and development, etc.

Dominant scholars from the West, for example, have come to understand and define peace largely as an "absence" of particular conditions, while for contemporary Muslims the word peace has no real meaning unless it signifies a "presence." For many Muslims, peace signifies a presence of justice, self-determination, and social equilibrium or harmony. These, at least, are central tendencies of thought within

Western and Islamic cultures; differences in value articulation and formulation *within* civilizational discourses are every bit as significant as differences between civilizations. Asymmetric power relations between the Muslim and Western worlds exacerbate the implications of the different articulation and formulation of the civilizational discourses. Thus certain Western policies are viewed as more legitimate and even marketed for Muslims and the world as the "only proper" discourse. While discourse from an Islamic perspective becomes threatening and delegitimized, the same dynamic occurs when most of Western discourse and narrative is selectively presented to Muslim communities by its exclusivist interpreters.

Like the West, Islam possesses multiple paradigms of thought and action on matters pertaining to peace, and it is only by recognizing the internal diversity of civilizations that we will be able to construct narratives of intercultural peacemaking. Thus essentializing each other's complex and diverse approaches to peace and war become a simple yet dangerous way of stereotyping and delegitimizing the other.

Both Islam and the West are truly between stories – between the stories of the past, and the story that they must now create together. All who identify with Islam and with the West can become coauthors of this new story. We are all heirs of the story of conflict. If we leave aside tired generalizations and seek to know one another, we can become the architects of a truly new order of cooperation. Muslims and Western people will not meet as rivals. Instead, Muslims will give the Western world the best of Islamic practices in exchange for receiving the best of the Western practices.

A Call for Fresh Thinking

As they sought to reframe problems in Western-Islamic relations, attendees at the Alexandria conference were by no means reluctant to call for fresh thinking on the part of Muslims. Troubled by what many perceived as a retreat from intellectual openness and dynamism in the Islamic world, they grappled with deeply important questions: How can Islam reclaim the best of its intellectual traditions, and revitalize them in a modern context? Can Muslims recover and build upon the spirit of intellectual openness that characterized Islamic civilization when it was at its historic zenith? This need for internal examination and self-reflection became a central focus for conversation once attendees asserted the importance of taking responsibility for the current state of Muslim societies. However unhelpful past Western policies may have been, Muslims should not further disempower themselves through a narrow focus on the misdeeds of others.

As many scholars have noted, the habit of viewing Islam ahistorically, as an *abstract theological doctrine*, has complicated efforts to understand how Islamic values can be applied to contemporary contexts. Static conceptions of Islam make it difficult for Muslims to respond creatively to new forms of knowledge and new cultural experiences. If Islam is understood as an abstract set of commandments that lack a meaningful relationship to specific historical contexts and experiences, Muslims are bound to face difficulties when seeking to discover how Islamic principles can be applied to meet the challenges of contemporary societies. Rather than formulate creative yet substantively Islamic positions on issues like democracy, development, cultural diversity, and peace, Muslims will compete for an elusive "authenticity" and face inevitable intellectual fragmentation. Reformers will be denounced as "outcasts," in accordance with an intellectual framework that devalues innovation and discourages impartial investigation of non-Islamic cultural experiences. Efforts to resolve contemporary social problems will be driven by simplistic ideological formulas ("Islam is the solution") and post-colonial identity politics rather than by disciplined programs for human and social development. In other words, Muslims will remain trapped by a defensive, reactive attitude that some scholars associate with a broader "psychology of the oppressed." Only by responding differently to these challenges can Muslims liberate their ways of thinking from self-defeating assumptions that perpetuate external domination and internal decay.

But how can Muslims respond differently as they confront the challenges of the modern world, while still preserving Islamic identity? Many of the conference participants concurred with the idea that Islam's journey over the centuries reveals that it is not so much a static doctrine as a *historical dynamic* that finds expression in the *lived experiences and circumstances* of people. In other words, the history of Islam is a story of never-ending efforts on the part of Muslims to comprehend the ideals of the Qur'an, and then to transform their understandings into reality. In this dynamic process of interpretation and action, the ideals of Islam are emergent rather than static.

From a theological perspective, this approach suggests that every historical period and cultural milieu has drawn forth a different *synthesis* of Islamic command-ments from the rich texts of Islamic faith and experience. Every generation in the Muslim world has developed a unique and yet integral Islamic synthesis which distinguishes that generation from previous ones. *Practicing Islam*, then, requires creative management of tensions between the real and the ideal, as well as between expectations and achievements. In the contemporary historical context, it requires that Muslims wrestle with challenging questions:

What is happening to the traditional synthesis of classical Islamic civilization as a result of changes and transformations in the world today – the challenge of modernity, the spread of literacy, the education of women, the emergence of more and more competing voices claiming Islamic legitimacy, the troubled relations of Muslim communities with the external world and with their own governments? What should Muslims aspire to preserve? What can they allow to change?

To what extent do emerging syntheses, such as those of revivalists and reformists, succeed in manifesting the historical legacy and unfolding ideals of Islam?

How can Muslims in the contemporary world find new meaning in their sacred texts?

What are the most important issues that *critical* Islamic thought must address? What does it mean to apply Islamic ethics to today's challenges?

How can Muslims project an Islamic vision that is *big enough* for the reality they are experiencing – a vision that is neither a superficial reflection of current Western norms nor a shortsighted rejection?

Where and how can Muslim scholars and practitioners expand their existing yet limited spaces for such open exchanges – spaces for self examination and internal dialogue?

Preview

The chapters in this volume are intended to stimulate further discussion of how a dynamic and contextually sensitive approach to Islamic faith and practice can facilitate the emergence of new Islamic syntheses that render faith meaningful in changing times. Readers of these essays will find that they address many of the most vitally important issues facing Muslims today with courage, insight, and intellectual integrity. They are required reading for all who seek insight into major problems in Islamic thought and in Islamic-Western relations.

The first section of this volume, entitled "The Many Voices of Islam: Cultivating Intellectual Pluralism," explores diverse views of Islamic interpretation and the impact of these views on Muslim societies. Particular emphasis is placed on need for dialogue among Muslims who approach revealed scripture and legal structures in different ways, in accordance with diverse intellectual traditions, cultural contexts, and social challenges. Some of the questions explored by the authors were: How do approaches to interpretation differ among "traditionalists," "reformists," "renewalists," and other types of contemporary Muslim thinkers? What are some of the potential benefits of dialogue among "competing" tendencies in Islamic thought? To what extent do problems faced by Islamic societies reflect a lack of synthesis within contemporary Islamic thought? On what grounds can Muslims affirm pluralistic approaches to interpretation? Should Muslims do more to support the principle of commonality in our multiplicity?

For Mustafa Ceric, the Grand Mufti of Bosnia and Herzegovina, the process of interpreting Islam in a modern context requires an attitude of openness and rediscovery – an affirmation of pluralistic possibilities inherent not only in contemporary cultural encounters, but also in the text of the Qur'an itself. More specifically, Muslims can choose to define their own authenticity as emerging from a rediscovery and affirmation of – rather than a negation of – the other, or to imagine tradition and modernity as realities that can be reconciled with each other. They should not hesitate to imagine the essence or ideals of their religious tradition as emergent and potentially dynamic rather than as static and rooted in a distant historical reality.

Like Ceric, who defends the idea of cultural and intellectual pluralism through references to a dynamic core of Islamic principles, Recep Senturk also concerns himself with the challenge of discerning how traditional Islamic ideals relate to contemporary contexts and especially to the concept of universal human rights. He argues that the historical legacy of Islamic legal thought presents contemporary Muslims with two options as they define their values and norms: an exclusivist school of thought and an inclusivist position. In his view, the latter, inclusivist approach provides the most viable and attractive option, because it proposes that all humans share basic rights regardless of religious or cultural background, and seeks to foster understanding through dialogical engagement rather than communalistic competition. Epistemologically as well as legally, the inclusive option demands a broad and participatory process in which members of estranged cultures rediscover their respective traditions and come to respect one another's deeper cultural values and motivations. While gaining access to empathetic understandings of other cultural systems, they also begin a process of broadening and reconstituting the cultural as well as intellectual foundations of their own identities: religiously, legally, and politically.

Where Senturk concerns himself with latent possibilities in Islamic normative discourse, A. Reza Sheikholeslami offers a sociological analysis of norms that are currently providing Muslim societies with a basis for communal cohesion. Gleaning from Durkheim's framework for studying religion as a social phenomenon, Sheikholeslami argues for new synthesis among those who study Islamic societies. In contrast to orientalist and "radical" syntheses that view Islamic societies alternately as frozen in time or as driven by hatred for outsiders, Sheikholeslami's preferred approach would focus on illuminating the bonds that hold Muslims together and the dynamics that move Muslims as members of a community. Rather than impose a misleading assumption of stasis on Islamic societies, this new synthesis would take into account sociocultural changes that have transformed Muslim world-views from other-worldly to this-worldly. For Sheikholeslami, sociological analysis is essential in efforts to demystify the character of Islamic societies and provide a basis for transcending "exceptionalist" perspectives that do a disservice both to Western academics and to the Muslims they purport to describe.

This section ends with a chapter by Meena Sharify-Funk in which she inquires into the origins and character of new Muslim discourses and self-critiques. Giving particular attention to problems inherent in conventional labels such as "modern" or "progressive" Islam, she argues that innovative tendencies in contemporary Islamic thought are best understood as manifestations of an emergent, transnational hermeneutic field that blends cultural influences in unexpected and sometimes unpredictable ways. Rather than transpose Western categories or posit continuities with more reactionary forms of "Islamism," Sharify-Funk represents contemporary Islam as a transboundary, pluralistic phenomenon characterized by constant renegotiations of sacred meaning.

The second section, "Applied Ethics of Political Participation," investigates the relationship between Islamic principles and political life, with particular attention to challenges of broadening participation in political processes, enhancing the accountability of governments to the governed, and promoting respect for both the dignity of individuals and the integrity of communities. Contributors discuss ways in which Muslims express both their political identity and their diverse interests with an Islamic vocabulary, seeking a cultural and not merely a technological future. Some questions addressed include: How can Islamic values promote accountable and participatory governance? What are the challenges facing Islamic societies that seek to democratize? What historical events and experiences have shaped contemporary

Muslim attitudes towards civil society and political participation? How could reform of political institutions in the Muslim world (e.g. democratization, accountability with respect to human rights) foster a stable social peace? How might Islamic values support the "flowering of the individual" in Muslim societies?

The first chapter in this section, by Armando Salvatore, provides a framework for exploring Islam's role in modern Europe, with particular attention to Islam's potential contributions to "public religion." After examining major debates concerning secularism and the role of religion in political society, Salvatore concludes that – despite secularist doubts about religion's impact – religions such as Islam can help to sustain political and cultural dialogue about the role of values in the public sphere.

Serif Mardin's chapter offers another analysis of the interaction between secularity and religiosity, with particular reference to the politics of modernization in the Ottoman Empire. In the process, he seeks to elucidate the roots of ideological conflicts that beset contemporary Turkish society. Though his examination of symbiosis between an aggressive secularism and a reactive Islamism is limited to the Turkish case, his assertions about overlooked possibilities for ideological accommodation are relevant to the study of many contemporary Muslim societies.

In her analysis of hotly contested debates about the role of women in Islamic societies, Zainah Anwar provides an illustration of religio-political conflict. She argues that, though contemporary Muslim governments and Islamic movements have often used the "status of women" issue in ways that convert conservative sentiments into political capital, many opportunities for progressive civic activism exist. Civil society organizations such as Malaysia's Sisters in Islam are actively contesting dominant tendencies, utilizing both the language of Islamic values and more cosmopolitan discourse on women's rights.

Farid Esack's chapter is concerned first and foremost with the challenge of developing a progressive Muslim ethic that effectively engages topics such as human rights and democracy without submissiveness to prevailing Western understandings. In Esack's view, an authentically Islamic perspective cannot easily be reconciled with prevailing practices of economic globalization and the ethos of competitive and corporate individualism. Unlike conservative and reactive Islamic movements, however, a progressive Muslim political project would seek common cause with other global social movements for women's rights and economic justice.

In the third section, entitled "Applied Ethics of Peace and Nonviolence in Islam," contributors analyze strengths of the Islamic faith and practice which contribute to peacemaking, social justice, and global peace. Particular attention is given to principles, values, and traditions within Islam which support the resolution of deeply rooted conflicts with a minimum of violence and coercion. In addition, authors look at Islamic conceptions of peace and their similarities and differences *vis-à-vis* Western understandings. Some questions explored were: What is the Islamic standpoint on violence and its justification? Is nonviolence to be located solely within the domain of personal morality and individual self-training, or could it be applied to the collective needs of society (both Muslim and non-Muslim) and of governance? What are some examples of constructive, nonviolent, Islamic actions and movements? What are the most important Islamic resources for peacebuilding and peacemaking? How can Islamic conceptions of social justice be applied for conflict prevention and resolution?

This section begins with Mohammed Abu-Nimer's investigation into the principles and practices of nonviolence found within Muslim traditions. Drawing upon the Qur'an and the Hadith literature, Abu-Nimer outlines the scriptural basis of Islamic values such as forgiveness, patience, equality, social solidarity, inclusivity, and pluralism. Abu-Nimer's chapter is followed by Nadia Mahmoud Mostafa's analysis of violence and nonviolence in Islam. Mostafa argues that a "middle view" is the most appropriate Islamic stance: while nonviolence is an important value, Islamic commitment to this value cannot and should not be absolute. In defense of this position, she outlines Western political practices that have been detrimental to Islamic values and interests.

Chaiwat Satha-Anand's contribution to this section proposes that Muslim nonviolent action can serve as a means for transforming terrorism. Despite obvious differences in method and outcome, nonviolent action and terrorism share two important similarities: both are based on an imperative to fight injustice in the world, and both presuppose willingness to die for a good cause. In making the case for nonviolent action, Satha-Anand argues for direct engagement with the rationales that are offered to justify terrorism. Muslims, he suggests, must not only condemn terrorism, but also offer rational and moral arguments for Muslim nonviolent action as an alternative political practice.

The final section, "Coexistence and Reconciliation: An Enduring Responsibility of the Muslim *Ummah*," examines the proposition that Islam transcends exclusive identification with either "East" or "West," and that Muslims can play a unique role in the world today – spiritually as well as culturally and politically – as a "Middle People." Contributions of Islamic values to reconciliation among cultures and to human solidarity receive special consideration. Some questions explored in this section include: How can an Islamic synthesis for today be derived from the diversity of Islamic interpretations and cultures? Can this synthesis establish common ground between Islam and the West without compromising core Islamic principles? How can the conception of Muslims as a "Middle People" be applied to efforts to resolve cultural and ideological conflicts within Islamic societies?

Mohammed Arkoun's chapter presents a multi-faceted critique of solipsistic tendencies both in Islamic thought and in political and social practice. He encourages Muslims to think the *unthinkable*, to transcend the impasse of what he calls "institutionalized ignorance" and to embrace the full range of intellectual and cultural resources that are openly available to Muslims in the modern world today. For Arkoun, Muslims cannot *disengage* or be *disembedded* from the modern construction of Islam: they cannot and should not create hermeneutic enclosures that bound interpretive experience to past "untouchable" discursive corpuses. Rather, Muslims need to live in creative *disclosure*: dynamic as well as transparent interactions within unlimited pluralistic spaces.

According to Arkoun, in order to think the *unthinkable* Muslims also need to understand processes that have bound themselves to "fixed" texts and contexts, and therefore to static conceptualizations and ideological "totalizations." Cognitive errors associated with static thinking negate new cultural experiences and insist that contemporary realities can only be understood within a past frame of reference that forms a limiting cultural enclosure. In Arkoun's view, this "totalized" viewpoint (which claims comprehensiveness) results in dichotomous thinking, logocentrism, and the monopolization of Truth itself.

Azyumardi Azra's chapter provides an exploration of cultural and political pluralism from the standpoint of the Southeast Asian Muslim experience. Focusing especially on the Indonesian context, he illustrates how Muslims have found bases in Islam for an ethos of moderation – a "Middle Path." In his view, this stance of moderation and pluralism can play an important role in a post-9/11 world.

Whereas the traditional hermeneutical approach directs all attention to the authoritative text while ignoring questions about *who* is interpreting and under what circumstances, Asma Barlas's chapter seeks to balance the claims of the text with consideration of the needs and existential circumstances of Muslim interpreters. Like many of her colleagues, she focuses on the interaction among text, interpreter, and context. Gleaning from such contemporary Muslim thinkers as Suroosh Irfani, Barlas calls for reflexive contextual understanding of one's place in the world. By understanding oneself through self-reflexivity, one becomes able to comprehend how others see and experience the world as well. Becoming conscious of one's own contextual relativity, she argues, is a basis for understanding how Islam's universalism is filtered and experienced within particular cultural and historical contexts. This awareness of unity and diversity within Islam, Barlas suggests, is an essential foundation of coexistence.

Taken together, the essays in this volume offer fresh resources for confronting one of the greatest challenges facing Muslim believers in the contemporary world: the challenge of making Islam a dynamic and living reality. Our intent in convening the two-day Alexandria conference was to create a space within which scholars could reflect deeply upon this challenge, opening space for new thinking about Islam – from within Islam, as well as from within a context of relationship to the world outside Islam. A key goal was to spur creative thinking about how present generations of Muslims can reconcile Islamic ideals with their social and political experiences, drawing new inspiration for troubled times. It is our hope that readers will seek to join this conversation, and add their own voices to those assembled here.

Part I

The Many Voices of Islam

Cultivating Intellectual Pluralism

1　The Many Voices of Islam

Cultivating intellectual pluralism

Mustafa Ceric
Grand Mufti of Bosnia and Herzegovina

Islamic Civilization as a Wheel

The phenomenon of the Islamic civilization may be seen as a wheel that is turning on the axis of a continuous divine message from the first human, Adam, to the last Messenger, Muhammad. This divine axis of the Islamic civilization has remained the same because it has the same meaning of the living spirit and because it is the same logic of the transcendental truth. The code of the axis is such that it moves the wheel of the Islamic civilization in different directions, but it remains in the vicinity of the axis. The dynamics of the movement of the wheel is faster at its edge than at its center. The axis of the Islamic civilization is the divine gift, which unfolds itself in the continuity of life and history. The wheel of Islamic civilization is the divine gift as well, but its movement is due to the human direction and speed.

Hence, the question is: Whither will the wheel of the Islamic civilization go? And with what speed will the wheel of the Islamic civilization move? But before dealing with these two questions, let me say that a civilization is more than a situation of urban comfort. A civilization, I believe, is an effort of human spirit to balance the memory of the past by the memory of the future time, to express the meaning of life, and to present the nature of human soul both in its hope and in its fear. Indeed, civilization is the state of mind which Ibn Khaldun called the 'aṣabiyyah', i.e. the passion[1] for a decent human life as it progresses from one stage to another with a purpose of self-actualization in history. Very important forces of the passion for human life are the freedom of human spirit and the strength of human mind.

The attribute "Islamic" to civilization should lead us to the notion of the coexistence of continuity and change in history and life.[2] That, I believe, is the crucial point whereby the course of the Islamic civilization has been determined in the past – its ability to comprehend the essential continuity of tradition with possible changes in history. It is, then, in this ever-demanding challenge – the appreciation of the continuity of tradition and the acceptance of changes in history – that I see as the real test for the future of the Islamic civilization both in terms of its spiritual boldness and its intellectual creativity. In fact, the idea of the coexistence of continuity and change is the major idea and the one which had provided the Islamic civilization with an unprecedented success in world history. The strength of it lies in the notion of affirmative (*hiero*) history[3] and the notion of guilt-free origin of man.

Affirmative History

The affirmative (*hiero*) history comes as the most convincing proof that the Qur'an is the culmination of an inclusive divine Message and that the Prophet Muhammad is the universal divine Messenger. In other words, the revelation of the Qur'an does not come as a surprise, it does not break the rules of the God-Man communication, and it does not begin from nowhere:

> And before this, was the Book of Moses as a guide and mercy: and this book affirms it in the Arabic tongue; to admonish the unjust, and as Glad Tidings to those who do right.
>
> (46:12)

> God! There is no god but He, – the Living, the Self-Subsisting, Eternal. It is He Who sent down to thee in truth, the Book, affirming what went before it and He sent down the Tawrat (the Law of Moses) and Injil (the Gospel of Jesus) before as a guide to mankind, and he sent down the Criterion of judgment between right and wrong.
>
> (3:1–3)

Consequently, the Prophet Muhammad is not the first, but the last Messenger of God. The history does not begin, nor does it end with Muhammad. He is not a rebellious revolutionary who negates everything that came before him.[4] The Prophet Muhammad is the Messenger of God who has come to affirm all the good things which preceded him, but also he is here to teach people how to avoid bad things in life and history from the experience of far-gone people and nations.

> Thus have we sent you amongst a people before whom (long since) have other peoples gone and passed away in order that you may rehearse unto them what We send down unto you by inspiration. Yet do they reject him the Most Gracious. Say: 'He is my Lord! There is no god but Him! On Him is my trust, and to Him do I turn'.
>
> (13:30)

The notion of the affirmative history (or *hiero*-history) has enriched Muslims with the idea of an inclusive approach to history[5] as a whole and, in turn, freed the Islamic history from an exclusive possession of it. Of course, the Muslims did take their consequential role as the heirs of *hiero*-history very seriously, but they have never denied the role of the others, especially the role of *Ahlal-kitab* ("People of the Book"), namely, the Jews and Christians.

The Holy Qur'an and Critique

While reading the Holy Qur'an, a Muslim cannot but feel the presence of the People of the Book, in almost every page of it. Similarly, Jews and Christians cannot read any relevant book of world history without recognition of the Muslim presence in all fields of human life. Surely, the Qur'an criticizes some Jews and Christians, but it does the same with particular Muslims as well. I guess it is the Muslim moral responsibility not to take advantage of the critique of others in the Holy Qur'an in order to cover the Muslims' own shortcomings. If nothing else, but for the fact that the Qur'an, as the word of God, is almost unique in appreciating the goodness of people of other religions, especially of the Jews and Christians, the Muslims have a duty to carry out the spirit of tolerance in the midst of religious pluralism. Here is one of many verses of the Holy Qur'an that clearly indicates to that effect:

> Verily, those who have attained to faith (in this divine writ), as well as those who follow the Jewish faith, and the Christians, and Sabians[6] – all who believe in God and the Last Day and do righteous deeds – shall have their reward with their Sustainer; and no fear need they have, and neither shall they grieve.
>
> (2:62)

Religious Pluralism

Of course, it would be naïve to conclude that there are no differences between Islam and other religions, namely, Judaism and Christianity. The point here is not a vague notion of poor flattering or cheap religious propaganda, but a sincere conviction based on the most important Islamic source that teaches Muslims how to cope with religious pluralism on their own. It also teaches how to appreciate the fact that this world is not made up of one religion or one nation, because if God wanted the world to be so, He could do it, but He wanted the people of this world to be multiple in their religions and nations so that they may compete with each other in good deeds.

This idea of the competition in good deeds applies, especially, to these three world religions of the Book: Judaism, Christianity and Islam, not only because of their claim to the similar heritage of the Book, but also because of their heritage of a unique historical interaction that could not be avoided in the past and their historical responsibility that cannot be ignored in the future. It is precisely in this historical unavoidability of Judaism, Christianity and Islam that I see hope, but also, I must say, I sense a kind of fear. My hope is based on the good heart of the majority, though very often silent in its goodness, of sincere Jews, Christians and Muslims who seek their own peace in the similarity of these religions rather than conflict.

Unfortunately, there is a very loud minority in all three religions who, in fact, see in the similarity of Judaism, Christianity and Islam the very reason for conflict rather than peace. This kind of attitude leads us almost to the conclusion that the similarity, and not the difference, provokes the conflict while the difference brings the respect. We are familiar with the history of a severe debate among the similar, not different, religious groups, a debate that has often turned into a very violent conflict. I have in mind some historical conflicts between the Sunnites and the Shiites in the Muslim religion and the conflict between the Catholics and Protestants in the case of Christianity. I am sure that such examples exist in Judaism as well.

The logic of this kind of conflict among those who are similar, whatever it may be, lies in the false notion that in order for me to keep the purity of my religion the deep difference must be seen of the other who is similar to me, but, at the same time, his/her difference is not tolerated. This is, I believe, the real issue of the relationship between Judaism, Christianity and Islam today: their similarity, not the difference in their spiritual roots, their hope, not fear from each other, their love, not hate of each other, and their justice toward each other, and not oppression of each other.[7]

I should remind you that the glorious time of the Islamic civilization had been the time of its interaction with other civilizations. The idea of isolation is strange to the Islamic civilization because the Prophet Muhammad was sent to all mankind and thus he is the witness over the world in the sense of bringing upon it the mercy and not the curse.

It is clear, then, that the Muslims in the past knew how to interact with others who had been both similar to and different from their faith and their expectations of life and history. They had been guided by the strong belief of the conformation rather than denunciation, the belief of sharing rather than the belief of staring. Furthermore, they knew how to appreciate the different opinions amongst themselves while keeping in mind the same direction towards the glory of the Islamic civilization as a common achievement of the whole *Ummah*, Muslim community.

Since we are not children of the moment, we must be able to balance the memory of the past by the memory of the future time. It is in this point (i.e., the balancing of the memory of the past by the memory of the future time) that I see the difficulty in the Muslim present. In other words, the Muslims have difficulty, on the one hand, to free themselves from the guilt of some previous historical events and to take the risk of the future by, on the other hand, fresh spiritualism and creative intellectualism.

Once again, I should remind you that the idea of guilt-free origin of man is one of the most important ideas of the so-called modernity, which has led the world to a spiritual and intellectual advancement, i.e., humanism and renaissance? The slogan: "We are all born free and all men are equal before God," is the reaction to the notion that all men are born with the sin of Adam and that some men are born as masters and the others are born as slaves. It took Europe centuries and many bloody wars to overcome these two general ideas: the idea of predetermined guilt and the idea of preordained slavery. I believe that one of the reasons why the Muslim world was in advance to the rest of the world lies in the fact that Islam had freed humanity of the guilt and had set the stage of equal chance for all to show their historical merit.

Cultural Insecurity

The current crisis of the Islamic civilization may be seen in the lack of self-confidence, which came as a result of a cultural insecurity, which was introduced with the time of losing the belief in freedom of guilt and the belief in the equal chance for a success in life and history. Consequently, generations of Muslims have lost their spiritual boldness and intellectual creativity. And instead we have seen a kind of spiritual shyness that has led the Islamic civilization into isolation, as well as an intellectual borrowing that was going to lead the Islamic civilization into assimilation. Here is a possible answer to the questions: Whither will the wheel of the Islamic civilization go? Or whither it ought to go from here? To isolation or to assimilation? Or will it make its way towards interaction and co-operation?

Neither Isolation, nor Assimilation, but Civilizational Co-operation

The Islamic civilization is not made either for isolation, or assimilation. It is made for interaction and co-operation. However, in order to go in that direction the Islamic civilization must reject the idea of historical guilt. It is being imposed nowadays upon the Muslims in the sense that the current generation of youth must correct all the mistakes of the previous generations before it thinks of correcting its immediate and long-term future of the *Ummah*.

In other words, the contemporary generation should hold fast to the belief[8] of freedom from past mistakes and thus take responsibility for the future of the world not in the way of isolation, nor in the way of assimilation, but in the way of equal cultural interaction and civilizational co-operation. The middle ground of historic interaction and rational co-operation is the right way out from the embarrassment of isolation and the risk of assimilation of the Islamic civilization.

It is now the time for the third historic interaction of the Islamic civilization with the rest of the world, especially the western world, after it had experienced the interaction in the time of the venture of Islam and then in the time of the great Islamic impact on both the spiritual and intellectual change in the West. This time, however, the situation is somewhat different from the two previous ones because the West does not feel the need to learn anything from the East as used to be the case.

On the contrary, the West believes that the East should imitate the West in everything, even in their strange moral behavior, which is against human decency as well as human reproduction. This situation though should not discourage Muslims from interaction with the West because of the permanent interdependence between the two worlds – the East and the West – which did not start yesterday and will not end by tomorrow.

Let me now address the second question as to: With what speed will the wheel of the Islamic civilization move? With the speed of its center? Or with the speed of its edge?

Center and Periphery

But, first is there a center of Islam? Yes, there is a center of Islam, but not so much in the sense of geographical compact, economical product, or political impact on the global development as in the sense of a universal identity, the time-space *Ka'ba-Qibla* orientation and of the faith-based solidarity among common Muslims all over the world. These rather abstract characteristics of the idea of the center of Islam will remain strong because the message of the Qur'an is strong in its universality and its credibility for the human salvation.

The issue here, then, is not about the obvious blessings of the Heaven, but about the use and misuse of those blessings by humans. No one can deny the bliss of the time of the Prophet and . . .

> No one can deny the glory of the caliphate, the might of the Ottomans or the transformative impact of modern Europe . . . The caliphs and sultans – at least some of them – deserve their fame . . . And above all, the story of Muhammad (a.s.) and early followers has been a linchpin of Islamic identity for fourteen centuries.[9]

Yet, continues Richard W. Bulliet, the view from the center leaves too many questions unanswered. Where did all those Muslims come from? Why did they develop a coherent culture or civilization while Europe, despite its Christian homogeneity, was so fractious and diverse?

The view from the center portrays Islamic history as an outgrowth from a single nucleus, a spreading inkblot labeled "the caliphate." But what other than a political label held Islam together? And why did its political cohesion evaporate after little more than two centuries, never to reoccur?

The view from the edge holds out the possibility of addressing questions like these. It starts from the fact that most Muslims outside the Arabian peninsula are not the descendents of the Arabs. Most of them learned about Islam after they entered the community, not before; and what they learned never assumed a homogeneous character, though from the fourteenth century on there was a strong impulse toward normative homogeneity.[10]

Furthermore, no one can deny the central role of the Arabs, the Persians and the Turks in the mainstream history of the Islamic civilization. But also no one can ignore the fact that the heaviest burden of the Islamic civilization for the last two centuries was put on the Arab shoulders. It is only recently that the edge or periphery[11] of Islam is beginning to emerge and to show some signs of rallying around the center expecting that the center will come with an initiative to strengthen the internal relationship of the *Ummah* on a global level.

The periphery of Islam is becoming impatient to see a practical action of the center (if the center is aware that it is really a center of Islam today, in terms of translating the unique spiritual richness of Islam that can be seen in the unity of faith, the unity of purpose, the unity of prayers and the unity of destiny). The periphery of Islam cannot understand why the center is slow in addressing so many contemporary issues which stay on the way for a moral, political and economic development of the global *Ummah*. It is difficult to explain to Muslims who rely on the Internet that they cannot determine the date of their *Eid* in advance. It is difficult to explain to rational people that the global Muslim policy is still based on the rule that one member of the *Ummah* must lose so that the other may survive. And it is hard for decent people to believe that the Muslims do not have the strategy for a global economy which could decrease poverty and increase literacy among the Muslims who are by all standards still suffering from these two social illnesses more than any other religious group in the world.

Search for Syntheses

I believe that Muslims do not have choice today but need to come to the realization that their future is in their ability to synthesize their past memory with the future history. This may unfold itself in the internal co-operation of all the aspects of rich spiritual gifts and intellectual fruits as well as in the external interaction of all the possibilities of the advancement of human life that a positive human knowledge may offer to an individual and society.

In addition to that, Muslims today must come to the point of self-respect so that others may respect them as well and they must know that today's world operates on the basis of mutual trust that requires much more time to build it than to destroy it.

Notes

1 *Passion* – a strong liking or desire for or devotion to some activity, object, or concept.
2 See John Lukacs's statement, " . . . history and life consist of the coexistence of continuity and change. Nothing vanishes entirely." *At the End of an Age*, New Haven: Yale University Press, 2002, p. 31.
3 The word (*hiero*) history (*hiero* – sacred) indicates to what is known as *Qiṣaṣ al-Anbiya'* (Stories of the Prophets) in Islamic literature.
4 Compare that with some recent revolutionary movements in the world especially that of the Marxist-Leninist type and see how destructive they had been in the name of change and fake progress. Even in some Muslim revolutionary movements we can notice the destructive force, which is entirely in contradiction to the spirit of Islam. The idea of *tajdid* is a strange idea and it does not correspond to the basic teaching of Islam and it does not reflect the real purpose of the progress in the Islamic civilization.
5 See John Lukacs's statement, "History is not a social science but an unavoidable form of thought. That 'we live forward but we can only think backward' is true not only of the present (which is always a fleeting illusion) but of our entire view of the future: for even when we think of the future we do this by *remembering* it." In *At the End of an Age*, New Haven: Yale University Press, 2002, p. 53.
6 "The Sabians seem to have been a monotheistic religious group intermediate between Judaism and Christianity." See *The Message of the Qur'an*, translated and explained by Muhammad Asad, Gilbraltar: Dar al-Andalus, 1984, p. 14, n. 49.
7 Cited from my paper presented at the Conference: "Beyond Violence: Religious Sources for Social Transformation" at The University of Southern California on the 5–7th May, 2003, under my topic: *Judaism, Christianity, Islam: Hope or Fear of our Time*.
8 See John Lukacs's statement, "After all, every thing a man does depends on some kind of belief. He will speak or act in a certain way because he thinks that this kind of speaking or acting is better than another." In *At the End of an Age*, New Haven: Yale University Press, 2002, p. 88.
9 Richard W. Bulliet, *Islam: the View from the Edge*, New York: Columbia University Press, 1994, p. 7.
10 Ibid. pp. 7–8.
11 See Ozay Mehmet, *Islamic Identity & Development: Studies of the Islamic Periphery*, London: Routledge, 1990.

2 Sociology of Rights

Inviolability of the Other in Islam between Universalism and Communalism

Recep Senturk

All religions known in the world are founded,
so far as they relate to man,
on the unity of man, as being all of one degree.

Thomas Paine

The world is anxious today to know how Muslims would treat the Other. But ironically, at the height of the so-called information age, a straightforward answer is difficult to obtain. Does Islamic law accord inviolability to the Other? Does Islam grant equal rights to all human beings at the universal level, regardless of their religion, or only to the co-believers? The perception of the non-Muslim public is divided on this question. The Other expects Muslims to offer assurances of inviolability from the perspective of Islam. But why cannot they get it?

Like the broader world community, the Muslim community is also anxious to know whether the West accepts the inviolability of the Other. They expect a clear, unanimous and permanent assurance from the Western countries about their inviolability. Yet, in the cacophony of disparate voices emerging from America and Europe, Muslims fail to find this assurance and this divides the Muslim public and the non-Western world into a range of competing perceptions of the West. Why can this community not find the assurance it seeks either?

Neither side can give or get such an assurance in unanimity. This is because, I argue, neither the Self nor the Other – from whichever perspective any one of us represents – speaks with a single voice. None is homogenous and unified. Each Self is divided into multiple avenues of approach to the Other and so has no unanimous response to offer to the Other about inviolability. Not only the general population but also scholars, experts and policy makers, be they Muslims or non-Muslims, are at odds on this issue. The question thus remains one of the most puzzling ones for today's Muslims and non-Muslims specializing in the fields of religion, politics, international relations and human rights law.[1]

Below, instead of taking one side, I will shed light on the origin of this divide in the classical Islamic legal theory and trace its evolution until modern times prior to offering my own view on why all human beings (should) have inviolability on the basis of their humanity. I then summarize my approach, which I ground in the tradition of the Universalistic School of Law in Islam, through the expression *I am therefore I have rights*. In other words, all human beings are sacred and inviolable by virtue of their existence irrespective of gender, race, religion and nationality.

Inviolability and Interconnectedness at the Age of Globalization

A symbolic border separates each society from the rest of the world and bestows upon it its social identity. These borders may not always converge with the geopolitical borders. It is the cleavage between the Self and the Other which I call the *we/they line*.[2] The terms of relationship between the Self and the Other is crucial for a concept of universal human rights which stipulates that the Self respect the inviolability of the Other and vice versa. Yet the distinction between the Self and the Other is not so clear-cut. Instead, it is, as Figure 2.1 illustrates, produced by a complicated matrix of relations within and between societies.

The line between the Self and the Other is fluid, contested, and constantly negotiated and redrawn. Both the Self and the Other, as well the terms of their relationship and the line between them, all constantly shift. It is a political process. Political power demonstrates itself in its ability to redraw these boundaries and redefine the terms of relationship between different sides. Those who enjoy more power are the ones who decide where the borders should be drawn and how the terms of relationship should be defined.

The same is true for the internal cleavages in a society concerning the approach to the Other. Neither side (the Self and the Other) is united. As Figure 2.1 illustrates, the cleavage between the universalists and the communalists divides both the Self and the Other. Although they belong to different societies, the universalists from both sides constitute a single group because they share the same universalistic values in their approach to the Other. Likewise, the communalists from different societies also constitute a category because they share the same exclusionist or communalistic approach to the Other.

From a universalist standpoint, a state of peace is taken as the default relationship between the Self and the Other. However, from a communalist perspective, the *de facto* relationship between them is war or contention unless otherwise proven. The universalists may easily relate themselves to the Other while the communalists would face serious problems in this regard because of their adversarial approach to the Other.

As Figure 2.1 illustrates, the two lines (the Self-Other line, and the Universalist-Communalist axis) that mark intersecting cleavages, give rise to a fourfold matrix of relations. This matrix has critical importance for the issue of the Other and their inviolability. Below I will illustrate how this matrix bears on the inviolability of the Other. The density or the volume of the relations between the Self and the Other has exponentially increased at our age which is characterized by interconnectedness,[3] flatness,[4] and death of distance.[5] Yet, ambivalence prevails on whether the increasing interconnectedness in the world has been paralleled by increasing inviolability and human rights.

Therefore, our investigation must pay attention to diverse and divergent views in Islam. There is no one among Muslims who can speak with God's voice and answer

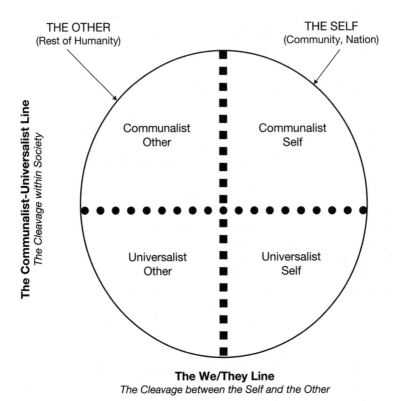

The We/They Line
The Cleavage between the Self and the Other

Figure 2.1 Intersecting Cleavages: Embattled lines separating the Self from the Other and the universalists from the communalists

the question about the inviolability of the Other in Islam. Nor is there an authoritative official voice, especially after the collapse of the Ottoman Caliphate, to speak for Islam. The historical survey of literature also defies any monolithic answer and one-sided story. If a Muslim affirms that Islam accepts the inviolability of the Other, then the following question is whether it was ever put in practice in Islamic history. If yes, can it be revived today? How compatible is it with the modern paradigm of human rights?

This is made more complex by the fact that Islam is a polyphonic civilization with numerous schools of thought in philosophy, law and Sufism most of which have been considered equally valid by the Muslim public over centuries. A comparative approach, taking into account historical and sociological aspects, helps us put things in perspective while trying to make sense out of what at first sights seems to be a confusing puzzle in Islam. Such an approach would demonstrate that there are universal social and cultural patterns to which Islamic culture and Muslim societies are no exception. Among these patterns is the divide between universalist and communalist groups in each society.

Consequently, in all societies, it is possible to find opposing exclusionist and inclusive views concerning the inviolability of the Other. Similar to the rest of the world in their approach to the Other, the cleavage between universalism and communalism divides Muslims as well. This divide is reflected in law as the dichotomy between two rival paradigms: human rights at the universal level *vis-à-vis* civil rights at the national level. This enduring tension between universalistic and communalistic perspectives in Islamic culture is far from being peculiar to Muslim community. Instead, it is a commonly observable aspect of all major cultures in the world.

Besides the common patterns between Islamic and Western laws emanating from universal patterns, one should also bear in mind more specific commonalities emanating from common origins and historical experiences. Islam is a Western religion, historians of religion unanimously agree, emanating from Abraham as Judaism and Christianity, which is common knowledge for the specialists, even if it remains a surprising discovery for the general public. So are Islamic law, science[6] and philosophy.[7] They reflect striking parallels because of a common history.[8] Islamic discourse may be seen as a continuation of the Judeo-Christian legacy (*Israiliyyat*). Furthermore, Islamic law inherited some aspects of Jewish law.

Islamic philosophy and science heavily derived from Greek philosophy and science through state-sponsored translations from Greek into Arabic during the eighth and ninth centuries. Muslim scholars preserved the Greek heritage against the religious bigotry prevalent in the West during the Middle Ages until the rational thinkers of early modern Europe reclaimed it through translations from Arabic to Latin. The legacy of such Greek thinkers as Socrates, Plato and Aristotle traveled to Europe through the Middle East. Islamic philosophy revered Aristotle as the First Teacher (*al-mu'allim al-awwal*) who was followed by al-Farabi (339/950[9]), the Second Teacher (*al-mu'allim al-thani*). Ibn Rushd or, as known in the West, Averroes, the "Commentator of Aristotle," is yet another renowned follower of Aristotle. Not only the rationalist Aristotle but also Plato had prominent Muslim followers such as Ibn Sina, the most prominent representative of Illumination (*ishraqiyyah*) in Islamic philosophy.[10]

Yet, Islam also internalized a broader cultural base especially during the first centuries of its history. Muslims were eager to claim the legacy of the entire humanity during the formative period of Islamic civilization. Not only the Greek classics but also the products of the Egyptian, Iranian and Indian cultures were also translated into Arabic – contributing to the creation of a highly cosmopolitan discourse which came to be known as Islamic culture. While some Muslims extended their interest endlessly, the others concentrated only on the core, the Qur'an and the Hadith, and blamed the former group with heresy. However, neither approach had been definitive on the fate of Islamic culture. Rather, they coexisted in tension, competing to gain more intellectual and social ground.

Since the axis of universalism and communalism divides all societies, peace is considerably contingent upon or best served by the coalition of universalists from the Self and the Other joining in a sense of common cause. Otherwise, if the communalists prevail, societies would find themselves on a collision course. For a sustainable world peace, the universalists who act with "value rationality"[11] from different societies should ensure each other about their respect for the Other's inviolability, but more importantly, try to curtail the propensity towards communalism inside their own society from reaching extremes.

For the universalist effort to succeed against communalists, the universalists in each society need the collaboration of the universalists from other societies. This is highly critical because one of the most important factors that triggers and feeds communalism is feeling threatened by the Other – which is the fuel of the communalistic ideologies, and the only way to overcome it is the insurance needed from the Other. Even if there is not such a threat, the communalists may on occasion try to invent it, or even fictively construct it, to increase their popularity because they need an outside enemy and an imminent external threat to compete against universalists. Consequently, forestalling international conflict depends on the triumph of universalists over communalists within each society more than anything else.

Communalism in a society feeds communalism in its neighbors while universalism feeds universalism. If communalism is on the rise in one society, the Other cannot say this is its problem – it has to overcome it by itself. This is because there is a great possibility that the actions of the communalists in one society might have spurred communalism in its neighbors. For this reason, the neighbors should check whether or not their own society, knowingly or unknowingly, contributed to the rise of the communalists in their neighbor.

Communalism may gain power in a society to an extent that it begins threatening or attacking its neighbors. In such a political and psychological context, universalism in the neighboring societies has little or no chance to survive until external attacks and threats disappear. No one would listen to intellectual arguments – regardless of how convincing they are, for the inviolability of the Other while they are violated by the same Other. The last two centuries of Muslim societies, as I will explain below in greater detail, testify to that. The Universalistic School of Law in Islam lost ground in Muslim societies as a result of colonization by Western powers. Each time Muslim society has been attacked or felt threatened, communalism gained ascendancy. In response, some of the communalist intellectuals blamed Muslims for it and claimed that this was a Muslim problem which can only be solved by them. In today's interconnected and flat world, this may be a misplaced focus and an unrealistic expectation. The same applies for the efforts of the universalists in the West who cannot succeed if the Muslim extremists continue attacking or threatening their societies.

Thus it is the actions of both sides that together determine whether the we/they line favors the upper hand by universalists or communalists. For the same reason, the communalism on one side can only be controlled by the collaboration of both sides. This is more so at the age of globalization, which successfully turned the globe into a small village but has yet to discover how to foster neighborly relations and the inviolability of the Other in that village.

Human Rights *Versus* Civil Rights

A society usually recognizes the inviolability of its members[12] yet the inviolability of the Other is a divisive question for the society under consideration. In the process of addressing this question, societies usually break up into two rival camps by what I call the we/they line. The we/they line is a line of exclusion and inclusion that separates the Self from the Other by distinguishing a society from the rest of humanity. Some of us would like the we/they line to be unbreakably thick and high while some want it to be transparent, thin and low. Consequently, the we/they line brings about a cleavage almost in every society based on its approach to the Other: the we-side is usually divided because of its approach to the they-side.

Hence originate the differences between the advocates of universal human rights and civil rights.[13] The universalist jurists argue that the we/they line is inconsequential as far as basic human rights are concerned; therefore all human beings (should) have equal rights. In contrast, the communalist jurists assert that the "we/they" line has consequences on rights and thus the people on the "they-side" are not qualified for equal rights as those who are on the "we-side" of the line. The former group is concerned with the wellbeing of humanity as a whole while the latter group is concerned primarily, if not exclusively, with the wellbeing of the citizens of its own society. Here lie the roots of the cleavage in Islamic and modern jurisprudence, in Europe and in the US, between the advocates of universal human rights and those of civil rights at the national level.

How to draw the "we/they" line has divided Muslims, as it did the rest of the world, in their approach to the Other. How thick should be the "we/they" line separating Muslim and non-Muslim societies? The answer divides Muslims into two camps between those who see no difference and those who see the Other as unqualified for equal rights with Muslims. The cleavage between universalism and communalism has also been a feature of Islamic thought and law.

A universalist position, from my perspective, is characterized by two features. First, it accords equal rights to all human beings on the basis of their humanity alone, by making no distinction between Us and the Other as far as human rights are concerned. Second, it acknowledges that the Other also stands for universal human rights and cares for us no less than we care for them.

From this perspective, all universal cultures in the world make some provision for universal human rights (albeit in their own terms), and the emanating discourses and paradigms are incommensurable. It would be contrary to universalism to claim that only our culture provides for the guarantee of universal human rights, and that all remaining world cultures cannot. Claiming monopoly on human rights discourse is but another form of subduing the rest of humanity to our cultural superiority with the very claim that we are all equals – which our culture, but not theirs, establishes. That is just another subtle way of saying we are still not equals.

Highlighting, at the outset, the duality between human rights and civil rights perspectives in the classical Islamic and modern secular legal systems is vital for the ultimate objective of this chapter: exploring the compatibility and the possibility of the synthesis between the universalist strands of legal thought concerning human rights in Islam and the West. If we compare the universalistic tradition on one side with the communalistic tradition on the Other, we are destined to arrive at the wrong conclusions. Both cultures house exclusionist and inclusive worldviews and the structure of their legal discourse reflects the tension between the same duality.

Therefore, we should be attentive to comparing the inclusive or universalist traditions from each culture. This is a crucial prerequisite for a viable attempt for understanding how compatible they are and if a synthesis is possible between the two. But if we contrast the universalist approach from one culture with an exclusionist approach from another – as most of the polemical and ideological literature does – then our attempt would certainly be bound to fail.

Muslim jurists since the eighth century CE have been divided on these issues – as I will elaborate below. Some jurists, led by Abu Hanifa (699–767), argued that all human beings are inviolable, regardless of their innate, inherited or gained qualities, for the sake of their humanity. The followers of Abu Hanifa postulated this as: *al-'ismah bi al-adamiyyah*.[14] In English, the term *'ismah* means inviolability and the term *adamiyyah* means humanity, personhood or adamhood.[15] From this perspective, inviolability arises on account of one's humanity. Abu Hanifa and his followers from Hanafi and other schools envisioned a world law based on a universal normative system. The subject of law for them was the human being, but not the citizen of a particular state. As I will explain below in further detail, the Universalist School solidified its claim by rational and scriptural arguments from the Qur'an and the Hadith.

Not all Muslims have agreed with this universalistic approach. The communalists also formulated their arguments deriving from the same Islamic scriptures, the Qur'an and the Hadith, sayings of Prophet Muhammad. They claimed that the jurisdiction of Islamic law cannot be extended towards non-Muslims who do not believe in it. Nor can Islamic law be enforced outside the Islamic state. They argued that if the non-citizens do not accept the authority of our legal system and we do not have the power to enforce our laws, then why should we make laws for them? They argue that a law must be made by the authority that can enforce it.

Here we observe a dialectical relationship, rather than a linear evolution from one to another, between two strong forces influential on the society. Societies oscillate between universalism and communalism and between exclusion and inclusion. Important historical events in the history of nations trigger either tendency in societies. The Muslim society swinging from a predominantly universalistic culture to a predominantly communalistic one – owing to the colonization during the last two centuries – provides an excellent example for this process. American history also reflects an instructive example where it is possible to trace the enduring tension between the universalists and the communalists since the time of the founding fathers, whose universalistic legacy has not always been maintained as carefully by the leadership from subsequent generations. The civil war and later the civil rights movement may be seen as the manifestations of this latent and enduring tension.

Similarly, once dominant in Islamic theology, law and mysticism, the universalist interpretations of Islam are no longer officially adopted by the so-called Muslim states. Nor are they represented and advocated by any Muslim intellectual or scholarly community except for scattered solitary voices here and there in the large geography of Islam.

Recognizing inviolability of the Other is not the only difference between the concepts of human rights and civil rights. Instead, there are other underlying philosophical and procedural differences. Universal human rights are based on a notion that there are certain rights that are "natural," "born," "God-given," and "inalienable."[16] From this perspective, since they are inherent in every human being, human rights cannot be taken away by any authority. In contrast, the civil rights are constitutional in the sense that they are granted by the state to its citizens and can be taken away by it. One of the main purposes behind the idea of inalienable human rights is to protect the individual human being from the oppression of the omnipotent state by limiting its authority on its subjects.

Since human rights are thought to exist independent of the state and against its possible intrusion, a different procedure is required to protect and enforce them. The creation of the United Nations with its relevant arms was a response to the need for an international organization, whose authority is accepted by the member nation states, to enforce the universal human rights. However, the UN has never had the enforcement power the nation states have had. Consequently, without sufficient enforcement at the international level, the Universal Declaration of Human Rights faces the risk of becoming a merely "moral," rather than a "legal," document.

Multiple Grounds for the Justification of Human Rights

Those who accept the universality of human rights are further divided over the question of justification: Why is the Other inviolable? What is the reason why all human beings (should) have equal rights on the sole basis of their humanity? This conceptual discussion about the justification of human rights is different than the purely legal issues in the practical law. This distinction may be indicated, following Perry, by calling the issue of justification the *morality of human rights*.[17]

There have been countless attempts in the world for the justification of human rights. Almost every one of them makes an exclusive claim that only it can provide a coherent and logical justification for the universal human rights and refuses the intelligibility of the other attempts for justification.[18] Yet, from the perspective outlined here, for me to be right in my justification, the Other does not have to be wrong all the time. Therefore, in order to prove my own justification, I do not always need to disprove the rest of the arguments for the justification of human rights. There is a possibility that our arguments may complement each other.

I argue that there is not a single way of justification for human rights. Nor does it have to be. There is no reason for us to exclude the possibility that human rights can be justified in a myriad of ways by arguments originating from different levels and dimensions of analysis. As long as they all conform to the same normative rules, there can be multiple and multiplex grounds for human rights, emanating from East and West, from religious and secular thought. Each universal culture and religion offers the universal human rights within a language of its own. Furthermore, we should also be aware about the diversity within the universalist camp in each culture, rather than taking it as a monolithic entity. In each culture there may emerge several ways of justifying human rights.

These paradigms that are used by different cultures to justify the inviolability of human beings for their humanity are incommensurable. We cannot judge the intelligibility or plausibility of one based on the other. Plausibility is cultural and relative. Consequently, the mechanisms of justification are also diverse. What looks sensible for a religious person may look nonsensical to an atheist and vice versa. What is most plausible for a Buddhist may look implausible to a Christian or a Jew.

In such a situation, the advocates of a paradigm may easily be tempted to discredit the Other's attempt for the justification of human rights and attempt to make an exclusionist claim that the sole justification emanates from their paradigm. Alternatively, as I call for here, each paradigm may refrain from the temptation of claiming monopoly over the terrain and acknowledge the legitimacy of the other attempts of justification as long as their advocates find it convincing for themselves and their communities.

These differences between cultures and within them add to the strength of the universal human rights paradigm and create a global synergy. However, conventionally, each universalist school of law claimed the exclusive honor of justifying human rights, which is self-defeating for the cause of human rights and counterproductive. For our human rights law to be universally acceptable and applicable, it should be open to different narratives and terminology used for the justification of human rights.

Islamic culture provides an instructive example to how universal human rights can be justified differently within the same culture. For instance, the rationalist Mutazilite scholars cannot be expected to use the same language as Mystic Sufis. The same is true for the theologians and jurists.

A survey of Islamic universalist discourse demonstrates that there have been multiple grounds for the inviolability of all human beings regardless of gender, religion, race and color. Numerous arguments have been advanced by different universalist schools of thought in Islam: all human beings are inviolable (1) for being created by God; (2) for being loved by God; (3) for being honored by God as the best of creation; (4) for being vicegerents of God on earth; (5) for God's plan to try human beings on earth cannot be realized otherwise; (6) for the principle of reciprocity – do unto others what you like them do to you – requires so; (7) for God commands so; (8) for it is good in itself to do so.

Some of these arguments belong exclusively to a particular school of thought while some are commonly shared. For instance, the first and the second arguments are typically Sufi arguments. The third, fourth and the fifth arguments are generally used by the rationalist jurists. The sixth and seventh arguments are advanced by the traditionalist scholars who support their claims by evidence from the Qur'an and the Hadith. The eighth argument reflects the view of the Mutazilites, the rationalist theologians, on what is good and bad. Our purpose here is only to demonstrate the multiple grounds in Islam for the justification of universal human rights; therefore, I will leave the task of further elaboration to another study.

From this perspective, the right to inviolability is thus a universal and inalienable right in Islam founded on multiple grounds by diverse schools of thought represented by theologians, Sufis, jurists, traditionalists and rationalists. Some Muslims appealed to law while some appealed to love while trying to justify universal human rights. Since intelligibility of arguments has been seen as incommensurable in the classical Islamic thought, all have been considered valid.

Furthermore, Islamic law makes no claim to be the sole protector of humanity – instead it acknowledges that at the very basic level it serves the same goal as other legal systems in the world. This approach instructs Muslims on two principles: they should care for the Other and know that the Other also cares for humanity.

It is unanimously agreed in Islamic theology that the objective of religion since Adam – not only Islam but all religions – is to protect these six sacred rights. Covered by the right to inviolability in Islamic law are: (1) sanctity of life; (2) sanctity of property; (3) sanctity of religion; (4) sanctity of mind; (5) sanctity of honor; and (6) sanctity of family.

From an Islamic perspective, these rights constituted the permanent core of perennial human law and morality. Muslim scholars assert that all universal normative systems share these values which serve as the common ground among them. Furthermore, expectedly, each of these normative systems relies on different mechanisms, discourses and narratives of justification.

Each one of these arguments advanced by different world cultures to justify universal human rights[19] is characterized by a common feature: they are all founded on a concept of universal human rights. Universal human rights are accorded to that abstract subject the construction and emergence of which precede the rise of universal human rights. The existence of such a concept makes human rights possible in a culture because otherwise there would be no subject to which human rights can be attributed.

The right to be human or a person precedes, both logically and chronologically, all other rights. If a person does not have the right to legal personhood, they are by definition disqualified for any right because rights are accorded to persons. Since Aristotle, the law focused on citizens who enjoyed legal personhood while the rest of the people were considered below the level of citizens. Because they lacked the right to personhood, non-citizens did not qualify for rights or duties defined by law.

One may expect a linear evolution in the human thought but here we have an example of the opposite. While Abu Hanifa served as the voice of the propensity towards universalism, Malik, Ahmad bin Hanbal and ash-Shafii adopted the role of serving as the voice of the propensity towards exclusion. The idea of universal human rights evolved out of communalism but it could never completely replace it. Abu Hanifa lived before some of the above mentioned advocates of the Communalistic School, who came later, and yet opposed him. The same is true in Western legal thought where universalism and communalism still coexist as two rivals.

Why do we need multiple grounds for the justification of the inviolability of the Other and universal human rights? No justification in the world is – and would possibly be – convincing for all human beings. Different arguments may be more effective in convincing different people to refrain from violating the Other. Since intelligibility and plausibility are relative and incommensurate, one argument may look reasonable and convincing for a group while it may have no impact on another group. What works is different in each social and cultural milieu.

Inviolability of the Other in Islamic Law: Who has the Right to 'Ismah?

Now, we can have a closer look at the debates in Islamic law concerning the inviolability of the Other. All Muslim jurists in the classical era agreed on what rights should be protected under the coverage of *'ismah*, but there was a question that divided them: Does the Other have the right to *'ismah*? Is the entirety of humanity qualified for *'ismah* or citizens of the Muslim state alone?[20] Can Islamic law legislate for non-citizens to grant them human rights? Does all of humanity or the citizenry of the Islamic state alone, composed of Muslims and non-Muslims, fall under the jurisdiction of Islamic law? To what extent are Muslims allowed to intervene on legal traditions under their rule and on what grounds?

There emerged two positions in Islamic law as to the relationship between *'ismah* and *adamiyyah* or, more plainly put, as to who possesses the six basic rights covered under the title of *'ismah*. Abu Hanifa and his followers from Hanafite and other schools attached *'ismah* with *adamiyyah*, while al-Shafii and his followers from his own and other schools attached it to *iman* (declaration of Islamic faith) or *aman* (making a treaty of security).

The divide between those who accord inviolability to humanity, which I call the Universalistic School, and those who accord it to the citizens of Muslim state, which I call the Communalistic School, has yet to be explored in Islamic law. Below, I will try to expose this enduring tension which has thus far remained latent. This may be seen as just another example of how the approach to the Other divides a community.

The Universalistic School: The Other is Inviolable

Ibn Abidin, a prominent Hanafi jurist who lived during the nineteenth century, stated that "a human being is inviolable legally even if he is a non-Muslim" (*Al-Adami mukarram shar'an wa law kafiran*).[21] When he stated this principle, he was not making a new revolutionary statement as his counterparts had done at that time in Europe and America. Instead, he was simply reiterating a basic principle in the Universalistic School of law in Islam.

The Universalistic School in Islamic law can be traced back to Abu Hanifa, the founder of the Hanafi School. Abu Hanifa's close circle of students recorded his lectures on Islamic law and disseminated them after his death. He authored a few small books on theology,[22] but none on law. Abu Yusuf (182/798) and Muhammad al-Shaybani (189/805), two of Abu Hanifa's leading students, played a key role in transmitting the doctrines of their mentor in writing to subsequent generations. Tahawi (321/933), Quduri (428/1037), Dabusi (430/1039), Sarakhsi (483/109), Kasani (587/1191), and Marghinani (593/1197), among many others, systemized these views in encyclopedic works. Sarakhsi's *magnum opus, al-Mabsut,* has occupied a significant role in the development of the early Hanafi literature. Later generations of Hanafi jurists expanded, modified and reinterpreted the legacy of Abu Hanifa and his prominent students. Among the prominent Hanafites from subsequent generations are Zaylai (762/1360), Fanari (834/1431), Molla Khusraw (885/1481), Ibn

Humam (861/1457), Ibn 'Abidin (1252/1836) and Ibn Nujaym (970/1563).[23] Babarti (786/1384), Timurtashi (1004/1596), Haskafi (1088/1677) and Khadimi (1176/1762) are also among prominent Hanafite jurists.[24] The work of the Ottoman reformist jurists during the second half of the nineteenth century, mainly led by Ahmed Cevdet Paşa (1312/1895), represents the first attempt to codify and enact the Ottoman civil law. *Majalla-i-Ahkam al-'Adliyya* is a product of that period and reflects the universalistic Hanafi approach.[25]

It would be misleading, however, to see the universalistic approach to the inviolability of the Other as an exclusively Hanafite perspective – despite the fact that it originates from Abu Hanifa – because the followers of the Universalistic School expands well beyond the Hanafi School. There are scholars from the other major schools of law, such as Maliki, Hanbali, Shafii, and also Shiite, who subscribe to the universalistic principles. Among these non-Hanafite scholars from the Universalistic School of Law are Ghazzali (d. 505/1111) from the Shafii School, Ibn Taymiyya (d. 728/1328) and Ibn al-Qayyim al-Jawziyya (d. 751/1350) from the Hanbali School, Ibn Rushd (d. 595/1198), Shatibi (d. 790/1388) and Ibn al-'Ashur (d. 1394/1973) from the Malikite School, and Muhammad Jawad Maghniyyah from the Ja'fari Shiite School. This list is far from being exhaustive.

For the Universalistic School of Law in Islam, humanity (*adamiyyah*) constitutes the subject of human rights law. At this level, non-Muslims are not the Other for Muslims. On the contrary, humanity as a whole is considered as one and equal with respect to the right to inviolability. The right to inviolability (of life, property, religion, mind, honor, and family)[26] is considered *daruri* – literally translated, necessary, self-evident, axiomatic or given. The aforementioned six basic rights are termed *daruriyyat*, or the axiomatic rights, indicating that they are self-evident and also that they serve as the foundation or justification of other rights. From the perspective of the Universalist School in Islamic law, since the basic human rights are axiomatic, all human beings, be they Muslims or non-Muslims, enjoy them without any question.

For a universalist Muslim jurist, who is the Other at one level becomes the Self at another. Non-Muslims are the Other for Muslims at the level of religious beliefs but not at the level of humanity and human rights. Figuratively speaking, there are two converging circles: the circle of humanity and the circle of Islam. The latter is smaller than the former but a part of it. From this perspective, humanity as a whole is seen as the *ummah* of Prophet Muhammad; some have already responded (*ummah al-ijabah*) while some are still being invited (*ummah al-da'wah*).

The root for the term *adamiyyah* is Adam, the name of the first human being God created – according to the Torah, the Bible and the Qur'an. It is one of the rare common words in Jewish, Christian and Islamic cultures and languages. In Hebrew, *adama* means "earth," similar to Latin *humanus*, human, which is related to *humus*, earth. The connotation is that human beings are created from earth and live on the earth.[27] The name Adam occurs in the Qur'an 208 times.

Abu Hanifa and his followers found a universalistic concept of human being already offered by the teachings of Prophet Muhammad, which is reflected in the Qur'an and the Hadith. Otherwise, if their cultural repertoire had not tolerated and facilitated them to develop and construct the abstract concept of humanity (*adamiyyah*) as a universal category, it would have been impossible for them to make such a concept the foundation of their legal reasoning. Now we can look closely at the concept of human being in the teachings of Prophet Muhammad.

The Qur'an is addressed to the children of Adam, as were other sacred scriptures before it.[28] According to the Qur'an, God created all human beings with perfect souls and bodies and bestowed upon them the *karamah*, honor and dignity. God privileged all the children of Adam by assigning them as His vicegerents on the earth to promote good and to prevent evil, by speaking to them, by granting them intelligence, knowledge and ability to express themselves and communicate with Him and each other. God created human beings so that they know Him and each other because He loves to be known and He loves His creatures to know each other for this would increase their knowledge about Him. He put differences among human beings such as gender, color and language so that they know each other. Yet He declared that the superiority belongs to those with a higher moral conduct and piety. God looks at the hearts and deeds, said Prophet Muhammad, but not at appearances and wealth. God commanded repeatedly that His creatures also look at each other with God's eye.

God's love, grace and providence are universal, embracing all human beings as the sunlight. Therefore, all human beings, including the infidels who deny God, have *karamah*, inviolability and dignity. Human beings are required to treat each other with dignity – the way God treats them. Human beings should treat others the way God treats them and the way they want God to treat them. Human beings are not allowed to punish others for denying God or going against His will. God made it explicit in the Qur'an that "*thy duty is to make (the Message) reach them: it is our part to call them to account.*"[29] God loves human beings.[30] He also puts love between them to enable them to love one other[31] – which is what they are repeatedly commanded to do in the Qur'an and the Hadith.

It is, the Qur'an states, a sign of God that He created human beings as two sexes and put love and compassion between them. The gender difference is a means God created to try people. Eve is not the sole responsible for the Fall from Paradise. God forgave both Adam and Eve as they repented from their sins after the Fall. Consequently, all human beings are born with equally pure souls, free of sins, and each one is judged according to their own deeds. Both men and women are charged with the same moral and religious duties, except for minor differences due to their physical differences.

Similarly, it is a sign of God that He created people in different colors and divided them into different races, nations, tribes and religious communities. The same applies to the class difference or the difference between the rich and the poor. The poor have a legal right in the wealth God granted to the rich.[32]

None of these natural or God-given differences may be used to justify different treatment of a human being before law. If God had wanted, the Qur'an states, He could have made all human beings one race and one faith but the divine wisdom required otherwise. These differences are signs of God's art and a means to test people to see whether they would discriminate against each other. Human beings are invited to realize that the variable qualities – over which one has no or little control – are not what make a human being who they are, but the heart which one is required to, and able to, purify and reform.

This brief illustration demonstrates what Abu Hanifa and early universalistic jurists found at their disposal – which reflects many commonalities with other universalistic traditions, in particular Judaism and Christianity – to build upon. The *adamiyyah* as a term does not occur in the Qur'an but the notion is there. The universal category of *adamiyyah* is the contribution of the Universalistic School to the Islamic legal thought. Since it does not exist verbatim in the scriptures of Islam, the traditionalists who concentrated on the letter of the scripture refused to adopt it. Instead they used religiously or politically defined categories such as Muslim versus non-Muslim or citizen versus non-citizen. (I should note that citizenship is an evolving concept and did not have the same meaning in the Middle Ages as it has today.)

The existence of the construct of universal humanity is the most important prerequisite for the rise of universal human rights in a culture. The right to be human, as I stated earlier, precedes all other human rights. Having shed some light on the conceptual sources of the universal category of humanity, with which the Universalistic School is distinguished, now we can explore the arguments for the justification of a universalistic position towards the Other from the perspective of Islamic law. More specifically, we will be searching for an answer why Abu Hanifa and his followers in the Universalistic School of law thought that all human beings (should) have the right to inviolability. Simply put, *why should a Muslim accept that the Other is inviolable?*

The scholars from the Universalistic School used rational and scriptural arguments to prove that all human beings are inviolable for their humanity. Islamic theology does not condemn – nor does it hold suspect – secular rationality and reason. On the contrary, it is an indispensable part of the Islamic jurisprudence, especially the methodology the so-called People of Opinion (*ahl al-ra'y*) developed and used. Rational arguments are intended to convince all human beings while the scriptural arguments are intended only to Muslims who believe in them. Sometimes both approaches are combined. I will provide a brief survey of these arguments.

God's purpose in creating humanity is to try them to see how they will relate to their Creator, their fellow humans and the rest of the world. Being tried by God (*ibtila*) is both the honor and the burden human beings have to carry (*taklif*) in this life. This purpose of God in creating humanity cannot be achieved unless every human being has the right to inviolability and basic freedoms. If human beings are not inviolable and free, it would be impossible to try them, an important prerequisite of which is allowing them to use their free-will and mind. Otherwise, either they will be forced to accept Islam – which is neither allowed nor considered a virtue because it is not out of free-will – or their life will be terminated – which is not what God intended when He created them. Consequently, the mind and religion of every one must be respected even if it is completely different from what we believe as the true religion of God. Using reason and free-will is the only way to make moral choices which entitles one to the reward of God. Freedom of thought is necessary to ensure that people study and understand the divine message prior to accepting or rejecting it. The great Hanafi jurist, Sarakhsi (483/1090), summarized this line of argument as follows:

> Upon creating human beings, God graciously bestowed upon them intelligence and the capability to carry responsibilities and rights (person-hood). This was to make them ready for the duties and rights that God determined. Then He granted them the right to inviolability, freedom and property to let them continue their lives so that they can perform the duties they have shouldered. Therefore, these rights to carry responsibility and enjoy inviolability, freedom and property exist with a human being when he is born. The insane person (like the child) and the sane person (or adult) are the same with respect to these rights. This is why proper person-hood is given to him when he is born for God to charge him with the rights and duties when he is born. In this regard, the insane/child and sane/adult are equal.[33]

In the above citation, Sarakhsi, following the Hanafi tradition, reiterates that human beings are born with basic rights and freedoms. These are God-given rights which are necessitated by His plan to test them which is His purpose in creating them. Consequently, violation of these rights amounts to violating the broader divine order in the world and disrupting God's plan. Because all human beings enjoy the same status, violating the rights of non-Muslims would be a great sin and no different than violating the rights of Muslims. It is also important to draw attention to a striking feature in the writing of Sarakhsi where he makes no reference to the state or judiciary – instead he grounds these rights on a higher plane in which the state cannot intervene.

The writings of scholars like Sarakhsi did not remain only on paper. Consequently, not only the People of Book, comprising Christians and Jews, but also Zoroastrians in Iran, Hindus and Buddhists in India were allowed to enjoy inviolability as they continued to practice their religion under Islamic rule for centuries. The category of *adamiyyah*, which is the legal ground for inviolability, is much broader than the category of the People of the Book, including polytheists and idol-worshippers, the minorities who have also been granted sanctity under Islamic rule.[34]

Another argument used to prove the inviolability of the non-Muslims can be summarized as follows: Disbelief, the Universalist School argued, will be punished by God, not by human beings. Human beings are not required to punish all the sins committed against the will of God. Law is required to punish crimes that violate other people's rights or disrupts social order, but not the sins that are harmless to other individuals and to the social order.

Since *adamiyyah* never ceases to exist, the right to inviolability also never ceases to exist with human beings. Al-Miydani (d. 1881), a Syrian scholar from Damascus, wrote at the end of the nineteenth century that the person has sanctity by virtue of their existence (*al-Hurr ma'sum bi nafsihi*).[35] The only exception to this rule is when one violates another person's inviolability in which case they jeopardize their own inviolability in turn, and deserve punishment for their crime. Even then, the right to inviolability is not completely lost. Instead, it is conditionally suspended in the area where the punishment, which is required to be determined through due process, will be applied. Consequently, the suspects cannot be penalized until a legitimate court issues a verdict about them. Even then, the violability must be limited to the exercise of the legally determined penalty.

In conjunction with this, there is another line of argument why all human beings are inviolable from an Islamic perspective. Every human being has dignity and sanctity for being created and loved by God who would not like His creation to be unduly mistreated or devastated. As I explained above, all human beings have *karamah* (honor, sanctity) which God equally bestowed upon them all. Violating the sanctity of the Other amounts to violating the divine *karamah*.

In addition to these rather rational attempts for justifying the inviolability of the Other, the scholars from the Universalistic School used arguments derived verbatim directly from the Qur'an and the Hadith. From this perspective, all human beings are inviolable because there are many verses and sayings in which God commands so. Killing, stealing, sacrilege of one's religion or sacred symbols, and dishonoring family is prohibited by the Qur'an and the Hadith. Similarly, the Qur'an explicitly prohibits imposing one religion on people. Even during the war, the innocent civilians, in particular women, children, elderly men and the clergy who do not take part in war – the teachings of Prophet Muhammad make it explicit – are inviolable.

The Communalistic School: The Citizenry Alone is Inviolable

Similar to the advocates of the civil rights paradigm who oppose the advocates of the universal human rights paradigm, the majority of the Shafii, Maliki, Hanbali and Shiite jurists opposed the Universalistic School. It is important to remember that, as I pointed out above, some scholars from the above mentioned schools subscribed to the views of the Universalist School regarding the inviolability of the Other. Consequently, it would be misleading to perceive this divide as a divide between Hanafis and the rest of the schools of law in Islam. Instead, it would be more precise to think of it as a network of scholars from different schools who have formed a hidden constituency. Among the most important representatives of the Communalist School are Malik (712–795) the founder of the Maliki School, Ahmad bin Hanbal (780–855) the founder of the Hanbali School, and al-Shafii (767–820) the founder of the Shafii School. Numerous scholars followed them during the subsequent centuries such as Dawud al-Zahiri, Ibn Hajar al-Haythami, Shirbini, Qurtubi, Qarafi, Bujayrimi, Qadi Abu Bakr Ibn Arabi, and Khallaf. The majority of the classical Shiite scholars, such as Tusi and Hilli, also adopted the same approach.

Like the concept of humanity, the concept of born right is also absent in the thought of the Communalist School. These scholars commonly argue that inviolability is due by virtue of faith in Islam or compact of security with a Muslim state (*al-'ismah bi al-iman aw bi al-aman*). From this perspective the right to inviolability or basic human rights is not born, innate or inalienable. On the contrary, it is a gained right. One is entitled to the right to inviolability through their actions, namely believing in Islam or making a treaty of security with Muslims.

The Communalistic School argues that the Other, the non-Muslims (*kuffar*) who are not the citizens of the Muslim state, is not qualified to have the right to inviola-bility. They defend their position by the following arguments. Disbelief (*kufr*), the communalist scholars argue, is a rebellion against God and should not be tolerated. Believers should do their best to erase disbelief from the face of the earth because it is the biggest sin.

However, the Universalist School asserts in its rebuttal, this argument does not hold given the fact that the non-Muslims who accept the authority of the Islamic state (the *dhimmis*) by making a treaty of security with it are still non-Muslims which demonstrate that the disbelief cannot be seen as a reason for their inviola-bility. If disbelief had been the reason for not having inviolability, the *dhimmis* would have never had the right to inviolability. However, it is unanimously accepted in Islamic law that the *dhimmis* enjoy the right to inviolability.

From the perspective of Communalist scholars, the disbelief is the reason for the absence of the right to inviolability. As a result, the *de facto* status of the Other is not inviolability. This status can be changed only by one of two ways: voluntarily embracing Islam or accepting the citizenship of the Muslim state. In other words, from a communalist perspective, the Other is the foe unless they prove otherwise.

The communalist jurists use verses from the Qur'an and the sayings of the Prophet Muhammad as evidence to defend their position. They argue that the divine command in the Qur'an to fight against the infidels is eternal and unconditional.[36] The most commonly cited Hadith in this literature is "I am commanded to fight against people until they say: there is no deity but God."

Another line of argument the Communalist School uses to support their position is that people who are not citizens of the Muslim state are outside its jurisdiction. Therefore, Muslims cannot make any law concerning their inviolability. Even if they do, they will not be able to enforce it. Based on this, the Communalist School argue that there is no point in making law concerning the rights and duties of non-citizens.

Two Rival Root Paradigms in Islamic Jurisprudence

The above described divide on the inviolability of the Other between Universalist and Communalist Schools of Islamic law is founded on some deeper philosophical and methodological differences. I will try to briefly highlight some of these differ-ences between these two rival root paradigms in Islamic law.

First of all, the primary identity of the subjects of law for the universalist Muslim jurists was not the citizenship of a particular state but the citizenship of the world where they are sent by God for a brief period of time. The universalist scholars were aware that they were not only a member of the Muslim *Ummah* but also humanity. They combined brotherhood in religion with brotherhood in humanity. They were human beings before they were citizens. Their thinking was distinguished by incor-porating the universal category of humanity.

In contrast, the primary identity of the subjects of law for the communal jurists was based on the citizenship of the Muslim state. They emphasized brotherhood in faith and the citizenship of a particular state. Humanity was the Other which remained outside these two categories. The Other was neither the co-believer nor the co-citizen. Their reasoning was distinguished by the absence of the universal category of humanity. Instead, they relied on non-universal categories such as citizenry and religious community, the *Ummah*.

Briefly put, the subject of law for the universalist jurists was the human being regardless of their faith, nationality, or innate, inherited and gained qualities, whereas for communalist jurists the subject of law was the citizen of a particular state. The Communalistic School is characterized by the nascent absence of a concept of universal human being. Instead, it relies on identities defined by membership in political and religious communities.

The refusal to use the abstract concept of humanity by the Communalist School is in conformity with their traditional methodology which focuses on the letter of the scriptures. These scholars are commonly called the People of Tradition, *ahl al-hadith*. In contrast, the Hanafis are called the People of Opinion, *ahl al-ra'y*. The former group of scholars strictly follow the text of holy scriptures, the Qur'an and the Hadith, while the latter group try to capture the general meaning conveyed by diverse verses concerning a particular issue, and postulate them as universal principles. These general principles would then serve as reference points, along with the actual texts of the verses from the Qur'an and the Hadith, which jurists use in solving legal conflicts.

Another important philosophical difference that lies beneath the different approaches adopted by Universalist and Communalist Schools in Islamic law was conveyed in the construction of the authority to legislate and enforce laws. The universalist jurists constructed the laws and normative principles and dealt with the issue of enforcement separately. In contrast, the communalist jurists did not accept that these kinds of laws, which are impossible to enforce, should be made even if they are correct morally at the abstract level. Yet, the universalist jurists argued that the enforcement of laws rely primarily on the morality of human beings while enforcement by state plays the secondary role. In addition, since the ultimate justice will be realized in the Day of Judgement, it is not pointless to state the rules even if the state is not going to be able to enforce them. Today, with the rise of international organizations to enforce universal human rights, we can say, with hindsight, that the vision of the Universalist School has proven to be far reaching.

Inviolability as the Foundation of a Universal Law and World Order

Using the rational methodology of jurisprudence and putting a distance between themselves and the state, the universalistic jurists in the classical era made the concept '*ismah* the foundation of a universal law, applicable in the cosmopolitan *Millets* system. The concept behind the system of *Millets* is based on a meta-jurisprudence; a legal philosophy intended to embrace all legal systems globally. It is a self-reflexive activity by the jurists about their own profession worldwide. What do jurists from all nations and religions stand for? What do all legal systems stand for? What is the common ground among divergent legal systems? Why should all legal systems be granted legitimacy? Where does legitimacy come from? Is there a limitation to the right to legal self-determination? These are some of the questions the universalistic jurists from the classical period tackled.

Therefore, *'ismah* is a key concept not only to understand Islamic law *per se*, but also the way Muslims looked at the legal systems of the world and the way they incorporated them within their own social order. Then, *what is law for Muslims?* This question cannot be answered without reference to the theory of *'ismah*. The paradigm of *'ismah* plays a role in the way one looks at himself/herself and relates to others. This is true on the individual, communal and global levels: the I, the we and the We, as well as their interrelationships, are defined based on the concept of *'ismah*.

All legal systems serve the purpose of protecting human sanctity, the classical jurists observed. Therefore, they concluded, every legal system is legitimate so long as they serve this objective. Hence, the legal tradition of each community should be protected and those who adhere to it should continue practicing it. Islamic law was not imposed on the conquered lands and communities during the Middle Ages. Instead, each society was allowed to maintain its laws. Yet if there was a practice in contradiction with the sanctity of human beings it was to be abolished forcefully. For this reason, practices like *sati* in India or virgin sacrifice to the Nile in Egypt were not allowed under Islamic rule. Each community was allowed to enjoy legal autonomy but not to the detriment of human sanctity.[37]

One should bear in mind that the concept of *'ismah* emerged in a political structure which was not characterized by nation states. Nor was it characterized by positive law or a monolithic system of law. In contrast, the term human rights emerged in the West at the age of nation states and positive law. The difference in the circumstances in which these two theories emerged must be taken into account when comparing them.

The concept of *'ismah* is not only a legal one in classical Islamic thought; it is at the same time a moral and religious concept. One is not allowed to violate their own *'ismah* and the *'ismah* of others. One should protect their own *'ismah* and the *'ismah* of everyone else on the earth. But why? Not only because one may suffer legal consequences, but more importantly, for moral and religious reasons. Violating *'ismah* or failing to protect it is a major sin; God will punish for it in the Hereafter. Protecting *'ismah*, however, is a moral and religious virtue; it will be rewarded by God in the Hereafter.

According to Islamic theology, God may forgive sins committed against Himself, but not against other human beings. If a sin involves violation of a person's *'ismah*, the victim is the only one who is entitled to forgive it. God does not forgive the violation of human rights (*huquq al-'ibad*) because these rights belong to their bearers. Consequently, if one commits a sin by violating the right of another person, he/she is required to compensate the damage before repenting for his/her sin. Repenting without compensating the harm is not acceptable. A robber must return the stolen property or pay reparation before standing in the presence of God to apologize for his/her sin. Likewise, the person who damaged the honor of another must repair the damage and make the victim content prior to turning to God for forgiveness.

Some of the rights covered by *'ismah* are considered "the rights of the persons" (*huquq al-'ibad*) while some are considered "the rights of law" (*huquq al-shar'*) or "the rights of God" (*huquq Allah*). The reasoning behind the latter category is that their violators cannot be forgiven by the victim since it involves causing damage to the public, not only to an individual victim. If the crime involves violation of a personal right, the victim is entitled to reach a settlement, accept reparation or forgive unconditionally. Rights of the person comprise right to life and property. Rights of the law include protection of religion, mind, honor and family.

Reparation is acceptable if the crime involves the violation of one of the rights of a person and can be monetarily assessed and compensated. Otherwise, if the crime involves the violation of one of the rights of law, which cannot be monetarily assessed and compensated, reparation is impossible. Punishment must be applied in these cases. The victim may forgive injury or theft. The family of the victim can also forgive murder. But a raped or slandered woman cannot uplift the punishment from the rapist or the slanderer by forgiving him. The latter is considered a violation of public order, not only the violation of individual sanctity.

From the perspective of universalistic jurists, the rights *'ismah* embraces are universally granted, in an indivisible, non-contingent, non-reciprocal and inalienable manner. They serve the most basic needs of a human being to lead a decent life. These needs are called the "axiomatic needs" (*daruriyyat*). The concept *"daruri"* means given, axiomatic, self-evident, inevitable, beyond discussion, and absolutely necessary. Classical jurisprudence recognizes three types of need: axiomatic or self-evident needs (*daruriyyat*), required needs (*haciyyat*),[38] and the accessories or embellishments (*tahsiniyyat*). The first category alone is protected universally as human rights. The others are also emphasized in varying degrees.

The objective of all political and legal systems (*maqasid al-shari'ah*) is to ensure the protection of human inviolability and provide the needs for a decent life for each human being. This is how the classical jurists defined it. Therefore, they stipulated, the implementation of a particular law in a particular setting may be revoked, suspended or even reversed, if it is going to be counterproductive. The "axiomatic needs" have the power to override all laws. A legal maxim stipulates: "the axiomatic needs turn the unlawful into lawful" (*al-darurat tubih al-mahzurat*). For instance, drinking alcoholic beverages is prohibited but in the absence of any other drink one must drink them to maintain one's life; in that case, it is no longer a sin but an obligation. The jurists in the classical era tried to determine the borders of the axiomatic needs clearly and strictly, to prevent misuse of the permissions emanating from them.

Although they have the power to override all laws, the axiomatic needs of a person do not have the power to override the rights of others. For instance, if one consumes the food owned by another, out of dire necessity to maintain his/her life, he/she must compensate for it, because his/her need does not negate the sanctity of another's property. The needy person has the right to take this property, but he/she is at the same time obliged to compensate for it at a later time.

The above example can be used to explore the hierarchy among rights and needs. Right to life is considered the most prominent above all other rights. In the case of a conflict, priority is always given to it. For instance, if circumstances dictate so, one has to take the property of another person to protect his/her life because right to life overrides the right to property. In a similar way, if the axiomatic need of a person conflicts with the required need or an accessory of another, the priority is given to the first one.

The legitimacy of a political and legal system, universalistic jurists argued, depends on whether it effectively fulfills the functions expected from it (*al-Masalih al-Mursalah*), which is the protection of *'ismah*. Protecting inviolability is the most fundamental benefit expected from a political system, or it otherwise loses its legitimacy. "The legitimacy of political authority is contingent upon providing basic human rights" (*al-Mulk manut 'ala al-maslahah*).[39] The theory of *maslahah* (function, utility) in classical Islamic jurisprudence features prominently. A law can be based solely on that principle. Furthermore, existing laws can be suspended on that principle in some circumstances if their implementation is going to function counterproductively by causing harm, rather than protection to human sanctity.

Each of the six basic human rights constitutes a source of law, *al-asl*, on which laws can be built. For this reason, they are called the governing principles or sources of law (*al-usul al-khamsah*).[40] Again, this goes back to the methodology of Islamic jurisprudence. The root principles of law or the legal maxims, *al-usul*, which had been produced through induction from scattered teachings in the Qur'an and the Hadith, summarize the common rationale in the laws and, in turn, serve as grounds for new legislation.

The *'ismah* of a person remains intact under all conditions. No authority has the right to usurp it from a person. Nor does the individual have the right and power to voluntarily abandon it. The only reason that causes the *'ismah* of an individual to fall is their violation of the *'ismah* of others. As explained above, violating sanctity brings about punishment or reparation, according to the Hanafi jurists, while the Shafii jurists claimed both are required. Inflicting a punishment, which is a harm, is impossible before one's *'ismah* becomes suspended through one's own fault.

This is how the *'ismah* is legally enforced through punishment and reparation. The violator loses their *'ismah*, but not completely. Hanafi scholars are stricter on the extent to which a criminal's sanctity falls. They advocate that only the segment where the punishment is going to be implemented (*mahall al-jaz̄a*) loses its sanctity. On this ground, they refuse coupling punishment with reparation. However, the Shafii jurists extend the fall of *'ismah* in such a way that it includes both punishment and reparation at the same time.

Islamic law charges every individual, community and state to protect their own *'ismah* and the *'ismah* of others. One is responsible for the entire world. This is a moral, religious and legal duty. Dying for one's own sanctity or others' is considered martyrdom, to be rewarded by Paradise. If a state fails in protecting the *'ismah* of a citizen, it is required to pay reparation to the victim's family. For instance if a prisoner is murdered in a state prison, the state has to pay blood money to their family. The family of the victim is not even required to prove that there was negligence on the part of the state. Since it is the responsibility of the state to protect the sanctity of life in prison, it has to compensate for its failure. Likewise, if a person is murdered in a neighborhood the entire neighborhood is required to pay blood money if the criminal is not found.

The theory of *'ismah* had thus served as the foundation of a cosmopolitan legal system during the Middle Ages up until the collapse of the Ottoman State, peacefully embracing the diverse and contradictory laws of Jews, Christians, Zoroastrains, Buddhists and Hindus, along with different schools of Islamic law. The universalistic Muslim jurists stipulated the principles regarding the protection of human sanctity to be applicable worldwide, across all legal systems, irrespective of the faith behind it. The legitimacy Muslims granted to non-Islamic legal systems can also be observed in the way they remained open to receiving laws from them. The Methodology of Islamic Jurisprudence (*Usul al-Fiqh*) lists among the sources of Islamic law "the laws of the previous peoples" (*shar'man qablana*). If the Islamic law is silent on an issue, this rule stipulates, Muslims are allowed to adopt the laws from other cultures. It may be seen as yet another sign that the openness of classical Islamic law is for universal cooperation and exchange.[41]

Conclusion: I am Therefore I have Rights

Building upon the universalist approach to human rights, I argue that the very existence of a human being in society qualifies them for inviolability. Yet my approach to human existence in this context is a sociological and relational one, not a metaphysical and essentialist one. If a human being exists as part of a society, they must have rights for the sake of their existence. I must have rights because I exist: *I am therefore I have rights*. If you accept that I exist – which you cannot deny – you must also accept my right to inviolability. If I accept that you exist – which I cannot possibly deny – I must also accept your right to inviolability. The first one is an "is" statement while the second is an "ought" statement. The former logically requires the latter.

Did Robinson Crusoe have rights? No. This is because one can only have rights when one exists as part of a social network, which we call society. Rights are not inherent in human beings from an essentialist perspective; instead, they are inherent in them from a relational perspective because they are connected to each other via social relations. Mere existence in a completely solitary manner is only a hypothetical case as far as human beings are concerned.

A human being who is born in a society is also born into many relations within that society. And each relationship comes with its own rights and duties. Therefore, the concept of right is a relational but not an essentialist one. I am born with relations and thus with rights and duties. Likewise, I continue to exist with relations and thus with rights and duties. When a relationship is terminated, the rights and duties it brought also ends. Be it love or war, each relationship is characterized by rights and duties.

Neither the relationships, nor the rights and duties emanating from them, are reified. Instead, they are all fluid and constantly refigured along with the identities of social actors on both sides. Two cleavages dynamically shape the rights and duties: the we/they line between societies which separates the Self from the Other, and the universalist-communalist line within each society. These two cleavages are dynamically linked to each other and constantly reconfigured by the matrix of relations within and between societies under concern. It takes two sides to fight or to make peace.

However, some believe that there is a fixed set of rights which we have come to call "human rights." Yet, the unfolding events after WWII have proved otherwise. Since the declaration of the Universal Declaration of Human Rights (UDHR), human rights have been constantly redefined and expanded. The second generation of rights followed the first generation of rights and now we have at our doorsteps what is called the third generation of rights. These changes in the understanding of human rights may be seen as evidence that human rights constantly redefined as the relations are ceaselessly reconfigured in the social networks.

Consequently, human rights are not just a legal but also a sociological issue. Their emergence and evolution cannot be understood fully without taking into account the social creature we call human being, the creator, interpreter and the bearer of human rights, and their dynamic relations within a fluid social network. The matrix of relations within and between societies determines who we are, and who the Other is to us. The Other may be seen as an extension of the Self at a broader level, or it may be seen as the enemy. From the first perspective, we grant inviolability to the Other, while from the second perspective the Other has no right to inviolability. The Other divides the Self as the Self constantly tries to redefine the terms of their relationship with the Other. This universal pattern repeats itself in Muslim societies as well. Yet the terms of justification for each position vary as the societies oscillate between universalism and communalism in their history.

The close connectedness we enjoy today at the age of globalization, if combined with threats, attacks and counterattacks, may cause humanity, including Muslims, in the East and the West, to swing towards more communalism. Intellectual arguments in defense of universalism would have little impact in such a context of fear and suspicion. Yet, the closely connected and interdependent global society, if combined with a coalition of universalists from all sides, may establish firmly, more than ever, the inviolability of the Other. It is crucial in this vague process that the universalists speak up for their own society and culture which offers, as I tried to demonstrate above, a multitude of arguments with which they can arm themselves. Who speaks for the majority of the Other with an authentic voice – this is also equally important to discern.

Notes

1   See Abdullahi A. An-Na'im and Francis M. Deng (eds), *Human Rights in Africa: Cross-Cultural Perspectives*, Washington, DC: Brookings Institution Press, 1990; Ann Elizabeth Mayer, *Islam and Human Rights: Tradition and Politics*, Boulder: Westview Press, 1991.
2   One may also call it the *us/them line*. The universalist interprets it as "we *and* they" whereas the communalist interprets it as "we *or* they."
3   See Duncan J. Watts, *Small Worlds: the Dynamics of Networks between Order and Randomness*, Princeton, NJ: Princeton University Press, 1999 and Duncan J. Watts, *Six Degrees: The Science of a Connected Age*, New York: Norton, W.W. & Company, Inc., 2003.

4 For the account of a prominent journalist, see Thomas Friedman, *The World is Flat: A Brief History of the Twenty-first Century*, New York: Farrar, Straus and Giroux, 2005.
5 Frances Cairncross, *The Death of Distance: How the Communications Revolution is Changing Our Lives*, Boston: Harvard Business School Press, 2001.
6 The historian of science, Marcia L. Colish, calls Judaism, Islam and Christianity "sister civilizations." See, Marcia L. Colish, *Medieval Foundations of the Western Intellectual Tradition 400–1400*, New Haven: Yale University Press, 1997.
7 For a sociological account of Islamic philosophy, see Randall Collins, *The Sociology of Philosophies: a Global Theory of Intellectual Change*, Cambridge, MA: Harvard University Press, 1998.
8 Richard Bulliet illustrates the common historical experience between Islam and Christianity in his book, *The Case for Islamo-Christian Civilization*, New York: Columbia University Press, 2004.
9 In this chapter, I use both the Muslim and Christian calendar dates: the first date before the slash is according to the Muslim (Hijra) calendar, beginning 622 CE with the flight of Prophet Muhammad from Mecca to Medina, while the second is according to common era (CE).
10 On a general history of Islamic philosophy, see M. Fakhry, *A History of Islamic Philosophy*, New York: Columbia University Press, 1983; O. Leaman, *An Introduction to Classical Islamic Philosophy*, Cambridge: Cambridge University Press, 2002.
11 For value rationality and its relationship with other types of rationality, see Guenther Roth and Claus Wittich (eds), *Weber, Max, Economy and Society: an Outline of Interpretive Sociology*, Ephraim Fischoff, *et al.* (trans.), Berkeley: University of California Press, 1978.
12 This was not always true historically because not every member of the society was granted citizenship. The expansion of equal citizenship to all members of society is a modern development in the West. A considerable portion of the Greek, Roman and the medieval European societies had been non-citizens. Islamic political and legal theory, on the other hand, granted citizenship to all members of society, except for slaves, at a very early time.
13 "The term 'civil rights' is sometimes used by the courts in the broad sense of rights enjoyed and protected under positive municipal law in contrast with so-called 'inherent rights' vesting in the individual by virtue of a supposed 'natural law;' more frequently it is used in the United States in a narrower technical sense acquired in constitutional discussion concerning the legal rights of free Negroes in the years before and immediately following the Civil War. It was often coupled by way of contrast with the term 'political rights' . . . " John Dickinson, "Civil Rights" in *Encyclopedia of Social Sciences*, New York: Macmillan Company [1930] 1935, vol. 2, p. 513. For a more detailed discussion on the difference between "human rights" and "civil rights," see Rex Martin, *A System of Rights*, Oxford: Oxford University Press, 1997, pp. 73–126.
14 See for instance, Burhanaddin 'Ali ibn Abi Bakr al-Marghinani (d. 593 H), *al-Hidayah Sharh Bidayah al-Mubtadi*, Muhammad Muhammad Tamir, Hafiz 'Ashur Hafiz (eds), Cairo: Dar al-Salam, 1420/2000, II, p. 852.
15 On the concept of *'ismah*, see Baber, Johansen *Contingency in a Sacred Law: Legal and Ethical Norms in the Muslim Fiqh*, Leiden: Brill, 1999. In the lexicon, the verb *'asama* means "he protected" which is considered synonymous to *waqâ* and *mana'a*. For instance, *'asamahu al-ta'am* as a sentence means "the food protected him from hunger." The infinitive *al-'ismah* means protection. See al-Fayruzabadi, *al-Qamus al-Muhit*, Beirut: Muessese al-Risala 1419/1998, p. 1198; Ibn al-Manzur, *Lisan al-'Arab*, Beirut: Dar al-Ihya al-Turath al-'Arabi, 1419/1999, pp. 244–247. In Islamic theology, the term *'ismah* corresponds to "infallibility" which does not concern us in this article. For the legal concept *al-'ismah*, see Muhammad Rawwas Qal'aji, *al-Mawsu'ah al-Fiqhiyya al-Muyassara*, Beirut: Dar al-Nafais, 2000/1421, vol. I, p. 1401; for the equivalent term *hurmah*, see ibid., vol. I, p. 745–747. For the usage of *'ismah* in Islamic law, see Recep Senturk, "Ismet," *TDV Islam Ansiklopedisi*, vol. 23, p. 137–138; *"ismah,"* in *al-Mawsu'ah al-Fiqhiyye*, vol. 30, pp. 137–140.

16 For the rise of the idea of natural rights in Europe, see Brian Tierney, *The Idea of Natural Rights: Studies on Natural Rights, Natural Law, and Church Law 1150–1625*, Grand Rapids, MC: William B. Eerdmans Publishing Co., 1997.

17 Michael Perry, *Toward a Theory of Human Rights: Religion, Law, Courts*, New York: Cambridge University Press, 2006.

18 Samuel Huntington claims that only the Western civilization provides the universal human rights in Samuel P. Huntington, *The Clash of Civilizations and the Remaking of World Order*, New York: Simon and Schuster, 1996. Michael Perry argues that only the religious arguments can justify the inviolability of the Other, but not the secular ones (see Michael Perry, *Under God? Religious Faith and Liberal Democracy*, Cambridge: Cambridge University Press, 2003. (See also ibid.) Jack Donnelly adopts a position that only the Western-secular ideologies can provide universal human rights, but not others in Jack Donnelly, *Universal Human Rights in Theory and Practice*, Ithaca: Cornell University Press, 1989. There is a dangerous tendency to use the claim that a culture does not provide human rights to violate the rights of its followers: if their culture does not have human rights, then why should we treat them in accordance with human rights?! This is a twisted logic to justify violating the inviolability of the Other.

19 John Witte Jr. and Johan D. van der Vyver (eds), *Religious Human Rights in Global Perspective* I-II, The Hague/Boston/London: Martinus Nijhoff Publishers, 1996.

20 See Recep Senturk, "Adamiyyah and 'Ismah: The Contested Relationship between Humanity and Human Rights in the Classical Islamic Law," *Turkish Journal of Islamic Studies*, 2002, 8, pp. 39–70.

21 Muhammad Amin Ibn 'Abidin, *Radd al-Mukhtar 'ala al-Durr al-Mukhtar Sharh Tanwir al-Absar*, Beirut: Dar el-Kitab el-'Ilmiyye, 1415/1994, volV, p. 58.

22 For the works of Abu Hanifa on theology see, Imam-i A'zam Numan b. Sabit el-Bagdadi Ebu Hanife (150/767), *İmam Azamın Beş Eseri*, Mustafa Öz (trans.), İstanbul: Marmara Üniversitesi İlahiyat Fakültesi Vakfı (FAV), 1992.

23 See Burhanaddin 'Ali ibn Abi Bakr al-Marghinani (d. 593 H), *al-Hidayah Sharh Bidayah al-Mubtadi*, Muhammad Muhammad Tamir, Hafiz 'Ashur Hafiz (eds), Cairo: Dar al-Salam, 1420/2000; Ala al-Din Abi Bakr ibn Mustafa al-Kasani, *Bedaiu's-Sanai' fi Tartib al-Sharai'*, Beirut 1406/1986; Ibn 'Abidin, *Hashiyet Redd al-Mukhtar*, Istanbul: Kahraman Yay'. 1984, vol. IV, pp. 160–161; vol. V, p,. 58.

24 On the history of the Hanefi School of Law, see "Hanefi Mezhebi" in *TDV İslam Ansiklopedisi*, XVI, pp.1–12.

25 Cevdet Paşa, *Açiklamalı Mecelle (Mecelle-i Ahkam-i-Adliye)*, Ali Himmet Berki (ed.), İstanbul: Hikmet Yayinlari, 1982. There are voluminous commentaries on the *Mejelle* by Hace Reşid Paşa, Atıf Mehmed, and Ali Haydar Efendi. For the reprint of the English translation of the *Mejelle* see, *The Mejelle*, C. R. Tyser, D. G. Demetriades and Ismail Hakki Efendi (trans.), Kuala Lumpur: The Other Press, 2001 [Originally printed by the Ottomans in Cyprus 1901].

26 In Arabic, *'ismah al-nafs* (inviolability of life), *'ismah al-mal* (inviolability of property), *'ismah al-deen* (inviolability of religion), *'ismah al-'aql* (inviolability of mind), and *'ismah al-'ird* (inviolability of honor and family). It should be noted that I translated the last right (*'ismah al-'ird*) into English as two separate rights because the Arabic term *'ird* stands for honor and family in English.

27 Robert Hendrickson, *QBP Encyclopedia of Word and Phrase Origins*, New York: Facts on File, Inc., 2004, p. 7.

28 The message of the Qur'an is to humanity as a whole: on several occasions (seven times), God calls on the "children of Adam" (*bani Adam*) while He more frequently (twenty–one times) calls on the humanity (*nas*).

29 Ar-Ra'd [13:40] which states, *"alayka al-balagh wa alayna al-hisab,"* "Thy duty is to make (The Message) reach them: It is Our part to call them into account."

30 Among the numerous attributes of God mentioned in the Qur'an, a considerable number reflect his endless love, grace, providence and mercy. For instance, God is the Most

Merciful (*al-Rahman* which is repeated in the Qur'an more than 150 times), the Most compassionate (*al-Rahim* which occurs in the Qur'an 627 times), and the Most Loving (*al-Wadud*) (see Hud 11:90; Buruj 85:14).

31 See the Qur'an, Al-Anfal 8:63 which states "And (moreover) He hath put affection between their hearts: not if thou hadst spent all that is in the earth, couldst thou have produced that affection, but Allah hath done it: for He is Exalted in Might, Wise." See also, Al-Hashr 59:9–10, Al-Mumtahinah 60:7.

32 Az-Zariyat [51:19] states, "And in their wealth and possessions (was remembered) the right of the (needy), him who asked, and him who (for some reason) was prevented (from asking)." Al-Ma'arig [70:24] states, "And those in whose wealth is a recognised right."

33 Sarakhsi, Usul, pp. 333–334. *"Li anna Allah ta'ala lemma khalaqa al-insan li haml amanatih akramahu bi al-'aql wa al-dhimmah li yakuna biha ahlan li wujub huquqillah ta'alah alayhi. Thumma athbata lahu al-'ismah wa al-hurriyyah wa al-malikiyyah li yabqa fa yatamakkana min ada'i ma hummila min al-amanati. Thumma hazihi al-amanah wa al-hurriyyah wa al-malikiyyah thabitah li al-mar'i min hinin yuladu, al-mumayyiz wa ghayr al-mumayyiz fihi sawaun. Fakazalika al-dhimmah al-saliha li wujub al-huquq fiha thabit lahu min hinin yulad yastawi fihi al-mumayyiz wa ghayr al-mumayyiz."*

34 See Recep Senturk, "Minority Rights in Islam: From *Dhimmi* to Citizen" in Shireen T. Hunter, with Huma Malik (ed.), *Islam and Human Rights: Advancing a U.S.-Muslim Dialogue*, Washington, DC: CSIS Press, 2005.

35 Al-Miydani, *al-Lubab fi al-Sharh al-Kitab*, Muhammad Muhyiddin Abdulhamid (ed.), Cairo, 1383/1963, vol. IV, p. 128.

36 See the Qur'an, Tawba 9:5; Anfal 8:39.

37 Turkey, which allowed several legal systems to concurrently operate during the Ottoman period, is the first Muslim nation to switch to Western laws, which had been eclectically collected from different European countries. A scholar like Ebulula Mardin, who was a prominent professor of Islamic law teaching at Istanbul University Law School, switched to teaching the new European laws. So did many scholars. How they could legitimize the transition in their minds still remains a question for most researchers. I believe that their legal philosophy deriving from the universalistic approach and the Ottoman tradition of legal pluralism must have played a significant role on shaping their attitude toward the secular and Western laws.

38 The required needs (*hawaij* or *al-hawaij al-asliyya*) include social and economic necessities for decent life. The means that to serve the satisfaction of these needs are granted exemption from the annual 2.5% alms tax, *zakat*. Housing, nourishment, clothing, employment, transportation, daily security, and the like are considered basic human needs. Consequently, one's house, car, workshop, weapon, sufficient amount of food for a period of time are exempted from *zakat*.

39 (*al-Mulk Manut 'ala al-Maslaha*) The legitimacy of political authority is contingent upon protecting human sanctity (*Mejelle*, Article 58).

40 I translate *'ismah al-'ird* as the inviolability of honor and family. Consequently, the number of rights are five in Arabic, while they become six when we list them in English, due to the lack of a single term in English corresponding to the concept of *'ird* in Arabic.

41 Human rights culture is rooted in a pluralist science culture, allowing coexistence of truth claims. On the concept of "open science," which serves as the scientific culture of an open society, seen my articles, "Towards an Open Science: Causality and Beyond – Learning from Ottoman Experience," *The Humanities on the Birth of the Third Millennium*, New York: Fatih University and Brigham Young University, 2002; "Toward an Open Science and Society: Multiplex Relations in Language, Religion and Society," *Turkish Journal of Islamic Studies*, no. 5, 2001.

3 From Individual Sacrament to Collective Salvation

Muslim Community in Transition

A. Reza Sheikholeslami

The Problem

We know the world through the stories that we construct; the stories we tell. Within the story, the heroes and events make a whole: a synthesis, so to speak, emerges from the interaction of parts which alone apparently have no meaning. The story, i.e., the synthesis, is merely our understanding of reality. But the story is a paradigm that answers our immediate queries and anxieties. When our story does not adequately explain the world, when new questions emerge, when our anxieties are unabated, then we alter the story. We construct a new one: a new tale that seems to answer the new questions that the old story could not, the new anxieties that have emerged. The new synthesis includes much of the old thesis, its ingredients, ideas and rhetoric, and it also includes the abstraction of the emergent social reality. However, it still is, and necessarily so, transient. The new worldview survives so long as the world does not change, and a new social reality has not made our present synthesis outmoded.

As far as Islam is concerned, we used to hear a different story in the past than we hear now. The story that the Orientalists told us seemed to put a complex if not a chaotic world in order. Observers of Islamic societies used to argue that the rapid development of the Islamic realm meant the subjugation of religion to the state.[1] The Sunni establishment was presumed to be dependent on state patronage; in Shiism, in the absence of the Mahdi (the messiah), all political acts were considered equally amoral.[2] The majority of Muslims, i.e., the Sunnis, parroted the state, and the minority, the Shiites, did not express any opposition, and at times even feigned unbelief, *taqqiyah*, to protect themselves. Active self-subjugation and passive quietism summed up the Islamic worldview. Conservatism was assumed to be the pillar of all religious thought in Islam.

Islam philologically and characteristically meant submission, and omnipotence and omnipresence of Allah did not permit Muslims to consider alternatives. Muslims were believed to have internalized submission. The prevailing theory was that Islam was fundamentally apolitical, other-worldly, and that it was a solid base on which to build traditional, unchallenging, political structures. Thus, Bernard Lewis states categorically that "the Western doctrine of the right to resist bad government is alien to Islamic thought. Instead, there is an Islamic doctrine of the duty to resist impious governments."[3] He goes on to place 1400 years of Islamic history from Spain to Indonesia in a narrow Procrustean bed. The ruler of the Islamic world, Lewis claims, "has the right moreover the exclusive right to be obeyed in all matters of governmental judgements, discretion and administration, such as beginning and ending military campaigns, [and] collecting and expending money . . . "[4] Such monolithic and totalitarian theory brushes over a history of disobedience, rebellion, coups, riots and revolutions.

The theories of the Orientalists had repercussions in the world of decision makers. The existing paradigm that represented the Islamic synthesis was responsive to the questions raised about the past Muslim societies. At present, the old story, the Orientalists' synthesis, is inadequate to explain the prevailing militant conditions. The struggle, the opposition, and the powerful cry of "I refuse to submit" cannot be explained within the complacency paradigm of yesteryear. In the last decades, particularly after the Iranian Revolution of 1978–79, the new Islamic synthesis, as it appears to the outsider, has been radically transformed. The observers of Islam, at first, re-evaluated their quietist interpretation of Shiism and contrasted the radicalization of Shiism with the absence of a Sunni clerical class to provide leadership and the depoliticization of the Sunni majority. In the last two decades, however, the Sunnis proved the professional observers wrong on a global scale. Some leading members of the scholarly community, without explaining the reasons for the past mistakes, simply produced new syntheses to describe the present conditions. Thus, no longer is Islam considered quietist. Rather, it is "enraged." It cannot be the pillar for pro-western systems once opposing communism, as was assumed in the past; it is itself the major destabilizing factor everywhere. Almost by definition, Islam is now assumed, by some scholars, particularly in the United States, to be anti-western, intolerant, and deeply and irrationally hateful.[5] A new generation of scholars of Islam has done their best to convince the media and the policy makers that these are the fundamental particles that make up what is called Islam. Rejection has replaced submission as an Islamic core value. The religion that sanctifies Christianity and Judaism and has much in common with them is considered to be essentially, ideationally, and historically opposed to both.[6] The theory has serious policy implications. The new generation of Islamic scholars may be just as misdirected as their predecessors were, but they are certainly more directly, though less responsibly, associated with policy makers. The seemingly innocuous scholastic endeavor has been indeed a matter of life or death for many. "Scholarship" on Islam is one of the few cases in history where theory affects actual policies of war and peace.

Outsiders tend to observe a phenomenon in accordance to the manner that it affects them politically and economically. No wonder that the essence of Islam seems to change as Muslims take positions, voice grievances and challenges, or maintain silence and remain supine. Islam, once conceived to be peaceful and tolerant, is now considered to have been at war against Christianity from the beginning. Acts of political disobedience are not understood in the context of the immediate situation nor are they understood individually. All such acts, no matter how secular and this-worldly, no matter how an oppressive political relationship may have brought them about, are presumed to be merely a millennial clash with the West, western culture, and rationalism, and are primordially Islamic. Many scholars who identify the conflict between some Muslims and the imperial West are not afflicted with "enthusiastic ignorance" as Rashid Khalidi suggests, but they appear to suffer from "ideological blindness."[7] As the outsider, at present, is dominant, some insiders internalize the power relations and accept the worldview of the dominant as the only valid worldview.

The two syntheses presented above are deeply influenced by the observer being an outsider, and, therefore, seeing Islam not as a belief system that supports, represents, and is rooted in the changing social reality of a historical community, but as it affects the observer's universe of ideational and ideological commitments. Both view Islam as "the other." The more recent synthesis views it as the hateful, irrational, and unchangeable "other." The earlier one takes a more benign and avuncular view of Islam.

It is, however, important to study Islam as it is perceived and practiced in Islamic countries, rather than concentrating on the challenges and opportunities it creates for the non-Islamic world. Muslims who have studied Islam are often dismissed as apologists. The access to the decision-making process and the credibility of many scholars who deny the truthfulness of the basic Islamic principles, however, are not seriously challenged. If primordial belief can affect one's scholarship adversely, surely, so does primordial disbelief.

What is fundamentally wrong in the first two syntheses is that they both take a historicist and anti-historical approach. They both assume that Islam as well as Muslims are frozen in a time frame. The possibilities of social and ideational trans-formations are implicitly dismissed. There is, consequently, need for a third synthesis that will take into consideration the bonds holding Muslims together and the dynamics that move Muslims as members of a community.

The emerging synthesis should take into account societal changes that have trans-formed the Muslims' worldview from other-worldly to this-worldly. Muslims as socially interactive individuals who function within a variety of social frameworks should be studied both sociologically and as a changing social reality. Contemporary Islamic belief systems need to be interpreted as they are understood by Muslims at the time and not as what an outsider determines it to be now or assumes what it might have been at a critical point in history. What could have been historically true once is not unchangeably true today. In doing so, the new synthesis should study Muslims and not Islam. The question of the belief or disbelief of the observer will thus not conflict with the process of observation.

Methodological and Conceptual Questions

Most studies on Islam belong to one of two schools of thought. One school argues that Islam has historically withheld legitimacy from the state and thus it has set the foundation for political instability and continuous political opposition. The other school emphasizes the absence of church in Islam and thus the delegation of all authority to the state.

In contrast to these historicist contentions, it is posited here, in the Durkheimian tradition, that religions, Islam included, are fundamentally social phenomena which symbolize the prevalent *representation collective*. This framework is dynamic enough to allow for change. It can serve as an explanatory model to analyze how a religion can be a source of opposition at one time and support the power structure at another.

What Durkheim neglects, however, is that religion can be correctly understood only within the trinity of interactive patterns of the meanings of its rituals and symbols, the social position of the carriers of religious ideas as a status group, and the larger systemic social class structure within which it operates. From this perspective it is possible to formulate an explanatory model of religious change that is more comprehensive than the Durkheimian conception of religion, which centers mainly on its integrative function.

In the case of much of the Islamic world, given the dominance of power as a factual relationship, Islam has until recently performed a conservative political function. The clerics, as junior members of the ruling class, legitimated the state and often participated in the process of rule application. The dialectical relation between Islam as belief system, i.e., a set of ideas collectively held, and the state was rooted in the class structure of the Islamic societies, where the majority of the society consisted of non-urban strata and the position of the clergy was as a high status group. The societal changes brought about in the nineteenth century and more prominently in the twentieth, accompanied by the clerics' loss of status, radically changed the relationship between the church and the state.[8] The changes in the meanings of Islamic symbols, which have taken place in modern times, represent the transformation of a peasant society to a mass society.

Generally, the relationship between religion and politics has been a curious one. Frequently religion has institutionally supported and morally legitimized political rulers. Thus the Greek historian of Rome, Polybius, considered the "scrupulous fear of the gods" as "the very thing which keeps the Roman commonwealth together."[9] In the same vein, but with more wit, Gibbon wrote that the various forms of worship prevalent in the Roman world at the time of the Antonines, "were considered by the people as equally true; by the philosopher as equally false; and by the magistrate as equally useful."[10] And in the words of Charles I of England, who fell to a revolution (1649) which often expressed itself religiously, "the dependency of the church upon the crown is the chiefest support of regal authority: People are governed by the pulpit rather than by the sword in time of peace."[11] The philosophical tradition of the Enlightenment, from Voltaire to Marx, has provided more argument regarding the conservative, even backward, nature of religiously inspired political action.

On the contrary, religion has indeed at times supported, or even brought about, revolutionary situations. New religious interpretations did much to undermine the authority of Charles I and the official English ecclesiastical structure, just as three centuries later the radicalization of religion terminated monarchial rule in Iran (1979) and still, unnoticed by observers of Iran, eroded the authority of the established clergy as well. At present, re-interpreted religious ideas feed the resistance movement in Palestine and feed oppositions that are religiously articulated and politically motivated where the battle lines are drawn.[12]

At times, the role of religion has been less violent, but perhaps more fundamental in replacing the old archaic structures with modern ones. For instance, "when asceticism was carried out of monastic cells into everyday life, and began to dominate worldly morality," Weber argues, "it did its part in building the tremendous cosmos of the modern economic order."[13] During extended social crises, many values of religion, such as its emphases on collective orientation, selflessness, sacrifice, exemplary behavior, and equality, may affect and legitimize social protest.

The writings on Islam, by and large, concentrate on the presumed impact of the belief system on the community. Only a few studies, almost all of them carried out by social scientists, attempt to establish the impact of the society on the belief system. To some, Islam, as a set of fixed ideas, has historically supported the status quo, and, thus, any variation is aberrant and non-Islamic. To others, Islam has meant the denial of authority to the temporal rulers.[14] The vocal and violent opposition to the prevailing and globally inferior positions of Muslims seemingly supports the latter view both politically and economically.

The methodological problem with both of these approaches is that religion is conceptualized as a set of identifiable, compatible, and permanent ideas which dominate but remain above and independent of the society. In contrast to this Platonic tradition, it is analytically more fruitful to look at religion within the Durkheimian framework, in which religion symbolizes the sense of social solidarity of a society and whose symbols and rituals in turn perpetuate and strengthen that solidarity.[15] What Durkheim ignores, and some of his writings implicitly dismiss, however, is that the nature of the class structure in the society has a profound effect on its conception of itself. The conception of solidarity in a bourgeois society is obviously different from a feudal one or from a pre-class Asiatic one. Similarly, Durkheim's analysis leaves out any discussion of the carriers of ideas, i.e., the guardians and interpreters of religion, which as a stratum are placed in a favorable social position to dominate the thought processes. Weberian analysis, on the other hand, is keenly cognizant that the social composition of the carriers of ideas has a significant impact on the content of ideas.

Within this framework, then, it is argued that Islam has been a conservative, as well as a revolutionary force, in accordance with the changing nature of the Muslim social structure. The cycle can be repeated indefinitely in the future. In the pre-World War I (1914–18) period, which was marked by the dominance of military norms and institutions over embryonic civil institutions, political anarchy ironically coexisting with a high degree of social stability and a generally tribal and peasant social structure, Islam was a conservative force which legitimized military rulers. The religious leadership, i.e., the 'ulama as carriers of ideas, tried to maintain its high social status by maintaining social order.

The twentieth century, particularly during its second half, witnessed a rapid transformation of the Muslim societies. The continuous secularization, urbanization, and class formation affected the social composition of the carriers of ideas as well as their ideas. The subsequent religious re-interpretations paralleled, and in fact followed, the transformation of an elite-dominated society into a mass society. The other-worldly religious concepts, symbols, and rituals came to be interpreted in a worldly and often a revolutionary manner, representing the social change that the society was going through. The historical failure of the high clergy to manipulate symbols and rituals, their inability to translate their social power into an organized structure, and their continuous adherence to scriptualism (as opposed to folk religion) permitted the quick erosion of their positions and the emergence of new carriers of ideas.

The contemporary "clergy" may not be as literate as those of the past, but they are certainly more able to manipulate symbols and rituals and to represent the mass society of today as opposed to the elite structure of the past. It is significant that the leaders of the community who articulate the sacred values today are very different from the past *ulama*. By and large, they are civilians who think and dress as the ordinary members of their respective societies. The major impact on the way the society thinks is brought about by a non-traditional group of carriers of ideas, like the Iranian Ali Shari'ati (d. 1977) and the Pakistani Abu al-'Ala Maududi (d. 1979), who represent the contemporary community in a way that the traditionally-structured *ulama* cannot. The preachers of today increasingly look like their followers in appearance. Young crowds who, until recently, were alien to expressions of religiosity are now flocking to hear religious sermons. They listen to people like themselves, articulating their concerns in a contemporary fashion. "No longer is the turbaned Azharite the trademark of the Muslim image; Islam is now available in far more accessible format, open to everyone." An educated urban man summed up the situation in the Arab street. "I want to listen to someone who is like me, who speaks my language and understands my problems – not someone who dresses differently . . . compromises with the regime and offers only the most noncommittal answers." Secular outlook, political commitment, and refusal to bend before the enemy are the characteristics that the younger urban Muslim requires from his preacher. Ideologically and characterologically the new preacher is unlike the old.[16]

Religion and Society

God not only represents the community, He also guarantees its success and survival. One of the most popular Shii prayers, *al-Sahifah al-Sajjadiyah* by the Fourth Shii Imam, Zain al-'Abidin (d. 712 AD), simply asks God for that. The prayer invokes God so that He may give us success. . . . in all of our days, to work for good, avoid evil. . . . follow traditions, stop innovations. . . . defend Islam, diminish falsehood. . . . O God, guide those who are astray and help the weak.[17]

In the famous prayer of 'Arafat, attributed to the Third Shii Imam, Husain (d. 680 AD), God is portrayed as a giving and protecting father of the believers. The supplicant asks him for "the highest reward, the largest treasure and the lastingness of ease." The supplicant, furthermore, requests him to forgive "our sins, all of them," and asks God to "destroy us not with those who perish."[18] In the same prayer and in reference to the Qur'an is the promise that "If God helps you, none can overcome" (chapter 3, verse 160).

In much of the Islamic liturgy, Sunni as well as Shii, and for that matter in the liturgy in many other faiths, God is spoken of as if He were a person, albeit one of superior power and wisdom. What makes Him special, however, is the intimate relationship that He maintains with the members of the community. It is, therefore, not surprising that during tests of communal survival, the special relationship with this Being should be stressed through such intense religiosity as evidenced during the Libyan, the Algerian and the Iranian Revolutions and now in the resistance movement in Palestine, and as a general reaction to imperialism at present and in the past.

Not only is God anthropomorphized and brought to earth (in spite of the strong Islamic claims to God's absoluteness and unity), where He comes to represent the Islamic Community, but man, the martyr or the oppressed, is almost deified and hence linked to God. Passages in the Qur'an put men at the center of the universe as the vice-regent or caliph of God (chapter 2, verse 30). Other verses in the Qur'an indicate that this special rank means man's dominance over the universe. Chapter 16, verse 12 reads "And He subjected to you the night and the day and the sun and the moon." Or again, "Have you not seen how God has subjected to you whatsoever is in the heavens and earth?" (chapter 31, verse 20).

Although man is assumed to have been created from earth, a most common substance, the Qur'an asserts that God blessed him with His own divine spirit (chapter 15, verse 29 and chapter 32, verse 9). Angels were instructed to prostrate before man (chapter 2, verse 30). In many Muslim prayers, as well as mystic poems, humanity is seen as the vessel of God. It is through mankind that the believer comes to see God. "There is no difference between them [mankind] and You [God]," a popular prayer continues, "except that they are Your servants and Your creation; their success and failure is in Your hands; they commence from You and end in You."[19] By conceptualizing such a divinity, mankind in general and the Muslims in particular are saved from the world of the ordinary and the accidental.

Religion strengthens the Muslim's belief in himself and his/her life as being a member of the collectivity develops meaning. In fact, many Islamic writings present the earthly life as a microcosm of the much larger macrocosm. Man, therefore, becomes associated with something permanent, grand and celestial. The later development of the concept of the infallibility of the imams in Shiism and the miraculous powers of the saints and sufis in Sunnism are the extension of the original idea which saw God as the leader of the community. Other examples of this phenomenon include some radical ideas of the fifteenth century which held that God at times takes the shape of a person and that Moses, Christ, Muhammad, and certain other saints were godheads. The popular philosophy associated with Ibn al-'Arabi argues that all creatures are manifestations of God. Prophets are merely the highest forms of this manifestation. Moreover, the belief system strengthens the tendency of the community to perceive God as its symbolic representation. The Alphabetical Order, Hurufiyah, established by Fadl al-Allah Hurufi in 1401 AD, went even further and believed most men were capable of becoming God.[20] The secret of this ascent was supposedly in the hidden (and sacred) meanings that the Arabic alphabet symbolized. Nor is this the only example of ordinary items becoming divine as they come to represent a society. Even today, the change of the Arabic alphabet, as a totem-like symbol of the social order, is regarded by many Muslims as a sacrilegious attack on the community by hostile and sinister forces.

The absence of a clearly structured church, whose dogmas would have separated the sacred and the profane, has permitted the relatively easy incorporation of much of the ordinary traditional life and practices into the religion.[21] A whole class of things such as trees, water fountains, buildings, and tombs became divine to the people who lived within their proximity. Many human activities were drawn into this sacred circle. As mundane as many of the items and practices might have been, they represented the community in which they were located in a way that the maple leaf on the Canadian flag represents Canada. They were a source of pride, not only of veneration. Religious symbols, therefore, have above all been representations of social solidarity. In this sense, God, as the highest and most comprehensive symbol of solidarity, Durkheim argues, "is only a figurative expression of the society."[22]

Through ritualized processes, holidays, parades, all societies need to affirm their collective personality, or as Durkheim called it, their "collective sentiments."[23] Such rituals indicate the depth and breadth of internal agreements which hold the society together. In the case of the Muslim world such rituals are predominantly religious. The secular national holidays declared by many governments are often hollow and uninspiring.

The central political authority in many societies has been theoretically and popularly conceived as a link between the sacred and the secular. Coronations in these societies have functioned in elevating the person from the realm of the profane to that of the divine, rendering the king into a symbol of solidarity.[24] The attempts by Muslim court historians and panegyrists to call the prince *zill-Allah* (the shadow of God) falls in this category. The absence of rites and rituals associated with succession within political rulership, however, indicates the failure of the attempt. There is no evidence that coronation in the Islamic world performed a sacred function, transforming the monarch from an actual power holder into the symbol of divinity. While the office of the ruler had a sacred dimension during the Abbasid caliphate (750–1258), there was little religious pretension in other dynasties, whose efficacy was maintained merely by actual control of power.

From the perspective outlined above, it is possible to formulate an explanatory model for religious change that is more comprehensive than Durkheim's conception of religion, which centers on integrative function alone. In case of Islam, given the dominance of power as a factual relationship, the fear of lawlessness, and the patrimonial political system where the state acted as the main monopolist of the means of the production, Islamic clergy acted as a conservative force, trying to maintain the community. The clerics, as junior members of the ruling elite, had an interest in legitimizing the prevalent power relations. The dialectical relationship between the church and state was further strengthened by the clerical position as a high status group.

The societal changes brought about in the last fifty years or so have been accompanied by loss of the clerical group's social status. Other groups have emerged to replace it. Technocrats and businessmen have become the junior partner to the state without conviction or authority to serve as carriers of ideas. There is a void in ideational leadership and community needs that others have stepped forward to fill. The dialectical relationship between the church and state has changed. As the carriers of ideas have changed, so have the ideas. As the needs of the community have changed so have the symbols of the community. As the community's integrity or survival is under attack from outside, social mobilization has become more intense. Finally, as the community has transformed itself from a predominantly peasant to an urban one, the meanings of the symbols have become this-worldly, and as the attack is immediate, they have also become more present-oriented rather than deferring things to the afterlife.

The Rites of Togetherness

Islam, like most other religions, sanctifies its community of believers, the *Ummah*. The community in a way is deemed infallible. The Prophet is reputed to have said that his community would not unite on falsehood, a tradition that became the justification for *ijma'*, a source of Islamic law.

Collective duties in Islam, such as pilgrimage to Mecca, *hajj*, payment of special taxes for maintaining the community, and propagating good and forbidding evil, (*amr bi al-ma'ruf wa nahy 'an al-munkar*), as externalities of religiosity seem to dominate the deeply internal, mystical, and individual search for salvation. Islam almost from the beginning was a government, a system of rulership. Muslims almost from the beginning developed as a self-governing society. The Islamic state almost negated the need for a church as an organizational mechanism. Islam, therefore, perhaps more than other religions, has been an expression of social reality, indicating the validity of Durkheim's thesis that religion is something eminently social, "and that religious representations are collective representations which express collective realities."

The many collective rites of Islam separate the individual from their daily secular routine and impress upon them the power of the society of believers. The community, through religious acts, periodically regenerates itself. It is often assumed that the division of labor, institutional differentiation, and the expanding authority of public bodies have made the modern man more dependent on the community than their presumably individualistic, actually atomized, ancestors. In the Arabian context where Islam sprang up and in the rest of the ancient world, into which Islam expanded, this was not the case. Men lived as members of associations: tribe, clan, and village. No life other than a collective one was possible in a nomadic or an agricultural society.

Communal association with others was not an idealistic end. It was the minimum requirement for survival. Such absolute dependence on the society generates in man a sentiment of religious respect for it. Consequently, it is the society, Durkheim argues, "which prescribes to the believer the dogmas he must believe in and the rites he must observe." Islam negates monasticism, other-worldliness, and any other form of rejection of the society.

The final ownership of worldly possessions is commonly attributed to God. He is the owner (*huwa al-malik*), and, consequently, the world of the profane is linked to the divine, and security in an insecure world is insured. Social success is, therefore, tolerated as a sign of divine trust. Islam, in fact, goes so far as to deny the possibility of resurrection for those who cannot make a living. Not only the social association but also its material implications become aspects of the religion and are sanctified.

The roots of religion can be traced to the practical demands of social life. The clan structure of the Arabian society was transformed through Islam into a pattern of values and symbols which strongly emphasized the role of the community, sacrifice, and altruism, and attempted to restrain egoism and to develop supra-individualism. In short, Islam was the expression of social totality. Muslims, therefore, utilized these patterns of symbols, concepts, and metaphors to understand the social reality that surrounded and included them. Religion not only made the social world intelligible, it also made it an aspect of divinity and turned the subjection to it into a religious duty.

The moral ethics of Islam, and for that matter of other monotheistic religions, primarily ensure the continuation of social life. Condemnation of thievery, falsehood, adultery, murder, and the obligation to extend assistance to fellow believers are essential if the society is to survive. Stressing that vengeance is the prerogative of God, not man, prohibits the individual from taking the law into his own hands. And Islamic law (*shari'ah*), becomes the symbolic indicator of the solidarity of the faithful. Its efficacy and legitimacy are linked to the concept of compensation. The law rewards moral compliance and punishes those who do not abide by it. Anyone who would escape the punishment of the law in the present is surely damned eventually. The belief in the inevitability of reckoning surely strengthens the communal bonds.

Law itself as the norm of behavior in a regulated society, and even more importantly as the external indicator of the social conception of morality, has been deeply affected by Islam. Many local practices were Islamicized to find room for them within the Islamic law. The social conception of morality deeply penetrates the individual life as we enter the most personal matters: marriage, divorce, inheritance and so on. To behave according to Islamic law is an ideal. The law is not a utilitarian tool: it creates a sacred symbolism, obedience to which is an ideal. Islamic law, regulating everyday life, goes on to bridge the gap between this world and the next, the profane and the secular.

The Community Besieged

The discussion so far has emphasized the extent to which the existence of a community is essential to Islam. Indeed, the existence of the community is a main prerequisite to Islam. Sociologically speaking, one cannot remain Islamic as an individual Muslim. It is not an act of private piety that allows for an ideal Islamic life. Rather it is living in and dedicating one's life to the community that allows for an Islamic life.

Meanwhile, the social structure of the community has radically changed. The peasant society has become increasingly urbanized and is continuously challenged by outsiders who seem to threaten its existence. Urbanization has affected the communal understanding of cause and effect. Calamities once presumed to be of divine origin, acts of God, are increasingly considered to be social miseries, socially created. Misery considered as an act of God does not generate political reaction. Misery assumed to be socially created generates rage. The extension of secularization has focused attention on this-worldly dangers to the communal existence. This-worldly threats require immediate and political reaction. The rescue of the community is still a sacred, religious duty. It should be carried out through communal mobilization. In carrying out this sacred act, one cannot be inhibited by traditions which can no longer make sense to an urban, politicized person.

This becomes more imperative when the carriers of ideas, the new clergy, are themselves non-traditional, politicized, and the crystallization of the ideals of the present community. The traditional interpretations of the value of human life, the rights of the non-combatants, and the sacredness of one's own life, have shadowy meanings in this new context. As one can have no life other than a communal life, one's sacrifice to maintain the community makes sense and becomes not only rational but religiously incumbent on members.

As the internal dynamics and the prevailing political culture of the community have radically changed, the community itself feels besieged, indeed attacked. As members of the community fall or rise in defiance, they are not individuals. Through their acts they represent the sacred community as a whole and they become through their stands the crystallization of the moral order. Their public acts cannot be explained through the scholastic, arcane analyses of the teachings of Islam, but they can be understood as men and women who risk their lives to defend the sacred community, and they are therefore the idealization of the community of believers. What is now truly sacred is not the act of individual piety, but sacrifice to uphold the community. What is endangered is not God because of believers' failure to pray, but the community because Muslims have failed to defend. The call for action rather than the call for prayer becomes the order of the day.

The community is sacred. A human's spirit is assumed to exist within his body. The human body, therefore, becomes more sacrosanct than other objects. Christ's body was envisaged as an immanence within the church. The church was, therefore, sacred. Similarly, God exists above but also within his community. He is the highest representation of the community. Reciting his name is a communal expression of pride. There are ultimate political meanings to ordinary acts of calling his name. There is an ultimate political/social meaning to the recitation of *La illaha illa Allah* ("There is no god, except God").

The communal boundaries are between "us" and "them", the normal and the deviant, the just and the unjust, between those who seek peace and those who wage war. The dichotomy is established through religious ritual. Its vernacular is religious. The more pronounced and threatening the outsiders become, the more radically integrated the community becomes. The more endangered it is, the more the community will seek out the primordial bonds of togetherness.

Collectivity realizes its distinctively corporate existence through a structural apparatus, which is empowered to make collective decisions and take collective actions. For national societies, the state carries out this function, expressing national goals, respecting national symbols, and defending national security. When the state collapses, or when the state does not exist, such tasks are left to the society itself. Such is the prevailing situation in Palestine today. On almost a daily basis, communal leaders are subject to target killing, and immediately others of whom we had never heard replace them.

The new Islamic synthesis is the conclusion to a dialectical interaction between primordial identification as a thesis and the violent negation of communal solidarity based on primordial sentiments as its antithesis. Like all syntheses, the Islamic response has integrated some of its rites, belief system, and language with the this-worldliness and violence of the modern world which it negates. Conflict over a prolonged period has historically created resemblances.

Meanwhile, the community is under attack, the habitual acts of collectivity have become reflective and dynamic. Membership is not passive any more but active and conscious. The collectivity is reborn, rejuvenated. The crimes committed against individuals are crimes against everyone. In fact, they are crimes against the sacred community. Threats to collective existence, the collective identity, result in a collective act of mobilization to hunt down the enemies and protect the collective identity. The individuals in the threatening community are not perceived as innocent individuals, living an ordinary life. They all represent the constituent parts of a hostile community. They are hunted not as individuals, but they are depersonalized as merely the representatives of their respective community. Individuality has ceased to exist. The traditional theories of respect for the life of the innocent do not hold and they may merit intellectual curiosity, but do not describe sociological reality.

Many a researcher in the past that assumed the resistance fighters in Palestine and elsewhere who welcomed certain death were alienated, psychologically pathetic, and culturally backward individuals. Recent studies show that this is substantially untrue. Those who welcome certain death are conceived as the best the community has to offer. In an unequal war, they are the elite who defend the weak. Most suicide bombers are from societies that are dominated by superior external forces that threaten communal solidarity.[25] The martyr in fact has a celebrated position in the community.[26] Others observe that the Lebanese Hezbollah at first tried to conceal its suicide missions lest it would offend the sensitivities of Muslims who traditionally are expected to condemn self-annihilation. However, the tradition of clerical findings already had been replaced by a new tradition in which the guardianship of the community was paramount to other religious observations. The concealment was replaced by a public cult of martyrdom in which the suicide fighter became a religious, saint-like icon. In a community that was weakened and threatened, the martyr became the hero who negated the existing relations of humiliation. The martyrs by and large do not come from traditional backgrounds. By and large they are modern with modern educations. There is little that is Islamic about their act. Theological studies and *ex post facto* analyses, historical narrations, or, worse, fabrications, do not help. Sociology and psychology may show the way. In fact, the mission of what is called Islamic terrorism is universal. All societies venerate and celebrate those who risk their lives in the defense of their community and destroy the enemy. Whether it is the kamikaze pilot or the Hollywood-generated conception of the American soldier-hero fighting the Germans or the Japanese, those who risk their lives and the lives of individuals unknown to them in order to avenge a presumed injustice are recognized as heroes. The important factor is to die not for oneself but for one's community.[27] What motivates those who are about to die is the popular acclaim that they receive and the common belief that the community is unjustly threatened and the procedural/normal means of resolving the problem are unavailable.

In this communal war, it is the communal order that is threatened. This is the sociology of deviance. What once existed, what was normal, the status quo, is being opposed by deviant behavior. Durkheimian sacred and profane in this sense is the same category as deviant and normal. The profane and the deviant both threaten the corporate order. They both symbolically and actually oppose the order. The order is communal togetherness. The sacred is its collective representation.

Notes

1   See Hamilton A. Gibb, William Polk and Stanford Shaw (eds), *Studies on the Civilization of Islam*, Princeton, NJ: Princeton University Press, 1990.
2   AKS. Lambton, *State and Government in Medieval Islam*, Oxford: Taylor and Francis, 1981, pp. 267 and 271, and AKS. Lambton, "Quis custodiet custodies? Some Reflections on the Persian Theory of Government," in *Studia Islamica*, vol. V, 1956.
3   Bernard Lewis, *Ideas, People, and Events in the Middle East*, Chicago: Open Court Publishing Co., 1993, p. 314.
4   Ibid., pp. 315–316.
5   Bernard Lewis, *What Went Wrong? Western Impact and the Middle East Response*, Oxford: Oxford University Press, 2002. See also his "The Roots of Muslim Rage," *Atlantic Monthly*, Sept. 1990, pp. 47–60. When he lays out the argument that is later popularized by Samuel P. Huntington as "the clash of civilizations."
6   It is significant that Lewis, reprinting his essays from the past fifty years, omitted the following passage in his *From Babel to Dragomans: Interpreting the Middle East*, Oxford: Oxford University Press, 2004. In it he states: "Islam is one of the world's great religions . . . Islam has brought comfort to countless millions of men and women. It has taught people of different races to live in brotherhood and people of different creeds to live side by side in reasonable tolerance. It inspired a great civilization in which others besides Muslims lived creative and useful lives and which, by its achievements enriched the whole world."
7   Rashid Khalidi, *Resurrecting Empire: Western Footprints and America's Perilous Path in the Middle East*, Boston: Beacon Press, 2004.
8   Islam is presumed to be different from Christianity partly due to the absence of church in Islam. However, the institutional absence of a church and a structured pyramid of sacred authority does not mean that ecclesiastical function is non-existent in Islam or that a set of less structured sub-systems do not functionally perform institutional tasks. It is significant that many men of religious influence in recent history have risen from the non-clerical strata. Ali Shariati in Iran, Sayyid Qutb and Hasan al-Banna in Egypt are only three examples of a much larger group.
9   Polybius, *The Histories of Polybius*, translated by Evelyn S. Shuckburgh, London: Macmillan, 1889.
10 Edward Gibbon, *The History of the Decline and Fall of the Roman Empire*, 3 vol, London: Penguin Publishers, 1903, vol. I, p. 165.
11 Cited by Christopher Hill, "Religion and Democracy in the Puritan Revolution," *Democracy*, vol. 2, no. 2, April 1982, p. 40.
12 For the study of the Puritan Revolution see Michael Walzer, *The Revolution of the Saints: A Study in the Origins of Radical Politics*, Cambridge, MA: Harvard University Press, 1965.
13 Max Weber, *The Protestant Ethic and the Spirit of Capitalism*, translated by Talcott Parsons, New York: Charles Scribner's Sons, 1930, p. 180.
14 See for example the different approaches to the Shi'ite branch of Islam in Hamid Algar in *Religion and State in Iran, 1785–1906: The Role of the Ulama in Qajar Iran*, Berkeley and Los Angeles: University of California Press, 1969, takes oppositional statements by some

ulama as to mean their denial of legitimacy to the state, dismissing the long history of cooperation between the *'ulama* and the state. Although the *ulama* chosen by Algar are not necessarily representative of the whole status group, and even then the case is not established, he concludes Shi'ism has always negated the state. Joseph Eliash in two cogently argued papers, "The Ithna 'Ashari-Shi'i Juristic Theory of Political and Legal Authority," *Studia Islamica*, 1969, pp. 2–30, and "Misconceptions Regarding the Juridical Status of the Iranian *'ulama"* *International Journal of Middle Eastern Studies*, vol. 10, no. 1, 1979, pp. 9–25, on the other hand, points out that Shii theory denied religious authority not only of the secular ruler, but to the *ulama*, as well. In the absence of the *imam*, therefore, secular authority, though not infallible, could be carried out by the ruler with no legitimate challenge from the *ulama*. Said Amir Arjomand, "Religion, Political Action and Legitimate Domination in Shi'ite Iran: Fourteenth to Eighteenth Centuries A.D.," *European Journal of Sociology*, vol. 20, 1979, pp. 59–109, traces the accommodation the *ulama* reached with the state. Neither Elias's nor Arjomand's arguments established a framework for the understanding the present Shi'ism. By relegating religion to the other world, they fail to recognize the interaction between the social change and religious adaptation.

15 Emile Durkheim, *The Elementary Forms of Religious Life*, translated from the French by Joseph Ward Swain, London: George Allen & Unwin Ltd., 1915.

16 "Religion Anyone?" *Al-Ahram Weekly*, 20–26 October 2005.

17 Imam Zain al-Abidin, *al-Sahifah al-Sajjadiah*, translated into Persian by M. A. Sharani, Terharn, n.d., pp. 32–33.

18 Again, another popular Shii prayer, presumably given to Shaikh Abu Jamar Muhammad, a caliph of the Twelfth Imam, the Mahdi, during the Lesser Occultation (872–939 AD), by the Imam himself, asks God in the same vein, "Preserve us from sins. Give us what you determine adequate. Bless us with your regard. Leave us to no other than yourself. Do not deny us your goodness . . . Bring us to the month of fasting and the days and years that come after it." See Abbas Qumi, *Miftah al-Jinan*, Tehran, 1961, pp. 280–281.

19 The prayer is compile in ibid., pp. 531–553.

20 N.V. Pigoulevskaya, A. You. Yakoubovsky, I.P. Petrouchevski, L.V. Stroeva, and A.U. Belenitsky, *The History of Iran: From the Ancient Period to the End of the Eighteenth Century*, 2 vols, translated from Russian into Persian by Karion Kechaverz, Tehran: Tehran University Press, 1967, vol. II, p. 466–469.

21 Weber argues that rationalization of religious life as opposed to sanctification of tradition takes place when a priesthood establishes itself as a power and status group. See Max Weber, *Economy and Society*, 3 vols, edited by Guenther Roth and Claus Wittich, New York: Bedminster Press, 1968, vol. , pp. 500–503.

22 Emile Durkheim, *The Elementary Forms of Religious Life*, p. 226.

23 Ibid., p. 427.

24 Lee Edward Shils and Michael Young's discussion of the function of coronation in England in "The Meaning of Coronation," *Sociological Review*, vol. 1, no. 1, 1953, pp. 67–80.

25 See Robert A. Pape, *Dying to Win: The Strategic Logic of Suicide Terrorism*, New York: Random House, 2005.

26 Anne Marie Oliver and Paul Steinberg, *The Road to Martyrs' Square: A Journey into the World of the Suicide Bomber*, New York: Oxford University Press, 2004.

27 See the excellent study of the Hezbollah by the Israeli author Ami Pedahzur, *Suicide Terrorism*, New York: Polity Press, 2005; see also Mia Bloom, *Dying to Kill: The Allure of Suicide Terror*, New York: Columbia University Press, 2005.

4 From Dichotomies to Dialogues

Trends in Contemporary Islamic Hermeneutics

Meena Sharify-Funk

In recent years scholars of contemporary Islam have devoted increasing attention to an emerging literature that reimagines the interpretive identities of Muslims and the Muslim *Ummah* within the context of a new, pluralistic hermeneutic field. While it does not yet provide the dominant reading of Muslim politics, this growing literature offers a basis for new approaches to the study of Islamic interpretation and activism. It suggests a need for direct engagement with contemporary Muslim intellectuals, in a search for answers to questions such as:

> How are cultural encounters shaping Muslim identity and the hermeneutics of Islam? Is a more "open" Islamic identity possible?
> How are the contours and boundaries of interpretive communities defined? What influences and persons shape interpretive practices and Muslim self-understandings? How is Islamic hermeneutics affecting the transnational character of Muslim life and identity – and vice versa?
> Can the classical juristic dichotomy of *dar al-Islam* (the "abode of Islam") and *dar al-Harb* ("the abode of war") dissolve into a greater dialogical continuum characterized by symbiosis – *dar al-Ahad* ("a unified abode," or single world community)?

For decades, scholars have struggled to formulate an adequate terminology for differentiating among diverse ideological tendencies within Islamic religious culture. Though scholarly terminology has often succeeded in illuminating Muslim attitudes toward Western culture, the study of Muslim hermeneutics and of Islamic-Western dialogue is still developing. A new "hermeneutic turn," however, promises to generate deeper insight into the processes and politics of Islamic interpretation, particularly as they relate to matters of identity and intercultural experiences.

Trends in Contemporary Islamic Interpretation

Commentators focusing on contemporary tendencies in Islamic interpretation are by no means of one mind in their efforts to classify thinkers who are receptive to new understandings of Islamic ethics and morality, particularly with respect to the status of women. In addition to the hostile labels that are placed on "innovative" interpretive tendencies by Muslim protagonists of "traditional" social roles, a number of differing labels have also been applied by Western scholars and media analysts. Drawing on nineteenth-century usage of the classical Islamic concept of *islah* ("reform") some scholars construe "pro-anything Western" interpretations as "reformist Islam." In contrast, those who see open-mindedness with respect to issues such as democratization, civil society development, human rights, and gender equality (to name just a few) as a counterpoint to a broader phenomenon of Islamic extremism use the language of "moderate Islam." Those who believe that these issues are quintessentially modern speak of a "modernist Islam," while still others use such terms as "liberal Islam," "critical Islam," or "progressive Islam." Though the media tend to use all of these labels interchangeably,[1] each of them is laden with implicit theoretical as well as strategic or rhetorical content.

The lack of consistency in terminology used by interpreters and those who study their efforts should not deter analysts seeking to make sense of significant trends in contemporary Islamic thought. Despite differences, those who are called reformists, moderates, modernists, liberals, critical thinkers, or progressives often share a number of distinctive motivations. Their interpretive practices include:

> questioning traditional interpretations and legalistic structures;
> engaging in critical debate, especially through revisiting the historicity of traditional analysis; and
> deciphering and elucidating new meaning through processes of reinterpretation, often in relation to new contexts of experience (e.g., temporal, hermeneutical, cultural, political).

Due to inherent pluralism and the diverse influences motivating contemporary reinterpretive projects, all interpretive labels are best understood as approximations of dynamic, variegated, and fluid processes. Moreover, broad labels for diverse social phenomena can never be more than "ideal types":[2] they are only approximations capturing general tendencies, or lenses that disclose specific categories of meaning while downplaying others. The various labels applied to "new" schools of Islamic interpretation – especially those that Western scholars are inclined to view as "positive," such as "reformist"/"moderate"/"modernist"/"liberal"/"critical"/"progressive" – tend to overlap to a considerable extent, in implied content if not always in semantics.

Although the boundaries implied by terminology about Islamic interpretation cannot be not rigidly defined, words that are chosen for "favorable" trends implicitly invoke other categories of Islamic interpretation from which they have been differentiated. The existence of a "moderate" Islam necessarily presupposes the existence of an "immoderate" or even "extremist" Islam.[3] "Modernist" Islam requires a "premodern" Islam,[4] while "liberal,"[5] "critical,"[6] and "progressive"[7] labels presuppose "illiberal/conservative," "uncritical," and "reactionary" Islamic counterparts respectively. While each linguistic approach highlights different aspects of Islamic intellectual thought and bears within itself distinctive conceptual as well as rhetorical advantages and disadvantages, the "reformist" label has been most consistently applied by Western scholars of Islam because it is perceived as carrying less cultural baggage than alternative labels. As conventionally used by scholars of Islam, "reformism" (in Arabic, *islah*) presupposes not only a "traditionalist" project (*taqlid*) that seeks to maintain past precedents and forms, but also a more populist phenomenon of "revivalism" or "renewalism" (*tajdid*) – a movement that involves change in the character and content of Islamic concepts, but not necessarily along a trajectory that leads Westward.[8] Even the reformist-traditionalist-revivalist paradigm has limitations, however, for it is arguable that many if not most Muslim individuals are dwelling "in between labels."

As interpretive tendencies are found in Islamic societies, "traditionalist Islam" is also known among Western scholars as "conservative Islam" or "customary Islam." Reformist Islam sometimes includes secularist tendencies, whereas "revivalist Islam" correlates with such phenomena as "Islamist brotherhoods," and often with what Western observers refer to as "fundamentalist Islam," "political Islam," "radical Islam," and "Muslim extremism." In addition to conveying a stance toward Islamic culture and tradition, each of these ideal-typical tendencies also implies an Islamic intellectual orientation toward Western culture, as represented in the following "conventional" equations:

Retrench = Traditionalist

Reject = Revivalist

Reflect = Secularist

Relate = Reformist

Even though all of these tendencies have their own stories, with historically key figures and significant moments, there is an absence of scholarship that traces *how* and *why* each has emerged in relation to the others, constructing and (re)constructing one another's boundaries of meaning. Such research would enrich understanding of interpretative identities in the Islamic world, and of their impacts on Muslim societies as well as on relations between Islamic and Western cultures.

Hermeneutical Traditionalist Tendencies

In the "modern" traditionalist literature, scholars give particular attention to the role of interpretation, in which they generally reject and denounce the revivalist/fundamentalist and modernist reinterpretations while upholding a premodern synthesis of hermeneutic practices and normative conclusions.[9] Even though traditionalists accept that there are varying traditional interpretive tendencies, they advance the thesis that a coherent and generalizable "traditionalist" provides an ideal, comprehensive model for understanding and emulating the teachings of the Qur'an (holy scripture of Islam), Hadith (sayings by the Prophet), the Sunnah (traditions of the Prophet) and Fiqh (i.e., early Muslim jurisprudential scholarship). These teachings, as traditionalists propose, can and should be applied to contemporary society, through adherence to specific historical practices. The traditionalist model then presents Islam in its classical form, and is therefore a more "authentic" expression of normative Islam, as reflected in the Qur'an and the example of the Prophet, than modernist, postmodernist, and revivalist/fundamentalist approaches. Although traditionalist arguments vary, they all have two hermeneutical methods in common: (1) reconstructing "past originality"; and (2) a minimalist hermeneutics in which the interpreter suppresses textual ambiguities while claiming that the text "speaks for itself."

Traditionalists such as Seyyed Hossein Nasr, a Professor of Islamic Studies at George Washington University in Washington, DC, defend Islamic Law as interpreted by the five classical schools of Islamic thought (Hanbali, Maliki, Shafi, Hanafi, and Jafari), and maintain that its historically derived forms are completely providential – Divine. The Law (for traditionalists, this is not "law" but "Law") is the concretized Divine Will, and is *not* open to casual debate or pragmatic reform. This belief that the practice of the earliest believers and the interpretations of early generations of jurists provide the ideal model for contemporary society, especially for relations within the family and the community, reinforces an inevitably "crystallized" view of the Law and the traditions supporting the Law. Emphasis is placed on the "perceived" virtue of past Islamic communities, while modern Islamic communities are evaluated pejoratively for their failure to live up to the standards of their fore-bearers. Therefore, present-day contexts, whether religious, social, political, cultural or economic, are reconstructions of early Islamic communities.[10]

This normative stasis as prescribed by traditionalist beliefs is best illustrated in the restrictions placed upon one controversial Islamic concept, *ijtihad* (independent juristic interpretation). Although most traditionalists believe that the "doors of *ijtihad*" closed after the schools of thought were formed and fully institutionalized (approximately seven or eight hundred years ago), there are others like Nasr who acknowledge the possibility of *ijtihad* but only under the constraints of other traditional legal principles such as *qiyas* (analogical reasoning as defined by the intellectual elite), *ijma* (consensus of the intellectual elite), and *istihsan* (application of discretion in a legal decision). Unfortunately, these constraints severely undermine the potential of *ijtihad* by emphasizing obedience to deterministic concepts. However, the traditionalist argues for these constraints due to a strongly felt obligation to preserve authentic religious forms. "Complete" knowledge is transmitted from generation to generation, with a priority placed on memorization and fidelity to the wisdom of great synthesizers of the past, resulting in a "locked-in" mentality that penalizes innovation and prizes the legacy of past male scholarship and the heritage of received wisdom.

Many critics of the traditionalist approach particularly critique its "atomistic" nature.[11] These critics suggest that traditionalism tends to universalize the particular (that is, to selectively generalize from specific historical practices, injunctions, and utterances) while offering no consistent methodological principle to justify the absence of contextualization, the suppression of textual richness, and selectiveness that this approach entails.[12] By universalizing the particular, traditionalist interpretive practices have locked Muslims into narrow, rigid, and inflexible ways of defining their values and their identity. This absence of flexibility in interpretation has been cited as a core cause of the identity crisis that Muslims are experiencing today.

Tendencies of a New Hermeneutic Field

The Lasting Influence of Fazlur Rahman

Such adherence to atomistic as well as fatalistic tendencies was deeply unsatisfying for one of the foremost thinkers of modern Islamic hermeneutics, Fazlur Rahman. One of the many positions Rahman held was on the Advisory Council of Islamic Ideology, a religious policy-making body in Pakistan which proposed policies for implementation by the Pakistani government. Although he met with great opposition and finally had to leave Pakistan in 1968, it was this practical experience of initiating political and legal reforms that encouraged Rahman for the rest of his life to advocate for the transformation of a whole intellectual tradition.

In the decades since Rahman began his reinterpretive project, his works have become a major touchstone for emergent, transnational trends in Islamic interpretation. What draws many to Rahman is his ability to emphasize the need for a new opening of sacred texts, and for pluralistic exchange of opinions among scholars. By engaging Western as well as Islamic sources in a dynamic and innovative manner, Rahman provided an example that has provided inspiration to many "reformist" thinkers, especially but not only among women and educators. As in all of his books, Rahman poses his life-long question: "How does Islam as a religious, cultural, political, and ethical heritage deal with a modernizing and rapidly changing world?"[13] This explicitly stated question relates closely to Rahman's other implicit preoccupations, which might be formulated in the following terms: "How do Muslim scholars develop a viable Islamic humanism without becoming vulnerable to delegitimization by adherents of traditional fatalism?" "How can a dialogic hermeneutics and historical method be developed wherein one can reevaluate the past and differentiate those practices which advanced Muslim society from those which resulted in stagnation?"

An important summation of Rahman's reevaluation of Islamic methodology and hermeneutics, *Revival and Reform in Islam: A Study of Islamic Fundamentalism*, was composed at the end of his life and reflects some of his most important contributions to scholarship. In this study of intellectual ferment within Islam, Rahman investigates, dissects and confronts the main tendencies of revivalist thought, which can be found at various stages of Islamic history. His work also included the more recent period dating from the late 1800s, when scholar-activists such as Jamal al-Din Afghani and Muhammad Abduh sought to rethink Islam to make it a more relevant force in the modern world. Noting that the term "fundamentalism" can apply to adherence to basic principles as opposed to haphazard affirmation of historically contextualized injunctions, Rahman seeks to reframe the debate on Islamic norms and hermeneutical methods and present a viable alternative to traditionalism.

Rahman, like Nasr, rejects the revivalist tendency to superficially and selectively "Islamize" externally derived knowledge systems. Revivalists, Rahman notes, are preoccupied with the dilemmas of reflecting or rejecting dominant Western cultural powers and corrupt secularized Muslim regimes. Although their interpretations resemble traditional tendencies (i.e., static, atomistic and selective practices), their approach is defensive in nature, populist in style, and often lacking in scholarly discipline. They aim to protect Muslim society against encroaching Western cultural and political power and attach specific symbolic importance to a reaffirmation of selected traditional interpretations and practices, which uphold a moral social order (for example, the appearance and role of women).

Although Rahman does not explicitly focus on women in this book he does implicitly denounce the revivalists' view of the woman as a politicized symbol that represents both authentic, traditional Islamic values with contemporary socio-moral order. Unfortunately, instead of being a bridge between tradition and modernity, the woman is utilized as a political tool and manipulated in the struggle for cultural hegemony or political influence. His groundbreaking ideas would inspire generations of scholars, including many women interpreters, to challenge the status quo for women under Islamic traditional norms.

The approach advocated by Rahman aims at a comprehensive but internally derived overhaul of the Islamic intellectual tradition, not piecemeal adaptation or defensive maneuvering. Citing medieval sources and such eminent philosophical thinkers as al-Ghazali and Ibn Taymiyya, Rahman challenges the static notion of *irja*, or predestination, as seen in both traditionalist and revivalist thought. He believed *irja* created a sense of moral apathy and degradation of Islamic intellectualism which in turn nurtured fatalistic doctrines of "predeterminism" as well as "concrete" (static, formalistic) attitudes of conformism. This "uniformism" of Islam presented a monolithic ideal, effectively disregarding de facto Islamic diversity in thought and practice. Ultimately, such thinking impoverished theological and philosophical constructions of *tawhid* (unity of God or, from a philosophical perspective, the unity of existence), and reinforced both metaphysical absolutism and political docility in the form of "unconditional obedience to the ruler, no matter if he be a tyrant, a transgressor against the law and usurps power."[14] Rahman challenges the traditional fixation on authority and fatalism by demonstrating how the thoughts of two philosophers, al-Ghazali and Ibn Tammiyya, were terribly misconstrued and "miserably truncated"[15] to such a point that their works were used to legitimize tyrannical practices.

Rahman claims that due to the lack of a comprehensive understanding or "whole-text" learning, especially on topics of political authority, many political, fundamentalist, movements (e.g., Wahhabi movement in Saudi Arabia) have dangerously misrepresented certain philosophers' thinking by "piecemealing" the philosopher's argument to their own political agenda. For instance, even though there are strong *irja* (deterministic) elements within the thought of Ibn Taymiyya, (1263–1328), there are also counterparts to these elements, such as his extensive thought on free will. In his argument against the religious leaders of his day, Ibn Taymiyya pointed out how scholars tended "to affirm the divine will but [did] not affirm wisdom and [affirmed] only [God's] all-compelling will (*mashi'a*) without affirming mercy (*rahma*), love (*mahabba*) and no gratitude [contentment] (*rida*)."[16]

God's transcendent, omnipotent qualities of commandments and prohibitions were emphasized but immanent qualities were overlooked, resulting in a denial of human freedom. However, Rahman also stresses the fact that Ibn Taymiyya did not dismiss the concept of *irja*; rather, he was warning about the misuse of *irja*, i.e., "put[ting] determinism forward as an excuse for one's errors." In summary, Ibn Taymiyya's ideal scenario was the synthesis between Divine responsibility and human responsibility.

Rahman argues that it is the duty of philosophers to struggle with paradoxical realities, concepts and sources within Islam. An attitude of passivity, as manifested in traditional master-student relationships, had no claim in the pursuit of knowledge and the development of the Islamic intellectual tradition. Therefore, Rahman reclassifies Islam in the twentieth–century as "neo-fundamentalist" Islam, a reconstruction of "fundamental" or original precepts and practices within Muslim traditions in order to meet the challenges of contemporary Islamic societies.

In another famous book, *Islam and Modernity: Transformation of an Intellectual Tradition*, through the process of reinterpretation, Rahman advocates a renewal of Islamic intellectualism as it relates to the moral improvement of mankind. In his historical investigation, which utilizes a *longue duree* approach, Rahman points out that traditional Islamic models of juristic reasoning, such as *qiyas* (analogical reasoning), greatly restricted the ability of Muslim intellectuals to apply Islamic values. These models were very atomistic in their hermeneutical approach (giving priority to injunctions without context, and without an integrated philosophical sense of underlying principles), preventing comprehensive analysis of the whole text of the Qur'an and resulting in the equation of Islamic values with specific historical practices. In other words, Muslims have long lacked a well-developed "Qur'anic *Weltanschauung*" that might help them differentiate that which is essential and relevant to the demands of a situation from that which is not.

Rahman's reinterpretive hermeneutical process depends upon a "double" intellectual movement: (1) formulating an understanding of the Qur'anic *Weltanschauung* (in terms of general principles) within its historical context, and (2) reevaluation of contemporary social and moral context(s) within which Islamic values may be applied. First, one must move from the concrete case treatments of the Qur'an – taking necessary and relevant social conditions of that time into account – to the general principles upon which the entire teaching converges. Second, from this general level there must be a movement back to specific legislation, taking into account the necessary and relevant social conditions.[17]

Gleaning from the insights of Western hermeneuticists, in particular Hans-Georg Gadamer's principle of "effective history," Rahman stresses the importance of knowing our predeterminations and questioning our self-awareness of historical influences. However, he also questions the reliability of "whose" effective history is being asserted:

> This means that the process of questioning and changing traditions – in the interests of preserving or restoring its normative quality in the case of its normative elements – can continue indefinitely and that there is no fixed or privileged point at which the predetermining effective history is immune from

such questioning and then being consciously confirmed or consciously changed. This is what is required for an adequate hermeneutical method of the Qur'an. . . . [18]

By pointing out the impermanent, ever-changing nature of reality, Rahman challenges traditional, static tendencies and stresses the need for the development of an Islamic dynamism or an Islamic theory of social evolution. Such a theory would be based in his "double" reform movement of historical context analysis and social and moral context analysis. One traditional belief was that if you cannot define a religious concept concretely and operationally (in terms of specific behavior demanded from it), it would tend to be avoided in practice, vanish from intellectual debate, or permit excessive scope for individual idiosyncrasies. The concept of *ijtihad* ("the effort to understand the meaning of a relevant text or precedent in the past, containing a rule, and to alter that rule by extending or restricting or otherwise modifying it in such a manner that a new situation can be subsumed under it by a new solution"[19]), independent juristic interpretation, provides a notable example. Due to its potentially boundless, individualistic nature, *ijtihad* could have been impossible to regulate. It contradicted the "absolute authority" of the consensus of learned male elders, *ijma*. Rather than give free rein to individual interpretive efforts, jurists sought to restrict them and eventually proclaimed that the "doors of *ijtihad*" had been closed. Rahman notes that, ironically, closing the doors of *ijtihad* implied closing the doors of intellectual *jihad* (striving) for both men and women. Ultimately, historical reflection and open debate were sacrificed to the fear of abandoning historical authenticity.[20]

According to Rahman the obvious solution for reconciling tradition with modernity would result in the reformation of traditional educational practices that in turn – to use Gramscian terminology – becomes the reformation of the "traditional" Islamic intellectual into the "organic" intellectual. In his analysis, Rahman distinguishes between two directions of orientation for reform: (1) Islamizing modern secular education, and (2) modernizing Islamic education. The first movement he describes as "classical modernism," which can be viewed as a "defense of Islam" against Western ideas, and the second movement he characterizes as "contemporary modernism" which is the rise of secular thought within Islam. Rahman favors the second orientation of the "organic" intellectual, as a vehicle for meeting the changing needs of Islamic societies (i.e., impact of globalization, modernization, secularization, industrialization, and cultivation of science and technology).[21]

A variety of Muslim reformist scholars of hermeneutics, often under the influence of Fazlur Rahman's initiatives, are also challenging dominant contemporary traditional interpretive practices by revisiting the historical, social, and cultural contexts of the traditionalist interpretations as well as analyzing the interaction of these interpretations with the contemporary revivalist intent of the religious texts. Their intent is to interpret by utilizing old and new hermeneutical techniques, to comprehensively understand divergent approaches to similar issues, and eventually to influence a "reconstruction" of Islamic values and precepts that can be translated into contemporary Islamic social norms.

Imagining Muslims and the Muslim Ummah *in "Trans-" Formation*

In an article entitled, "The Coming Transformation of the Muslim World," Dale F. Eickelman, a cultural anthropologist at Dartmouth College, America, proclaims that Muslims are, indeed, living in a "profound era" of intellectual, social, and political transformation of their world:

> What distinguishes the present era from prior ones is the large numbers of believers engaged in "reconstruction" of religion, community, and society. In an earlier era, political or religious leaders would prescribe, and others were supposed to follow. Today, the major impetus for change in religious and political values comes from below. . . . These transformations include a greater sense of autonomy for both women and men and the emergence of a public sphere in which politics and religion are subtly intertwined. . . . In changing the style and scale of possible discourse, [Muslims engaged in such a discourse] reconfigure the nature of religious thought and action, create new forms of public space, and encourage debate over meaning.[22]

As suggested by Eickelman, more Muslims are expanding their perceptions of themselves and others, moving beyond premodern consensual thinking towards more self-reflexive thinking. These authors are suggesting that there is no one definitive discourse of Islam that can definitely label or shape Muslim identity. Rather, Muslims through transnational as well as transcultural conversations/negotiations are becoming interpretive agents of multifaceted textual and contextual realities.

This "trans"-formational nature of Muslim public experience has been described in a variety of ways, and some of the recurring characteristic tendencies include movement towards symbiosis in intercultural relations, notions of dynamism, and a "both/and" attitude of openness toward differences. Whereas discursive frames for discussing authentic identity have previously underscored the necessity of choosing between pure "Islamic" or "Western" options – presenting the intellectual with an "either/or" option – emergent approaches to interpretation underscore possibilities for reconciliation.

As pointed out by Farish A. Noor, a Malaysian human rights activist and academic, the new voices of Islam are products of this "symbiotic" relationship between tradition and modernity, between global and local, between West and East.[23] This relational symbiosis is the act of living together in a more intimate association or close union of dissimilar otherness, whether temporal or spatial. Transcending the bifurcation of the world based in static, separated preconceived concepts of self and other, symbiotic thinking encourages more organic awareness of "hybrid" or "creolized" identity as an ever-changing whole with endless frontiers.[24] In an article entitled, "Muslims Need Creative Pluralism," Tariq Ramadan[25] states a similar argument: Muslims (especially Canadian Muslims) need to embrace the multiplicity of their identity as well as their common humanity.

> Muslims must reform themselves; it is not for others to change. . . . It is a complex and difficult challenge that requires knowledge and analysis of traditional

Islamic sources as well as the Canadian environment, its history, its institutions, and its culture. We are only at the beginning of this process, but evolution is much more significant and tangible among younger generations of Canadian Muslims, particularly women. Society cannot disregard new realities transforming it from the inside. . . . What should bring us together today is our common citizenship: We live in the same society, we share the same challenges and future.[26]

An attitude of symbiosis between tradition and modernity as well as between culturally and geographically defined identities (e.g., Islamic/Western) creates space for relation, enabling all Muslims (whatever their walks of life) to openly discuss the complexity of being Muslim in the new contemporary contexts while simultaneously embracing context of humanity as a whole. Such symbiosis, as Noor suggests, is opening new constitutive spaces of debate, discussion and dialogue amongst different individuals on issues of identity, society, nationalism, and hermeneutics.

Contemporary Muslim commentators who argue for new conceptions of Islamic identity seek to ground their calls for change in basic reconceptualizations of Islam and Islamic tradition. Their approaches to communal values underscore dynamic relativity and the importance of context. As Abdul Aziz Said, the current occupant of the Mohammed Said Farsi Islamic Peace Chair at American University in Washington, DC, eloquently suggests:

Islam may be likened to a "river" rather than a "lake." Islam is in motion through history, and has never been static. Like a river, Islam has sometimes picked up sediments that are not particularly Islamic, yet the soils over which Islam has flowed have sometimes enriched Islam by providing new, culturally diverse ways for the universalism of the tradition to manifest. Islam is dynamic rather than static, and can be reconciled with modernity.[27]

Said's metaphor helps interpreters to conceive of Islam as something other than a static set of theological propositions. Interpreters must view Islam in living, historical contexts, as a tradition that is flexible and adaptive yet continuous across time. Encounters with new cultural and historical realities may sometimes "compromise" core Islamic notions, yet they also present opportunities for new discoveries and angles of vision.

In his exploration of emerging tendencies in modern Islamic thought, Sanjay Kabir Bavikatte, a professor of law and development at the University of Guyana in Guyana, South America, extols the importance of relativization:

[Globalised culture] links together previously encapsulated and formerly homogenous cultural niches forcing each to relativize itself to others. This relativization may take the form of either reflexive self-examination in which certain principles (projected as fundamental) are reasserted in the face of threatening alternatives or the absorption of some elements of other cultures. Second, it allows for development of genuinely trans-national cultures not linked to any particular nation-state-society that may be either novel or syncretistic.[28]

The process of relativizing is connected to another tendency: an attitude of openness and rediscovery – an affirmation of "both/and" possibilities inherent in contemporary cultural encounters and interpretive processes. In other words, it becomes possible to conceive one's own authenticity as in relation to the Other wherein tradition and modernity are rediscovered as realities that can be reconciled with each other. It also becomes possible to imagine life and religious ideals as emergent, rather than as static and concretized in a distant historical reality.

Another contemporary Muslim whose writings affirm such interpretive possibilities is Recep Senturk, Chair of History of Science at the Center for Islamic Studies (ISAM) in Istanbul, Turkey. In "Toward an Open Science and Society: Multiplex Relations in Language, Religion and Society," Senturk argues for an "open ontology" as well as a "multiplex epistemology" – that is, a more complex vision of the world that can accommodate different kinds of truths, including the truths of modern physical, social and human sciences as well as those of premodern metaphysical speculation.

> . . . [T]he essentialist and the relational approaches can coexist and complement if they are combined in a stratified image of the world and applied simultaneously. For such an inclusive approach we need to operationalize what I term an "open ontology," which postulates an "open world," a multiplex structure with multiple layers complementing each other. . . . Our worldview becomes "open" when we discontinue excluding layers and dimensions that are accessible to different perspectives and intellectual communities.[29]

For Senturk contemporary identity in any context needs to be approached with an all-inclusive, open-ended worldview. Ideally, such thinking promotes dialogical understanding and egalitarian cultural engagement. Epistemologically, it demands a broad and participatory process in which members of estranged cultures rediscover their respective traditions and come to respect one another's deeper cultural values and motivations. While gaining access to empathetic understandings of other cultural systems, they also begin a process of broadening and reconstituting the cultural as well as intellectual foundations of their own identities.

Through their questioning, a common pattern is developing: each is searching and promoting a new reflexive methodology. They seek to reinterpret religious traditions *holistically*, in terms of overarching as well as overlooked textual and contextual values, in order to articulate understandings that promote not only the empowerment of women, but also the initiation of reflexive change of Muslim societies. Such reflexivity encourages open dialogue among Muslims in search of forms of present-day originality that do not reduce the meaning of Islam to specific historical practices.

Muslims must reformulate their understandings of early and medieval Islam, extract essential Islamic values, principles and goals from the root sources, and move beyond legalistic reduction towards a more integrated, systematic and reflective methodology. Basically, Muslims must carefully examine relations between the sacred text and the contemporary, experiential contexts in which precepts must be translated into practice. Articulating the role of hermeneutics through which the Qur'anic ethos could be grasped as a dynamic whole, these scholars provide a compass for the application of Islamic values to modern problems. Though their interpretive efforts do not exclude traditionalist and revivalist perspectives from the circle of dialogue, their approach does presuppose a broader conversation. The new hermeneutic field that they seek to construct demands a softening of attitudes characterized by static certitude, and openness to previously "unthought" and "unthinkable" positions.

Conclusion

As this chapter has affirmed, a new hermeneutic field is opening within the contemporary Muslim *Ummah*. Though still struggling for recognition and legitimacy – many continue to deny its authenticity, and thereby put innovative interpreters on the defensive – an increasing number of Muslim interpreters are grappling with profound questions that demand hermeneutical engagement and scholarly sophistication. Given the importance of these questions for cultural and social change efforts in the Muslim world, much might be gained from a more systematic investigation of key issues that continue to be at stake. The following questions are particularly important for further exploration:

1) How are intercultural encounters shaping the identity and hermeneutics of interpreters who fall into the new hermeneutic field – especially among Muslim women? Is an "open" Islamic identity a viable cultural and intellectual possibility for them?

2) How is transnationalism affecting the way contemporary Muslim activists and intellectuals – especially those engaged in conversations about the status of women as "authorities" in Muslim societies – perceive their identities and engage in activism?

3) Is transnationalism facilitating the efforts of these Muslims to become agents of interpretation and social change?

4) What aspects of transnationalism do these Muslim activists and intellectuals find most empowering or significant? What does transnationalism *mean* to them, and how does it affect their perceptions of identity and social agency?

5) To what extent are Muslims who engage in "women and Islam" debates experiencing a "hermeneutic turn"? Are explicit ideas about Islamic hermeneutics shaping their identities and strategies?

6) How do contemporary interpreters and advocates of "progressive" reform respond to cultural and geographical dichotomies that have restricted the scope and character of Islamic identity – dichotomies that oppose the Islamic and the Western?

The search for answers to these questions will require direct interaction with contemporary interpreters, in a manner that elicits personal narratives as a basis for analyzing the impact of experiences with transnational dialogue. It will also require an ethos of participatory inquiry – a spirit of encountering the other, in a cooperative effort to understand how experiences of intercultural dialogue are shaping Muslim identities, and opening new horizons in the field of Islamic hermeneutics.

Notes

1   A good example is an article by Karim Rasian, "Indonesia's Moderate Islamists," in *Foreign Policy* (July–August 2002), which uses most of these terms (i.e., "progressive Muslims," "liberal Islamists," and "moderate Muslims") to define a new breed of Muslim thinkers.

2   The notion of an "ideal-type" was initiated into the context of social sciences by Max Weber in his chapter entitled, "'Objectivity' in Social Science and Social Policy," in *Max Weber on the Methodology of the Social Sciences*, Edward A. Shils and Henry Finch (eds), Glencoe, IL: Free Press, 1949, pp. 49–112. According to Weber, an "ideal-type" is a processual representation of "revealing concrete cultural phenomenon in their interdependence, causal conditions, and their *significance.*"

3   After the tragic events of September 11th, 2001, you find numerous articles, reports as well as initiatives supporting the project of "moderate Islam," all of which share a common objective: the prevention of terrorism by Muslim extremists. For example, some newspaper articles were Daniel Yankelovich, "To Defeat Al-Qaeda, US Must Build Trust of Moderate Muslims," *The Christian Science Monitor*, 20 September 2004, p. 9, and Radwan Masmoudi, "Why the US Should Engage Moderate Muslims Everywhere," *The Daily Star*, 26 October 2004. Other examples of supporting a "moderate Islam" agenda are found in the mainstream American institutions like the RAND Corporation's project and subsequent report, "Civil Democratic Islam: Partners, Resources, and Strategies." (For more information see articles by Paul Reynolds, "Preventing a Clash of Civilizations," *BBC News Online, World Affairs*, April 13, 2004: http://news.bbc.co.uk/1/hi/world/americas/3578429.stm [accessed 5 February, 2006], and Yvonne Haddad, "The Quest for a 'Moderate Islam,'" *Al-Hewar Magazine*, vol. 15, no. 2 (Winter/Spring 2004), pp. 8–12. The Carnegie Council on Ethics and International Affairs also sponsored a program entitled, "The War for Muslim Minds" (September 2004) in which Gilles Kepel, a French Arabist, argued with Ian Buruma, author of books dealing with radical Islam, that moderate Muslims (especially living in the Muslim diaspora found in Europe) may be more powerful than previously perceived. There are also Muslim organizations, like the Center for the Study of Islam and Democracy (CSID), which also advocate the project of "moderate/liberal" Muslims. However, as pointed out by Radwan Masmoudi (Executive Director of CSID), to be labeled a "moderate Muslim" may benefit a Muslim in a Western context (i.e., backing as well as funding from Western political institutions) and simultaneously delegitimize a Muslim in an Islamic context (i.e., all your projects are seen as Western conspiracies). See the article, Radwan Masmoudi, "The Silenced Majority," *Journal of Democracy*, vol. 14, no. 2, April 2003, pp. 40–44. This thought is shared by many other Muslim scholars and activists who promote the modernization of Islam but know they are stereotyped as being less authentic, less committed, and less solidly established in communal faith and doctrinal truth.

4   Charles Kurzman views the first wave of reformists from the last century as "modernist" Muslims (e.g., Muhammad 'Abduh, Muhammad Rashid Rida, Sayyid Jamal al-Din al-Afghani, Sayyid Ahmad Khan), distinguished by distancing themselves from the secularists who downplayed the importance of Islam while "privileging nationalism, socialism and other ideologies" and by differentiating themselves from the revivalist Muslim brotherhoods who advocated modern values but downplayed modernity by "privileging authenticity and divine mandates" in Charles Kurzman (ed.), *Modernist Islam, 1840–1940: A Sourcebook*, Oxford: Oxford University Press, 2002, p. 4. These Muslim individuals started some of the great modern debates, such as "Should the Islamic faith use traditional scholarship or

reimagine Islam in modern contexts?" and "Should the Islamic faith be engaged in original precepts or in modernizing original precepts to meet today's changes?"

5 Kurzman regards the second wave of reform ("or subset of modernist Islam" or "neo-modernist") from the last century as "liberal" Islam. In his view, a number of Muslim thinkers (e.g., Ali Shariati, Fazlur Rahman, Mahmoud Muhammad Taha, Abdullahi an-Na'im, Fatima Mernissi, Amina Wadud, Muhammad Shahrour) revived as well as extended the modernist Islamic discourse by providing new methodological frameworks of interpretation concerning Islamic scripture and law. They also began to reconcile Islam with the precepts and practices of Western liberalism; especially in the subjects of individual liberties, democratic processes, pluralism, civil society and gender equality. Resources: Charles Kurzman, *Liberal Islam: A Sourcebook*, Oxford: Oxford University Press, 1998. The National Endowment for Democracy (NED) has hosted many discussions on the "concerning prospects for Liberal Islam;" one conference was held on September 25, 2002, in which the keynote speaker, Nurcholish Madjid, as senior researcher at the University of Paramadina in Jakarta, Indonesia, and who also ran for the presidency in 2003, "explained how concepts of modernity, pluralism, and human rights do exist within Islamic tradition. He [also] argued that even when Muslims use modern secular institutions, their behavior can still be governed by Islamic ethical principles." *NED Newsletter*, Fall 2002, p. 5.

6 Peter Mandaville, in *Transnational Muslim Politics: Reimagining the Umma*, London: Routledge, 2001, analyzes an emerging trend comprised of men and women throughout most of the Muslim world who are negotiating the processes for meaning of Muslim identity in modern contexts through critical reflexivity and activity. These critical Muslims (e.g., Mohammad Arkoun) are "increasingly willing to take Islam into their own hands, relying on their own readings and interpretations of the classical sources or following 'reformist' intellectuals who question traditional dogmas and challenge the claims of the *ulama* to be privileged sources of religious knowledge" (p. 178).

7 Many new Muslim virtual as well as non-virtual organizations, especially found in North America, have emerged in the last five years with their identity being linked to "Progressive Islam" or "Progressive Muslims." Such formal virtual organizations are "The Muslim Meet-Up" (http://islam.meetup.com), "Progressive Muslim Network" (www.progressivemuslims.com), and "Muslim WakeUp!" (http://muslimwakeup.com) and a non-virtual organization called "Progressive Muslim Union of North America." According to Saadia Yacoob, a founder of the Progressive Muslim Network in Washington, DC, these Muslim individuals particularly advocate "a radical reinterpretation of societal structures and ideals, rather than proposing reforms that do not question the inherent oppressive foundations upon which the societal structures were built" in a conference paper entitled, "Developing Identities: What is Progressive Islam and Who are Progressive Muslims?" for the 33rd Annual AMSS Conference, September 24–26, 2004. Additionally, a colleague of Ms. Yacoob, Sanjay Bavikatte, defines Progressive Islam in an online paper entitled, "Allah is in the Details: Towards a Theory of Progressive Islam," found in *Qalandar* (an online journal which specializes on Islam and Interfaith Relations in South Asia), available at: http://www.islaminterfaith.org/issue.html [accessed 1 July 2003]:

> . . . as an ideology [which] emerges at the node of [a] complex matrix of reflexivity, relativization, and trans-nationalization. More specifically, Progressive Islam is a process of self-examination that results in attempts at cultural legitimization and assertion within Islam of specific 'progressive' ideas. These ideas may be both the result of absorption of elements of other cultures and a resurrection of previously marginalized ideas/fragments of belief within Islam itself.

See also insightful articles, such as Leslie Scrivener, "Progressive Muslims Challenge Tradition," *Toronto Star*, 16 October 2004, A1 and A26; and Leslie Scrivener,

"Progressive Muslims Responding to Very Narrow Version of Islam," *Toronto Star*, 14 November 2004, F7. See also Omid Safi (ed.), *Progressive Muslims: On Justice, Gender and Pluralism*, Oxford: Oneworld Publications, 2003.

8 For a good comparison of *tajdid* and *islah* see John O. Voll, "Renewal and Reform in Islamic History: *Tajdid* and *Islah*," in *Voices of Resurgent Islam*, John Esposito (ed.), Oxford: Oxford University Press, 1983, pp. 32–47.

9 See Seyyed Hossein Nasr, *Ideals and Realities of Islam*, Boston: Beacon Press, 1966, pp. 93–118.

10 See critique by Amina Wadud in "Muslim Women as Citizens?," in *The Many Faces of Islam: Perspectives on a Resurgent Civilization*, Nissim Rejwan (ed.), Gainesville, FL: University Press of Florida, 2000, pp. 206–209.

11 See Fazlur Rahman, *Islam and Modernity: Transformation of an Intellectual Tradition*, Chicago, IL: The University of Chicago Press, 1982; Wadud, *Qur'an and Woman*, Kuala Lumpur, Malaysia: Penerbit Fajar Bakti Sdn. Bhd., 1992; and Abdullahi an-Naim, *Toward an Islamic Reformation*, New York: Syracuse University Press, 1990.

12 Amina Wadud, *Qur'an and Woman*, p. 2.

13 Fazlur Rahman, *Revival and Reform in Islam: A Study of Islamic Fundamentalism*, Oxford: Oneworld Publications, 2000, p. 4.

14 Rahman, *Revival and Reform in Islam*, p. 80.

15 Ibid., p. 132.

16 Ibid., p. 149.

17 Fazlur Rahman, *Islam and Modernity: Transformation of an Intellectual Tradition*, Chicago: University of Chicago Press, 1982, p. 20.

18 Rahman, *Islam and Modernity*, p. 11.

19 Ibid., p. 8.

20 There have been many individuals to follow and further develop Rahman's arguments about *ijtihad* debates (i.e., Abdullahi An-Na'im, Azizah Al-Hibri). One of the more recent public discussions about *ijtihad* was at the United States Institute of Peace's workshop entitled, "Ijtihad: Reinterpreting Islamic Principles for the Twenty-First Century." For a summary of this discussion see the Special Report 125, USIP, Online. Available at: http://www.usip.org/pubs/specialreports/sr125.html [accessed 5 February 2006].

21 Interesting insights emerge when we juxtapose Rahman's project with the social and political thought of Antonio Gramsci. Gramsci's conceptions of political contestation, ideology, and "organic intellectuals" have influenced many Muslim feminists (once again demonstrating the transnational character of "Islamic" intellectual space). Although Gramsci stated that "all *men* are intellectuals," he also stated that "although one can speak of intellectuals, one cannot speak of non-intellectuals, because non-intellectuals do not exist" (see Antonio Gramsci, *Selections from the Prison Notebooks*, edited and translated by Quintin Hoare and Geoffrey Nowell Smith, New York: International Publishers, 1971, p. 9); hence, *men* may imply human (this of course could be a result of a translated oversight). Given his experiences in Pakistan, Rahman might agree with Gramsci that intellectuals are "subaltern functionaries" of Islamic superstructures: they can either form and maintain a hegemonic state or construct and sustain a counter-hegemonic movement. Rahman and most reformist thinkers promote the idea that "organic" reformist intellectuals play a key role in developing critical awareness as well as actively engaging in the formation of political and ideological consensus. In addition, followers of Rahman's initiatives would go one step further and reinforce what was stated by Edward Said, who is greatly inspired by Gramsci's insights:

> . . . the intellectual is an individual with a specific role in society that cannot be reduced simply to being a faceless professional, a competent member of class just going about her/his business. . . . [Instead,] the intellectual is an individual endowed

with a faculty for representing, embodying, articulating a message, a view, an attitude, philosophy or opinion to, as well as for, a public.
(see Edward Said, *Representations of the Intellectual: 1993 Reith Lectures*, New York: Pantheon Books, 1994, p. 11.)

Said clearly beseeches intellectuals to avoid the assimilated traps of "subaltern functionaries" and give their active consent to counter-hegemonic movements by representing the "weak and unrepresented" (Said, *Representations of the Intellectual*, p. 22). This "art of representing" in a critical manner is crucial for the emancipation of Muslim women. As stated by Said, "the purpose of the intellectual's activity is to advance human freedom and knowledge" (ibid., p. 17). Gleaning from the analysis of the intellectual by Gramsci and Said, other questions to explore in further research are raised: How organically developed are the intellectual strata of Islamic societies? What is the degree of connection that reformist intellectuals have with fundamental, traditional social groups? And how established are the gradations of their functions and of the gender-hegemonic superstructures?

22 Dale F. Eickelman, "The Coming Transformation of the Muslim World," in *Middle East Review of International Affairs*, vol. 3, no. 3 (September 1999) or Online. Available at: http://www.biu.ac.il/SOC/besa/meria/journal/1999/issue3/jv3n3a8.html [accessed 28 January 2006].

23 Farish A. Noor (ed.), *The New Voices of Islam*, Leiden, Netherlands: ISIM Publications, 2002, p. 1. Noor edited this volume when he was a visiting fellow at the International Institute for the Study of Islam in the Modern World (ISIM). For more information about ISIM and its research projects, go to: http://www.isim.nl. Noor also was the Secretary General of the International Movement for a Just World (JUST) and has taught at the Centre for Civilizational Dialogue at the University of Malaya.

24 See Daniel Williams, "'Modern Muslims' Forge Hybrid Culture," *The Washington Post*, 24 July 2004, A15; and Jon W. Anderson's paper, "Muslim Networks, Muslim Selves in Cyberspace: Islam in the Post-Modern Public Sphere," Online. Available at: http://www.mafhoum.com/press3/102S22.htm [accessed 28 January 2006].

25 See Jane Lampman, "Muslim Scholar Barred from US Preaches Tolerance," *The Christian Science Monitor*, 21 September 2004, p. 16. This article describes the controversy over Homeland Security's decision to revoke the visa of Tariq Ramadan, who had been offered the position of the Henry R. Luce Professor of Religion, Conflict and Peacebuilding at the University of Notre Dame's Joan Kroc Institute. There were many other articles by concerned scholars demonstrating their support for Ramadan's scholarship, such as Paul Donnelly, "The Ban on a Muslim Scholar," *The Washington Post*, 28 August 2004, A25 and Diana L. Eck, "Why Exclude a Muslim Voice?," *The Boston Globe*, 4 September 2004. Tariq Ramadan also wrote in petition an op-ed article, "Too Scary for the Classroom?," *The New York Times*, 1 September 2004. Although Ramadan has been critical about the position of the US towards war in Iraq and the US-Israeli policies in Israel/Palestine, many of these American scholars state that there is no justification for denying Ramadan entrance into America which upholds the right to freely express and criticize; especially when one's intention is towards efforts of reform and dialogue.

26 Tariq Ramadan, "Muslims Need Creative Pluralism," *The Globe and Mail*, 19 February 2005, A23. In another article, Peter Ford, "Europe's Rising Class of Believers: Muslims," *The Christian Science Monitor*, 24 February 2005, Ramadan also stated, "Muslims living in Europe have an opportunity to reread our [religious] source. . . . We are going through a reassessment and the most important subject is women. Our experience in Europe has made it clear we must speak about equality." A friend and colleague of Ramadan on various projects, Azizah Al-Hibri, a Professor of Law at the T.C. Williams School of Law in Richmond, VA, stated a similar argument that was, however, applied not to Canadian or European Muslims but to American Muslims:

In order to be good Americans in this country, first of all you have to be good Muslims. . . . We need to be psychologically bound to this land, because this is where we are going to live and die. We need to understand that we are engaged in nation-building . . . We also need to understand that democracy is a work in progress. There are still a lot of defects in this democracy, and certainly Muslims have suffered from some of these defects . . . but that is no reason to despair. That is a reason to start a civil rights movement.

How do you start a civil rights movement for Muslims, or for Arabs, or other groups? First you have to know the history of the civil rights movement in this country. You have to know what Martin Luther King, Jr. and Malcolm X and others did. We need to rediscover our history, rediscover America's history, redefine it and redefine ourselves. . . .

For more of Al-Hibri's speech see "Dr. Azizah Al-Hibri Explores What it Means To Be an American Muslim," in *The American Arab Dialogue: English Supplement of Al-Hewar Magazine*, vol. 16, no. 2, (Winter/Spring 2005).

27 Abdul Aziz Said, "Toward a Contemporary Islamic Synthesis," opening speech for the international conference, "Contemporary Islamic Synthesis" at the Library of Alexandria in Egypt, 4–5 October, 2003, p. 1.

28 For more on Bavikatte's thoughts on the competing visions within Muslim thought see "Promises of a Brave New World," in *CHOWK On-Line*. Available at: http://www.chowk.com/show_article.cgi?aid=00001418&channel=university%20ave &start=0&end=9&chapter=1&page=1 (accessed 5 February, 2006).

29 Recep Senturk, "Toward an Open Science and Society: Multiplex Relations in Language, Religion, and Society," *Islam: Arastirmalari Dergisi (Turkish Journal of Islamic Studies)*, Sayi 6, 2001, p. 101.

Part II

Applied Ethics of Political Participation

5 Public Religion, Ethics of Participation, and Cultural Dialogue

Islam in Europe

Armando Salvatore

In this chapter I will, firstly, review a key controversy on the idea of "public religion" as a possible vehicle of a religious ethics of political participation. Secondly, I will illustrate a conceptual approach for defining the anthropological and philosophical basis of a religious ethics of political participation through bridging the tension between the real and ideal dimensions in human history. Thirdly, I will reexamine public religion as applied to Islam with regard to the chances of "cultural dialogue" in a European context. This chosen structure is important for two reasons: since ethics of political participation can no longer be contained within a nation-state oriented notion of citizenship, and because as the "secular continent" and the cradle of modernity, Europe is a crucial terrain for testing notions and practices of public religion, in particular in view of the inherited historical conflicts with Islam.

Public Religion and Islam

A seminal contribution that revisits the controversial and overloaded notion of secularization in view of reassessing the chances of religion's contribution to the ethics of political participation is in the work of José Casanova. From his book *Public Religions in the Modern World* to more recent essays explicitly embracing Islam as the present and future candidate, to play a positive role as a "public religion," Casanova has brought fresh insights into a conceptual deadlock concerning the following question: whether secularity, or what Talal Asad has called the "formations of the secular," allows or prevents the rising and thriving of public religion(s). According to Asad, the "secular" is not simply a discourse or an ideology (called "secularism") but, simultaneously, a life form and a way of governance produced by the formation and transformation of the modern European state. It also connects to notions of citizenship, from the so-called Wars of Religion of the sixteenth and seventeenth centuries to the gradual formation, after the Second World War, of a European Community, more recently Union. In numerous writings and especially in his recent book *Formations of the Secular*, Asad has expressed doubts about the possibility that Islam might even be allowed to produce and institute ethics of participation in a secular, and in particular, in a European socio-political context, due to the institutional rigidities of the European secular formations. José Casanova is instead more optimistic, and bases his argument on a comparative analysis of the public role of religion in various socio-political arenas from North to South America, and from Western to Eastern Europe, and has more recently – albeit tentatively and speculatively – started to apply his model to some national cases in the Muslim majority world.[1]

Without venturing into the technicalities of Casanova's thesis, to the extent they are formulated in the specific vocabulary of the sociology of religion, it is possible to summarize his main argument in the following way. He holds that religious traditions in general, and specifically those sprouting from the Abrahamic tree, have the potential to contribute decisively to public discussions of issues involving basic human and societal values, like justice, the protection of human life and of the environment, peace, solidarity with disadvantaged social strata, etc. Indeed, we all know that religions in general, and Abrahamic religions in particular, contribute articulate views of forbearance, piety, caritas ("doing good to the other"), and friendship. They configure, more than abstract values, dispositional methods for turning those values concrete, in the crucial, albeit elementary relation between ego and alter that grounds the "social link." However, Casanova contends, this potential of religions to sustain public action can only become effective if religious authorities play by the rules of the game of democratic politics. In other words, public representatives of a given religion, like or even more than any other social and political actor accessing the public sphere, have to rely on persuasion via public discourse and cannot invoke traditional authority and the concomitant repertoires of authoritative means for disciplining religious practitioners into complying with religious norms and ethics.

Therefore, religious values of justice, humanness, solidarity, and peace can and should contribute to the common good, according to Casanova, but as part of discourses geared to persuade the general public, or its majority. In Casanova's view, this is the positive legacy of secularization. Religion has a potential, a particularly strong one, for addressing the common good in secular polities and motivate citizens into civic and political participation in the name of universal values that secular doctrines too often proclaim but neglect, due to the frequent prevalence of particularistic interests and egoism. In a sense, Casanova regards religion as the permanent and most secure source of those universal values, so that a secular political formation without public religion might be in danger of losing touch with these underlying values. He has been explicit in maintaining that:

> The very resurgence or reassertion of religious traditions may be viewed as a sign of the failure of the Enlightenment to redeem its own promises. Religious traditions are now confronting the differentiated secular spheres, challenging them to face their own obscurantist, ideological, and inauthentic claims. In many of these confrontations, it is religion which, as often as not, appears to be on the side of human enlightenment.[2]

However, this potential of religious traditions can only be invested into the secular rules of the game, laying a premium on the capacity to mobilize and persuade without threatening the state's monopoly of the institutional instruments of coercion and consensus-building, and without impinging on citizens' freedom of conscience.

Indeed, it is on this latter point that Asad's critique has been implacably focusing, and I will later refer to some of the key points he raised.

Both Casanova and Asad view Europe as a major ground for testing and assessing the "secular," and therefore the chances and limits of public religion. A first general problem raised by the approach of Casanova is that, while it deflates the notion of secularization by eliminating its underlying teleological assumption about the decline of religion and its normative assumption about the privatization of religion, it preserves as the hub of public religion the idea of secularization as an institutional differentiation between religion and politics. The model of public religion is based on the normative presupposition that whoever has legitimate credentials to speak in the name of a religion or of a religious group is called to distill "values" out of the religious imperatives, and build on their basis a persuasive ethical discourse that can legitimately insert into the political process. Now, even a superficial look at the European history of formation of modern secular nation-states, and lately of European integration, shows that the separation between religion and politics has never been fully institutionalized as the discourse of secularization claims it to be. Let us see how and why the relation between religion and politics within European modernity – whatever the claims of the official discourses of public authorities – crystallized into a field of permanent and shifting tensions rather than into a stable configuration of institutional and constitutional separation. In other words, let us see how the fairness of the so-called secular rules of the public game, as assumed by Casanova's thesis, cannot be taken for granted, not just in their application (all games might be rigged), but also in their very formulation.

The Burdens of European History

Relations of tension and compromise between religious communities or institutions, on one hand, and the rising nation-states, on the other, have been constitutive of modern European societies. The variety of arrangements resulting from this ongoing relation are inscribed in the social and legal charters of the various European societies and inform contemporary national political cultures. It should be emphasized – as also stressed by Casanova – that the principle of religious neutrality of the state was often promoted by non-conformist and non-established religious groups. While this principle was the result of a "movement," in order to be accepted and institutionalized it had to feed into the logic of concentration and sophistication of power and control that became the brand mark of the state formation in Europe. Therefore, at the basis of the principle of religious neutrality there is an inherent tension between the tolerance and even the recognition of the other, and the constraining of this potential openness into rigid rules enforced by the state. The twin principles of the religious neutrality of the state and of religious tolerance imposed as a rule on all citizens also operate as factors of regulation of civic life, commerce, and public order but might be inimical to communication and dialogue, which inherently imply the risk of confrontation. In its variety of institutional and ideological forms characterizing European history – from *laïcité* in France to state church in some Scandinavian countries – the separation between religion and politics is far from unproblematic at the very stage when it is formulated and institutionalized. The main problem seems to be that fear of confrontation might inhibit dialogue, which is the main testing ground of any effective public sphere, and therefore also a condition for a vital public religion, which is in turn, according to Casanova, an essential component of public life.

In a replication of these dynamics under changed social conditions, Muslim immigrants in Europe have since the 1950s experienced that the trade-off associated with state neutrality is, while positive for established churches and religions, Islamic, like other non-established groups, are placed outside or, at best, at the margins of these arrangements. Since after the crisis of trust generated by the Rushdie affair in the UK and *l'affaire du foulard* in France (both erupted in 1989), public disputes affecting or raised by Muslim groups have directly exposed the fragility of the self-understanding and the normative aspects of the secular character of European societies. It has become increasingly evident that the significance and implications of these crises and controversies for future regulations transcend sharply the specific problems raised by the presence and activity in Europe of a consistent and growing population of Muslim religious backgrounds. As evidenced by the French sociologist Danièle Hervieu-Léger,[3] the Muslim diasporas in Europe are an indicator and an anticipator of a much wider and deeper transformation of the religious field and of the crisis of the capacity of governance of the secular states. This has been clearly evidenced by the authoritarian backlash of French *laïcité* in the early 2004 law against "ostentatious" religious symbols (mainly but not only the Islamic headscarf) in state schools.[4]

Let us reconsider this process and its institutional limitations with reference to Casanova's notion of public religion, its role, and its conditions. While the diversity of national trajectories and arrangements in Europe testifies to different solutions and fields of tension, the common legacy of all these processes is a diffuse understanding that state institutions have de-legitimized any pretension of religious authorities to have a say in the political process. They have therefore gained – in various relations of collaboration and compromise with the religious communities – a legally pinpointed control of the "religious field." That the practice of religion has been incorporated in a field with clearly defined borders – at least toward the state institutions – authorizing a limited range of Church "community" activities, is one of the main markers of the successful emergence of the nation-state in Europe. This new political formation emerged through the lengthy dissolution of the idea of an Empire, a *sacrum imperium*, incorporating the ideals of the *respublica christiana* (a "Christian republic" embracing the entire Latin Christian Europe) and based on a concerted harmony between spiritual and temporal powers. However, during the sixteenth and seventeenth centuries several legal acts and theories, culminating in the work of the leading legal philosopher Hugo Grotius, were formulated under the heading of the "Turkish Threat." This label identified the continuing military and political advances of the Ottomans into a Europe perceived as the last stronghold of Christianity.[5] In these texts, the "Christian republic" was explicitly considered the political entity – and corresponding identity – under threat by the Muslim armies. Tracts and treaties called to the *unitas christiana* ("Christian unity") in the very epoch during which this unity had internally collapsed and given way to what Eric Voegelin has called the reciprocally schismatic formations of the modern nation-states. In other words, the internal division in Europe – political and religious – and the search for an overarching ideological cohesion went hand in hand.

The decline of the political and military power of the Ottoman Empire in the nineteenth century and the construction of colonial empires by the European powers increasingly secularized the European religious self-understanding into the racial-ized idea of the "white man's burden" in the task of civilizing non-Europe. The culmination of the rivalry between European imperial powers into the two devas-tating world wars gave way, in the second half of the twentieth century, to a process of economic and later political integration that was marked, quite at its beginning, by a renewed search for a collective European identity.

What are the implications of the historical burden of Europe's internal and external conflicts on the issues at stake here? It is difficult to overlook how slowly and reluctantly, in this long-term trajectory, even on the part of some of the intellectual heroes of European modernity, the idea of a Christian republic, the historical religious antecedent to the secular idea of Europe, came to be replaced by the conse-cration of a differentiation and separation of competencies between "religion" and "politics" within the emerging nation-states. The prevalent post-Christian, post-Enlightenment and post-colonial understanding of religion, common to the whole of Europe despite all differences, is intimately connected to these differentiation processes, and therefore to the idea of a religious field regulating religious belief and practice, along with the range of social (not political) competencies radiating from religious commitment. And here Casanova is right in reinterpreting secularization as differentiation of social spheres, and not as an inevitable decline and privatization of religion, ergo – since religion is neither disappearing nor becoming privatized – as a process that favors a renewed public role of religion. The problem is that this legally pinpointed differentiation, and concomitant institutional arrangements, are, in Europe, on the one hand, the least common denominator representing the basic secular character of the institutional landscape. On the other, they cannot account for the complexity and at times fluidity of the relationship between religious and political cultures – and here the limits to "public religion" become manifest.

A condition for public religion to unfold and thrive is that the religious groups and institutions are allowed to play a crucial role within the reproduction and nego-tiation of value systems. They provide spaces for encounters on different levels – the parish church, the educational programs, and the ecumenical dialogue with other denominations – and inform individual and collective strategies of cultural dialogue. This is hardly surprising, since the counterpart to state control is the autonomy of actors in the religious field, within its boundaries. The presupposition is that religious authorities accept and internalize this border. However, while the institutional and legal principle is clear, its implementation is far more ambiguous, and indeed Casanova himself admits that religious actors might act so as to redesign and make more porous the institutionally and legally rigid borders between private and public spheres. A rigid application of the principle of separation would indeed imply the full social paralysis of religious groups, since all activities oriented to social solidarity can be interpreted as having an at least implicit political potential. Due to the still privileged position attributed in many European countries (and even in the laic France) to specific churches, and to the ideologically post-Christian character of the European self-understanding that views Christianity as a necessary antecedent to humanism and the Enlightenment, it is not surprising that the best example of the institutional limits to "public religion" in contemporary Europe is in the quite narrow range of options allowed to any public manifestation of Islam.

Look at the efforts of the French government to institutionalize the representation of Islam in French society through the *Conseil Français du Culte Musulman*, in order to create an *Islam de France*. This strategy does not represent a real break with the historic, colonial and post-colonial cooptation of Muslim leaders in order to secularize and discipline Muslims into national citizenship. This approach is a dubious application of the already ambiguous separation principle as inherited from the history of European nation-states. According to this principle, it is the state's prerogative to legislate on, and organize administratively, the separation of religion and politics, but not to influence the selection of the speakers of the religious groups or even to preemptively define the type of Islam to be (re)constructed as fitting the imperatives of the nation-state.[6] Not surprisingly, some Muslim groups on the ground that it violates the separation of religion and politics and the concomitant principle of state neutrality have initially criticized this ambivalent approach. Within these kinds of tensions or, at best, unbalanced dialogues, Muslims of a variety of political orientations and committed to different life forms often play the same role earlier played in Europe by non-established religious groups in invoking the autonomy of the religious field.

This contentious process illustrates how Muslims are – much more clearly than they could be twenty-five years ago – an actively contending part in the complex socio-political mechanisms of European societies, and are not just heterogeneous cultural groups "implanted" from outside and seeking a mere "representation" of their rights and claims. On the other hand, they are no mere atomized entities in the process to learn to live in a pacified liberal individualistic society either. The political struggles on the accession of Turkey dramatically highlight the process through which Islam is becoming again – as it already was, through the heritage of al-Andalus and the Ottoman Empire – increasingly integral to Europe. This is in spite of all resistance based on the memories of the "Turkish Threat" and of colonial confrontations with various parts of the Muslim world, including other regions of the Ottoman Empire. Is this the promising, albeit turbulent beginning of a "cultural dialogue" or just the more recent chapter of an old "clash of civilizations"?

Talal Asad, both in his critique of Casanova and in his wider argument from his two books *Genealogies of Religion* and *Formations of the Secular*,[7] warns us that the root of the problem, and the limitation of the solutions currently traded, lie in the fact that secularism is not easily soluble into post-secular arrangements based on cultural dialogue. He adds that this is because the institutional kernel, the institutions of modern citizenship within nation-states, is intrinsically built on the European post-imperial, cultural self-understanding of majorities. These are intended – i.e., understand themselves – not merely as fluctuating political-electoral, but as stable cultural and national majorities. Every group not belonging to such a majority is therefore considered a minority to watch and monitor, continuously in need to prove its loyalty. Therefore, hopes for a cultural dialogue depend on whether a dialogic refoundation of the European public sphere, by eroding the mythically ethnic and cultural foundations of the nation-states, will dissolve the idea of cultural majorities and overcome the limitations of political and religious tolerance as conceived and practiced so far. They will thus open the way to a European version of public Islam[8] – as a crucial instantiation of public religion as identified by Casanova – to become one of the factors of the new Europe.

These hopes and perspectives cannot be advanced by the sheer inertia of socio-economic forces, like those envisaged in deterministic equations between development and prosperity, between democracy and tolerance, between an economic and a political union, between an enlargement process and the promise of a general inclusiveness, as also manifested in the rejection of the European constitu-tional treaty in France and the Netherlands in May and June 2005. A permanent warning should be the memory of the fact that the persecutions of the European Jewry culminating in the holocaust occurred at the end of a period of major economic crisis. The seeds for the otherization of the Jews, of the process that made them a suspect and potentially dangerous minority, were laid as part of the trajec-tory through which the idea itself of a cultural majority of the nation found its institutional and ideological underpinnings. Talal Asad asks that:

> time and place should be made for weaker groups within spaces and times commanded by a dominant one. Muslims in Europe . . . should be able to find institutional representation as a minority in a democratic state that consists only of minorities. For where there are only minorities the possibilities to forge alliances between them will be greater than in a state with a majority presiding over several competing minorities.[9]

Seeds of Dialogue in European Modernity

While Asad's diagnosis is as impeccable as his critique is implacable, we need to focus the attention and elaborate upon a patrimony of reflections and discussions that have had a formative influence on Europe and its values. I refer in particular to the manifestation of an early suspicion and criticism of the logic of concentration and monopolization of power and control that grew into nation-state formations, and which risks nowadays being transferred into European institutions. What I invoke here are not nostalgic and backward-looking theories and views, but a highly systematic and consciously innovative work of an author from the so-called Neapolitan Enlightenment. His ambition was no less than grounding a "new science" encompassing and systematizing what we would call today social theory, i.e. a coherent view of the genesis and development of human social institutions, religious and civil. The author of this ambitious theory was Giambattista Vico, and his work culminated in successive editions of his *Scienza nuova*.[10] The importance of Vico for the modern social sciences has been widely acknowledged and does not stop generating novel recognitions and interpretations. My own attention is directed to the fact that his theory includes the main ingredients at stake in the contemporary discussions and challenges of public religion just discussed.

The choice of Vico is also due to the need to counterbalance emerging views of "multiple" or "alternative modernities" that bracket out earlier traditions of questioning modernity from within the process of construction of its cultural and institutional underpinnings. In his book *Provincializing Europe*, Dipesh Chakrabarti[11] traces alternative trajectories of modernity that show how European modernity's centrality and intimations of standards of normality and normativity for the modern citizen should be relativized, or are indeed *de facto* relativized by the post-imperial predicament of Europe. However, and in spite of the existence of strong common denominators in Europe as to, e.g., the attempted institutionalization of principles of religious neutrality and tolerance into the secular shell of the modern European state, European modernity itself, if conceived singularly, is an elusive entity, internally even more than externally. There are several trajectories that have contributed to the present predicament of Europe, whose intersecting genealogies one should actively trace, instead of indulging in sketching one grand genealogy of a singular trajectory leading to what Asad calls the "formations of the secular." The fast pace of European enlargement eastwards, including the South-East, and the active and growing presence of groups of population of various religious background (not only Muslim, but also, e.g., Christian neo-Pentecostal and charismatic) point out indeed that in the background of any discussion on public religion and public Islam in Europe or also on the relations between Europe and various parts of the Muslim world (especially the former European colonies), one should dig out the seeds of an alternative modernity cultivated within Europe itself. This endeavor is necessary not for the sake of archaeological curiosity but precisely in order to reinvigorate arguments for making European societies and public spheres more pluralistic, reflexive and self-critical. This is also necessary for making space for Muslims in Europe in a logic that goes beyond the norm of protection of minorities, a norm that is (as rightly stressed by Asad) destined to keep these minorities in a subordinated status, subject to ongoing special monitoring and control, beyond all legitimate security reasons that are appropriate for holding in check the tiny minority of extremist groups. This step is necessary in order to reopen the thus far narrow spaces allowed – theoretically and practically – for public religion to take root and thrive.

My contribution to a possible enrichment of the discussion requires an excursus that links modern views of man, society, and history, to theoretical issues in the philosophy of law. Vico's project was ingenious in that it included a combined genealogy of religious, legal, civil and political institutions, without producing any rigid and transhistorical norm of the moral being or the "citizen" and his underlying patterns of humanity and rationality. In Vico's approach, he consciously and openly challenged the Dutch thinker Hugo Grotius, largely considered till our days the champion of modern European legal theory and philosophy of law. Vico's opposition to Grotius was due to what he saw as the singularly unsociological character of the latter's theory. This shortfall affects particularly the modern approaches to natural law. The key fallacy here, according to Vico, is in the arbitrary sense in which the idea of "nature" was used – ranging from an analogy with specific natural sciences to a quite elastic reference to a variety of social phenomena – by Grotius and others, for reconstructing what they took to be the "essence" of man. In his *Respublica Christiana*, Grotius had argued for a metamorphosis of this kind of *respublica* that had been understood, in the Middle Ages, as a mystical body. This body had simply disappeared from his view in the Europe of rising nation-states. He searched instead for a generic and unitary character of mankind, whose civilized nature he saw in the most affluent and powerful nations of North-Western Europe, in opposition to what he saw as the uncivilized or less civilized non-nations of the rest of the world. This type of European white man became the standard of mankind's essence at the moment he was getting ready for an unbroken series of colonial and imperial under-takings lasting till our days, and effectively emptying out any universal idea of law. This is particularly evident in Grotius's *The Freedom of the Seas, or The Right which Belongs to the Dutch to Take Part in the East Indian Trade*, an unmistakable title for a book that theorized about the right of the Western sea powers to arrange and lead the mercantile exploitation of the world. He stated that denying this kind of law was tantamount to erasing the fundaments of human fellowship, mutual service, and of nature itself. Putting the will to power at the basis of law could not have been more explicit.

Vico's *Diritto universale* ("Universal law"), his main work before the *Scienza nuova* ("New Science") for which he is mainly known, is an implacable indictment of this theory of law. Targeting Grotius and other authors, he deconstructed their theories by deploying a philologically and historically sophisticated argument focusing on the genesis of Roman law and Roman political institutions. This was the platform for a more general argument about the genesis of law and institutions. He showed how far apart the origins of Roman law and Roman political institutions were from the imagination of the new natural law theorists, who still declared their commit-ment to the Roman law tradition at the very moment they started to talk about an a-historical essence of man, in reality modeled on contingent political ambitions of white man. Vico exposed the basic fault of his rivals as being of a genuine ethnocen-tric nature, manifest in the assumption that if a law is given and legitimate in a specific social and institutional context, it must be equally legitimate in any other social constellation. The fatal error of this theory resided in the idea that "society" is based on a type of contract whose presuppositions are enshrined in the practices and interests of a rising, modern bourgeois civility.[12]

What these philosophers of law fatally took for granted was that they tackled human nature as already civilized by religion and law, and bracketed out the labo-rious processes that produce and reproduce religious, civic and legal institutions. Vico summarized this fallacy as rooted in the twin "conceits," i.e. of the scholars, and of the nations. In other words, in their pursuit of worldly power, the modern European thinkers unconsciously lost sight of their positioning *within* a civiliza-tional discourse, so that the only option left by this blindness was between being a liberal and a libertine: to erect one's civilizational values of right into an absolute system (therefore effecting an implosion of the civilizing tradition and its complexity), or to reject those values wholesale (what amounted to a collapse of the civilizational tradition). The only way out of this dilemma that threatened the collapse of inherited civilizational formulas of education, discourse, and law was for Vico in the pursuit of a genealogical method of understanding one's own historicity. He stressed the need to bring the mythical evocations contained in the civilizational formulas within closer intellectual and analytic grasp, and finally to situate oneself critically towards the original and permanent engine of the civilizing process, whose critical hub he saw in the *sensus communis*, i.e. the common sense, the practical knowledge of the commoners.

While in *De iure belli ac pacis*, Grotius attempted to ground justice on a rational, minimalist conception of human sociability, therefore providing a direct antecedent to the theory of civil society developed by the Scottish Enlightenment in the eighteenth century. Vico rejected the notion that natural law is profitably treated as if it were detached from the historical development of customs, and of the laws that grow out of those customs. His key argument was that natural law should be understood simultaneously as an ideal of eternal truth and as an historical development of the customs and traditions of human society.[13] There are several apparent and latent similarities between Vico's approach and the method of the fourteenth century Muslim Maliki Andalusian *faqih* and philosopher of law al-Shatibi. This convergence is probably more than a theoretical affinity, since a genealogical link – though tenuous, on the basis of available evidence – seems to be available. As stressed by the leading contemporary Muslim intellectual, Khalid Masud, both in his book on al-Shatibi[14] and on other occasions, the two Thomist Christian Spanish theorists of the law, Francisco de Victoria and Francisco Suarez, who lived after al-Shatibi and before Vico (between the sixteenth and seventeenth centuries) show a resemblance not only of content but also of methods with the Andalusian scholar, and they were also two major authorities invoked by Vico for constructing his legal theory. For sure, their view of the natural rights of colonizers and colonized was antithetical to that of Grotius.[15]

The lesson we draw from Vico is that the reconstruction of natural law intrinsically requires a genealogical method. Human beings' increasingly adequate concept of justice is based on a historical expansion of the *aequum bonum*, the notion of common good rooted in communication and social interaction. Instead of reproducing the philosophers' myths of a state of nature, the Neapolitan thinker pointed out that the criteria for the distribution of goods and pains were always dependent on the apprehension of the good allowed by a given stage of human development.[16] Hiding this normativity behind a transhistorical view of man and natural rights was for Vico the most insidious error to confute in the battle for modernity's soul and for determining the type of social science that matters for the work of reconstructing the type of sociality and morality required by modernity. Vico decried the "conceit of the nations," the self-illusion of cultural uniqueness and unity entertained by various peoples since the antiquity, as one of the main dangers to the integrity of the prudential knowledge necessary to build the rules and institutions of civic life. With the new instruments and techniques of power, monitoring and control nourished by the strengthening of the power machinery of the modern state, the danger highlighted by Vico became ever more manifest and acute. This is also why he criticized the leading French political philosopher Jean Bodin for not grasping the composite nature of the political body and for simply endorsing the political fact of modern nation-states that had been emerging, in particular in North-Western Europe, as mythically compact political entities, replacing the view of the mystical body considered thus far incarnate in the *respublica christiana*. This process of substitution engendered sectarian groups and separated national communities that reframed the civic, legal and even religious institutions inherited from the medieval order. By the time of Vico, i.e. by the eighteenth century, the various national communities were advancing in deploying ever more comprehensive ideologies of the nation that turned symbolic assets of a shared mystical body (a Christian idea) into fully-fledged, increasingly secular, political ideas. By this process, however, the *telos* of the original symbolic power was perverted and reconverted, and the civic, legal and religious institutions were subjected to totalizing visions of power.[17]

It has been stated that "Vico traces modern rigorism to a desperate and prideful attempt to escape from contingency."[18] To remedy this trap, the Neapolitan philosopher consciously managed the sense of contingency that emerged out of the implosion of medieval traditions. He used this historicized sense of contingency to counter the totalizing ambitions of sacred national interest. He did so by trying to adequately reflect the complexities and polarities of reality, and the inherently pluralistic world of needs, significations and discourses. He considered the new discourse of power especially inadequate to tackle man's continuous creation of the *mondo civile*, the civil world, via a refraction of divine truth grounding the human capacity to envisage and equalize the needs and interests of a multitude of men. The crux of this process – this is Vico's legacy in a nutshell – consists in translating the pursuit of this *aequum bonum* into common participation in reconstructing social relations, via turning the principle of equity and common good into patterns of dialogue, understanding and agreement among human beings and co-citizens.

But the peak of Vico's argument is when he shows how the pursuit of the common good cannot be simply a matter of making rational sense out of a complex social reality, but has to face the hard and risky business of encountering and dealing with otherness. Only dealing with otherness can finally vindicate public reasoning. The image obsessively evoked in the "Poetic Economy" section of the *New Science* is the refugee or guest. This is the section where Vico primarily tackles the crucial issue of the origin of cities, which he finds in patrician families, colonies, and asylums. In the asylums, which were the first hospices, the strangers received were automatically considered guests.[19] This encounter between the host/autochthonous and the guest/stranger was the type of ego-alter relationship that received the strongest sacralization. Zeus/Jupiter is not only the god of thunder who insinuates fear, but also the guest-god who protects all strangers and punishes any wrong committed against them. Therefore, the arrival itself of the stranger (something to which the host/citizen should be permanently prepared, since it is utterly and inherently unpredictable – a motive recently taken up by Derrida, almost three centuries after Vico) testifies the existence and importance of the other, not only as a singular other, but as representing social worlds, needs and fears other than one's own. These social worlds are to be made, under the threat of godly sanctions, mutually accessible.

This is, for Vico, the meaning of asylum as the civic institution necessarily antecedent to what we call the "city."

The relationship between host and guest is not one-sided but inherently reciprocal. The notion itself of reciprocity is always imperfectly incorporated in all proto-institutions of patronage and marriage, entailing inherent, mostly gross, power imbalances. The asylum is no exception, and indeed it expands the power over servants and slaves, wife and children, of the *pater familias* into a more encompassing patriciate. At the same time, however, it consecrates the litmus testing ground of an even exchange via the idea of friendship, an inviolable gift that binds forever ego and alter and is the grounding stone of the social link. This institution is prior to – and the condition for – prophetic discourse and any ensuing injunction of commanding good. However, Vico is well aware that the constructed relation between ego and alter cannot erase power gaps and strangeness, which linger on. This is the juncture where prophetic discourse finds its place and launches into what Eric Voegelin called a "leap of faith," which pinpoints the triangular relationship of ego, alter and Alter/ God, and the concomitant partnership in faith between ego and alter.

Before that leap occurs, and the pride and force of the patrician host is tamed, *hostis* means both guest and enemy. Vico embarks on an archaeology of civic unrest, grounded on the fact that the citizens and guests in Rome – taken by Vico as a better scenario for theorizing about the social link than an elusive "state of nature" – turned into the conflicting classes of the patricians and plebeians. It is not an expansion of the gift of forbearance and friendship that grounds alone the public sphere, but, realistically, the civil war. It is the rebellion of the plebeians against the patricians' egoism and lack of justice, and against the want of transparence of the laws enacted by them, that produced the idea itself of public, and indeed of the *respublica*. In order to rebel against injustice, however, there should be seeds of justice in the common sense entertained by the plebeians. Without these seeds, neither rebellion, nor its resolution, could occur. The motor of the history of Roman society – that Vico takes as the prototype of a society based on law and on the crucial notion of *respublica*, which is much more basic to the social link than "republic" as a form of government – was in this combination of perpetual conflict and permanent recreation of the social link. It is this dynamic combination that established the necessity of new laws and a potentially democratic progression in the form of government, like the shift of the Roman state from monarchy to republic. This process was supported by new transformations at the social level, resulting from the grounding of new cities, further military conquests, and the influx of new guests/refugees. The use of a paradigm drawn from Roman history and Roman law helps Vico to paint a theoretically much richer picture which not only references an abstract "state of nature," but also to the Athenian *polis*, an overloaded, recurring icon of European self-understanding until today (as evidenced by the preamble of the draft of the constitution of the European Union). Correspondingly, from Vico's perspective it is clear that Aristotle's view of the polity as based on a quite static class society is not enough. The Greek philosopher is particularly unsuitable to appreciate the importance of the moral imperative of piety that is at the root of the right of asylum.[20]

Cultural Dialogue: Towards a New Public Sphere of Agonic Civility and Mutual Forbearance?

While loyalties to the nation-states were originally and by definition exclusive, religious allegiances entailed the seeds of openness to the other (at least to the other as a potential convert, but often as a brother by a Godly-consecrated bond of nature). It often depended on political circumstances whether this openness became a factor of inclusion and integration, or recoiled into exclusion and conflict. It should be recalled that the early modern European Wars of Religion, unlike medieval crusades against infidels and heretics, were not purely religious conflicts, as they were already entangled in clashes among rising national interests. Also, it should be noted that this tendency didn't stop in Europe until the insane catastrophe of the Second World War that some historians have identified as the culmination of a longer "European civil war," which bears some resemblance to the Vichian prototype of the war between patricians and plebeians; especially, since it could only be vindicated, providentially and dialectically in Vico's sense, by the rise of a new type of *respublica*.

Can the new Europe be such a kind of *respublica*? The possible reviving of the seeds of an alternative articulation of modernity implanted in the thought of European and Muslim thinkers of the past and revived by their present heirs depends on making the current process of European integration sensible to the development of horizontal ties of trust, solidarity and civic participation. It also depends on the contribution by evolving religious cultures, both in their reciprocal relationships as well as with regard to the secular, philosophical and humanistic traditions of Europe. Cultural dialogue, intended both as a direct interaction and in its more institutional or semi-institutional forms – as "regimes of dialogue" – is simultaneously the conceptual kernel and analytical key to approach this process.

Yet while invoking moments and dimensions of dialogue we should not ignore numerous imbalances of power within and around the "religious field" which make clear that dialogue is sometimes not easy or even impossible, and, if feasible, often stems from conflicted situations. As far as Western Europe is concerned, the history and experience of colonialism has been the main agent of the view of Islam as a "culture" in such a state of either decadence or infancy to justify a civilizing mission by Europeans that, in some cases, also assumed an explicitly religious dimension (e.g. with the installing of religious missions in various colonies). The variety of political and institutional arrangements among EU member states in dealing with religion and also the diversity of their colonial past that has oriented their migration policies might explain the European reluctance to produce a more articulated discussion of its complex religious identity. This cannot be reduced to the enigmatic contours of a "Judeo-Christian tradition," which Alisdair MacIntyre has dubbed a "fictitious amalgam" that is by today almost synonymous to the no less vague notion of "Western values." This amalgam is often brandished as a weapon – often by secular politicians – for otherizing and re-orientalizing Islam. The European acceptance of Judaism into the white-men club is itself a result of the sense of guilt that followed the quasi-annihilation, by white Europeans, of the European Jewry. Indeed, a crystallization of this reluctance to spell out the complex and contradictory religious heritage of Europe might damage the transparency needed in the value-setting process of the construction of Europe, in the definition of the discrete goods to pursue and of the common good or *aequum bonum* that should guide their pursuit. For example, the emergence of a clear anti-Turkey accession front by the end of 2002 was a rather defensive reaction to an enlargement process that can nowadays hardly be reduced to its economic or human rights dimensions, as it has entered a highly controversial constitutional stage. At the same time, the deadlock in the debate – or, more realistically, power game – about the introduction of a reference to the "religious common heritage" of the EU in the preamble of the future constitutional charter is also a relevant illustration of the problems, for the EU to date, to create a space for discussing such sensitive matters.

The practical significance of this approach is highlighted by the predicament of Muslim groups as part of an emerging European problematic field defined by inter-religious dynamics. The hope that cultural dialogue, and not an exclusive civilizational narrative, can emerge as a model for Europe can only be sustained by the rediscovery and application of an alternative, genealogical and critical, but finally constructive view of the inherent complexity of European modernity and of its institutional underpinnings. These are certainly related to the so-called "formation of the secular," whose institutional entrenchment is defied or at least eroded by several developments that took place during the 1990s. If we want to consider religiously motivated social and public action by Muslims in Europe as "public Islam," and therefore as an instantiation of the public religion of Casanovian shape mentioned at the beginning, we need to go beyond a shallow pluralism and multiculturalism, and look for transversal connections between the mainstream Abrahamic faiths and European political cultures. The chances for shaping a new European public sphere depend upon the extent one will be able to create interlocking spaces for different cultural traditions and place incentives on their mutual engagement in terms of public and dialogic communication, instead of watching with suspicion any non-prepoliced public speech.

Talal Asad, in his diagnosis and indictment of the democratic limitations of the dominant secular formations in Europe, has pointed out some possible paths out of those limitations that appear related to the seeds of an alternative modernity that we have detected in the thought of the Neapolitan thinker. In this context Asad praises John Millbank's idea that social spaces cannot be indefinitely homogenized along the abstracting and idealizing path of European nation-states and their rigid patterns of inclusion and exclusion. Asad concludes that "the sovereign state cannot (never could) contain all practices, relations, and loyalties of its citizens," and that indeed a heritage common to Christianity and Islam is in that they both "recognized a multiplicity of overlapping bonds and identities."[21]

There is a lesson we ought to draw from the seeds of an alternative modernity exemplified by Vico's thought and channeled into the concerns voiced by Asad. We need to reconstruct a plural tradition of modernity respectful of religious diversity while mindful of the strength and limits of existing patterns of secularity tied to the historic model of the European nation-states, which does not represent the end of history. What an alternative view on the tradition of modernity, adapted to the present circumstances, teaches us is that the two fields, the religious and the political/secular fields, while claiming autonomy within their own domains, are intertwined in the public sphere because of the anthropological condition of religion and its relevance to configurations of authority and power. The autonomy of the religious field is what religious groups gain in the European arrangements of separation. Without this, such deals would be unfair, and the political community based on citizenship would betray its own path of legitimization. But it cannot be bracketed out that any advance on the sheer level of rights - claiming can only be the result of collective action, which again very often unites Muslims as Muslims, across national divides related both to their countries of origin and to their places of residence or actual citizenship. The often invoked politics of recognition – as the hub of a new, fairer view of secularity – would be optimally the beginning and not the end of a process of engagement in a participatory, and in this sense, public articulation of key ethical tenets of Islam. An intermediate rationale of this public Islam is that the acquisition of autonomous spaces for socio-religious life be used as a school for participation in the affairs of the wider society.

What most socio-religious groups and religiously inspired individual actors share are the values of justice, service to the other, and sometimes the pride that goes with a feeling of being just and solidarity-oriented. All such values cannot be completely subsumed under the logic of exchange, ordered competition, and fair discussion that characterize the normative understanding – though not necessarily the practice – of European public spheres. The importance of discourses of justice, human solidarity and peace is increasingly voiced by those religious groups that see their mandate as global.[22] They also resonate with non-religious understandings of the democratic enrichment of the public sphere in the post-welfarist era of non-labor-based "new social movements." What is demanded to all religious and political cultures is to watch against the danger of "overcoding" political symbols. Talal Asad has raised this point by reference to the thought and suggestions of William Connolly to transform pluralism "from a majority nation presiding over numerous minorities in a democratic state to a democratic state of multiple minorities contending and collaborating within a general ethos of forbearance and critical responsiveness."[23] While the preservation and fostering of civility and overlapping exchange and communication as the kernel of secularity is not questioned by the largest majority of Muslim groups in Europe, historically proven formulas for establishing a secular public sphere (and corresponding, different institutional deals between states and religious groups) cannot be equated with the public sphere itself. The root of the public sphere, in Abrahamic religious traditions as much as in Greek philosophy and Roman law, resides in notions of the common good, the *aequum bonum* masterly reconstructed by Vico, and comparable with al-Shatibi's *maslaha/istislah*, a pair of key concepts denoting the common good/interest and the method to recognize and adjudicate it.

Conclusion: Some Practical and Political Implications

The issue of the participation of religious groups in general, and of Muslims in particular, within European post-national and post-secular public spheres, should therefore be addressed from a perspective of a cultural dialogue expanding public space. This approach should be different from sheer "public recognition," which is based on given and restricted views of a public sphere minimalistically conceived as a disciplinary space in need of regulation through self-policing and predictable practices. While shallow formulas of multiculturalism die out, as they inhabit no notion of public sphere whatsoever, we witness a juridification of religious issues, which further reifies religion into a discourse of mere rights. On the other hand, we observe different uses of institutional opportunities, whereby the existence of spaces of rights and liberties is genuinely sought by Muslims and other religious minorities, starting from the acquisition of full or double citizenship, through organizing religious teaching in state schools, to instituting private religious schools. While these processes are important, the significance of rights-claiming and a politics of recognition remain thus far entrenched in the normative character of European public spheres, which cannot contain the aspirations of Muslims as well as of other non-established groups whose members express various degrees of commitment to disparate religious traditions in the organization of their lives.

Instead of applying theorems of institutionalization and internalization of notions of border and separation inherited from a traumatic European history, one should investigate more openly how a variety of associational forms (both formal and informal) express the collective identities and goals of religious communities *vis-à-vis* the goods, goals and programs of the wider associational bonds of all citizens under a secular state sensible towards diversity and inclined to invest in its richness. The reflexive rationalization of life experiences and lifestyles, projects and goals, as well as of cultural attachments, are key to the Enlightenment project and the social sciences more generally. This is a precious achievement that has emerged through the vicissitudes of Europe in the modern era and, for this same reason, should not be a yardstick pre-delimiting the patterns of "integration" of religious groups, Muslim or other. Rather, the conditions for reflexive rationalization should be permanently re-created as the institutional contribution to the process through which different groups interact and sometimes conflict in a public sphere, also through the differing assumptions they carry about how the public goods should be attained and through which existential, expressive, and practical modes of engagement they should be framed. And one should keep in mind that, behind any such reflexive rationalization, and underlying or accompanying notions of agency, responsibility, and social reform, there are, to quote Asad once more, "Judeo-Christian-Islamic traditions of obligation." These are for many citizens relevant platforms of agency and reflexivity, yet they cannot be completely absorbed, not to speak erased, by overarching secular norms.

Other research projects that are well under way highlight the complex "micropolitics" of articulation of such traditions in everyday life, like in the predicament of young educated, religiously committed (and often headscarf wearing) Muslim women. This type of politics represents an important – and very sensitive – vector of appropriation of public space.[24] As Amir-Moazami has shown, contingent and tactical uses of the veil are only possible in relation to a living tradition, and they are neither a strictly individual choice nor the marker of an exclusive Muslim subjectivity.[25] However, we cannot here indulge in seeing a – however conflict-laden – "normalization" of Muslim traditions into factors of self-formation in Europe, as evidenced from the ongoing contestation of theorems of separation propagated by public opinion makers considering public manifestations of Muslim religiosity and, first of all, the iconic veil as endangering *laïcité*. The frequent answer to these reassertions of secular orthodoxy is less a hybridization of identities (French, Muslim), intended as *bricolage* and narcissistic display, than a laborious and daily work of reconstructing viable strategies of survival in settings characterized by tensions between different cultures or traditions, and even more between the state's monitoring and educating prerogatives and the partial autonomy of socio-religious actors. In her work on young daughters of labour migrants born in the 1970s,[26] Nökel ascertains that school is the main arena of identity-formation for young Muslim women in Germany. At school they learn and internalize the techniques of self-creation and self-assertion transmitted by public education. The result of the process is frequently the "creation of a female Islamic actor, overcoming boundaries and deconstructing essentialization, compelled and empowered by the rules of public spaces and discourses, but at the same time subordinating herself to these rules."[27] Compared with the complexity and ambivalence of such micropolitics, even the widely acknowledged public discourse of a leading thinker like Tariq Ramadan risks legitimizing patterns of "over-regulation." Such Muslim women are mostly not interested to submit to a kind of generalized "Islamic rationalization," i.e. to construct a Muslim subjectivity valid for all aspects of their life. They rather strive to preserve individual creativity and a feeling of self-empowerment that could be thwarted by an over-regulation and institutionalization managed by professionals who are in charge of the pedagogical-political machine, so essential to the bureaucratic steering of European states.[28]

Notes

1 José Casanova, "Civil Society and Religion: Retrospective Reflections on Catholicism and Prospective Reflections on Islam," *Social Research*, 2001, vol. 68, no. 4: 1041–1080.

2 José Casanova, *Public Religions in the Modern World*, Chicago: University of Chicago Press, 1994, pp. 233–234.

3 Danièle Hervieu-Léger, *La religion en mouvement: Le pèlerin et le converti*, Paris: Flammarion, 1999.

4 See Talal Asad, "Reflections on Laicité & the Public Sphere," *Social Science Research Council. Items and Issues*, 2005, vol. 5, no. 3: http://www.ssrc.org/publications/items/v5n3/

5 Almut Höfert, "The Order of Things and the Discourse of the Turkish Threat: The Conceptualisation of Islam in the Rise of Occidental Anthropology in the Fifteenth and Sixteenth Centuries," in *Between Europe and Islam: Shaping Modernity in a Transcultural Space*, Almut Höfert and Armando Salvatore (eds), Brussels: P.I.E.-Peter Lang, 2000, pp. 39–68.

6 See Valerie Amiraux, "CFCM: A French Touch?" *ISIM Newsletter*, 2003, 12: 24–25.

7 Talal Asad, *Genealogies of Religion: Discipline and Reasons of Power in Christianity and Islam*, Baltimore, MD: Johns Hopkins University Press, 1993 and Talal Asad, *Formations of the Secular: Christianity, Islam, Modernity*, Stanford: Stanford University Press, 2003.

8 See Armando Salvatore (ed.), *Muslim Traditions and Modern Techniques of Power. Yearbook of the Sociology of Islam*, 2001, vol. 3. Hamburg: Lit; New Brunswick, NJ: Transaction. Armando Salvatore and Dale F. Eickelman (eds), *Public Islam and the Common Good*,

Leiden: Brill, 2004. Armando Salvatore and Mark LeVine (eds), *Religion, Social Practice, and Contested Hegemonies: Reconstructing the Public Sphere in Muslim Majority Societies*, New York: Palgrave Macmillan, 2005.

9   Talal Asad, *Formations of the Secular: Christianity, Islam, Modernity*, Stanford: Stanford University Press, 2003, p. 178.

10 Giambattista Vico, *New Science: Principles of the New Science Concerning the Common Nature of the Nations*, 3rd ed., David Marsh (trans.), London: Penguin, 1999 [1744].

11 Dipesh Chakrabarti, *Provincializing Europe: Post-colonial Thought and Historical Difference*, Princeton, NJ: Princeton University Press, 2000.

12 Barry Cooper, *Eric Voegelin and the Foundations of Modern Political Science*, Columbia, MO: University of Missouri Press, 1999.

13 Robert C. Miner, *Vico, Genealogist of Modernity*, Notre Dame, IN: University of Notre Dame Press, 2002, pp. 37–38.

14 Khalid Masud, *Shatibi's Philosophy of Islamic Law*, Kuala Lumpur: Islamic Book Trust, 1995 [1977], p. 59.

15 Anthony Pagden, "Dispossessing the Barbarian: the Language of Spanish Thomism and the Debate over the Property Rights of the American Indians," in Anthony Pagden (ed.), *The Languages of Political Theory in Early-Modern Europe*, Cambridge: Cambridge University Press, 1990, pp. 79–98.

16 Robert C. Miner, *Vico, Genealogist of Modernity*, Notre Dame, IN: University of Notre Dame Press, 2002, pp. 43–46.

17 See Barry Cooper, *Eric Voegelin and the Foundations of Modern Political Science*, Columbia, MO: University of Missouri Press, 1999.

18 Robert C. Miner, *Vico, Genealogist of Modernity*, Notre Dame, IN: University of Notre Dame Press, 2002, p. 9.

19 Giambattista Vico, *New Science: Principles of the New Science Concerning the Common Nature of the Nations*, 3rd ed., David Marsh (trans.), London: Penguin, 1999 [1744], p. 174.

20 Giuseppe Mazzotta, *The New Map of the World: The Poetic Philosophy of Giambattista Vico*, Princeton, NJ: Princeton University Press, 1998, p. 175.

21 Talal Asad, *Formations of the Secular: Christianity, Islam, Modernity*, Stanford: Stanford University Press, 2003, p. 179.

22 See José Casanova, "Civil Society and Religion: Retrospective Reflections on Catholicism and Prospective Reflections on Islam," *Social Research*, 2001, vol. 68, no. 4: 1041–1080.

23 Talal Asad, *Formations of the Secular: Christianity, Islam, Modernity*, Stanford: Stanford University Press, 2003, p. 177.

24 See Armando Salvatore, "Making Public Space: Chances and Limits of Collective Action Among Muslims in Europe," *Journal of Ethnic and Migration Studies*, 2004, vol 30, no 5: 1013–1031.

25 Amir-Moazami, "Hybridity and Anti-hybridity: the Islamic Headscarf and Its Opponents in the French Public Sphere", in Armando Salvatore (ed.) *Muslim Traditions and Modern Techniques of Power: Yearbook of the Sociology of Islam*, vol. 3. Hamburg: Lit; New Brunswick, NJ: Transaction, 2001, pp. 309–329.

26 Sigrid Nökel, "Personal Identity and Public Spaces: Micropolitics of Muslim Women in Germany," in *Jahrbuch 2000/2001*, Essen: Kulturwissenschaftliches Institut im Wissenschaftszentrum NRW, 2001, p. 131.

27 Ibid., p. 145.

28 Sigrid Nökel, "Being Muslim in Europe Between Body Politics and Bio-Politics," in Sigrid Nökel and Levent Tezcan (eds), *Islam in the New Europe: Challenge of Continuity, Chance for Change: Yearbook of the Sociology of Islam*, vol. 6, Bielefeld: Transcript; New Brunswick, NJ: Transaction, 2005.

6   Continuity and Change in the Modernization of Turkey

Serif Mardin

Some of the recent developments that have underlined the secularity of the Turkish state have been explained in relation to the element of "laicism" one finds in the Constitution of the Turkish Republic. This may well be true but then the secularist regime of Turkey itself is part of a continuity of which one finds roots in the Ottoman Empire. I myself have underlined this development in a study of the Tanzimat published many years ago. However, I believe we can go even further back in the history of the Ottoman Empire to trace the roots of this "secularity."

A glance at the structural components of the Ottoman Empire at the time of its nadir reminds us of the ways in which such a tradition may have developed. The components of the Ottoman political establishment are the elements that provide us with a clue. Were one to summarize the make-up of the ruling class in the Ottoman Empire the best description would be to fasten on the "orders," the specialized operational codes of three more or less distinct groups among the rulers. What we find here are the "sword wielders" the *seyfiyye*, the Doctors of Islamic Law (*ulama*) and the record keepers (*kalemiyye*) with a less distinct order being that of the "Sufi" orders (*sufiyye*).

There has now accumulated considerable information about the Ottoman Political Elite.[1] Halil İnalcık was the first to indicate that while the Doctors of Islamic Law (*ulama*) had a central role to play in the Ottoman Empire, there existed a rivalry that set *ulama* against the carriers of the Ottoman political discourse formed in the Palace and the scribal class established in "bureaus" of the Ottoman administration.[2] This rivalry was in fact the rivalry of two discourses: one clearly targeted to the preservation of the Ottoman state and the second aimed at keeping a state of equilibrium in the complex social structure of the Empire, giving its due both to individuals and to the Ottoman equivalent of established social institution.

Although there existed an overlap between these discourses there also could be distinguished a dividing line separating the discourse of the bureaucracy – more "secular" – and that of the Doctors of Islamic Law – more "religious." An early example of the "secularity" of the bureaucratic discourse may be found in the work of the seventeenth-century polymath Kâtip Çelebi. Both his organicist theories of the state and his adoption of the Haldunian view of the rise and demise of states differ from the argumentation of the earlier, more moralistic classical discourse of Kınalızâde that has a more clearly Islamic foundation.[3]

Kâtip Çelebi's indictment of the mefarious effects of the religious strife of his time as well as his critique of Ottoman Islamic religious education place him in a special spot even within the discourse of Ottoman scribal personnel. While we do not know whether this seventeenth-century Ottoman critique was a harbinger of more general secularist trends it is quite clear that the eighteenth century brought about a number of cumulative changes that promoted the "secularist" aspect of the discourse of the Ottoman bureaucracy. One of these changes was the creation of a new bureau (Amedi Odası) through which flowed all communication with Western states.[4] The employees of this bureau were now increasingly exposed to information about the major European states. Antedating this change already in the 1730s there had been an increase in the number of bureaucrats who were sent to various European capitals to observe Western "ways." An innovation of the same years was the practice of these envoys of writing reports about their missions upon their return. What is striking about these reports is the "materiality" of their content. The reports did not contrast the religious or political institutions they found in the West with their Ottoman equivalents but focused on the material elements of daily life in the West as well as on items of daily life. These included such things as the construction in stone of buildings both military and civilian, the organization of leisure activities such as the theater, and the precision of the observation of new astronomical observatories.

In the case of 28 Çelebi Mehmed Efendi, the envoy to France in 1720:

> [W]hat he evokes − principally − and with what astonishment and wonder is the achievements science and technology and those of the different arts, following in that respect, his instructions. But his curiosity and his interest also cover natural phenomena and animal species: the tides, or the early bloom of hyacaints and violets in Bordeaux . . . plants of the Jardin de Roi 'unknown in Turkey'. The animals of the new world he discovers in the menagery in Chantilly.[5]

The most interesting part of his report, however, is Mehmet Çelebi's summarizing of his experiences, i.e., the *hadis* to the effect that the world is the prison of the believer and the paradise of the infidel. This, of course, is pure irony and opens another window on the discourse of the Ottoman bureaucrats. An aspect of the Ottoman bureaucratic style which is in harmony with this bureaucratic irony is the strong influences in Ottoman state bureaus of Persian culture and its classics, an anathema to more Orthodox *ulama*.

No Doctor of Islamic Law was chosen for these foreign missions even though the bureaucrats that were selected carried the same disadvantages of the *ulama* of not knowing the languages of the countries in which they were on mission. Such personnel did, however, emerge increasingly from the Amedi Bureau with time. A most extraordinary example of the emphasis on what I have called "materiality" is the report on Austria of Ebubekir Ratip Efendi.[6] During the 227 days he spent in Austria in 1792–1793 Ebubekir Ratip Efendi was able to compile an extraordinarily detailed description of the military, financial and economic organization of that country. Only in one instance does one encounter a statement about religions in the entire report[7] and that relates to Islam being a better mobilizer of recruits into the army than the West.

In short, the reports of the envoys had a "positivistic" flavor that recreated the tacit elements of the bureaucrats' discourse. No wonder then that the foundation of the nineteenth-century reform movement known as the Tanzimat was modeled on the theories of the Austro-German Cameralists, those reformers of state structures whose view adumbrated the later positivists and Saint-Simonians. The entire reform movement of the Tanzimat secreted the positivistic view of the social engineer.[8] In the 1790s a doorway into that worldview had been the similarly, necessarily "positivistic" cast of military education.[9]

The founders of the Ottoman reform movement of the nineteenth century (the Tanzimat 1839–76) thus already had a foundation that enabled them to look with sympathy at a European development of the eighteenth century we know as "Cameralism." The latter has been placed in context by William Doyle:

> The period between Locke's Second Treatise and the publication in 1748 of the Spirit of Laws, a period that saw the flowering and the maturity of the Enlightenment, produced no notable developments in political theory. Men's minds were elsewhere, and most were content to say, with the Pope,
> 'To forms of Government let fools contest. Whate'er is best administered is best'.
> The writings of the German cameralists exemplify this attitude very well. Writers such as Seekendorff, Becher, Hornigk, Shröder or Justi were more interested in what states should do than the authority by which they did it. Their writings were with references to the quality of various forms of government, but there was no unanimity among them and often little consistency in the works of individual writers. None set out to construct a coherent theory of political obligation; a government justified itself in cameralist eyes if it used its power wisely. Their aim was to suggest the ends of government should pursue and to prescribe the best administrative arrangements for doing so. Cameralism was bureaucratic, rather than political, theory. The writings of its exponents derived more from the well-established German university tradition of administrative studies that from the advanced thought of the day.[10]

The religious neutrality of a theory of administration admirably suited the Ottoman reformist statesmen of the 1830s. But in the long run it was not this mentality but the relegating to the background of the *ulama* that emerged from the policies of reform.

A simple description of the institutional changes of the Tanzimat brings the double faces of reform – administrative rationalization and gradual secularization – in focus. Sultan Mahmud II had initiated such a rationalization of institutions during his reign. Military rationalization and creation of a new army followed upon the dispersion of the Janissaries in 1826. In 1832 offices of the state were reorganized to fit few principal categories. New ministries were established where duties encroached upon those of the *ulama*, such for instance was the state takeover of the administration of pious foundation. The position of employees of the central admin-istration (the "Porte") was reinforced by the granting of regular salaries. Entirely new ministries, increasing the control of the state over society such as the Ministry of Finance were established. The day-by-day control of policies of the Grand Vizier and other ministers and established through the formation of a Council of Ministers (*Meclis-i Hass*) in 1835 was reinforced with the help of a new police system.

In a document written in 1829 the Secretary for Foreign Affairs, Pertev Efendi, enumerated a theory of government in which of the four fundamental orders making up the state he gave precedence to the "men of the sword" and the "men of the pen" without even bothering to mention the *ulama*.[11]

Particularly teeling with regard to the position occupied by the *ulama* was the creation of new secular tribunals and the new law codes (such as the commercial code of 1850). In 1864 a new law for provincial administration began to be applied. The greatest blow to the status of the *ulama* and their position in which they controlled the main educational institutions, the *medrese* or religious schools and colleges, was the gradual founding of a secular system of state education. Here the graduate of normal schools replaced (although admittedly very slowly) the *alim* or *müderris* (holding religious diplomas).

Altogether the *Tanzimat* may be seen as having gradually "secularized" the Ottoman. In administration this was done by abolishing the administrative func-tions of the *kadı*, or judge, in the court system by the introduction of secular courts and law codes and in education by replacing the *alim* with the schoolmaster. The compromise concerning the place of Islamic law in the administration of the Empire, the codification known as the *mecelle*, was in fact a rationalization of basic principles of Islam expressed in the language of the modern jurist.

All of this did result in protest from the interested; in 1859 a Nakşibandi Sheikh organized an unsuccessful regicide. The first constitutionalist democrats, the Young Ottomans, placed the religious law back into the foundation of their project. When examined more clearly, however, Sultan Abdülhamit's apparent Islamic inclination reveals a continuation of the institutional project of the *Tanzimat* and a manipulation of the Islamist discourse for Imperial consolidation. By the end of the nineteenth-century, in the foundational principles that inspired it, the Ottoman state could be easily compared with Austria or the Russian Empire.

To institutional forces with a secularizing influence we have to add the influence of currents of thought from the West that became sources of inspiration for Ottoman intellectuals. Realism and naturalism as well as the mid-century materialism of Büchner had an important influence in this respect. But the greatest deviation from the times when the *ulama* and Islamic Law were incorporated in the Empire was the pervasive influence on the Young Turks, in power after 1908, of Social Darwinism.

This influence has been related in a recent doctorate dissertation of Marmara University. What this dissertation does not cover is an element that for the moment has to remain speculative but which is probably primordial in leading from the thoughts of the Young Turks to the secularism of the Turkish Republic. The present legitimation of this speculation relies on the way in which Charles Taylor approaches modernity, namely the place one should give to the tacit as well as the explicit when trying to reconstruct forces that lead to modernity.

In the case of the first two decades of the twentieth century there is no doubt that humanistic-democratic political thought had been considerably eroded by the worldview of philosophers of the end of the nineteenth century such as Nietzsche, Michels and Sorel. The mainstream of European thought was to replace the optimistic constitutionalist theories of the nineteenth century by investigation of "iron laws" of social structuration and the ways in which one could avail oneself of a control over those "iron laws." Action as a principle of polities replaced the argumentation that Marx had already seen as *passé*! In the thought of the Young Turks in exile, action and construction from the ground up had begun to show up as an element of their ideology. The politics of the Young Turks is power – despite its overt acceptance of constitutionalism – turned out to be a theory of action, a praxis that had, in fact, no theoretical foundation only a tacit acceptance of the urgency of action. Shaping the nation, mobilizing education, restructuring political parties to one that could move society would seem to have been a new addition to a continuity of secular structuring that went back to Ottoman times. In this respect the laicism of the Turkish Republic does not consist simply of an ideological discourse but can be seen as a construction in which secular continuities going back to Ottoman times have been given a new shape by conjoining them with action as a tacit principle of political organization.

The process by which these elements were taken up by the A. K. Parti, the most recent political party whose overwhelming presence in the Turkish Parliament was at one time interpreted as the victory of an "Islamist" political party, is another story. That story is one in which in reality it is not so much the laicism of the Republic but the practices, inspired by a new mode of knowledge construction that has "infiltrated" all of Turkish society in the last eighty years and affected "Islamists." Economic rationality and an unstated element in the discourse of the Republic have led to the rise of a new class of Anatolian entrepreneurs and would seem to be central here. A new type of knowledge about economic action has transformed the *esnaf* (the "*bazari*") into a businessman and the latter's demands are very reminiscent of the demands of his Western equivalents. Similarly, politics seen as a game, another tacit item of knowledge derived from the background of rationality of the Republic has now become a central factor in the worldview of persons somewhat too easily classified as "Islamist."

Notes

1 Carter Vaughn Findley, *Ottoman Civil Officialdom: A Social History*, Princeton, NJ: Princeton University Press, 1989.
2 See for instance Halil İnalcık, *The Ottoman Empire: The Classical Age 1300–1600*, Norman Itzkowitz and Colin Imber (trans.), London: Weidenfeld & Nicholson, 1973, pp. 100–103.
3 For Katip Çelebi see Hilmi Ziya Ülken, "Katip Çelebi ve Fikir Hayatımız," in *Katip Çelebi Hayatı ve Eserleri Hakkında İncelemeler*, Ankara: Türk Tarih Kurumu, 1991, pp. 177–196 and for Kızade see Baki Tezcan, "The Definition of Sultanic Legitimacy in the

Sixteenth Century Ottoman Empire," Master of Arts Thesis, Program in Near Eastern Studies, Princeton University, 1996.

4 Halil İnalcık, "Reis-ül-Küttab," in *İslam Ansiklopedisi*, vol. 9, pp. 671–683.

5 Mehmed Efendi, *Le Paradis des Infidèles*, Gilles Veinstein (trans., notes and annexed texts), Paris: Maspero, 1981, p. 21.

6 For the text see Sema Arıkan, "Nizam-Cedit Kaynaklarından Ebubekir Ratip Efendi'nin Büyük Layihası," Unpublished PhD thesis, Istanbul University, Institute of Social Science, 1996.

7 Ibid., p. 36.

8 One of the first works that attempted to show how the newly established Ottoman engineering school had kept up with the times was a book by one of the graduates where the author described all the books he had read by French experts on military science: *Diatribe de l'ingenieur Mustafa sur l'état actuel de l'art militaire du Genie et des Sciences a Constantinople*, Üsküdar, 1218/1803.

9 Kemal Beydilli, *Türk Bilim ve Matbaacılık Tarihinde Mühendishane Mühendishane Matbaası ve Kütüphanesi (1776–1826)*, İstanbul: Eren Yayınları, 1995.

10 William Doyle, *The Old European Order: 1660–1800*, Oxford: Oxford University Press, 1990 [1978], p. 235.

11 See Serif Mardin, *Genesis of Young Ottoman Thought: A Study in the Modernization of Turkish Political Ideas*, New York: Syracuse University Press, 2000, pp. 149–154.

7 When Silence is Not Golden

Muslim Women Speak Out

Zainah Anwar

Background

The Islamic resurgence that has engulfed most Muslim countries today has thrown forth different levels of tension and competing ideologies within these societies, leaving Muslims to ask: what Islam and whose Islam is the right Islam? Very often, when answering this question, the status and rights of women become the first casualty in this battleground.

The struggle for equality and justice for Muslim women must therefore be placed within the context of women living in Muslim societies where Islam is increasingly shaping and redefining our lives. Since the early 1970s, Muslim societies in all parts of the world have been caught up in the throes of a resurgent Islam. However, all too often, in the turn to Islam as a way of life and the source for solutions to the ills and injustices that beset our societies, it seems that the place of women has become the first (and easiest) measure of a group's or society's commitment to the faith. It is as if those who have turned to Islam cannot cope with the monumental challenges posed by the outside world that is galloping ahead and changing in ways and directions that are beyond their control, that they choose the disempowered and weakest in society to prove their power and ability to dominate and bring about change . . . in the name of Islam, as they claim.

It is therefore not surprising that in many Muslim countries today, women's groups are at the forefront in challenging traditional religious authorities and Islamist political movements and their use of Islam to justify women's subordination and inferior status, and most perniciously, to use religion to silence dissenting voices.

For most Muslim women, rejecting religion is not an option. We are believers, and as believers we want to find liberation, truth and justice from within our own faith. We feel strongly that we have a right to reclaim our religion, to redefine it, to participate and contribute to an understanding of Islam, how it is codified and implemented – in ways that take into consideration the realities and experience of women's lives today.

September 11th, the bombings in Bali, Riyadh, Casablanca, and London, have ironically been positive for those of us who are pushing the boundaries of public engagement on Islamic matters. One important impact of these tragedies in much of the Muslim world today has been the opening of the public space for debate, for discussion, for a diversity of voices and opinions on Islam and Islamic issues to be heard in the public sphere. There is greater engagement by ordinary citizens – Muslims and non-Muslims, civil society, and intellectuals – in shaping the direction of Islam in their own country. There is greater awareness that if Islam is used as a source of law and public policy to govern the public and private lives of citizens, then the question of *who* decides what is Islamic and what is not is of paramount importance.

This, of course, poses a particular challenge in Muslim societies. Most Muslims have traditionally been educated to believe that only the *ulama* have a right to talk about religion. But what are the implications to democratic governance, if only a small group of people, the *ulama*, as traditionally believed, have the right to interpret the Qur'an, and codify the text. Their interpretation often isolates the text from the socio-historical context of its revelation, isolates classical juristic opinion especially on women's issues, from the socio-historical context of the lives of the founding jurists of Islam, and isolates our textual heritage from the context of contemporary society, the world that we live in today. At a time when Islam plays an increasingly dominant role in reshaping and redefining our lives, the *ulama* can no longer have the monopoly over issues of religion.

Increasingly in Malaysia today, in many small ways, women's groups, human rights groups, NGOs, the media, and concerned individuals are beginning to speak up to engage publicly in the Islamic discourse. More people are beginning to speak out on some very key questions about the shape of the nation-state and the place of religion in this: What is the role of religion in politics? Is Islam compatible with democracy? Who has the right to interpret Islam and codify Islamic teachings into laws and public policies? How do we deal with the conflict between our constitutional provisions of fundamental liberties and equality with religious laws and policies that violate these provisions? Should the state legislate on morality? Is it the duty of the state, in order to bring about a moral society, to turn all sins into crimes against the state? Can there be one truth and one final interpretation of Islam that must govern the lives of every Muslim citizen of the country? Should the massive coercive powers of a modern nation-state be used to impose that one truth on all citizens? How do we deal with the new universal morality of democracy, of human rights, of women's rights, and where is the place of Islam in this dominant ethical paradigm of the modern world?

The search for answers to all these important questions on the role of Islam in today's modern nation-state cannot remain the exclusive preserve of the religious authorities, be they the *ulama* in government or in the opposition parties or Islamist activists pushing for an Islamic state and *Shari'ah* law. Muslims and all citizens have to take responsibility for the kind of Islam that develops in our societies.

The Political Context

In Malaysia, the two main Malay political parties, UMNO, the dominant party in the ruling coalition and PAS, the Islamic party in power in two states, have been engaged in an escalating holier-than-thou battle for the hearts and minds of the Malay electorate, each desperate to out-do the other to prove their religious credentials within a society engulfed by the forces of Islamic revivalism. In the 1990s, a slew of Islamic laws were introduced or existing laws were amended as part of the government's effort to upgrade the status of Islam in Malaysia and also to prove its Islamic credentials *vis-à-vis* PAS. *Shari'ah* criminal laws were passed designed to ensure that the Muslim lifestyle does not transgress Islamic teachings. New offenses were created, and moral surveillance, enforcement and more severe punitive punishment of Muslims were introduced. Eating in public during the month of Ramadan, consuming alcoholic beverages in public, women or men indulging in cross-dressing, homosexuality, lesbianism, and indecent behavior all became punishable *shari'ah* crimes.

The Islamic Family Law, one of the most enlightened personal status laws in the Muslim world, was amended to make divorce and polygamy easier for men and to reduce men's financial responsibilities towards women. The Administration of Islamic Law was amended to make *fatwas* issued by the state Mufti be given the automatic force of law – once they are gazetted – without going through the legislative process. Only the Mufti has the sole power to revoke or amend a *fatwa*. This was accompanied by new amendments to the *Shari'ah* Criminal Offenses Act which provided that any violation of the *fatwa*, any effort to dispute or to give an opinion contrary to the *fatwa* constitutes a criminal offense. To even possess books on Islam that are contrary to a *fatwa* that is currently in force is also an offense.

In Kelantan and Terengganu, the state governments under PAS control, which contain contentious provisions for *hudud* punishments such as flogging, amputation of limbs, stoning to death and crucifixion, and which grossly discriminate against Muslim women and non-Muslims, passed the *hudud* laws. Women are disqualified as witnesses; a single woman who is pregnant is assumed to have committed adultery; a woman reporting rape will be charged for *qazaf* and lashed eighty times if she cannot prove it.

This race to measure one's piety and Islamic credentials based the severity of punishment one imposes on those who transgress the teachings of the religion, on the way one dresses, and the status and control of women in one's society, and is a reflection of the reality in many Muslim societies when religion is transformed into an ideology for political struggle and a source of legitimacy.

SIS Strategies

In such a climate of intense religio-political contestation for power, the production of knowledge, laws and rulings in the name of Islam is guided more by political ideology and expediency. Islam is used and abused for purposes of political mobilization while Islam as a faith and source of ethical values are secondary. In such a situation, more than ever, civil society groups such as women's rights and human rights NGOs play a crucial role to change the terms of public engagement on religion and participate in the definition and codification of laws in the name of Islam.

In Malaysia, Sisters in Islam (SIS) has been at the forefront in creating and expanding the space for public discussion on laws and policies made in the name of religion that discriminate against women and infringe constitutional provisions on fundamental liberties and equality. Women and ordinary citizens, Muslims and non-Muslims who are not traditionally trained in religion, now regularly comment on all kinds of Islamic issues.

With our first letter to the editor published in 1990 in all the major newspapers in the country questioning the interpretation and practice of polygamy, SIS paved the way for the lay public to question, challenge, criticize and offer alternative views on laws, policies and pronouncements made in the name of Islam. We justified our right to have our voices heard, our concerns considered on the following grounds:

> We asserted that given the use of Islam as a political ideology and a source of law to govern our lives, Islam can no longer remain the exclusive preserve of the *ulama*.
> We pointed out that there exists in the rich and complex Islamic juristic heritage a diversity of positions and interpretations on a whole range of issues in Islam. Therefore, the one position taken by the religious authorities may not necessarily be the only "authentic" Islamic position.
> We stressed at every opportunity possible that there is a difference between what is the revealed word of God and what is human understanding of the word of God. The former is divine; the latter is fallible and changeable in accordance with changing times and circumstances.

Advocacy

SIS began as a research and advocacy group with a focus on interventions in the law and policy-making process on matters of religion. Our advocacy work takes two forms: as memorandums or letters to the Government on law or policy reform; and as letters to the editor on current issues to educate the public and build a constituency that would support a more enlightened interpretation of Islam on specific issues that are in contention.

Central to our advocacy work is our research into the interpretation of the Qur'an as that work feeds into our writing and press statements on contentious issues where the conservative religious authority or the Islamic movements are pushing for laws and policies that discriminate against women or violate fundamental liberties. This work is important, because first, we are believers, and as believers we want to fight for change from within our religion. Second, the knowledge that the Qur'an supports the universal values of equality, justice and a life of dignity for women is so empowering and liberating to us that it gives us the courage and conviction to stand up and argue with those who claim, also using the interpretations of the Qur'an, that women and men are not equal in Islam. It is this knowledge that gives us the confidence and conviction to speak out in public on alternative views on the subject and challenge the obscurantist view which discriminates against women and which is detrimental to the best interest of a modernizing, industrializing, multiracial and multireligious society.

In recent years, SIS advocacy and research work has expanded from the area of women's rights to issues of democracy and fundamental liberties. This is a natural progression as it becomes increasingly clear that without that democratic space and right to speak out and offer alternative views, and without any respect for the fundamental liberties of citizens in a democratic society, then the space to speak on women's rights would eventually disappear. Thus, we have taken public positions on critical issues such as freedom of religion and freedom of expression as well.

Advocacy through Memorandums to the Government

As part of our effort to influence law and policy-making, SIS has submitted several memoranda and letters to the Government on issues such as the appointment of women as judges in *Shari'ah* courts, the right of Muslim women to equal guardianship, the Domestic Violence Act and its application to Muslim women, Reform of the Laws on Polygamy specifically, Reform of the Islamic Family Law as a whole and the Administration of Justice in the *Shari'ah* System, Reform of the *Shari'ah* Criminal Laws and Conflict with Fundamental Liberties, the *Hudud* Law and Discrimination against Women.

In these memoranda and letters, we expressed our concerns on provisions in the law or policy that discriminate against women in substance or implementation, or violate fundamental liberties, offered a justification for why they should be amended and then provided specific wordings or position to make clear the changes that we want to see take place. We use sources in the Qur'an, the juristic heritage, and the real life experience and documented cases of abuse to justify the reforms we propose. SIS then submits these memoranda to the targeted minister in charge of the subject and then follows up with consultations on the matter, at the ministerial level and also through the press.

The results have been mixed. While most ministers are responsive initially to begin a process of negotiation and consultation, there has been no staying power to deliver on the demands made. In our experience, it is much more difficult to reform existing laws than to stop new laws from being introduced. We successfully got the Government to withdraw its effort to provide for a one-year mandatory detention for rehabilitation of those who want to leave Islam. We were successful in getting the Domestic Violence Act to apply to Muslims in the face of attempts to keep it exclusive to non-Muslims while Muslims involved in cases of domestic violence would be dealt under the Islamic Family Law.

Our efforts in trying to push for reform of the discriminatory provisions of the Islamic Family Law is stuck at the negotiation stage with the Ministry of Women, the Islamic Development Department, and the Attorney General's Chambers. At this stage, we only managed to delay the passage of a new draft Islamic Family Law Bill with amendments that further discriminate against women.

Advocacy through Letters to the Editor

Our memorandums to the Government are often, though not necessarily, accompanied by letters to the editor which we send to the major newspapers in the country to educate the public about alternative positions in Islam on a particular issue and hopefully, through this process, to help engender a more informed public discussion on the issue and build a constituency that would support our advocacy for a more enlightened and progressive Islam to take root in Malaysia.

This is a very important strategy because SIS is not a grassroots group and the fastest and most effective way for us to reach a wide audience with our alternative position is through the newspapers. The major newspapers in Malaysia have been very supportive of SIS work and have given us much valuable space to print, most of the time without any editing, our very long letters, which sometimes run to four or five single spaced pages.

As a strategy, too, some of our letters to the editor and to the government are submitted jointly with other women's and human rights organizations to show that our voice is not an isolated voice and that the women's movement and human rights groups are speaking in one voice on a particular issue.

For example, when the Ulama Association of Malaysia tried to charge me and five other writers for insulting Islam in January 2002, SIS mobilized the NGO movement and prominent individuals to sign a press statement to condemn the act. In a campaign against the *Hudud* Law of Terengganu, SIS mobilized eleven other women's groups to submit a letter to the editor to condemn the law. Press briefings were held with input from *shari'ah* and constitutional lawyers to educate journalists on the issues at stake and provided the Minister for Women with arguments and cases in Nigeria and Pakistan to assist her to publicly support our position.

While the *Hudud* bill was still adopted by the Terengganu State Assembly with some unsatisfactory amendments, the debate we generated and the bad press it received served as notice to the Terengganu government and its supporters that it enforces the *Hudud* law at its own peril.

The important lesson learnt from all our years of advocacy is that change cannot happen behind closed doors. We need to mobilize public opinion and win media support. Political leaders respond best to public outrage and press coverage of a particular issue.

Public Education

Another important strategy used is public education to build that core group of activists and opinion-makers such as journalists, policy-makers, human rights activists, and political party activists to be exposed to ideas in progressive Islam.

Seminars and Workshops: SIS regularly organizes such forums to discuss issues of significance to Islam, nationally and regionally. This includes issues such as Islam and the Modern Nation State; Islam, Culture and Democracy; Islam, Reproductive Health and Women's Rights; Islamic Family Law and Justice for Muslim Women.

These workshops bring together activists, progressive Islamic scholars and policy-makers from the region to come out with solutions and best practices to the challenges faced in each issue area.

Public Lecture: Our Public Lecture Series aims to expose the general Malaysian public to alternative progressive thinking in Islam by eminent progressive Islamic scholars. We've had Fathi Osman talk on Islam and Modernity; Amina Wadud on Islam, Qur'an and the Female Voice; Abdel Rahim Omran on Contraception, Abortion, and Reproductive Genetic Engineering; and Abdullahi an-Naim on Human Rights, Religion and Secularism. While these scholars are in Malaysia, we identify key journalists to interview them on issues relevant to the Malaysian context; we organize additional meetings or talks with other activist groups or government officials. The intent here is to expose more and more Malaysians to progressive thinking in Islam.

Gender Training on Women's Rights in Islam: SIS has developed a module on the subject and is intensifying its training program (monthly) targeting young women and men, students and professionals, journalists, human rights lawyers, young political leaders and grassroots service providers. The response has been enthusiastic and in the following years we intend to conduct the training workshops in other states.

Networking

As an advocacy group, the success and ability of SIS to mobilize support and influence laws and policies made in the name of Islam is very dependent on an effective networking strategy. We network at three levels with:

> Key state actors, including the Ministry of Women, the Ministry of Law, the Islamic Development Department, and the Attorney-General's chambers.
> NGOs, especially women's groups and human rights groups. In the past few years especially, the non-Muslims in Malaysia have begun to realize the impact of Islamization and Islamic laws on their rights as citizens of this country and have been more willing to publicly take positions on Islamic matters which in the past they saw as the sole preserve of the Muslims. Many non-Muslim activists have begun to attend our study sessions, public lectures and training programs regularly.
> Traditionalist women's groups and Islamist groups. As the SIS voice is increasingly recognized, these two sectors have begun to engage with SIS, especially in areas of common concern. SIS was able to mobilize traditionalist women's groups such as the Association of Police Wives, the Muslim Women's Welfare Board, and the Association of Women Public Servants to join us in our Monogamy campaign in March this year and they remain a part of the coalition researching the impact of polygamy on the family institution. A few members from two Islamist groups, the Muslim Youth Movement and the Islamic Reform Movement, now attend our study sessions. For the first time ever, the Islamic party PAS officially invited SIS to its general assembly this year.

Backlash

Of course, SIS achievements have come at a cost. The work that we do is often considered controversial. We are often attacked and condemned by the Islamic party PAS and Islamist activists and others in government and in the media who don't agree with what they see as our liberal Islam or our feminist perspective on issues. They say these are nothing but alien western values that we are trying to impose on Islam. The attacks usually take three forms.

First, they undermine our right and our legitimacy to speak on Islam by questioning our credentials to speak on religion. They say we have no right to speak on Islam because we are not traditionally educated in religious schools, we do not have a degree in Islam from a recognized Arab university, we do not speak Arabic, and we do not cover our heads. They say we are western educated feminists representing an elite strata of society who are trying to impose western values on Islam and the *Ummah*. To them, the discourse on Islam is therefore exclusive only to a certain group of Muslims, the *ulama* with the right education, status, and position. Others do not have the right to express their opinions on Islam.

Second, they accuse us of having deviated from our faith. They equate our questioning and challenging of their obscurantist views on women and fundamental liberties, and their interpretations of the Qur'an as questioning the word of God, and therefore they say we doubt the infallibility of God and the perfection of the message. Consequently, we are accused of being against Islam. They allege we locate our arguments on an incorrect and unsystematic methodology of interpretation of the Qur'an. They also accuse us of using our brains, logic and reason (*akal*) instead of referring to classical exegetical and jurisprudential texts of the early centuries of Islam. They claim that these texts by the great theologians and jurists of centuries past have perfected the understanding of Islam and the doors of *ijtihad* should therefore remain closed.

Third, they contend that it is dangerous to offer alternative opinions and interpretations of the religion as this could confuse the *ummah* and lead to disunity. There can only be one interpretation to be decided upon by the *ulama* and all citizens must abide by this interpretation. Alternative views that differ from the mainstream views are an insult to the Qur'an, inculcate hatred against *shari'ah*, and degrade women, they assert.

It is ironic that many of those who often criticize us, themselves do not speak Arabic and have not been traditionally schooled in Islam studies. Their right to speak out, however, is not questioned. The issue therefore is not so much about who has a right to speak on Islam, but what is one's position on various issues in Islam.

If one supports the death penalty for apostasy, the *Hudud* law, and the Islamic state and imposition of *Shari'ah* law, then one will enjoy the freedom and space to speak on Islam even if one is only a third-rate engineering graduate from a third-rate American university. But if one does not believe in the death penalty for apostasy, does not agree to an Islamic state and *Hudud* law, then one is demanded to have the right credentials before one can speak out. This is because what is being said does not serve the political agenda of those who use Islam as a tool to mobilize public support for their political cause.

Sisters in Islam believe that when we as Muslims are expected to lead a life according to the teachings of Islam, and laws are being made to stone us to death, flog us 100 or 80 lashes, chop off our limbs, send us to jail, and fine us if we violate the tenets of Islam, then we have a right to engage in defining what Islam means to us and how it should govern our lives within our democratic constitutional frame-work. When three-quarters of Malaysian citizens – all women and all non-Muslims – will be denied the right to be witnesses in the *Hudud* Enactment as adopted by the Kelantan and Terengganu State Legislative Assemblies, how could we be expected to remain silent when it is we who will suffer the consequences of grave injustice and discrimination?

Every so often, there are attempts by segments of the religious authorities to ban those with "no in-depth knowledge" of Islam from expressing themselves publicly on Islamic issues. While some of them recognize the validity of our concerns, they however felt that it was best that we raised these issues privately with them behind closed doors so as not to cause disharmony, alarm and confusion.

We have publicly resisted such attempts to silence lay Muslim scholars and activists from engaging publicly in the discourse on Islam in Malaysia. In one letter to the editor, we questioned why should the right of those who preach hatred, misogyny, intolerance and extremism be recognized and protected while our right to challenge them and to preach an Islam that stands for justice, equality, tolerance and moderation be denied? We raised the concern we felt of the silence that reigns among Muslim scholars who are reluctant to speak out in public for fear of being embroiled in any controversy or accused of being anti-Islam by colleagues in the fraternity. Others just prefer to remain detached and isolated in their ivory tower where they lead privileged and protected lives.

It is then left to women's groups and lay Muslim scholars and activists like us to claim the public space and right to offer an alternative view of Islam as a religion that upholds the principles of equality, justice, freedom and dignity. These are the groups that are often accused of having no knowledge of Islam even though their effort to offer alternative views is done after much in-depth research and study of Islam and consultation with highly qualified Islamic scholars.

If we, as citizens of a democratic country, have the right to participate fully in the economic, social and political development of the country, why is it when it comes to religion, we must suddenly shut up and be denied the right of public participation? We pose this challenge to those in the vanguard of the Islamic move-ment that wants to turn Malaysia into an Islamic state. Why would Malaysians support the concept of an Islamic state which asserts different rights for Muslim men, Muslim women and non-Muslims and minorities, rather than equal rights for all? Why would those whose equal status and rights are recognized by a democratic system support the creation of such a discriminatory Islamic state? If an Islamic state means an authoritarian, theocratic political system committed to enforcing androcentric doctrinal and legal rulings, and silencing or even eliminating those who challenge its authority and its understanding of Islam, then why would those whose fundamental liberties are protected by a democratic state support an Islamic state?

These are real dilemmas that must be dealt with by those who want to create an Islamic state in multiethnic and multireligious democratic societies. If as believers we want to live a life according to the tenets of our faith, a simplistic call to return to an idealized golden age of Islam that has little bearing to the realities of today's world cannot be the answer. And yet the answers can be found within our faith – if only we have the intellectual vigor, the moral courage, and the political will to strive for a more enlightened and progressive interpretation of the Qur'an in our search for answers to deal with our changing times and circumstances. For us in Sisters in Islam, this is not heretical, but an imperative if religion is to be relevant to our lives today.

8   The Contemporary Democracy and the Human Rights Project for Muslim Societies

Challenges for the Progressive Muslim Intellectual

Farid Esack

> The richest treasure that you may covet should be the treasure of good deeds. Maintain justice in administration and impose it on your own self and seek the consent of the people, for the discontent of the masses sterilizes the contentment of the privileged few and the discontent of the few loses itself in the contentment of the many. So live in close contact with the masses and be mindful of their welfare.
>
> (Ali ibn Abi Talib, in his epistle to Malik Ashtar, upon the latter's appointment as Governor of Egypt).[1]

Introduction

The first section of this chapter critiques the immediate (post-September 11th 2001) as well as broader ideological context of the global human rights and democracy project and its possible function as the Trojan horse of recolonization. It raises the question of cultural imperialism that may mask the emergence of the *homo aeconomicus* and asks if the simplistic translation of democracy and human rights discourse into the language of Islam is not really a substitute for genuine dialogue. Such dialogue can only occur between equals and when one acknowledges the substantial differences both in historicity and cosmovisions of the human rights project and Islam.

The second section deals with the challenge for Progressive Muslims to develop an ethic that transcends the immediate needs of the political expedience that utilizes "moderate" Islam as the "flavor of the month" for the current ascending tendency or for political control over ordinary people. It argues the need for Muslim intellectuals to seek greater critical engagement with the emerging social movements and to find more authentic appreciations of human rights and democracy based on this engagement.

The Current Context of the Islam, Democracy and Human Rights Discourse

The importance of both the personal and ideological context for and of critical scholarship has been widely acknowledged in post-colonial discourse, cultural studies, feminist studies and in liberation theology. For me, the question is "What is my context as a progressive African Muslim scholar?" Where is my authenticity located when I uncritically embrace the intellectual and political constructs and urgencies of others as my own and desperately seek to redefine a 14,000 year old tradition – albeit an ever-changing one – in the face of external demands? (Even if these demands were generated by a complex array of factors wherein that tradition is not entirely innocent.)

As for my personal context, the questions of pluralism, gender justice, human rights, democracy, etc., have for long been ones that I have been engaged with and with a sense of principled urgency that has its origins in a rather different context than the current dominant one. My own engagement with the South African liberation struggle and that of my comrades, my work as a Commissioner for Gender Equality for five years, and my current work with Muslims who are living with HIV and AIDS have often infused many of those elsewhere who share our ideals with pride – a sense that Muslims can be part of a vision larger than obscurantist fundamentalism. It is, ironically, precisely this location of my own scholarship within a principled vision of a just world that makes me so profoundly suspicious of the dominant urgency to rethink Islam in "contemporary terms."

We are witnessing – and participating in – an intense and even ruthless battle for the soul of Islam; a ruthlessness that often escapes many of us who are keen to nurture and imagine a faith that is peaceful and compatible with the values of dignity, democracy and human rights. For many non-Muslim Westerners who are driven by conservative ideological imperatives, Islam and Muslims have become the ultimate other. Many liberals, on the other hand, move from the assumption that "global harmonies remain elusive because of cultural conflicts."[2] Hence, the desperation to nudge Islam and Muslims into a more "moderate" corner, to transform the Muslim other into a Muslim version of the accommodating and "peaceful" self without in any way raising critical questions about that western self and the economic system that fuels the need for compliant subjects throughout the Empire.

Muslims' too, are conflicted about their relationship with both "outsiders" as well as to the tradition of Islam and its ideals. The tension of being in a world wherein the vast majority of Muslims feel trapped between the demands imposed on them in their existences as subjects of the Empire on the one hand, and the violent convulsions of a fascist-like Islamically invoked response by the co-religionists on the other, are palpable.[3] At every step of our encounter with our non-Muslim neighbors, colleagues, students and immigration officers, those of us – committed or nominal Muslim, confessional or cultural – living or working in the West have to justify our existences, our faith, our humanness and our non-violent intentions.

Declarations that Muslim societies must be democratized are fairly easy and there is no shortage of publications that argue against the idea that Muslim societies or Islam are inherently opposed to democracy or that Islam is compatible with democracy.[4] The question really is what does democracy really mean and what does the cover of democracy really hide?

Islam, like every other religious tradition, is the product of both its heritage – itself the synthesis of ideas, beliefs and the concrete lived experience of the earlier

Muslims and the way that heritage is interpreted by every generation. "Generations" though is not a disaggregated, disembowelled, classless social category. It is thus impossible to speak about an Islamic synthesis for our age as if "our age" is valueless or interest-free. When we thus approach the theme of "Toward a Contemporary Islamic Synthesis," we must ask "for what and in whose interest?" There is nothing neutral about this quest. The origins of the dominant urgency to re-articulate Islam in ways acceptable to the Empire must be interrogated if we are to come up with anything beyond *ad hoc* accommodationist responses meant to placate the Empire or to smooth our existences or advancement in the belly of the beast.

As I was writing this chapter I found myself overwhelmed by the shadow of the tragic events in the United States of America on September 11th 2001 and its aftermath. I am an African and, notwithstanding my own commitment to working with those living and dying with HIV and AIDS, it is not the reality of millions of deaths on this continent and millions more dying that forms the backdrop to my thoughts on some of the challenges facing Islamic thinking. My thoughts are, instead, shaped by a compulsion to ensure that all our theological questions and responses, all searches for an Islamic synthesis must be engaged in through the prisms of the wounded Empire and premised on the culprit and his community's contrition. Democracy and accountability, human rights and gender justice . . . the urgency for all of these are palpable and the impression that it is all part of an attempt to humanize the barbarian is inescapable.

I am not suggesting that these are issues that have not been dealt with in Islamic scholarship before 11th of September 2001. I am concerned that the teacher with a formidable cane had sent all of us into a corner after one of our classmates sullied his new book or did something unspeakable in his coffee cup. Discerning a lack of complete and unqualified remorse – even some rejoicing – the entire class is now subjected to collective punishment. And so, all now have to write a thousand times, "I shall behave – I shall be democratic – I shall respect human rights – I shall be peaceful." As it is, the class – Muslim societies – is a "remedial one" for "slow learners" and we are on probation. (Some of my classmates have successfully escaped into a much smaller but "real" class next door.) Meanwhile, many of the other kids are dying around me (e.g. in the case of Africa and indeed in much of the Third World, quite literally). We are living in a world where more than 1.5 billion live on less than a dollar fifty a day, where the gap between the lowest 20 per cent and the top 20 per cent of the word's population has increased from a ratio of 1:30 in 1960 to 1:174 in 1997. Yet, my major project is to get into the good books of the teacher, to present myself as worthy of his acceptance, as different from the barbarian who did what he did.

Besides the immediate reality of the children dying around me, there are, of course, other realities around me including coercion, the irony of violence being used to impose a language of peace, the larger context of education and schooling which pretends to be ideology-less. Neither the elite nor the aspirant elites of our generation, so desperate to "succeed" within the system, have ever been too interested to engage the works of thinkers such as Paul Goodman, Paulo Freire and Ivan Illich. Too tantalizing is the promise of entry into the domain of the establishment subject to turning a blind eye to its inherent injustice, the demand for uniformity, the reduction of human beings to empty vessels to be molded to serve a particular kind of society with particular economic needs, the transformation of *insan* into *homo aeconomicus*.

Both traditional – particularly those aligned to the power structures of Muslim states – as well as modern Islamic scholarship are under enormous pressure to ensure that the dominant Islamic synthesis that emerges is one that fits into the immediate demands of the teacher. Just a few days after September 11th, the *National Post* newspaper had a story titled "Globalization Is So Yesterday." The immediate demands of the teacher had nothing to do with hunger, poverty, exploitation, socio-economic justice, HIV/AIDS and affordable treatment. Instead we were compelled to deal with madrasas, Wahhabism, the clash of civilizations, terrorism, Islam as peace . . .

In many ways, scholarly elites are represented by the student who is desperate to outdo his fellow students in appeasing the teacher. For these students threats are unnecessary; the promise of acceptance by the teacher and the concomitant material advantages are sufficient incentives. Despite the protestations of benign objectives of advancing education and learning, the teacher is there as part of a larger project – a project that is politically unwise to interrogate; in an authoritarian system or moment spending "valuable" time on challenging teachers means losing marks . . . it is "unscholarly, it lacks intellectual depth, does not have the sang froid of true scholarship . . . "[5]

As with the learners, the teacher is also not a disembowelled human being. He comes from the city and it is a village school. There are larger civilizational and ideological issues at stake, including understandings of development and its price, culture, the commodity value attached to people and land and the supremacy of rationalist forms of thinking. The issue of the teacher's sullied cup represents only the sharper edge of the frustration, anger and agenda, the rise and march of the Reconstituted Empire. The larger context of this is globalization for which we require the intellectual courage and political will to also historicize and unravel its implications when we consider issues of human rights and democracy in relation to Islam today.

The Wider Context of Human Rights and its Function as a Trojan Horse of Recolonization

Can one really speak of the political participation of the social majorities of the Muslim world when their voices are de-legitimized by asking them to speak a discursive language of rights that may not be something that resonates with their cosmovision?

Human rights are only two hundred years old. The ideology and the institutional arrangements of human rights were born after unprecedented forms of social and personal deprivation took root among the "developed" peoples of the world. The regime of the nation-state fusing nationalism and statehood was constructed at this same time, to keep the social order in a society exposed to forces of the modern market reducing the human condition to that of *homo aeconomicus*.

Tawhid (the unicity of God), and the establishment of *Tawhidi* society (one recognizing the indivisibility of mankind), and other religious and cultural ideals are quite obviously irrelevant, ineffective or even counter-productive for societies designed towards economic development or "progress". The social majorities are now trying to resist the economization of their lives by using the state's language of "rights" to curb its intrusions. While still using it to struggle against power abuses of imperialism and the state, they are drawing upon their own cultural and religious resources for moral insights needed to overcome their contemporary ills, regenerating their commons.

The dilemma I am raising isn't an absolute cultural relativist position but rather one of how does one escape from a human rights monoculture and engage communities in ways that take stock of their cosmovisions. The issue is twofold: First, how does one speak of ethics within one's own tradition in the context of human rights. This is an issue of cultural affirmation. Second, what is the nature of the individual in the liberal rights discourse and what are its problems. Both of this has to be addressed in the context of Islam.

Authentic dialogue is about entering the other's world while holding on to yours, with the willingness to be transformed. It isn't a space where trade deals are struck. One cannot speak of genuine political participation, integrity of communities etc., unless one can reach some kind of consensus on a shared system of ethics. The context of power wherein the current drive for such conversation is driven by the Empire's agenda makes it exceedingly difficult, if not impossible, to have any kind of authentic conversation that holds within it an openness to mutual transformation.

Shifting the Context for Re-thinking Islam

An Islamic synthesis is invariably the product of intra-Muslim conversation as well as an inter-penetration of discourses. For reasons outlined above, I want to move away from a dominant hegemonic discourse on rights and democracy and open other avenues for engagement that will lead to a more profound interrogation of our tradition and, hopefully, a more humane Islamic response to the challenges facing Muslims and others today.

The global village is not a village for the real villagers of the globe. Never before have there been so many "have-nots" in the world. If we were in a "global village," they would be visible to all. But they are hidden from the view of the defenders of the "global village." They are the under-pariahs, kept out of sight, hidden in three-quarters of the Third World. The experience of globalization is a profoundly disempowering experience for the impoverished and marginalized, the social majorities.

Proclamations of "thinking globally" or of "universality" does not automatically make one's discourse global or universal – as always, the crucial question is "Whose universe?" Uninterrogated global thinking is essentially located in a kind of Orientalist scholarship that was used in the service of power for the sake of colonialist and neo-colonialist expansion. It embodies one of the central features of the

Orientalist discourse of the objective outsider being able to observe, analyze and provide solutions to lesser cultures and peoples. These solutions will be mass-produced and applied universally.

Its harshest manifestations are in the IMF prescriptions of developing countries regarding financial austerity, and its more insidious forms are how the social majorities are given prescriptions about what is good for them by the social minorities.[6] What occurs here is that the social majorities are viewed as inert populations with limited perspectives that need to be mapped as populations and later molded into docile and useful global citizens. In the material realm this implies two things for the social majorities: First, a feeling of being overwhelmed by the sheer enormity of the global problems from the depletion of the ozone layer to the war on Iraq. Second, a feeling of constant inadequacy that one doesn't really have any answers and at best one can put a blind trust in one's so-called representatives, whether the government or the international institutions or even the human rights lawyer, to provide the solutions.

This is hardly empowering since the daily experiences and innovative struggles of the social majorities are dismissed under the broad rubric of the term "the masses" or the *"ammah al-nas."* This, when done by the human rights activist, the local Marxists or the *ulama,* essentially mirrors the discourse of the Empire.

The insidiousness of the Empire lays not so much in its naked repression but its ability to prescribe the good life for the vast social majorities. Even if the progressive Muslim or the strident human rights activist takes over the reigns of power tomorrow, that will not solve the problem – as we see in South Africa.[7] The root of the problem lies in a historical moment in the West, the supremacy of rationalist forms of thinking, through which the world can be broken up into its constituent parts, observed and solutions prescribed and secondly, in the reduction of persons – carriers of the spirit of God to *homo aeconomicus*. It is the inbuilt arrogance in the very structure of contemporary power that is the problem and that co-opts even the best of us. It is representation of social majorities by intellectuals/activists/government officials who will "articulate" their suffering in conference halls of academia, the boardrooms of the World Bank and international summits where the landless peasant, the woman with HIV and the worker are rendered speechless. They have not been schooled in the ways of power, i.e. haven't been to schools, can't speak English, do not know how to debate, haven't read important books on economics, theology, etc. So what can they possibly know?

This is not an argument for anti-intellectualism nor a suggestion that there should not be a global vision. What I oppose is an abstract identification with uninterrogated buzzwords, global solutions that are hammered out in the corridors of the Empire of which not only armies, but often the academy is the vanguard. They are exported wholesale into the lives of social majorities, the classifying of social majorities as people who don't know what's good for them and thereby taking away the most significant of their weapons i.e., their ability to speak from their lived experience, make their own mistakes and learn from them.

This is especially important in the context of the human rights discourse almost smacking of cultural imperialism in the way it is deployed to invade countries and subjugate people. If this context is not unpacked we effectively become the prefects employed by the teacher to help keep an "eye on the class" while he goes off and works his second and more lucrative job elsewhere – a job as bulldozer of the cultural and religious values of my parents to make way for Wal-Mart, Haliburton and KFC even as I drink from his poisoned chalice in the name of education. I am not saying that there can be no cross-cultural conversation. All I am saying is that we have to guard against shallow translations in the name of dialogue. When we fail to, then we are mere paid agents and emissaries of accommodationism unto our communities. The Islam that emerges from such a function will necessarily reflect our games of accommodation. Thus we see the emergence of *fatwas* arguing that the basic message of the Qur'an is really the same as the USA constitution. "So, democracy is that you would like to have on the menu today? Excellent, we do have it, more than you have ever had before and even better than any other restaurants in the whole wide world." There is no critical or ethical interrogation of the text, of the one placing the order, nor of the origins of the appetite. What makes us all that different from the Empire anyway is really to use Ashis Nandy's term, "an intimate enemy," seemingly out there but really inside?

Challenges for the Progressive Muslim Intellectual

There are a number of challenges for the progressive Muslim intellectual who continues to identify with Islam and who derives her or his inspiration from it. I will address these in the context of an Islamic appreciation of human rights and democracy. First, to live in fidelity to this heritage; second, to speak the truth to power; and third, to re-interpret the Islamic heritage in terms of the primary urgencies.

To Attempt to Live in Fidelity to the Islamic Heritage

In some ways this seems like an impossible task; it is certainly one that cannot be measured because heritage is not fossilized but ever mutating. The suggestion is in fact that one lives with a loyalty to a partner, Islam, and commits oneself to be in a faithful relationship with it in a manner that both gives and takes for one's own growth. The believers whom we seek to transform are entitled to know whether we are really insiders or outsiders masquerading as insiders. When Muslim intellectuals do not feel a genuine affinity with Islam nor try to live in fidelity to it then this faith is reduced to a utilitarian tool to transform others, "those Muslims" out there. This is somewhat akin to learning Arabic or Pushto in the US Army and then not wearing a uniform in order to blend in with the natives; the language is a learnt one or an inherited one but the message is one of and for the Empire. We were paid interlocutors and translators. There may be periods of tension, alienation, and even divorce between the engaged Muslim intellectual and Islam. However, if we are seeking to be a part of transforming our faith communities in ways that also nurture democracy and human rights then a pre-condition for this is transparency.

Speaking Truth to Power

This speaking truth to power is both a path and an objective, for a Muslim's life and witness as a returnee to God have implications beyond the here and now. Viewing ourselves as returnees to God enables us to take a more long-term view of things wherein optimism and pessimism or expediency is not the great variable but constancy in God. Yet, it is a constancy that does not lead to the appropriation of God by fundamentalism because certainty is seen as only belonging to God.

In the current context there are three primary audiences that need to be addressed as we struggle to speak our truths to power; the conversation with all three takes place simultaneously and each inform the other: a) the personal self, b) the Empire and c)the Muslim community.

Engaging the Self: I have spoken about the need for the intellectual to be self-critical of his or her context. The element embedded in all formal Islamic religious discourses is invaluable here; *"usikum was nafsi awwalan . . . "* (I counsel you and, first of all, myself) or in the other form *"usikum wa iyyaya . . . "* (I counsel you and myself). It is the relentless self-critique that enables the scholar to be true to the ideals of a just society in a way that also prevents his or her co-optation by those who have their own agendas or the expansion of the Empires as their primary reason for wanting to engage Islam.

Engaging the Empire: The Empire needs to be engaged about the way it deals with Islam, a 1400 year old faith, as a cheap restaurant that caters to all needs and tastes. The Empire enters with its allies, flaunt their wallets and muscle and demand *"jihad"* on the menu when that suits their very power-driven palates. And Muslims are expected to deliver – as we indeed did in the *jihad* against communism in Afghanistan. After a few years, they shift gears and demand "peace" on the menu – as all dominant Empires demand of their subjects, never of themselves. And now the dutiful restauranteurs are expected to nod, smile and go around proclaiming that "Islam means peace." Islam is far more complex than this and as a self-respecting Muslim – or a restauranteur with integrity – the Muslim intellectual can respond by saying, "I am awfully sorry, but you may be in the wrong restaurant." (Mahmud Mamdani has recently written an excellent study, *Good Muslim, Bad Muslim*, detailing the way the Muslim subjects are expected to flip-flop in terms of varying requirements of the United States and its adventures into the Muslim world.)

It goes without saying that the Empire is also more complex than this and in whatever ways that we engage with it, for our sakes and for that of our future vision, we must always recognize the intrinsic humanity of those who comprise the Empire. When we fail to do thus then the methods that we decide on engaging the Empire can so easy reflect its own violence and lack of humanity. We cannot become the evil that we abhor.

Engaging the Ummah: Like all individuals and societies Muslims are never powerless in the absolute sense. In relation to the Empire we may be having less power but others have less in relation to us in the various ways in which this us-ness is defined. The appropriation of the human rights and democracy discourse by the Empire does not mean that Muslims can dismiss these; indeed hide their own unwillingness to confront the lack of these behind the guise of protecting Muslim society from the Empire. Hassan Hanafi has described the dual nature of this challenge as "confronting imperialism outside and resisting oppression within." For Muslims, the challenge is that of the Mafia banging on the door of their restaurant while the restauranteur is employing slave labor to run it – the restauranteur may have less power in relation to the Mafia at his door but this does not exonerate him from not replicating patterns of exploitation and injustice with those who may share his/her religious identity but who have less power than him. The questions thus are: How does one challenge the Mafia in ways that simultaneously address the absence of the values underpinning democracy and human rights in Muslim society? How do we ensure that the alternative vision in the wake of the inevitable death of the Empire? (So much of Muslim invective directed at the Empire does not stem from a principled abhorrence imperialism but because we – Muslim men – are not the ones running the Empire.)

When we welcome the voices in the United States of America saying that "dissent is patriotic" then we need to understand that the same applies to us. How we deal with our internal "others" is really the only truthful measure of what our values are really all about – all else are minorities or the less-powerful posturing for a better position at the banquet of the self-same Mafia banging on the door.

Re-interpreting the Islamic Heritage in Terms of the Primary Urgencies

There is nothing "traditional" about religious traditions; regardless of the fervor with which believers cling to notions of tradition – it is constantly being shaped. While I may refuse to participate in the shaping of my faith in response to the demands of the Empire, as a believer, I am never freed from the responsibility of shaping it. For me the question is in response to whose demands do I re-think the meaning and implications of my faith?

As a progressive Muslim theologian I consciously locate my own work among the marginalized, not as a sociological category but as a real in-context condition. Acknowledging that it is always a question of "less-power-ness" rather than powerlessness, this social location of the progressive thinker does not become a question of identifying with "Black persons" or "women" *per se* but with specific communities in these groups who are being marginalized. While I can, for example, be in solidarity with a male Black worker in respect of the exploitation that he experiences at work, I ought to be in solidarity with his abused wife in the home context. While I can be in solidarity with the Muslim male who is being racially or religiously profiled at airports, I can be in solidarity with the marginalized Christian who lives in the same Muslim country that the Muslim male comes from.

This principled solidarity is related to my notion of prophetic Islam where Islam is in a state of submission in its ever changing forms for communities and individuals rather than normative Islam; i.e., as a sociological label which enables one to claim virtue or victimhood regardless of how one relates to the paradigm of "less-power-ness." The engagement of Islamic tradition with actual contexts of injustice rather than with sociological or national communities leads to a principled or prophetic solidarity rather than the expedient or situational ethics that dominate current Muslim public discourse. (It is always "why do they do this to us in, say Abu Ghraib," never "what are we doing to others in, say, Darfur.")

Towards a Progressive Islamic Synthesis

Anouar Majid in his *Unveiling Tradition: – Post-colonial Islam in a Polycentric World* traces the ideas of secularism to the late eighteenth and early nineteenth century products of Enlightenment thought and classical liberal philosophy which called for the re-calibration of human morality in ways that attempted to exclude traditional religious commitments. The emergence of natural rights that were later articulated as human rights were forged as a part of the liberal discourse where the individual was constructed as a bundle of rights and the new society was seen as an arithmetic sum of individual aims. This in many ways may have been an important development. However, Majid seems to suggest that this entire process was deeply embedded within capitalism where an ideology of infinite progress, profit and private property was buttressed by liberalism. With colonialism these ideas were exported to Asia and Africa to create conditions that are conducive to capital. Majid argues that most Third World post-colonial theorists, despite pointing out that colonialism was a rupture in traditional societies, have been unable to come to grips with colonialism transforming itself into neo-colonialism. The export of the Enlightenment ideas of liberalism and secularism have been under-interrogated in a number of post-colonial countries and somehow their links to rogue capital have not been taken seriously. Instead, he argues, we still think in terms of western dichotomies of religion versus reason, tradition versus modernity, regressive versus progressive, etc. These crude binaries tend to reduce religion and reconstruct it through the eyes of the Empire where the reality of religion as a living culture fraught with debate and dissent undergoes an erasure.

Majid calls for a re-theorization by the "natives" of the discourse of the "Empire" where ideas such as secularism, liberalism, nation-state, individual rights, etc., are looked at through different eyes, this time through the eyes of the post-colonial. This process of understanding these ideas as historically contextual to the West and not universal will liberate us from being forced to think in these categories. Instead we can now begin the process of re-imagining a polycentric world by liberating suppressed progressive traditions within our own cultures and religions. For progressive Islam, he argues, to provide a genuine alternative, it needs to stop configuring itself in western categories but instead unearth progressive practices within the tradition itself. This, according to him, is not merely a strategic way of countering both the Empire and religious absolutists but the only genuine pluralistic alternative to the capital's attempt at McDonaldization of society.

Progressive Muslims have less to do with linguistic hegemony of the West, the essence of the Arab identity or even Islam as national identity. We aren't so much demanding an Islamic revivalism as a socio-cultural or spiritual fight against the West. Our concerns relate far more directly to global structures of oppression, whether economic, gender, sexual, etc., and ensuring that the oppressed are once again active agents of history. This fight for us involves the centrality of God, the imagining of mankind as *al-nas* – a carrier of the spirit of God and an appreciation of Islam as a liberatory discourse.

Here we are not merely attempting to break the monopoly of the West in the production of the discourses of modernity. We also attempt to reclaim modernist discourses of feminism, socio-economic justice and restating them in Islamic terms. We are simultaneously engaged in the task of articulating interpretative traditions within Islam that embody these values thus challenging the notion that modernity is distinctly a Western project.

Our goals embody a diversity of liberation projects that include those of new social movements such as rights of indigenous communities and sexual minorities. We are not really concerned about re-establishing the primacy of Islam as a shield against what some of the Islamists considered "western moral corruption." On the contrary we are engaged in the task of finding common ground with other liberatory social movements spawned by modernity and recognizing the emancipatory potential of other religions. Ours is not so much an Islamic universe but a pluriverse of liberatory discourses (Islam being one of them) in cross-cultural conversation with each other, forming alliances that fight oppression anywhere.

Ours is a cross-cultural conversation in progress and the voices of western Muslims with their distinctive histories have as much place in it as those of Muslims from the south. What we have here is emblematic of a global Islam where we may share a faith but have dissimilar cultural contexts. What binds us together is neither geography nor history but more a belief in the trans-historical and trans-geographic liberatory potential of our faith.

The progressive Muslims demand not an imposition of western analytic categories but instead a dialogue. We ask for the abandonment of a positivist epistemology both within Islam and outside that sustains a conception of understanding as discovering the objective and final truth. Instead we believe understanding is the result of a dialogue between two horizons of meaning neither of which can claim a monopoly over truth. Here the demand is for a willingness to risk oneself into a transformative process in which the status of the self and other are constantly renegotiated. We believe in the inexhaustibility of meaning of texts and challenge the possibility of an objectively valid interpretation.

At the same time as progressive Muslims we ought to be attentive to the radical inequality between the partners to the conversation and are conscious of the political, cultural and economic – and radically unequal – conditions that shape the terms of the dialogue. The pluriverse we therefore imagine is not culturally isolated factions but an ongoing dialogue for radical social change that will create the conditions for genuine dialogue.

Notes

1   "Muslim Conduct of State," in *Concept of Islamic State*, London: Islamic Council of Europe, 1979, pp. 32–33.
2   Anouar Majid, *Unveiling Traditions: Postcolonial Islam in a Polycentric World*, Durham, NC: Duke University Press, 2000, p. 3.

128   *Farid Esack*

3   These demands are imposed in such a blanket manner that it has compelled all who are connected to the world of Islam and who had long since ceased thinking of themselves as Muslims to again embrace this identity, however reluctantly or unwillingly. See, for example, Tarek Ali, *The Clash of Fundamentalism: Crusades, Jihads and Modernity*, London: Verso, 2003. Ali has ceased to write about himself as a Muslim is now accepting the mantle, even it is imposed.

4   Noah Feldman, *After Jihad: America and the Struggle for Islamic Democracy*, New York: Farrar, Straus & Giroux, 2003. Abdullahi An-Na'im, *Toward an Islamic Reformation: Civil Liberties, Human Rights and International Law*, New York: Syracuse University Press, 1990. Khaled Abou El Fadl, *The Place of Tolerance in Islam*, Boston: Beacon Press, 2002. Abdelaziz Sachedina, *Islamic Roots of Democratic Pluralism*, New York: Oxford University Press, 2001.

5   Anouar Majid, *Unveiling Traditions: Postcolonial Islam in a Polycentric World*, Durham, NC: Duke University Press, 2000, p. 2.

6   I use the term social minorities to describe the social formations at the top and their discourse and others who knowingly or unknowingly become agents of it, i.e., economists, academics, development planners, human rights experts, etc.

7   South Africa today is one of the freest countries in the world; it is, in fact, the dream of many human rights activists come true. Yet, as we celebrate our first ten years of democracy we find that the poorest of our people have gone much poorer and the liberation movement is rapidly being transformed into a boring political party where money speaks every bit as loud as it does in the more stable democracies. A vibrant independent country that paid for its freedom in blood and tears and with the goodwill of the entire Two-Third World is being rapidly reduced to a local municipality, with its security and economic policies largely determined by the powers in Washington DC.

Part III

Applied Ethics of Peace and Nonviolence in Islam

9 Framework for Nonviolence and Peacebuilding in Islam

Mohammed Abu-Nimer

Introduction

Today, there is little debate that a paradigm shift is occurring in the field of international conflict resolution; where experts laud the effectiveness of peaceful means of ending disputes compared with the use of force or violence. This paradigm shift is reflected in the increasing number of academic and applied programs in peacebuilding in Eastern Europe, Latin America, Africa, South and East Asia, and the Middle East, including conflict resolution workshops, projects for building civil societies, and nonviolent resistance mobilization.[1] In peacebuilding contexts, scholars and practitioners are seeking to integrate authentic, indigenous and local cultural methods of conflict analysis and intervention, which are replacing the generic conflict resolution applications developed by western practitioners in United States and Europe.[2]

In their efforts to disseminate peacebuilding approaches, practitioners have carried conflict resolution methods to Muslim communities.[3] However, their progress has been hampered by a well-publicized Western assumption that Islamic religion and culture contradict the principles of peacebuilding, conflict resolution, nonviolence, and even democracy. Western media reports and policy documents often reflect these violent and aggressive images of Islam.[4] Academic literature on the subject is no less tinged with such stereotypes. For example, when one searches the Library of Congress subject catalogue for resources on"'Islam and nonviolent", fewer than five items appear on the screen. However, thousands of items are listed when "violence and Islam" are the search words.[5]

Scholarly interest in researching Islamic theories of peacebuilding also stems from the recent significant expansions in the study of religion and peace. Scholars and practitioners in peace studies and conflict resolution have begun exploring the role of religion in shaping the theory and practice of their field.[6] This new wave of research aims to shift the focus away from religion as the cause of war and conflict to the ways in which religious values, beliefs, and rituals are a rich source for the study of conflict resolution, peace, and change. Muslim scholars and practitioners have joined the examination of the potential formulation and application of a systematic peacebuilding approach derived from their religious and cultural background.

This chapter is an attempt to contribute to a theory of nonviolence and peace-building principles and values from an Islamic perspective and within an Islamic context. The objective of this chapter is not to defend Islam or offer an apologetic justification for the past use of violence in the Islamic "world," but to actively promote peacebuilding and nonviolent strategies and values based on an indigenous Islamic religious context. The first part discusses some of the assumptions that must attend any research addressing Islamic conflict resolution, nonviolence, and peace. The second part reviews some of the research that has been done on Islam and nonviolence and peace. The third part focuses on the identification of Islamic values, stories and worldviews that support peacebuilding practices. It highlights the basic assumptions, principles, and values of nonviolent methods found in Islamic primary religious sources. The chapter concludes with a set of guiding principles that can function as a framework for the application of peacebuilding in the Islamic context; it also calls for further research to explore the reflection of these values in the daily lives of Muslims.

Approaches to the Study of Islam and Peacebuilding

Before one describes the principles that underlie conflict resolution and nonviolent methods and determines their relationship to Islamic religion and tradition, it is imperative to establish fundamental distinctions and definitions which guide any discussion of nonviolence and peacebuilding in Islam.[7] It is also important to describe the assumptions used by scholars and practitioners like myself who examine Islam and nonviolence in order to contribute to a deeper understanding of the discussion and the objectives of the research.

First, the full potential of Islam to address social and political conflicts is yet to be fully realized. Both Islamic religion and tradition have a multitude of resources with which conflicts can be resolved peacefully and nonviolently. Islamic scripture and religious teachings are rich sources of values, beliefs, and strategies that promote the peaceful and nonviolent resolution of conflicts. Awareness of the Qur'an, the Prophetic tradition, and the early Islamic period is indispensable for understanding Islam, since these scriptures and traditions have continued to provide a paradigm for emulation by Muslims and Islamic movements in every age,[8] and their influence can be traced in every philosophical, ideological, and scientific inquiry among Muslims. Moreover, the impact of the Islamic early period and the Qur'an is clearly discernible even in modern nonviolent movements, such as Mahatma Gandhi's philosophy and methods of nonviolence, as McDonough and Satha-Anand show.[9]

Second, Islamic scholars and practitioners need to reconsider and constantly reevaluate our understanding and application of Islam in various historical periods when we consider nonviolence and peacebuilding. The process of deconstructing the meaning of historical realities is legitimate and necessary to the collective and individual survival of Muslim communities. Islam is subject to diverse interpretations and perspectives that may be legitimately pursued by sincere and knowledgeable Muslim scholars from different nations, cultures and schools.[10] Therefore, knowledge and interpretations should not be treated as the property of small, privileged, and particular elites. Interpreting and viewing Islamic religion, tradition, and cultural patterns through nonviolence and peacebuilding lenses becomes important in accurately understanding and capturing the meaning of Islam.

Third, many Muslims themselves lack a comprehensive Islamic knowledge and hermeneutics relevant to nonviolent conflict transformation through its peaceful teachings. Most extant academic research and writing on Islam and conflict, not only by Orientalists, but even by Muslim scholars, is aimed at the study and interpretation of war, violence, power, political systems or legal arrangements. Approaching Islamic tradition and religion from these perspectives only perpetuates negative images and perceptions, particularly by Westerners.

Fourth, though a wide variety of Islamic religious teachings and practices address conflicts and peacebuilding, the validity of their application depends on the type of interaction involved in the conflict situation, including whether conflicts involve interpersonal, family, or community relations internal to the Islamic community or involve non-Muslims. However, Islam yields a set of peacebuilding values that, if consistently and systematically applied, can transcend and govern all types and levels of conflict, values such as justice (*adl*), beneficence (*ihsan*), and wisdom (*hikmah*) which constitute core principles in peacemaking strategies and frameworks.

Expanded awareness and use of these four assumptions in research and proposals on integrating Islam and peacebuilding can assist both Muslim and non-Muslim researchers in expanding their understanding of the relationship between the concepts and practices of nonviolence, peacebuilding, and Islamic culture, religion and tradition. Perhaps as importantly, such awareness can reduce the negative characterizations of Islamic society and religion in both popular and academic literature, particularly eradicating ill-founded generalizations about Islamic ways of thinking, believing, or living.

Finally, utilization of these assumptions can provide researchers with a way to avoid oversimplified literal interpretations of Qur'anic verses and prophetic sayings that do not follow the Islamic interpretive tradition of considering the historical context or social, political, and cultural forces that influence the lives of Muslims and non-Muslims as well.

Current Studies of Peace and Nonviolence in Islam

Currently published studies that focus on whether and how Islam as a religion supports principles and values of nonviolence, peace, and war can be divided into three main categories, each with its own research issues, perspectives, and interpretations of Islamic religion and tradition: (1) studies of war and *jihad*; (2) studies of war and peace; (3) studies of nonviolence and peacebuilding.

Studies of War and Jihad

Unfortunately, most modern studies of *jihad* and war attempt to provide support for the hypothesis that Islamic religion and tradition lend themselves easily and in a unique way to the justification of war and violence as the primary means of settlement of conflicts. Some writers in this group have argued that Islam is a religion of "war," and that violence is an integral part of the Islamic religion and tradition; and conversely, all writers in this group consider "pacifism" or "non-violence foreign" concepts to Islam.[11]

In this group of studies, scholars have overemphasized, and some seem to have been "obsessed" with, the principle of *jihad* (self-exertion) in Islam. Violent *jihad* has been described as an ultimate method that Muslims employ to settle their internal and external differences. In this group of studies, scholars and policy-makers view the behaviors and expressions of Muslims solely through a *"jihad* lens,"[12] equating the rise of interest in Islamic religion with Islamic fundamentalism, the emergence of radical Islamic movements and the perception that Islam unequivocally legitimizes the use of force by government and religious movements as well.

Studies of War and Peace

By contrast to the *"jihad*-lens" group of studies, those studies in what may be called "war and peace" hypothesize that Islamic religion and tradition justify the use of violence and force only in certain limited and well-defined contexts. Scholars and writers in this group have focused on the conditions and circumstances in which Islam as a religion and tradition has allowed the use of force and violence to settle conflicts or as a way of dealing with others.[13] In illustrating their perspectives, these scholars often rely on the following Qur'anic verses:[14] "Permission to fight is granted to those upon whom war is made, because they are oppressed" (22:39). "Fight in the way of God with those who fight with you, and do not exceed this limit" (2:190). Thus, pacifism in its "Christian" sense cannot intersect with authentic Islamic teachings.

Scholars in the "war and peace group" put the highest emphasis on the struggle for justice and perceive the discussion of nonviolence as a means to an end and thus secondary in its importance in Islam. This approach as an alternative to nonviolence conceived as an end in itself is best described by Jaggi:

> In one form or another, the principle of nonviolence has an important place in every religion. Some religions limit its practice to human beings; others encompass the entire world of living beings. Some consider it the highest virtue, and others regard it as second only to social justice."[15]

However, the relegation of nonviolence to a secondary place in the "war and peace" literature may stem from the intellectual base for these studies, and its limited definition of pacifism or nonviolence. Many of these scholars aim to objectively present Islamic interpretations of war and peace, but they have all approached this topic from a framework of security, war, and strategic studies, or from a classic Islamic studies perspective instead of grounding it in peace and conflict resolution studies. Since these scholars' analytical and disciplinary frameworks are outside of the peace and conflict resolution fields, they have often defined nonviolence and pacifism as a method or state of surrender to the enemy or the other party. They have concluded, based on this limited definition of nonviolence, that Islam cannot be described as a pacifist religion.

Both the writings of Sohail Hashimi and Abdelaziz Sachedina capture well the argument of this group. Hashimi identifies several essential points from the Qur'an[16] that underlie Islamic discussions of the propriety of the use of peaceful and violent conflict resolution methods:

1) The human person's fundamental nature is one of moral innocence, that is freedom from sin;
2) Human nature is characterized by the will to live on earth in a state of harmony and peace with other living things. (This is the ultimate import of the responsibility assigned by God to man, his vicegerent on this planet. (Qur'an 2:30)) Peace (*salaam*) is therefore not merely an absence of war; it is the elimination of the grounds for strife or conflict, and resulting waste and corruption (*fasad*) they create. Peace, not war or violence, is God's true purpose of humanity;
3) Given the human person's capacity for wrongdoing, there will always be some who choose to violate nature and transgress against God's commandments;
4) Each prophet encounters opposition from those (always a majority) who will persist in their rebellion against God, and justify their actions through various self-delusions, through *kufr* (unbelief) and *zulm* (oppression);
5) *Salaam* (peace) is attainable only when human beings surrender to God's will and live according to God's laws; and
6) Because it is unlikely that individuals or societies will ever conform fully to the precepts of Islam, Muslims must always be prepared to fight to preserve the Islamic faith and Islamic principles.

(8:60, 73)

These Islamic principles identified by Hashimi clearly provide a strong base for a solid peacebuilding and conflict resolution approach within Islam. According to these principles, human nature is to aspire to peace and not to war or violence. Humans seek harmony with nature and other living beings. In addition, humans can learn to be peaceful and change their wrongdoing since they are born innocent and not evil. The third and fourth assumptions illustrate an important principle of conflict transformation: conflict is a natural phenomenon and it will always be part of the human reality. Therefore, those who reject God and oppress others will constantly struggle with those who attained peace by surrendering to God's will. Being a good and faithful Muslim becomes the condition necessary to achieving internal and external peace and harmony.

The last principle, which requires Muslims to defend the Islamic faith, is mainly a call for action and resistance to *kufr* and oppression. Hashimi, like other researchers in his discipline of international relations, dwells on this point in particular to argue that Islam cannot be a pacifist religion, and that Islam justifies the acts of violence, war, and the use of force under certain conditions. He provides a well-developed set of conditions that should guide Muslims using violence. However, Hashimi's main argument is that although Islam allows the use of violence and force, it prohibits aggression; and its main objective is achieving peace through justice and the preservation of the faith and values. Like other scholars in this group, Hashimi assumes that defending Islam, and attaining justice and peace, does not take place via nonviolence; consequently, the use of limited or conditional force is a necessary step.

John Kelsay, who examined the nature of peace according to classic Sunnite perspectives, provided a similar analysis. Kelsay notes four main basic features of peace:

1) a conception of human responsibility in which humans were endowed with knowledge that makes them responsible for their actions;
2) the possibility of human choice: humans select the way of headlessness or ignorance (*jahiliyyah*) or the way of submission (*islam*);
3) the political result of these choices: the way of submission as institutionalized in the existence of Islamic and non-Islamic political entities. The territory of Islam (*dar al-islam*) and the territory of war (*dar al-harb*) are respectively viewed as such political institutes;
4) a program of action in which *jihad* is a means to extend the boundaries of *dar al-islam* or the territory of Islam (*salaam*).

Kelsay concludes by stating: "Sunni theorists understood force to be a possible and useful means of extending the territory of Islam and thus a tool in the quest for peace."[17]

In their attempt to explain the hypothesis that Islam is not a pacifist religion, and that war and force are permitted and justified in Islam, scholars in the war and peace group have had to address the conditions that permit the use of violence. Therefore, like scholars in the first category, they too have focused a great deal on the concept of *jihad* in Islam. Like Hashimi and others in this category, Kelsay spends the greater portion of his study investigating the application of *jihad* in *dar al-harb* (the territory of war) and attempting to support the existence and applicability of such rules of violent engagement.

These scholars have also had to investigate the question whether Islam is compatible with pacifism. While they are clear that war is permitted in the defense of the Muslim state and the self, they also agree that Islam prohibits wars of aggression, expansion or prestige. They suggest, however, that the possibility of unconditional pacifism is undermined in Islam by verses such as:

> Fighting is prescribed for you, even though it be hateful to you; but it may well be that you hate something that is in fact good for you, and that you love a thing that is in fact bad for you: and God knows, whereas you do not.
>
> (2:216)

Hashimi concludes that:

> The Islamic discourse on war and peace begins from the a priori assumption that some types of war are permissible – indeed required by God – and that all other forms of violence are, therefore, forbidden.[18]

The use of force, then, as far as the Qur'an is concerned, is defensive and limited to the violation of interpersonal human conduct. Sachedina also rejects the notion of pacifism in Islam:

Pacifism in the sense of rejecting all forms of violence and opposing all war and armed hostility before justice is established has no place in the Qur'anic doctrine of human faith or its inevitable projection into not only identifying with the cause of justice but working for it on earth.[19]

Saiyidain too supports this notion:

> It cannot, therefore, be said that Islam does not envisage the possibility of the use of force at all, or does not sharply reprimand and stand up against those who go out of their way to deprive other people of the right to follow "Truth" as they see it.[20]

Thus according to this perspective, for a Muslim to be denied the right of worship is a valid reason and cause to apply force, because such a condition qualifies as a *kufr* (unbelief).

Thus, the "war and peace" group of scholars does not fundamentally associate Islam with violence, or expansion. On the contrary, these scholars suggest that non-aggression, pursuit of justice, and even peaceful and nonviolent means are natural and proper in the propagation of the Islamic faith. They find a warrant for peaceful means in the Qur'an and the Prophet's commitment to nonviolent resistance during his early years in Mecca. Even the Prophet's reluctant endorsement of limited warfare after his move to Medina has been taken to support the view that fighting is undesirable for Muslims, and that it is permissible only if there is no other effective way to resist aggression against the faith.[21]

Ayoub, Sachedina, and others, have proposed that Muslims practice "quietism" rather than pacifism, arguing that Islam views human existence as caught up in contradictions and conflicts between darkness and light, guided and misguided ways, justice and injustice, and that it is an ongoing moral struggle to achieve justice. Scholars in this category argue that Islam has always encouraged its followers to adopt the middle course, to follow the realistic path in solving day-to-day issues. Islam instructs them to keep in mind the spirit of equality, brotherhood, love, and purity of character. Thus, absolute nonviolence would not be a middle way, but limited force and struggle is permitted under certain conditions.

> We ordained for the children of Israel that if anyone slew a person – unless it be for murder or for spreading mischief in the land – it would be as if he slew the whole people: and if anyone saved a life it would be as if he saved the life of the whole people.
>
> (5:35)

Many scholars in the war and peace group can be criticized for discounting the second part of the verse that emphasizes the sacredness of life in Islam and instead using the entire verse to provide a proof for the inevitable need to use force. Unfortunately, analyses like theirs narrow the definition of nonviolence to passive pacifism and, as described by Sachedina, associate pacifism with a life of simplicity and poverty, one that prohibits bearing arms.[22] Yet, such analysts never consider Gandhian nonviolence as a pacifist option even though it has produced a strong political and social impact on millions of people around the world and it can hardly be said that Gandhi's pacifism was a form of submission to the oppressor.

In short, "war and peace" scholarship that criticizes descriptions of Islam as a religion of peace that has nothing to do with war is ultimately misleading, detracting from the wisdom that might be gained if the conditions of war and use of violence are explored in Islam. Kelsay suggests, as others in this category do, that nonviolence ought to be evaluated in light of the overall Islamic goal of establishing a just social reality. Therefore the focus should not be on whether Islam provides support for nonviolence, but where, how, and when nonviolent strategies serve the goal of establishing and maintaining the just social reality which Muslims pursue. Framing the issue in this way excludes the possibility of moral and credal pacifism or nonviolence, and assumes that the instrumental and pragmatic nonviolent approach is more appropriate in the Islamic context. However, several examples in Islamic history and tradition contradict the above assumption that credal pacifism or nonviolence cannot possibly be adopted based on Islamic principles or beliefs. For example, the nonviolent struggle of Abdul Ghaffar Khan, a Muslim leader who created a nonviolent social and political movement based on the Qur'an to fight the British colonial forces in Pashtun (currently in Pakistan), is a clear example of a credal or morally absolute nonviolent approach.[23]

Studies of Nonviolence and Peacebuilding in Islam

Scholars and writers in "nonviolence" studies groups have acknowledged the existence and legitimacy of limited violence in Islamic scripture. Nevertheless, they view and emphasize the great potential for nonviolence as a philosophy in Islam. They identify values and principles that make such a claim possible, such as: Islam's basic belief in the unity of mankind, the supreme love of the Creator, the obligation of mercy, and Muslims' duty of subjection of their passions and accountability for all actions. Scholars writing "nonviolence" studies are guided/motivated by peace and nonviolent frameworks. Starting with the hypothesis "[t]here is no theological reason that an Islamic society could not take a lead in developing nonviolence today, and there is every reason that some of them should,"[24] they attempt to contextualize principles of peace and nonviolence in Islamic tradition and religion.[25] A few of these writers justify the use of restricted violence under certain strict conditions. However, without exception their overall perspective is based on the potential pacifist and nonviolent nature and characteristics of Islamic religion and tradition. For instance, Saiyidain argues:

> There are circumstances in which Islam contemplates the possibility of war, for instance, to avert worse disasters like the denial of freedom to human conscience, but the essential thing in life is peace. It is toward the achievement of peace that all human efforts must be sincerely diverted.[26]

Satha-Anand's pioneering list of eight theses of nonviolence which flow from Islamic teachings illustrates such a notion as well:

1) For Muslims the problem of violence is an integral part of the Islamic moral sphere;
2) Violence, if any, used by Muslims must be governed by rules prescribed in the Qur'an and Hadith;
3) If violence used cannot discriminate between combatants and noncombatants, then it is unacceptable to Islam;
4) Modern technologies of destruction render discrimination virtually impossible at present;
5) In the modern world, Muslims cannot use violence;
6) Islam teaches Muslims to fight for justice with the understanding that human lives, as all parts of God's creation, are purposeful and sacred;
7) In order to be true to Islam, Muslims must utilize nonviolent action as a new mode of struggle; and
8) Islam itself is fertile soil for nonviolence because of its potential for disobedience, strong discipline, sharing and social responsibility, perseverance and self-sacrifice, and the belief in the unity of the Muslim community and the oneness of humanity. Although in his second thesis, Satha-Anand allows the use of limited violence, nevertheless his fifth thesis clearly prevents the current use of violence.[27]

As scholars and practitioners of peacebuilding in Islam explain the need for an Islamic nonviolent paradigm, they point to certain conditions:

1) The historical period has changed and, therefore, the use of violence as a means to resolve differences or to spread the faith is no longer religiously permissible. Whatever Muslims used to create, establish, or spread their faith fourteen hundred years ago is not valid for today's reality. Therefore, if Islamic culture and tradition would thrive and prosper again, both Muslim leaders and people have to adopt a nonviolent approach to address their differences and conduct their lives.
2) The status of the Muslim community in a global system and in local communities has changed enormously, and it does not permit the use of violence. Many Muslim communities live as minorities in the world; their economic, social, and political status is different from six to seven centuries ago, when they were the majority or the dominant force in their regions and outside of them.
3) Global economic and political systems that have been developing over the last century prohibit the use of violence, particularly weapons of mass destruction, in settling conflicts.
4) The new global reality, weaponry systems, and warfare leave neither Muslims nor Christians any choice but to abandon violence because the prescribed limits of violence cannot be assured.[28]
5) The use of violence as a means to address conflict was a minor element in the life of the Prophet and in Scripture; therefore, it should not occupy as much attention or importance today. The Hadith and Islamic tradition, and history and culture are all rich sources for examples of nonviolence and peacebuilding.

Scholars in the peacebuilding category attempt to reinterpret historical symbols, stories, and other events in Islamic tradition to change Muslims' approaches to life in general and to conflicts in particular. Searching for scriptural proofs that legitimize shunning violence in all its forms has been another primary focus of researchers in this category. These scholars emphasize Islamic sources that condemn violence and war in any context, particularly Qur'anic versus such as: "Whenever they kindle the fire of war, God extinguishes it. They strive to create disorder on earth and God loves not those who create disorder" (5:64). Tolerance and kindness toward all other people without exception are also emphasized: "God commands you to treat (everyone) justly, generously and with kindness" (16:90).

Supporters of the nonviolent Islam hypothesis often rely on the Meccan period of the Prophet's life (610–622 CE), when the Prophet showed no inclination toward the use of force in any form, even for self-defense. He lived a life of nonviolent resistance, which was reflected in all his instructions and teaching during that period when Muslims were a minority. The Prophet's teachings were focused on values of patience and steadfastness in facing oppression.

Of the 23-year period of prophethood, the Prophet spent the initial 13 years in Mecca. The Prophet fully adopted the way of pacifism or nonviolence during this time. There were many such issues in Mecca at the time which could have been the subject of clash and confrontation. But, by avoiding all such issues, the Prophet of Islam strictly limited his sphere to peaceful propagation of the word of God.[29]

Moreover, many Hadiths identified by peacebuilding writers and researchers illustrate the importance of peacebuilding and patience. Jawdat Said best summarizes several of these sayings in an attempt to prove the pacifist nature of Islam, particularly when the dispute involves two Muslims:

> I don't see anyone in this world who clearly explained when it is incumbent upon a Muslim to behave like (Abel) the son of Adam! Nor does anyone teach the Muslims that the Messenger of God said to his companion Sa'd Ibn Abi Waqqas, '*kun ka-ibni Adam* (Be as the son of Adam)!' at the time when Muslims turn to fight one another. The Prophet(s) said to his companion Abu Dharr al Ghifari in a similar situation, when Abu Dharr asked him, 'But what if someone entered into my home (to kill me)?' The Prophet replied: 'If you fear to look upon the gleam of the sword raised to strike you, then cover your face with your robe. Thus will he bear the sin of killing you as well as his own sin.' And in the same situation, the Prophet(s) told his companion Abu Musa al-Asha'ri: 'Break your bows, sever your strings, beat stones on your swords (to break the blades); and when infringed upon by one of the perpetrators, be as the best of Adam's two sons.'[30]

This lesson from the Qur'an supports a nonviolent response, even in a confrontational context. It is reflected in the story of Cain (*Qabil*) and Abel (*Habil*), personalities representing the two opposing ways of approaching life and conflict. Abel is representative of justice and righteousness, refusing to soil his hands with blood. Cain represents aggression and readiness to use violence or even kill on any pretext.

> God accepts the sacrifice only of those who are righteous. If He has not accepted your sacrifice, how is it my fault? If you will lift your hand to slay me, I shall not lift mine to slay you. I am afraid of God's displeasure, who is the Creator of the worlds.
>
> (5:27–28)

Peacemaking and negotiation are recommended as the first strategy to resolve conflicts, as clearly expressed in the Qur'anic verse: "if they incline to peace, you should also incline to it, and trust in God" (8:39).

Even if justice rather than nonviolence and peace were the ultimate goal of Islamic religious teaching, pursuing peace through nonviolent strategies is a viable and effective method to achieving that justice, particularly when such methods are used to empower the victims of injustice. Kishtainy identifies several principles and techniques in Islam that support nonviolent resistance, such as tolerance, persuasion, arguing, suffering, patience, civil disobedience and withdrawal of cooperation, rejecting injustice, strikes, emigration, boycotting, diplomacy, publicity, propaganda, and special rituals (fasting, parallel lines of prayer, religious chanting).[31] This approach rejects either unjust solutions to problems or attempts to convince victims of oppression that they should endure an unjust reality; rather, it assumes that nonviolent methods, if applied correctly and systematically, will lead to justice.

Peacebuilding scholars argue that Muslims already possess the values and principles in both their religion and daily practice which are compatible with the adoption of nonviolent actions as tools to fight injustice. Anand-Satha suggests that the values that underlie the five pillars of Islam are also core values for Muslim nonviolence action, the duties:

1) to obey God and the Prophet only and disobey others if necessary;
2) to practice discipline through prayers;
3) to show solidarity and support for the poor through *zakah*, the tax to support the poor;
4) to practice self-sacrifice, suffering and patience through fasting;
5) to embrace unity and brotherhood through pilgrimage.[32]

In conclusion, the peacebuilding group of scholars would argue that active pacifism or nonviolence is not a strange concept but a core concept in Islamic Scripture and tradition. Islam as a religion and tradition has a set of values, beliefs, and strategies which facilitate nonviolence and peacebuilding. Those elements can be found in the Qur'an and the Hadith, as well as in cultural practices. The rest of this article will be devoted to framing a set of nonviolent and conflict resolution principles that exist in Islamic religion and exploring their correspondence with the theory and practice of nonviolence and peacebuilding.

Islamic Peacebuilding Principles and Values

Many Muslim and non-Muslim scholars have identified values and principles in Islam such as unity, supreme love of the Creator, mercy, subjection to passion, accountability for all actions. These values are supported by innumerable verses in the Qur'an, commanding believers to be righteous and level-headed in their dealings with their fellow beings. Forgiveness and mercy are recommended as virtues of the true faithful. Other Islamic values especially emphasized which relate directly to peacebuilding include *adl* (justice), *ihsan* (benevolence), *rahmah* (compassion)[33] and *hikmah* (wisdom). Islam emphasizes social justice, brotherhood, equality of mankind (including the abolishment of slavery, and racial and ethnic barriers), tolerance, submission to God, and the recognition of the rights of others. This section identifies and discusses a set of these values and principles supported by the Qur'an and Hadith. These values and principles constitute a peacebuilding framework which may guide scholars and practitioners who are interested in promoting such concepts in a Muslim community context. In many cases the principle's connection to peacebuilding is self evident; in others, the relationship is briefly clarified.

Pursuit of Justice

A main call of the Islamic religion is to establish a just social reality. Thus, the evaluation of any act or statement should be measured according to whether, how, and when it will accomplish the desired social reality. In Islam, acting for the cause of God is synonymous with pursuing justice. Islam calls for action to do justice whether one is strong or weak. The following Qur'anic verses are commonly identified by scholars as carrying a strong message concerning the social justice and responsibility reflected in Islam. They describe the Muslim's duty to work for justice and reject oppression and injustice on interpersonal and structural levels.

> Allah commands justice, the doing of good, and liberality to kith and kin, and He forbids all shameful deeds, and injustice and rebellion.
>
> (16:90)

> Allah does command you to render back your trusts to those to whom they are due; And when you judge between man and man, that you judge with justice.
>
> (4:58)

> You who believe! Stand out firmly for justice, as witnesses to Allah, even as against yourselves, or your parents, or your kin, whether it be (against) rich or poor: for Allah can best protect both. . . . Follow not the lusts (of your hearts), lest you swerve, and if you distort (justice) or decline to do justice, verily Allah is well-acquainted with all that you do.
>
> (4:135)

O you who believe, stand out firmly for God, as witnesses to justice and let not the enmity of others make you swerve from the path of justice. Be just: that is next to righteousness, and fear God. Indeed, God is well acquainted with all that you do.

(5:9)

Continuously, the Qur'an reminds Muslims of the value of justice, thus it does not simply favor, but rather divinely orders the followers and believers to pursue justice.[34] Justice is an absolute and not a relative value, and it is the duty of the believer to seek justice and apply it. The early Caliphs were known for their strong pursuit of justice, particularly Umar Ibn al-Khattab who left a distinctive tradition in pursuing justice.

The connection of peacebuilding with justice is thus never far from the surface in Islam. Peace is the product of order and justice. One must strive for peace with justice. This is the obligation of the believer as well as the ruler. More than that, it is a natural obligation of all humanity:

'God does command you to render back your trust to those to whom they are due. And when you judge between people, that you judge with justice. Indeed, how excellent is the teaching that He gives you. For verily God hears and sees all things.' (4:58) [and] 'God loves those who are just.' (60:8)

Islamic scripture also sends a consistent message that Muslims must resist and correct conditions of injustice which can be corrected, both through activism and third party intervention, and through divine intervention. Justice and peace are interconnected and interdependent. Many peacebuilding researchers and activists echo the notion that peace cannot be achieved without justice.[35] In addition, the Qur'an and the Prophet have called Muslims to mobilize and stand fast against injustice, even if the injustice is generated by a Muslim:

O you who believe! Stand out firmly for justice, as witness to Allah, even as against yourselves, or your parents, or kin, and whether it be (against) rich or poor: For Allah can best protect both. Follow not the lusts (of your hearts), lest you swerve, and if you distort (justice) or decline to do justice, verily Allah is well acquainted with all that you do.

(4:135)[36]

Islam distinguishes between *adl* (justice) and *qist* (equity, fair play).[37] While there are many teachings in the Qur'an about social and economic justice, scholars agree that several Islamic institutes and values are central to ensure such justice. Promoting economic justice in Islam is an important principle applied through a number of channels, such as those Islamic institutes and values identified by Raquibuz Zaman:

1) *Zakah*, one of the five pillars of Islam, requires Muslims who have the basic necessities and comforts of life to pay a share of their wealth in order to purify their wealth on behalf of the poor. *Zakah* should be exclusively used to support

the poor and needy. The administrators of *zakah* are those whose hearts have been reconciled to Islam. It is used for the ransoming of slaves, in the cause of God, and for the wayfarer.

2) The giving of voluntary charity (*sadaqah*) is a responsibility beyond the obligatory payment of *zakah*. God urges all people to give generously in charity from whatever wealth He bestowed on them.

3) Contributing to the *waqf*, an institution which handles the assistance to the poor, is another form of voluntary charity. Individuals may leave part of their wealth for *waqf*, and the resources of *waqf* are used to benefit the poor and needy among Muslims.

4) Other occasions to give to the poor are *Id al-adha* (the feast of immolation), the sacrifice of animal and *kaffarah* (expiation and atonement). Muslims distribute food and give money to the poor during the feast.

5) Muslims also do justice through *Wasiyah* (will), which permits Muslims to leave a third of the property passing through their will to charity. Contribution to charitable foundations and organizations is an important way to promote social and economic justice.

6) *Irth* (Islamic law of inheritance) promotes economic justice and equality by distributing an estate among all members of family.

Other Islamic laws and cultural practices similarly encourage mutual support and cooperation to ensure economic justice. They include:

1) *Diyah* (blood money), which obligates the family of the criminal offender to pay money to the victim's family.

2) *Musharakah* (the law of sharing), which obligates Muslims to share their harvest of crops with those who cannot afford to buy them. Similarly, inheritors should remember the needy when they divide their inheritance (4:8); and

3) *Diyafah* (the law of hospitality) based on the prophetic tradition, which holds that there is a social obligation to treat the guest graciously:

> He who believes in God and the last day must honor his guest for one day and one night as well as granting him hospitality for three days. More than this minimum is considered *sadaqah*. A guest, then, should not stay longer in order that he might embarrass his host.[38]

While some of these methods are more central to Islam and more known than others, all are specific Islamic methods to promote economic justice and the equitable distribution of resources. They illustrate the strong Islamic emphasis on both distributive and procedural aspects of justice. The Qur'an supports these notions when it describes the Muslim community as a just one (3:110).

The concern for justice as prescribed by Islamic principles and teachings is compatible with approaches of nonviolence that mobilize communities to resist injustice in society. Contrary to the popular misperception among opponents of nonviolent conflict resolution, the nonviolent approach does not mean submission or passivity to aggression and injustice. Nonviolence and conflict transformation change the structural violence that exists in the conflict situation. The primary end of nonviolent engagement is to abolish the structural violence on both micro and macro levels. Such changes are necessary to establish a just society.[39]

Social Empowerment through Doing Good (Khayr and Ihsan)

Social empowerment of the oppressed through the two critical Islamic values of *ihsan* (beneficence) and *khayr* (doing good) is important to accomplish justice as well. As a religion, Islam spread in large measure because of its foundations of helping and empowering the weak and the disempowered, and it continues to be characterized as a religion of dynamism and activism. Struggling against oppression (*zulm*), assisting the poor, and pursuing equality among all humans are core religious values emphasized throughout the Qur'an and Hadith. Islam demands that one should do good (*ihsan*) not only to one's parents and relations but also to the orphans, the needy, the helpless, and the neighbor whether he/she is related to oneself in any way or not at all.[40] The emphasis in Islam is on doing good (*khayr*), not on power and force (*quwwah*). Good deeds are associated with *al-sirat al-mustaqim* (straight path) and with all the virtue of the Prophet.

> And there may spring from you a nation who invites to goodness and enjoins right conduct and forbids indecency. Such are they who are successful.
>
> (3:104)

> Those who believe (in the Prophet of Islam) and those who are Jews and Christians and the Sabians (that is who belong to a religious group) who believe in God and the Last Day of Judgment and whose deeds are good, shall have their reward with their Lord. On them there shall be no fear nor shall they grieve.
>
> (2:62)

Khayr (doing good) in Islam is among the many teachings, rules, and institutes that insure social justice (distributive, administrative, or restorative) and empowerment. Acts of social and economic justice are so important in Islam that they are even equated with other ways of worshiping God. The value of *zakah* (almsgiving) and *sadaqah* (voluntary charity) relate to individual and collective responsibility.[41] These obligatory and voluntary duties are intended for the poor, stipulating fixed shares of inheritance for women, children, and a host of regulations regarding the just treatment of debtors, widows, the orphans (90:13–16) and slaves (24:33).[42] *Zakah* and *sadaqah* are central virtues for doing good in life and helping others, particularly needy people. *Zakah*, one of the five main pillars of Islam, is aimed at insuring distributive social justice and empowerment of the weak. Charity is a good deed which every Muslim has to carry out within his/her limits. The Prophet said: "There is a *sadaqah* to be given for every joint of the human body; and for every day on which the sun rises there is a reward of *sadaqah* for the one who establishes justice among people."[43] Charity is prescribed in at least 25 Qur'anic verses. All encourage Muslims to take more responsibility for the social injustice systems that exist in their communities.

It is not righteousness that you turn your faces towards east or west; but it is righteousness to believe in Allah and the last day, and the book, and the messengers; to spend your substance, out of love for him, for your kin, for orphans, for the needy, for the warfarer, for those who ask, for the ransom of slaves; to be steadfast in prayer, and practice charity, to fulfill the contract that you have made, and to be firm and patient in pain (or suffering) and adversity.

(2:177)

People are responsible for and have obligations toward those who are underprivileged in their community. Islam repeatedly stresses such principles. "Did He not find you an orphan and provide for you shelter (and care). And He found you wandering and gave you guidance and He found you in need and made you independent (in the financial sense)" (93:7–9).

The Prophet's compassion as reflected in his treatment of the underprivileged who suffered personal misfortune or from social and economic injustices was not the result of the Qur'anic teaching only, but was born from his own experience as well. The expectation that the Muslim should do the good is not only on behalf of people that the Muslim knows, but, as the Prophet said: "I and the person who looks after an orphan and provides for him, will be in paradise like this, putting his index and middle fingers together."[44] The Qur'an supports the responsibility for such compassion: "Therefore treat not the orphan with harshness, nor repulse the petitioner (unheard)" (93:9–10). Thus, the Muslim ought to give charity and provide assistance to those who are poor and in need of help. Caring and helping those underprivileged constitute a central mechanism for social empowerment and for maintaining a sense of community. For example, the abolition of slavery was a clear result of the ethical standpoints and principles which guided Muslims in addressing issues of oppression, poverty, and human suffering.

On the interpersonal level, preserving good relationships with others is an expectation that a Muslim must fulfill. "No Muslim can become a *mu'min* (genuine believer) unless he seeks for all others (not only Muslims) what he seeks for himself and he makes friends with them for God's sake."[45] "God commands you to treat (everyone) justly, generously and with kindness" (16:90). "Be good and kind to others even as God is to you" (28:77).

Doing good extends beyond the interpersonal to a group or community level. A nation cannot survive, according to Islam, without making fair and adequate arrangements for the sustenance and welfare of all the poor, underprivileged and destitute members of the community. The ultimate goal Islam points toward is a world in which suffering and poverty can be eliminated. In addition to individual *zakah* or charity, the state is obligated to provide for its poor through *zakah* and *bayt-al-mal* (public treasury). *Zakah* was even recognized, with offering prayer, as a minimal condition to recognizing a community as a community of true Muslims.[46] Thus economic justice is a major component of Qur'anic teachings, which describe in detail the proper distribution of wealth.

In short, for a Muslim, justice and doing good are expected to be achieved and pursued in all interactions with other Muslims and non-Muslims. Both the Prophet and the Qur'an praised these as central virtues. Justice, along with those values and principles that insure it, can be utilized in collective movements and mobilization for solidarity and sympathy among Muslims both on national and local levels. These values also directly relate generally to social and economic development and to peace-building in particular because they are focused on social empowerment and their orientation is people-centered. The processes and outcome of nonviolent conflict reso-lution are supposed to empower the parties involved in the conflict, by providing equal access to decision-making and by giving the parties ownership of the conflict. Therefore, many mediators emphasize the need for equal access among the parties around the negotiation table since these nonviolent strategies are designed to empower, mobilize, and engage people in the process of resolving their conflicts.

Universality and Human Dignity

Islam sends a firm and clear message through the Qur'an and Hadith of the univer-sality of the human person. Universal humanity is a central value in Islam conveyed through Muslims' beliefs in the equality of origins, and their calls for equal rights, treatment, and solidarity among all people. The human is an integral part of an ocean of creation, and is the most dignified and exalted of all creatures. The human has the potential to learn and know, the ability to decide which actions to take, and to bear the consequences of his/her actions. The human is God's vicegerent on earth. The Qur'an states: "when your Lord said to the angels verily I am going to appoint a vicegerent on earth" (2:30).

Thus, the protection of human life and respect for human dignity are sacred in Islam. The honor that God bestowed on humans is also stressed. "We have honored the sons of Adam; provided them with transport on land and sea; given them for sustenance things good and pure; and conferred on them special favors, above a great part of Our creation" (17:70). Thus, the work, worship, and life of a person should be aimed at preserving, protecting, and achieving human pride and dignity as main principles and values in Islam. Islamic scholars have cited several Qur'anic verses to establish the importance of human dignity and pride:

We have indeed created man in the best of moulds.

(95:4)

It is We who created you and gave you shape; then We bade the angels bow down to Adam, and they bowed down; not so *Iblis*; he refused to be of those who bow down.

(7:11)

Behold, thy Lord said to the angels: 'I will create a vicegerent on earth.' They said: 'will You place therein one who will make mischief therein and shed blood? While we do celebrate Your praises and glorify Your holy (name)?' He said: 'I know what you know not.'

(2:30)

It is considered a good deed to intervene or act to protect the basic dignity and pride of the person, because the creation of the human by God makes him/her a creature who deserves respect and protection.

> In Islam, within every person there is sacredness; that person is protected and sacrosanct until the person violates this sanctity. The person removes with his/her own hands such blanket protection by committing a crime thus removing part of his/her immunity. With this dignity, Islam protects its enemies, as well as its children and elders. This dignity, which God blessed humanity with, is the base for all human relationships.[47]

Thus, in addressing conflicts through Islamic values, promoting and preserving the dignity of the parties involved becomes an important motivation in resolving the conflict. In fact, protecting and insuring the dignity of underprivileged groups in society is the core value that underlies many of the peacebuilding and nonviolent strategies.

Equality

Islamic teachings go beyond intervention to reach a settlement in a specific dispute; they aspire to achieve the value of one human family. The value of equality among all members of the community is prevalent in the Islamic tradition and values. It is promoted and acknowledged as a basic value because of the oneness and common human origin of all people:

> O mankind! We created you from a single (pair), a male and female, and made you into nations and tribes, that you may know each other (not that you may despise each other). Verily the most honoured of you in the sight of Allah is the most righteous of you. And Allah has full knowledge and is well-acquainted (with all things).
>
> (49:13)

In Islam, there is no privilege granted based on race, ethnicity or tribal association. The only two criteria to be deployed in recognizing good Muslims are their faith and good deeds. There is no difference whatsoever between people except in their devotion to Allah, since He is the common creator of all humans. A well-known *Hadith* confirms this principle of equality:

> All people are equal, as equal as the teeth of a comb. There is no claim of merit of an Arab over a Persian (non-Arab), or of a white over a black person, or of a male over female. Only God-fearing people merit a preference with God.[48]

Ibn Taymiyyah (a well-known Muslim scholar 1263–1328) argued in these terms: "The desire to be above other people is injustice because all people are of the same species. A man's desire to put himself higher and reduce the others is unjust."[49]

Islam underscores that all people are the children of Adam and Eve, and such sayings are often cited by traditional mediators and arbitrators as a recommendation or a call for brotherhood and harmony.

Sacredness of Human Life

Peacebuilding approaches assume that human life is valuable and must be saved and protected, and that resources should be utilized to preserve life and prevent violence. A central teaching of Islam is that there is a purpose and meaning (of wisdom and justice) in the creation of the universe, including humans: "Not for (idle) sport did We create the heavens and the earth and all that is between!" (21:16, see also 44:38). The Qur'an clearly suggests the sacredness of human life, "And if any one saved a life, It would be as if he saved the life of the whole people" (5:32). "Nor take life – which Allah has made sacred – except for just cause" (17:33). Islam respects the unique meaning of each person's life: it is an integral part of the great cosmic purpose. Consequently, what each person does matters profoundly.

Thus, destruction and waste of resources that serve human life are prohibited. Even when Muslims in the early period launched an armed conflict, their rulers instructed them to avoid destruction and restrict their wars. According to a well-known speech made by the first *khalifah* Abu Bakr, when he dispatched his army on an expedition to the Syrian borders:

> Stop, O people, that I may give you ten rules for your guidance in the battle-field. Do not commit treachery or deviate from the right path. You must not mutilate dead bodies. Neither kill a child, nor a woman or an aged man. Bring no harm to the trees, nor burn them with fire, especially those which are fruitful. Slay not any of the enemy's flock, save for your food. You are likely to pass by people who have devoted their lives to monastic services, leave them alone.[50]

In a similar context, Imam Ali, reacting to his followers' pressure to go to war, was forced to utter the following words to convey the importance of the values of saving lives, as well as patience and the duty to avoid violence:

> If I order you to march on them on warm days, you say 'This is the fire of summer. Give us time until the heat is over.' If I ask you to march on them in winter, you say 'This is the bite of the frost. Give us time until the cold is over.' All this and you flee from the heat and the cold, but, by God, you are more in flight from the sword.[51]

In short, peacebuilding initiatives in Islam ought to preserve and improve the conditions for protecting human rights and dignity, and promote equality among all people. Accomplishing those objectives through intervention is encouraged regardless of race, ethnicity, or religious affiliation of the people.

A Quest for Peace

Peace in Islam is a state of physical, mental, spiritual and social harmony. Living at peace with God through submission, and living at peace with fellow beings by avoiding mischief on earth, is real Islam. Islam is a religion that preaches and obligates its believers to seek peace in all life's domains. The ultimate purpose of one's existence is to live in a peaceful as well as a just social reality. While, as will be described,

> [t]here are circumstances in which Islam contemplates the possibility of war, for instance, to avert worse disasters like the denial of freedom to human conscience . . . the essential thing in life is peace. It is towards the achievement of peace that all human efforts must be sincerely diverted.[52]

Peace is viewed as an outcome and goal of life to be achieved only after the full submission to the will of God. Thus, peace has internal, personal, as well as social applications, and God is the source and sustainer of such peace. Accordingly, the best way to insure peace is by total submission to God's will and to Islam.[53] Shunning violence and aggression in all its forms has been another primary focus of Islamic values and tradition. Many Qur'anic verses stress this principle, among them: "Whenever they kindle the fire of war, God extinguishes it. They strive to create disorder on earth and God loves not those who create disorder" (5:64). Tolerance, kindness to other people, and dealing with all people in such a manner with no exception is also emphasized in these verses: "God commands you to treat (everyone) justly, generously and with kindness" (16:90); "Repel evil (not with evil) with that which is best: We are well-acquainted with the things they say" (23:96). Thus when evil is done to you it is better not to reply with evil, "but to do what best repels the evil. Two evils do not make a good."[54] The Prophet's tradition also supports the shunning of violence and calls for restraint. Such teaching is clear in the Hadith:

> The Jews came to the Prophet and said, 'Death overtake you!' Aishah said, 'And you, may Allah curse you and may Allah's wrath descend on you'. He (the Prophet) said: 'Gently, O Aishah! Be courteous, and keep yourself away from roughness.'[55]

Forgiveness and amnesty are also recommended and viewed as the best reaction to anger and conflict.[56] Even in situations or relationships of conflict and fighting, Islam calls on its followers to prefer peace over war or violent confrontation. This notion is best reflected in the well-known verse: "But if the enemy inclines towards peace, do you (also) incline towards peace, and trust in Allah: for He is the one that hears and knows (all things)" (8:61). "Nor can goodness and evil be equal. Repel with what is better: then will he between whom and you was hatred become as it were your friend and intimate!" (41:34).

The quest for peace is also clear in the Prophet's tradition and life. The use of violence as a mean to address conflict was rare in the Prophet's life and in the

Qur'an. During the Meccan period of the Prophet's life (610–622 CE), he showed no inclination toward the use of force in any form, even for self-defense. He emphasized nonviolent resistance in all his instructions and teaching during that period in which Muslims were a minority. The Prophet's teachings were focused on the value of patience and steadfastness in facing the oppression. For 13 years, the Prophet fully adopted nonviolent methods, relying on his spiritual preaching in dealing with aggression and confrontation. This period of the Prophet's life has been cited as a source of nonviolent inspiration and teachings of peaceful preaching. During this time, though he was tortured, accused of blasphemy, and humiliated, and his family and supporters were ostracized, he did not curse his enemies or encourage violence. On the contrary, his teachings were centered around prayer and hope for enlightenment and peace. Ibn Umar relates that someone asked the Prophet, "Who is the best Muslim?" He replied, "That one whose hand and tongue leave other Muslims in peace."[57]

In Islam, the quest for peace extends to both interpersonal and community cases of quarrel or disagreement. Muslims should not use violence to settle their differences, but rely on arbitration or other forms of intervention. The Qur'an explains, "[y]ou should always refer it (disputes) to God and to His Prophet." "And obey Allah and His Messenger; and fall into no disputes, lest you lose heart and your power depart; and be patient and persevering: for Allah is with those who patiently persevere" (8:46).

Peace in Islam is reflected in the meaning of the word itself in Arabic. The word Islam means the "making of peace;" thus, the idea of "peace" is the dominant one in Islam. A Muslim, according to the Qur'an, is a person who has made peace with God and others. Peace with God implies complete submission to His will, which is the source of all purity and goodness, and peace with others implies the doing of good to fellow humans: "Nay, whoever submits himself entirely to God, and is the doer of good to others, he has his reward from His Lord. . . ." (2:112). The centrality of "peace" is reflected in the daily greetings of Muslims of *"al-salam 'alaykum"* "peace be upon you." The Qur'an states: "And the servants of Allah most gracious are those who walk the earth in humility and when others address them, they say peace!" (25:63); "And their greeting therein shall be, Peace" (10:10); "Peace" is also a reward which the believers will enjoy in paradise: "They shall hear therein no vain or sinful talk, but only the saying, Peace, Peace" (56:25–26). Peace is the ideal that Muslims strive to achieve and they are constantly reminded of this value through the names of God such as "Abode of peace" (10:25).

Islamic principles and values of peace cannot be fully explained without addressing the value of *jihad*.[58] Scholars agree that there are conditions which permit the use of force, and there have been massive amounts of debates and research by Muslims and non-Muslims to provide interpretations of the context and meaning of *jihad*. Many of these studies concluded that *jihad* does not mean the constant use of the sword to resolve problems with non-Muslim enemies, or among Muslims. In addition to the Qur'anic verses which indicate the possibility of peaceful and nonviolent *jihad*, different sects in Islam have emphasized the principle that there are several levels of *jihad* and that the self-*jihad* is the most difficult to achieve.[59]

Peacemaking

Open communication and face-to-face confrontation of conflicts are more productive than avoidance of problems or the use of violence to resolve them. Communication and confrontation reduce the cost of an ongoing conflict, and address all the grievances of the parties. The role of the third party, as an integral part of peace-building intervention, is mainly to facilitate communication, reduce tension, and assist in rebuilding relationships. Such interaction is described as functional and necessary to engage the parties in a true peacebuilding process. Islam encourages such process through an active intervention, particularly among Muslims themselves.

> If two parties among the believers fall into a quarrel, make your peace between them. But, if one of them transgresses beyond bounds against the other, then fight against the one that transgresses until it complies with the command of Allah. But, when it so complies, then make peace between them with justice and be fair. For, God loves those who are fair. The believers are but a single brotherhood; so make peace between your brothers and fear Allah that you may receive mercy.
>
> (49:9–10)

Though these verses have been used by scholars who justify the use of violence in Islam, and to disqualify the pacifist hypotheses, nevertheless they clearly support the concept of mediation and third party intervention to resolve disputes using fairness and justice as the primary values of intervention. In addition, they reflect a core Islamic value of shunning away aggression. Muslims should not be involved in aggression at all. " . . . And let not the hatred of some people in shutting you out of the sacred mosque lead you to transgression (and hostility on your part). Help one another in righteousness and piety. But help you not one another in sin and rancor" (5:2). Lack of tolerance and hatred should not lead an individual to become the "aggressor" or hostile to the other disputant, even if they shut him out of the house of God, which is an act of exclusion and violence. Rather, Muslims must settle their conflicts peacefully based on both the Qur'an and the Prophet's tradition, as shown in the verses, "[t]he believers are but a single brotherhood: so make peace and reconciliation between your two (contending) brothers. . . . " (49:10) and "[s]hould they (two) reconcile with each other and a reconciliation is best" (4:128). Also there is a clear call in the Qur'an for peacemaking and reconciliation in verse 4:114: "In most of their secret talks, save (in) him who orders charity or kindness, or conciliation between mankind and he who do this seeking the good pleasure of Allah, we shall give him great reward."

Peacemaking and reconciliation of differences and conflict are preferred and highlighted by the Prophet's tradition. He instructed his followers: "He who makes peace between the people is not a liar."[60] The Prophet's intervention in resolving the problem of the Black Stone in Mecca is based on a well-known Hadith – as a classic example of peacebuilding.[61] It illustrates the creativity of a peaceful problem-solving approach conducted by a third party intervenor (in this case, the Prophet himself). Mecca clans had a dispute over the *Ka'ba*'s building and the lifting of the Black Stone to its higher location. The clans asked for the Prophet's advice and intervention, due to his reputation as a trustworthy and faithful person. The Prophet proposed a simple yet creative method to resolve the dispute. He placed the stone on a cloak and asked each clan to hold one side of the cloak and jointly lift the stone to the required height, then he placed the Black Stone in its new location.[62] The resolution of this problem implies the denunciation of violence and competition, and appreciates values of joint problem-solving, and creativity. In fact, there are many accounts of interventions by the Prophet in which he utilized such skills and principles in settling disputes.

In short, based on Islamic values, aggression and violent confrontation, bigotry, and exclusion are less effective than peacebuilding and nonviolent methods in resolving problems. Methods of peacemaking and the pursuit of justice rather than violence can be employed to resolve differences. Such values correspond to those identified by practitioners and scholars in conflict resolution and peace studies as a fundamental strategy which should guide conflict resolvers in the field of conflict resolution, too.[63]

Forgiveness

In Islam, as in many religions, it is a higher virtue to forgive than to maintain hatred. Justice ought to be pursued and evil should be fought. Nevertheless, forgiveness remains a higher virtue (42:40 and 24:43). Forgiveness is the way people (Muslim and non-Muslim) ought to deal with each other, "Keep to forgiveness (O Muhammad) and enjoin kindness, and turn away from the ignorant" (7:199) and Muslims are instructed to "[r]epel evil (not with evil) but with something that is better (*ahsan*) – that is, with forgiveness and amnesty" (23:96). In fact, believers are urged to "forgive even when they are angry" (42:37).

The Prophet himself, when he entered Mecca with his Muslim followers, set an example of a great forgiving attitude towards Meccans who fought him by declaring it as a sanctuary.[64] The Prophet always prayed when he was persecuted during the Mecca period, saying: "Forgive them Lord, for they know not what they do."[65]

Being merciful is another quality or behavior expected from a Muslim. "God has mercy upon those who are merciful to others."[66] Mercy is an important step in the process of forgiveness and reconciliation. The value of forgiveness and its relationship to mercy is similarly supported by a story about some of the Prophet's followers who asked him to invoke the wrath of God upon the Meccans because of their persecution of Muslims, His reply was: "I have not been sent to curse anyone but to be a source of *rahmah* (compassion and mercy) to all."[67]

Forgiveness and reconciliation are central values and practices in Western peacebuilding and conflict resolution approaches too. Theories and practices of conflict transformation and resolution have focused on reconciliation as the most desired outcome of a conflict resolution process.[68]

Deeds, Actions, and Individual Responsibility and Choice

Islam puts emphasis on doing and deeds; the real test of a Muslim's faith is in action. Lip service is not enough. As for those who have faith and have done good deeds, God will take them for his friends. "On those who believe and work deeds of righteousness, will (Allah) Most Gracious bestow love" (19:96). "If you do good, it will be for your own self; if you do evil, against yourselves you did it" (17:7). An individual is responsible for his/her deeds; no one else can guide him or bear the responsibility of someone else's actions:

> Whosoever brings a good deed will receive tenfold the like thereof, while whosoever brings an ill deed will be awarded but the like thereof; and they will not be wronged.
>
> (6:160)

> It is not that We wronged them but they wronged themselves.
>
> (11:101)

> Whoever acts righteously, man or women, and has the faith, verily We will give such a person a good life and give his reward in the hereafter also, according to the best of their actions.
>
> (16:97)

According to Islam a person has three major types of responsibilities according to which he/she will be judged by God:

1) responsibility towards Allah to be fulfilled through the performance of religious duties faithfully;
2) responsibility to oneself by living in harmony with oneself; and
3) responsibility to live in harmony and peace with other fellow humans.

Deeds are central in measuring the person's obligation in meeting these responsibilities.

Similarly, the emphasis on "actions and doing" is central in peacebuilding, particularly when parties attempt to go beyond the dialogue and exchange of opinions. Believing in the importance of behavioral changes and implementation of values through specific actions is a central factor that promotes peacebuilding and change. Moving the other by persuasion and allowing him the free will to make a choice are two important principles in Islam. Both indicate that individuals carry the responsibility of their own actions. Even the Prophet himself was not responsible for the decisions of others: "But if they turn away, Say: 'Allah suffices me: there is no god but He: in Him is my trust − He the Lord of the Throne (of Glory) Supreme!'" (9:129). The Prophet emphasized that if others do not accept your message, it is their choice; therefore, the person is only responsible for his/her actions.[69] Allah is the sole arbitrator who judges the choices of the people:

Now then, for that (reason), call (them to the faith) and stand steadfast as you are commanded, nor follow you their vain desires; but say: 'I believe in the Book which Allah has sent down; and I am commanded to judge justly between (us and) you. Allah is our Lord and your Lord; For us (is the responsibility for) our deeds, and for you for your deeds. There is no contention between us and you . . . .'[70]

(42:15)

The sense of individual choice and call for involvement extends to the political governing system in which the ruler expects his followers to take full responsibility and stop injustice if it is committed. Abu Bakr told the people: "I am no better than you. I am just like any one of you. If you see that I am pursuing a proper course, then follow me; and if you see me err, then set me straight."[71] Thus, the emphasis on persuasion is a strong indicator that humans are in charge of their own fate, and should personally reason about the effects of their own individual actions. Persuasion is a main strategy in the Qur'an, as reflected in the great number of verses that present the arguments of those who opposed the Prophet, and the systematic negation of these arguments through proof and evidence in the Qur'an.

Naqvi establishes the importance of "free will" and choice in Islam by deducing this value from its basic axioms. He states: "In the Islamic ethical scheme, man is the cynosure of God's creation. He is God's vicegerent on earth: 'He it is Who has placed you as vicegerent of the earth. . . . '" (6:165).[72] Hence, the purpose of human life is to realize one's status as a "free" agent, invested with free will and able to make choices between good and evil, right and wrong. By virtue of their freedom, humans can either realize their destiny of being God's vicegerent on earth or deny themselves this exalted station by making the wrong choice. In other words, humans will be held accountable for the choices they make in their individual capacity.

Involvement and actions in community life are favored channels for meaningful deeds by Muslims, because deeds and individual responsibility are so central in Islam. Therefore, Muslims are encouraged to improve their communal life, to support each other, and abolish poverty and help the needy. Such goals can be attained only through actions and deeds, important criteria which God and the Prophet instructed the followers to adopt. They are essential and central to the judgment of Muslims. Thus, peacebuilding in Islam must be based on such principles of individual responsibility and orientation to act upon his/her choices in supporting the development of their community.

Patience (Sabr)

Muslims are encouraged to be patient and to wait on their judgment of others, whether they are Muslims or non-Muslims. *Sabr* (patience) is a virtue of the believer who can endure enormous difficulties and still maintain his strong belief in God. In Arabic, the word *sabr* implies a multiplicity of meanings which cannot be translated into one English word, including:

1) patience in the sense of being thorough, not hasty;
2) patient perseverance, constancy, steadfastness, firmness, of purpose;
3) systematic as opposed to spasmodic, or chance action;
4) a cheerful attitude of resignation and understanding in sorrow, defeat, or suffering, as opposed to murmuring or rebellion, but saved from mere passivity or listlessness, by the element of constancy or steadfastness.[73]

As the Prophet said:

> Nay, seek (Allah's) help with patience and perseverance and prayer: it is indeed hard, except to those who bring a lowly spirit.
>
> (2:45)

> You who believe! Seek help with patient perseverance and prayer: for Allah is with those who patiently persevere. (2:153). . . . but if you persevere patiently, and guard against evil, then that will be a determining factor in all affairs. (3:186) O you who believe! Persevere in patience and constancy; vie in such perseverance; strengthen each other; and fear Allah; that you may prosper. (3:200)

At least fifteen additional Qur'anic verses encourage Muslims to be patient and persevere in their daily lives and in their pursuit of a just life.[74] The way in which Muslims should live out the virtue of patience is described as follows: "Therefore do you hold patience – a patience of beautiful (contentment)" (70:5). This deep commitment to God is the source of patience that empowers people in crisis or when they are persecuted. It is the belief that their cause will be victorious. Patience, according to Islam, can be a source of solidarity among people who resist their persecution with patience: "O you who believe! Persevere in patience and constancy; vie in such perseverance; strengthen each other; and fear Allah; that you may prosper" (3:200).

Patience is also associated with making a personal and individual sacrifice. "O you who believe! Seek help and prayer: for Allah is with those who patiently persevere" (2:153). "Be sure we shall test you with something of fear and hunger, some loss in goods or lives or the fruits (of your toil), but give glad tidings to those who patiently persevere" (2:155). "Patience and perseverance" as interpreted by Yusuf Ali is not mere passivity. It is active striving in the way of truth, which is the way of Allah. Thus, oppression and persecution can be resisted and faced with praying and active patience. Patience and restraint are better than revenge. The Prophet said that: "power resides not in being able to strike another, but in being able to keep the self under control when anger arises."[75] Even when arguing or engaging in a conflict, the Prophet said:

> Whoever has (these) four qualities is a hypocrite, and whoever has any one of them has one quality of hypocrisy until he gives it up. These are: whenever he talks, he tells a lie; whenever he makes promise, he breaks it; whenever he

makes a covenant, he proves treacherous, and whenever he quarrels, he behaves impudently in an evil-insulting manner.[76]

And if you catch them out, catch them out no worse than they catch you out: but if you show patience, that is indeed the best (course) for those who are patient. And do you be patient, for your patience is but from Allah; nor grieve over them: and distress not yourself because of their plots. For Allah is with those who restrain themselves. And those who do good.

(16:126–128)

In commenting on these verses, Yusuf Ali says:

> The context of this passage refers to controversies and discussions, but the words are wide enough to cover all human struggles, disputes, and fights. In strictest equity you are not entitled to give a worse blow than is given to you. But those who have reached a higher spiritual standard do not even do that. . . . Lest you should think that such patience only gives an advantage to the adversary, you are told that the contrary is the case: the advantage with the patient, self possessed, those who do not lose their temper or forget their own principles of conduct.[77]

This is a strong command that instructs Muslims on how to use patience and self-restraint in reacting to conflicts, a type of patience that will give them the advantage. *Sabr* is an important quality of the believers – as agents of change – in Islam, the same characteristic required for peacebuilders and for those who engage in nonviolent resistance campaigns. This type of patience is very appropriate to peacebuilding, since an intervener in such a context would need a great deal of patience to carry out initiatives for peace and development in the community, and the receiver's patience is also required for a peaceful coexistence in conflict areas.

Ummah, *Collaborative Actions, and Solidarity*

Peacebuilding approaches assume that collaborative and joint efforts to resolve a problem are more productive than competitive efforts by individuals only. The principle of one *Ummah* or community, and collaborative efforts based on that principle, are often utilized to motivate disputants to reach an agreement, achieve unity, gain strength, and be empowered by working together. *Ummah* also embraces the idea of reducing cost and damage that might be incurred by individuals if they stand alone in a conflict. It is used to mobilize unity and support against the outside enemy, and to motivate people to avoid political and social split or rivalries (*fitnah*). As a collaborative approach to life's challenges, *Ummah* assists in social and political mobilization, and can be employed for collective actions in a social or economic development or peacebuilding context.

In Islam the base for solidarity is wider than the Muslim community alone. God has created all humans equal, and they have a common origin. Therefore, they should assist one another and not neglect each other's needs.

O people, fear your Lord who has created you from a single soul and created from it its pair and spread from this too many men and women. . . . Fear Allah, in whose name you plead with one another, and honour the mothers who bore you. Allah is ever watching over you.

(4:1)

Solidarity among Muslims is a central value too, reflected in the well-known traditional saying:

'Help your brother, whether he is an oppressor or he is an oppressed one.' People asked: 'O Allah's Apostle! It is all right to help him if he is oppressed, but how should we help him if he is an oppressor?' The prophet said: 'By preventing him from oppressing others.'[78]

The Prophet also declared that: "None among you has faith until you desire for your fellow Muslims what he/she desires for him/herself."[79] This is a clear message to avoid the use of violence and prevent aggression by Muslims against other Muslims and non-Muslims. Solidarity in this context is different from tribal solidarity (*asabiyyah* – assisting members of the same tribe/clan/family against outsiders, regardless of the conditions).[80] Thus, nonviolent strategies in Islam are most effective if they are based on collective approaches and political and social solidarity.

The concept of *Ummah* has functioned as a base for collective action since the Prophet's time. During the early period of Islam, in Mecca, the Prophet utilized the values of collaboration and collectivism to mobilize his followers and to respond nonviolently to accusations and to the force of those who did not follow his prophecy.

Contrary to the notion that the sense of *Ummah* has vanished due to the different political regimes in the Muslim world, and that it existed only when Muslims were all under the same political authority, Farid Esack argues "The notion of *Ummah* has not only survived but continues to give Muslims a deep sense of belonging." As suggested previously, the *Ummah* has even expanded to include non-Muslims, for all those who believe in God are members of this community, too. Esack stresses that "[t]he universal community under God has always been a significant element in Muslim discourse against tribalism and racism."[81] Other scholars note that the "People of the Book," as recipients of the divine revelation, were recognized as part of the *Ummah*, based on the Qur'anic verse: " . . . and surely this, your community (*Ummah*), is a single community" (23:52). The charter of Medina – the first constitution created by the Prophet – is another proof of such an inclusive and religiously diverse community.[82]

The Prophet reminded his followers on many occasions on the importance of unity and solidarity between the believers and non-Muslims. He instructed Muslims to avoid causes of dissension and to support each other, comparing their relationship to the organs of the body that communicate pain if one part is ill, or to a building which is strengthened by the strength of its various parts. "A believer to another believer is like a building whose different parts enforce each other. The Prophet then clasped his hands with fingers interlaced (while saying that)."[83]

Islam has been considered a religion of structural transformation and change, particularly in its impact on pre-Islamic civilizations. In this context, the principle of *Ummah*, in both its specific and general meanings, has emerged in Muslim history as a powerful mechanism for social and political transformation.[84]

Peacebuilding initiatives can preserve a community's structure and identity by careful planning, implementation, and follow up. The inclusion of Muslim-defined communal solidarity in these phases can contribute to the success of peacebuilding initiatives and serve as an effective forum for social mobilization. Nonviolence and peacebuilding are based on similar collective and collaborative approaches that aim to respond to the needs and interests of the parties, and to create future bonds, relationships, and agreements between disputing parties. Collective approaches utilized by the victims of injustice or the less powerful party to exert influence and power over the other side can create a change in the behavior of the other side, as demonstrated by leaders of nonviolent movements on both political and social levels. *Ummah* offers a powerful mobilizing frame for various Muslim communities to pursue justice, realize their power base, and assert themselves nonviolently to systematically resist structurally unjust arrangements.

Inclusivity and Participatory Processes

Participatory forums and inclusive procedures are more productive and effective than authoritarian, hierarchical, and exclusionary decision-making approaches. Peacebuilding strategies are based on either assisting parties in joint interest-based negotiation or bringing a third party in to facilitate such a process.

Similarly, the Qur'an's main premise is that the idea of inclusiveness is superior to exclusiveness, that justice must replace injustice. These principles are best reflected in the Muslim tradition of mutual consultation (*shura*) in the governing process. The meaning of *shura* is the solidarity in society based on the principle of free consultation and genuine dialogue, reflecting equality in thinking and expression of opinion.[85] Through public and private consultation, the governor (the leader) should seek active advice and input from his followers prior to making a decision. "Those who harken to their Lord, and establish regular prayer; who (conduct) their affairs by mutual consultation; who spend what We bestow on them for sustenance" (42:38). Whether the ruler must consult is not a matter subject to differing interpretation in Islam due to the imperative form in which the *shura* was communicated to the Prophet.[86]

The central role that *shura* plays in Islamic governance systems has been widely discussed by Islamic scholars, particularly those who support the notion that democracy is not necessarily contradictory to Islam. Despite scholarly debates on when and who can be consulted in important community decisions, the fact remains that consultation and input in decision-making is expected from the whole *Ummah*, the general community and its leaders through a process of *shura*. Thus, *shura* was a hallmark of early Islamic governance.

For Islamic scholars who have emphasized its central role, *shura* is not merely a consultation by the rulers and their advisers only, but it is an inclusive process.

Shura involves all matters concerning the *Ummah*, not simply those in which they might be likely to have expertise. The people of the *shura* represent all the segments of the society, differing from the people of *ijtihad* who are the Islamic *fuqaha'* (pl. of *faqih*) or experts of jurisprudence. The Prophet encouraged Muslims to consult with each other and with experts. He repeatedly consulted with other Muslims and followed their advice even when he disagreed with the person.[87]

Scholars have identified major principles which support the democratic and inclusive procedures in Islam. Some of these principles are:

1) Governance is for the *Ummah*: its approval is a *sine qua non* for the continuation of the rulers. Thus the legitimacy for governance is based on the *Ummah*'s satisfaction and approval rather than on the *khalifah*'s:[88] "The Prophet said that if all Muslims agreed on a matter, then it cannot be wrong."[89]

2) The community is obligated to pursuing religion, building a good life, and looking after public interests; these are not the responsibility of the rulers only. In addition to the Qur'anic verses supporting this principle, almsgiving (*zakah*) is the best evidence for the mutual responsibility of the people in supporting each other. Helping others and sharing part of their wealth become a right and duty of Muslims towards each other.[90]

3) Freedom is a right for all. Freedom is the other side of monotheism. By acknowledging his loyalty to God alone, a person is free from all others.[91] Individual freedom of decision is expected and favored by the Prophet who says "Do not be a conformist, who says I am with the people, if they do good I do good, and if they do harm, I do harm."[92] If freedom of expression of all people is not guaranteed then *shura* is not practiced.

4) All people are equal in their origin. They are all humans and from one father. They were all created from the same soul.[93]

5) The other – the different one – has legitimacy, which provides him with the right to protection by virtue of his being human. For example, the Prophet stood to respect a funeral and when he was told that it was a Jewish funeral, he wondered aloud: "Is not that a soul!"[94]

6) Oppression is prohibited and opposing it is a duty. *Zulm* (unjust treatment) is one of the most prohibited acts because it defies Islam's chief message of justice.[95]

7) The law of *shura* is above all. Islamic law is to be followed by both the rulers and the people. Such a principle has the potential to protect the people from governments and technocrats who might manipulate and change the rules to serve their interests.

In addition to *shura*, *ijma'* (consensus building) is an important mechanism of Islamic decision-making because, with *shura*, it supports collaborative and consensus building processes rather than authoritative, competitive, or confrontational procedures for dealing with differences. These principles in Islamic tradition and religion, practiced by the Prophet, mandate involvement and responsibility among people to resist *zulm*, rather than passivity or acceptance of oppression.[96] Moreover, regardless of the level or nature of the conflict (community/interpersonal, or political/social), consensus and inclusivity frameworks are simply more effective than authoritative decision-making and coercion in resolving conflicts or implementing projects. They can achieve sustainable agreement (particularly on community and public policy levels) in many areas of conflict.

Pluralism and Diversity

Pluralism and diversity are core values in Islamic tradition and religion. The Qur'an recognizes diversity and tolerance of differences based on gender (49:13; 53:45); skin color, language (30:22); beliefs and ranks (64:2; 6:165). Harmony between the different social grouping and communities is praised, and competition and control of any person by another is condemned.[97] The Qur'an asserts that differences are inherent in human life. Thus, ethnic, tribal, and national differences have no real bearing on closeness to God. Rather, as suggested in discussing *Ummah*, only their degree of faith is the solemn criterion by which those groups will be judged.

Differences among people, inevitable in humanity, are a basic assumption in Islam. "If your Lord had so willed, He could have made mankind one people: But they will not cease to dispute" (11:118). These differences are integrally related to the free will that God has bestowed on humanity, for people should be expected to be diverse not only in nationality and affiliation, but also in the expression of their faith and the path that they choose to follow (10:99). Such a principle of free will and the individual's responsibility for all his/her actions is reflected in the Qur'an: "If Allah so willed, He could make you all one people: but He leaves straying whom He pleases, and He guides whom He pleases: but you shall certainly be called to account for all your actions" (16:93).

Tolerance of the "others" (particularly non-Muslim people of the Book) is repeatedly accepted and emphasized in Islam. The equality of the followers of different religions is reiterated in both the Qur'an and Hadith many times. Muslims are asked to remember that there is no difference in the treatment of people of different religions except in their faith and deeds (3:113–114; 2:62; 5:69). The Qur'an calls on Muslims to abandon fighting and coexist peacefully with other religions, reaffirming the validity of the other religions and requiring its followers to respect their scriptures. In fact, the expansion of Islam through *da'wa* in Asia and Africa or the Pacific region has taken place mainly among non-Muslims. Under such circumstances Islam could not have survived or prospered without having been strongly pluralistic and accepting of diversity.[98] The Qur'an reflects this celebration of diversity of people and belief:

Say, 'O People of the Book! Come to common terms as between us and you:
That we worship none but Allah; That we associate no partners with Him;
That we erect not, from among ourselves, lords and patrons other than Allah.'
If they turn their back, say you: 'Bear witness that we (at least) are Muslims
(bowing to Allah's Will).'

(3:64)

> Say, 'O People of the Book, you have no ground to stand upon unless you stand
> fast by the Torah and the Gospel and all that has been revealed to you from your
> Lord. . . . Those who believe (in the Qur'an), those who follow the Jewish scrip-
> tures and the Sabians and the Christians – any people who believe in God, the
> Day of Judgment and do good deeds, on them shall be no fear nor shall they
> grieve.'
>
> (5:71–72)

Among Muslims themselves, pluralism historically existed in the early Muslim
community. There was no single Islamic law or constitution, nor standardization of
the Islamic law. For example, the Sunni tradition produced four legitimate schools of
thoughts, not limited to legal traditions. In fact, the development of Qur'anic interpretation legitimizes the validity of differences (*ikhtilaf*): several interpretations of
the Qur'an coexisted in the same period and space. On the other hand, Islam is least
tolerant of non-believers or infidels. Throughout history those who were cast as
kafirun (pl. of *kafir* – unbeliever) were persecuted and punished by rulers and other
followers.[99]

The Medinah charter, which was contracted between the Prophet and the various
tribes, is an example of the high level of tolerance and respect of diversity assumed
by Islam. Under the charter, all Muslims and Jewish tribes (apparently, no Christians
were involved) are considered one community, but each tribe retains its identity,
customs, and internal relations. The charter was supplemented by a set of rules
derived from the Qur'an and *sunnah* to protect the rights of each group. The freedom
of religion, and the right not to be guilty because of the deed of an ally, were among
the protected rights.[100]

Proceeding from this recognition of diversity, seven main principles, or *usul*, can
be derived from the Qur'an supporting coexistence and tolerance:[101]

1) Human dignity deserves absolute protection regardless of the person's religion,
   ethnicity, and intellectual opinion orientation (17:70). This dignity is a form of
   individual protection given by God.
2) All humans are related and from the same origin (4:1; 6:98; 5:32).
3) Differences among people are designated by God and are part of His creation
   and rules (*sunnan*), thus differences in ethnicity, race, culture, etc., are a natural
   part of life (30:22; 10:99; 11:118, 199). God had the power to create us all the
   same, but He did not (11:118).
4) Islam acknowledges other religions and asserts their unity of origin (42:13;
   2:136) Because differences are a given in Islam, there is no justification for
   violating people's rights to existence and movement due to their different religious affiliation (42:15).
5) Muslims have the freedom of choice and decision after the calling or the
   message has been delivered (2:256; 18:29; 17:107; 109:4–6).
6) God is the only judge of people's actions. People are responsible for their decisions and deeds when they face judgment. The Prophet only carried the
   message, only God is responsible for the judgment (42:48; 16:124; 31:23;
   88:25, 26).

7) Muslims should observe good deeds, justice, and equity in dealing with all human beings (5:9; 4:135; 60:8).

The principles of Islam were not consumed by other cultures and did not reject them either; instead Islam created a new civilization, multicultural and pluralist in practice. Although Asian, African, or European Muslims have widely different cultural practices, nevertheless, as Muslims, they are expected to tolerate each other's cultural differences and those of non-Muslims in their communities.

Unfortunately, the social and political movements that attempt to mobilize the masses to pursue political control have been engaged in redefining multicultural and pluralist Islam as a more "centralist and narrow" view of the world.[102] Muslim scholars are still reacting to proposals attempting to redefine Islam in relationship to the principles of diversity and tolerance of difference. For example, Esack expresses some skepticism about the consequences of the embrace of all diversity to the Muslim community. He cautions against an automatic acceptance of all differences for two reasons. First, he points out the theological challenge of determining how Islam can set the limits on diversity and find an orderly path toward either affirmation or change of traditional practices, such as women leading Friday prayers. Second, he cautions that Western values and cultures underlie pluralism, which may unwittingly serve as an extension of hegemonic interests over the so-called underdeveloped world. Esack proposes that

> diversity be understood in Islamic not as the mere willingness to let every idea and practice exist, but as aimed towards specific Islamic objectives, such as freeing mankind from injustice and servitude to others, so that we may be free to worship God.[103]

In peacebuilding, diversity and tolerance of differences are core principles of practice. In their efforts, peacebuilders hope to bring people to the realization that they are different, and that such differences should not constitute a basis for discrimination or bias. Moreover, it is harmful and unjust to deprive people of their rights because of their national, racial, religious, or other affiliation. These values have been made integral parts of Islam since its inception. In short, for Muslims diversity and tolerance of difference are God's wish, because if God had wished He could have created all humans alike. Instead he created a pluralist world with different humans.

Conclusion

This chapter has only begun to describe the principles and assumptions which characterize conflict resolution and nonviolent beliefs and practices in Islam. As illustrated, all values are strongly supported by Islamic text and tradition (Qur'an and Hadith). The set of values and principles identified in this research constitutes a framework for Islamic peacebuilding that confirms Satha-Anand's eighth thesis which reveals the connectedness between nonviolence and peacemaking and Islam:

> Islam itself is fertile soil for nonviolence because of its potential for disobedience, strong discipline, sharing and social responsibility, perseverance and self-sacrifice, and the belief in the unity of the Muslim community and the oneness of mankind.[104]

The adoption of this framework can have significant implications on various aspects of internal and external intervention programs and forces in any Muslim community. If it is applied in a community context, this framework can promote objectives such as:

a)   an increase of solidarity among members of the community;
b)   bridging the gap of social and economic injustice;
c)   relieving the suffering of people and sparing human lives;
d)   empowering people through participation and inclusivity;
e)   promoting equality among all members of the community; and
f)   encouraging the values of diversity and tolerance.

On an applied peacebuilding level, Islam as a religion is conducive to nonviolence and peacebuilding methods through its various rituals and traditions. For instance, the weekly Friday prayer is a natural place for gathering which has been utilized by many political leaders and movements. In the last decade, scholars such as Chaiwat Satha-Anand, Robert Johansen, Karim Crow, and others have began examining Islamic traditions and religion to identify other rituals and practices that can be effective in applying nonviolent action strategies.[105] For example, the obligation of fasting is an excellent training for hunger strikes. Second, the ritualistic prayers and the formation of the worshipers into parallel lines, and practice of speaking and moving in strict uniformity, prepare people for engagement in disciplined actions. Third, religious chanting can be a main channel for peaceful marches, meetings, and principles.[106] All these are excellent preparation techniques for the discipline needed for nonviolent demonstrations, sit-ins, and assemblies. The utilization of nonviolence and peacebuilding strategies based on an Islamic framework is appropriate for both conflicts that involve only Muslims and those that involve non-Muslims too.

In both conflict resolution and development work, proven strategies to bring change to the life of disadvantaged communities always depend on the use of local and indigenous traditions and experience. Intense involvement of the community in the processes of change and resolution of its problems (organizing, applying, and evaluating) tends to increase the impact of the intervention. Muslim communities are not an exception to such a rule. Utilizing Islamic values and principles suggested in this framework will increase the possibility for peaceful change and development in such communities.

On a policy-making level, the incorporation of such values into decision-making and orientation of leaders as well as followers to these values can bring new momentum to any community. As social change agents in the various Muslim communities attempt to mobilize their people to engage in social and political movements, they often neglect the importance and power of such religious and cultural values in appealing to their masses. The values in this framework can constitute a way of communication for change among Muslims.

In the area of economic and social development initiatives, particularly those carried out by outside agencies and organizations, the use of these values and norms in their local projects can contribute to the success and sustainability of these initiatives. When such programs are developed based on these values, the outcome and the process has to empower the local communities and members who were involved. For example, when a World Bank micro-economics project in Cairo incorporates the values in this peacebuilding framework within the design and implementation phases, the outcome of such a project was necessarily different from a project that was based on criteria derived from American or Western values and approaches.

At present these are religious ideals. The present reality of the Muslim communities is far from achieving or applying such ideals on a massive political or social scale. In fact, many of today's Muslims seem not to follow these values and principles in their daily lives. Nevertheless, these ideals continue to exist and are transmitted to new generations through cultural, religious beliefs and practices, and other forms of socialization. In fact, much of the frustration among many Muslims expresses itself in the failure of Islamic leaders and communities to apply these values and principles.

The discussion in this chapter reflects a major gap between the Islamic basis for a peacebuilding approach to life in general and the interpretation of Islam as a warlike religion. This gap cries for the need for a more solid "community of interpreters" to study Islam and peacebuilding, interpreters who will attempt to contextualize Islamic religious and traditional values within peacebuilding and nonviolent frameworks, rather than in war and conflict frameworks. This effort to reconstruct legitimate social, religious, and political nonviolent alternatives to resolve internal and external conflicts in Muslim societies is most needed to promote socio-economic development on all levels.

Finally, by identifying the principles and values of peacebuilding in an Islamic context, the question of their existence in Islamic tradition and religion becomes irrelevant. Thus, future research and studies can focus on the next step: examining the application of such principles in day-to-day contexts, and identifying the obstacles that prevent their application. Another area of future research is to document successful day-to-day initiatives of peacebuilding and conflict resolution conducted in Muslim communities. By examining such case studies, scholars and practitioners can promote the conditions for effective peaceful intervention to resolve political, social, and other types of conflicts which are tearing apart many Muslim communities.

Notes

1   Ron Fisher, *Interactive Conflict Resolution*, Syracuse, NY: Syracuse University Press, 1997.
2   See *Conflict Resolution: Cross-Cultural Perspectives*, Kevin Avruch, P. Black and Joe Scemicca (eds), New York: Greenwood Press, 1991; John Paul Lederach, *Preparing for Peace: Conflict Transformation Across Cultures*, Syracuse, NY: Syracuse University Press, 1995;

Mohammed Abu-Nimer, "Conflict Resolution Training in the Middle East: Lessons to be Learned," 3 *Intl. Negot.* 99, 1998 [hereinafter Abu-Nimer, "Conflict Resolution Training"]; Mohammed Abu-Nimer, "Conflict Resolution Approaches: Western and Middle Eastern Lessons and Possibilities," 55 *Am. J. Econ. and Sociology* 35, 1996,; [hereinafter Abu-Nimer, "Conflict Resolution Approaches"].

3   Training workshops in peacebuilding have been conducted in the Middle East, Philippines, and Indonesia by Search For Common Ground, Catholic Relief Services, Institute for Multi-Track Diplomacy, and others.

4   Azizah al-Hibri highlights some of the negative depictions of Islam in American and European historical writing in Azizah al-Hibri, "Islamic and American Constitutional Law: Borrowing Possibilities or a History of Borrowing?," 1 *U. Pa. J. Const. L.* 491, 1999, pp. 493–527.

5   See list of such studies, *infra* n. 11.

6   See *Religion: The Missing Dimension of Statecraft*, Douglas Johnston and Cynthia Sampson (eds), New York: Oxford University Press, 1994; Abu-Nimer, "Conflict Resolution Approaches".

7   It should be noted that although the boundaries and distinctions between peace and conflict resolution fields are still being defined, nevertheless, in this study no distinction is made between them. Peacebuilding is used as an overarching term for nonviolent strategies and conflict resolution methods. They all share the assumption that to resolve a conflict, parties must be committed to nonviolent approaches and means. For further literature on such conflict resolution approach see John Burton, *Conflict Resolution and Prevention*, New York: St. Martin's Press, 1990; Louise Diamond and John McDonald, *Multi-Track Diplomacy: a System Guide and Analysis*, Grinnell: Iowa Peace Inst., 1991; Fisher, *supra* n. 1.

8   John Esposito, *The Islamic Threat*, New York: Oxford University Press, 1992.

9   Fasting is one of the main values and practices with which Gandhi associated Islam, particularly during his early imprisonment. See Sheila McDonough, *Gandhi's Responses to Islam*, New Delhi: D.K. Printworld, 1994, p.122; Chaiwat Satha-Anand, "Core Values for Peacemaking in Islam: The Prophet's Practice as Paradigm," in *Building Peace in the Middle East: Challenges for States and Civil Society*, Elise Boulding (ed.), Boulder, CO: Lynne Reinner Publishers, 1993.

10 Many scholars have written on the legitimacy and importance of the different interpretations of Islamic texts. See Farid Esack, *On Being a Muslim: Finding a Religious Path in the World Today*, Oxford: Oneworld, 1999; Azizah al-Hibri, "Islamic Constitutionalism and the Concept of Democracy," 24 *J. Intl. L.*, 1992, pp. 1–27.

11 Due to the scope and purpose of this article, the discussion of this category is brief. However, there have been several studies in English and many in Arabic that reviewed these studies and uncovered their cultural biases and limitations. For example, see Esposito, *supra* n. 8, at p. 26; John Esposito and John Voll, *Islam and Democracy*, New York: Oxford University Press, 1996. A sample of the studies conducted from war and *jihad* perspective includes Johannes Jansen, *The Neglected Duty: the Creed of Sadat's Assassins and Islamic Resurgence in the Middle East*, New York: Macmillan, 1986; Giles Kepel, *The Revenge of God: the Resurgence of Islam, Christianity, and Judaism in the Modern World*, University Park: Pennsylvania State University Press, 1994; Bruce Lawrence, *Defenders of God: the Fundamentalist Revolt Against the Modern Age*, New York: Harper and Row, 1986; Bernard Lewis, *Political Language of Islam*, Chicago: University of Chicago Press, 1988; David Pryce-Jones, *At War With Modernity: Islam's Challenge to the West*, London: Alliance Pub. for the Inst. European Def. and Strategic Stud., 1992; Emmanuel Sivan, *Radical Islam: Medieval; Theology and Modern Politic*, New Haven: Yale University Press, 1990; Michael Dunn, "Revivalist Islam and Democracy: Thinking About the Algerian Quandary, Middle East Policy 16, 1992, p. 1; Gudrun Krämer, "Islamist Notion of Democracy," 23 *Middle East Rpt.* 2, 1993; Martin Kramer, Islam vs Democracy, 95 *Contemporary* 2, 1993; "Islam and Liberal Democracy," 271 *A. Mthly.* 89, 1993; Steven

Emerson, "Islamic Fundamentalism's Terrible Threat to the West," 27 *San Diego Union-Trib.* G3, June 27, 1993; Daniel Pipes, "Fundamental Questions About Muslims," 30 *Wall St. J.* A11, October 30, 1992.

12 Dan Quayle, Patrick Buchanan, Daniel Pipes, and others best represent such policy-makers and politicians, who often have compared Islam with communism and Nazism. See Esposito, *supra* n. 8, at p. 168.

13 A few of those works are: Akbar Ahmed, *Discovering Islam: Making Sense of Muslim History and Society*, London: Routledge and Kegan Paul, 1988; Mahmoud Ayoub, a speech and a panel discussion at a conference on "Nonviolence in Islam," sponsored by Nonviolence International and Mohammed Said Farsi, Chair of Islamic Peace, American University, Washington DC, February 14, 1997; Lardner Carmody and Tully Carmody, *Peace and Justice in the Scriptures of the World Religions: Reflections on Non-Christian Scriptures*, New York: Paulist Press, 1988; Sohail Hashimi, "Interpreting the Islamic Ethics of War and Peace," in *The Ethics of War and Peace: Religious and Secular Perspectives*, Terry Nardin (ed.), Princeton, NJ: Princeton University Press, 1996, p. 146; Fazlur Rahman, "The Islamic Concept of Justice," in *Islamic Identity and the Struggle for Justice*, Nimat Barazangi, M. Raquibuz Zaman and Omar Afzal (eds), Gainesville, FL: University Press of Florida, 1996; John Kelsay, *Islam and War: a Study in Comparative Ethics*, Westminster: John Knox Press, 1993; Abdulaziz Sachedina, "Justification for Violence in Islam," in *War and its Discontents: Pacifism and Quietism in the Abrahamic Traditions*, J. Patout Burn (ed.), Washington, DC: Georgetown University Press, 1996.

14 For the translation of the Qur'an, the author relied on: Abdullah Yusuf Ali, *The Meaning of the Holy Qur'an*, Brentwood, MD: Amana Corp., 1991, except in cases in which the quoted scholars have used other editions of the Qur'an.

15 Peter O. Jaggi, *Religion, Practice and Science of Nonviolence*, New Delhi: Musshiram Manoharlal, 1974, p 25.

16 Hashimi, *supra* n. 13, at p. 142. See Sachedina, *supra* n. 13.

17 Kelsay, *supra* n. 13, at p. 35.

18 Hashimi, *supra* n. 13, at p. 151.

19 Sachedina, *supra* n. 13, at p. 147.

20 Khwaja Gulam (K.G.) Saiyidain, *Islam: the Religion of Peace*, 2nd ed., New Delhi: Har-Anand Pub., 1994, p. 175. In support of this strong argument against pacifism, several verses in the Qur'an have been identified: "Nor slay such life as Allah has made sacred, except for just cause, nor commit fornication; and any that does this (not only) meets punishment, (but) the penalty on the Day of Judgment will be doubled to him" (25:68–69). See also Qur'an 17:33; 6:151.

21 See e.g. Wahiduddin Khan, "Nonviolence and Islam," in *Forum on Islam and Peace in the 21st Century*, DC: American University, 1998 p. 5.

22 See Ayoub, *supra* n. 13; Sachedina, *supra* n. 13, at p. 74.

23 For full information on this case see Eknath Easwaran, *A Man to Match His Mountains: Badshuh Khan, Nonviolent Soldier of Islam*, Petaluma, CA: Nilgiri Press, 1984.

24 Patout Burns, *War and its Discontents: Pacifism and Quietism in the Abrahamic Traditions*, Washington DC: Georgetown University Press, 1996, p. 165.

25 See e.g. Eknath Easwaran, *A Man to Match in Mountains*; Ashgar Engineer, "Sources of Nonviolence in Islam," in *Nonviolence: Contemporary Issues and Challenges*, M. Kumar (ed.), New Delhi: Gandhi Peace Foundation, 1994; Khalid Kishtainy (see also Khalid al-Qishttini), "Violent and Nonviolent Struggle in Arab History," in *Arab Nonviolent Political Struggle in the Middle East*, Ralph E. Crow, P. Grant and Saad E. Ibrahim (eds), Boulder, CO: Lynne Rienner Publishers, 1990, pp. 9–25; "The Nonviolent Crescent: Eight Theses on Muslim Nonviolent Actions," in *Islam and Nonviolence*, Glenn Paige, Chaiwat Satha-Anand and Sarah Gilliat (eds), Honolulu, Hawaii: Center for Global Nonviolence Planning. Project, Matsunaga Inst. for Peace, University of Hawaii, 1993, pp. 7–26; Mohammed Abu-Nimer, "Conflict Resolution in an Islamic Context," 21 *Peace and Change*, 1996, pp. 22–40; Karim Crow, "Nurturing an Islamic Peace Discourse,"

168 *Mohammed Abu-Nimer*

American Journal of Islamic Social Science, vol. 17, no. 3, 2000, pp. 54–69. Abdul Aziz Said, "Cultural Context of Conflict Resolution: a Reference to An Arab-Islamic Perspective," 1994, unpublished paper; Jawdat Sai'd, "Peace – Or Nonviolence – in History and with the Prophets," 1997, unpublished paper; Chaiwat Satha-Anand, "Muslim Communal Nonviolent Actions: Minority Coexistence in a Non-Muslim Society", in *Cultural Diversity and Islam*, Abdul Aziz Said and Meena Sharify-Funk (eds), Lanham MD: University Press of America, 2003; see also Abdurahman Wahid, "Islam and Nonviolence: National Transformation," in *Islam and Nonviolence*, Glenn Paige, Chaiwat Satha-Anand and Sarah Gilliat (eds), Honolulu, Hawaii: Ctr. for Global Nonviolence Planning Project, Matsunaga Inst. for Peace, University of Hawaii, 1993, pp. 53–59; Wahiduddin Khan, *supra* n. 21.

26 See Saiyidain, *supra* n. 20.

27 Satha-Anand, *supra* n. 9.

28 Satha-Anand discusses the potential destruction which might result from nuclear warfare and concludes that such warfare is prohibited by Islamic teachings and principles. *Supra* n. 25, at p. 15. A similar conclusion was reached by K.G. Saiyidain as early as 1968 in a conference presentation on Islam and peace. He suggested that any type of total war cannot be carried out within the condition envisioned by Islam. See Jack Homer (ed.), *World Religions and World Peace*, Boston: Beacon Press, 1968. See the following sources located, *supra* n. 25: Easwaran; Engineer; Janner; Wahiduddin Khan; Paige; Jawdat Sa'id; Satha-Anand; and Wahid.

29 Wahiduddin Khan, *supra* n. 21, at p. 5.

30 Sunan Abu-Dawud, bk. 35, no. 4246, by Abu Dawud Sulayman ibn Ash'ath. This reprinted edition was reviewed and verified by Muhammad 'Awwamah, Jiddah: Dar al-Qiblah lil-Thaqafah al-Islamiyyah, 1998. Also cited by Jawdat Sa'id, *supra* n. 25, at p. 13.

31 Kishtainy, *supra* n. 25.

32 Satha-Anand, *supra* n. 25, at p. 17.

33 Several Qur'anic verses emphasize the value of compassion among people; see for example verse 90:17. Al-Tarmidhi stressed the same value: "He who does not show compassion to his fellow men is undeserving of God's compassion." Al-Bukhari Muhammad ibn Isama'il, *al-Adab al-Mufrad*, Cairo, 1959, bk. 34, ch. 53, pp. 47–48.

34 See particularly verses 5:8; 57:25; 16:90; 4:58; 42:15.

35 See John Lederach, *Peacebuilding in Divided Societies*, New York: Syracuse University Press, 1997; Heidi Burgess and Guy Burgess, "Justice Without Violence: a Theoretical Framework," in *Justice Without Violence*, Paul Wehr, Heidi Burgess, and Guy Burgess (eds), Boulder, CO: Lynne Reinner Publishers, 1994.

36 See other verses 5:9; 57:25; 7:29.

37 Verse 3:18 in the Qur'an states: "There is no god but He: That is the witness of Allah, His angels, and those endued with knowledge, standing firm on justice (*Qist*). There is no god but He the exalted in power, the Wise." Relying on this verse and others (55:9; 60:8), Mahmoud Ayoub, *supra* n. 13, at p. 43, emphasizes *Qist* is social justice in its broadest sense – first in our relationship to God and second in our relationship to society. We have to treat each other with *qist*. Justice also has a legal meaning when we refer to just laws. Similarly relying on verse 2:143: "Thus have We made of you an *Ummah* justly balanced, that ye might be witnesses over the nations, and the Messenger a witness over yourself;" Ayoub describes *wasat* as being the characteristics of fairness in Islam.

The prophetic tradition supports such notion of moderation and fairness: "You should act in moderation." Sahih al-Bukhari, vol. 7, bk. 70, no. 577; vol. 8, bk. 76, no. 470. Except where it is indicated, all Sahih al-Bukhari *Hadiths* in this article are based on the translation of Muhammad Muhsin Khan, *The Translation of the Meaning of Sahih al-Bukhari: Arabic-English*, Ankara: Hilal Yayinlari, 1972. These were verified with the Arabic edition of *Sahih Al-Bukhari*, vols 1–8, Bayrut: Dar al-Kutub al-'Ilmiya, 1992.

38 Sahih al-Bukhari, vol. 8, bk. 73, no. 156. Several of those values and institutions were cited by Raquibuz Zaman in "Economic Justice in Islam, Ideals and reality: The Cases of

Malaysia, Pakistan, and Saudi Arabia," in *Islamic Identity and the Struggle for Justice*, Nimat Barazangi, M. Raquibuz Zaman and Omar Afzal (eds), Gainesville, FL: University Press of Florida, 1996. Raquibuz Zaman based his examples on Yusuf al-Qaradawi, *Economic Security in Islam*, Muhammed Iqbal Siddiqi (trans.), Lahore: Kazi Publications, 1981.

39 In peace studies there is an emphasis on all aspects of justice (distributive, procedural, as well as, restorative components). Johan Galtung, "Peace, Violence, and Peace Research," 6, *J. Peace Research*, 1969, pp. 67–191.

40 See the Qur'an 17:26.

41 See the Qur'an 2:110 in which regular charity is emphasized like regular prayer; also verse 2:3 describes believers as those who keep regular prayer and spend out in charity.

42 Zakah is also encouraged and described in detail with its rewards in the Qur'an 2:262–272.

43 Sahih al-Bukhari, vol. 3, bk. 49, no. 870.

44 Sahih al-Bukhari, vol. 7, bk. 63.

45 See al-Tirmidhi, bk. 39, ch. 19, and bk. 45, ch. 98 (cited in Saiyidain, *supra* n. 20).

46 See Qur'an 2:262, 177 and 5:55.

47 Sheik Muhammed Abdallah Draz, *Observations in Islam* (n.d.), cited by Fahmi Howeidy, *Al-Islam wa al-Dimuqratiyyah*, in *Islam and Democracy*, Cairo: Al Ahram Pub. and Translation Ctr, 1993, p. 164.

48 Muhammad Ali, *A Manual of Hadith*, Lahore: Ahmadiyya Anjuman, 1941.

49 Al-Sharif al-Radi, *Nahj al-Balagha*, Beirut: Mu'assasat al-A'lami lil-Matbu'at, 1978, vol. 1, p. 77. Reviewed and classified by Muhammad Baqir al-Mahmudi. Kishtainy, *supra* n. 25, at p. 12.

50 Sahih Muslim, vol. 3, bk. 19, no. 4456. This also appears in Al-Tabari (Mohammad b. Jarir), *Kitab al-Umam wa-al-Muluk*, vol. III, Cairo: Dar-al-Ma'arif, 1969, pp. 226–227. See Satha-Anand, *supra* n. 25, at p. 11.

51 Al-Sharif al-Radi, *supra* n. 49, at p. 77, cited by Kishtainy, *supra* n. 25, at p. 12.

52 Saiyidain, *supra* n. 20, at p. 164.

53 The principle of total submission to God's will is central to Islam; thus, peace, as well as justice, cannot be fully accomplished without this principle. See Kelsay; Hashimi; and Sachedina, *supra* n. 13.

54 Abdullah Yusuf Ali, commentary notes, *supra* n. 14, at p. 895.

55 *A Manual of Hadith*, Muhammad Ali (trans.), Lahore: Ahmadiyya anjuman ishaat-I-Islam, 1944, p. 386.

56 In support of such interpretation see the Qur'an 41:34; 7:56; 7:199; 28:54 in which Muslims are expected to exercise self-restraint, and control their anger and reaction to evil doing.

57 Sahih al-Bukhari, vol. 1, bk. 2, no. 10; the complete saying is translated by Mohammad Muhsin Khan, *supra* n. 37, as the Prophet said: "A Muslim is the one who avoids harming Muslims with his tongue and hands. And a *Muhajir* (emigrant) is the one who gives up (abandons) all what Allah has forbidden."

58 See review of studies in text accompanying *supra* nn. 11–12.

59 There are Muslim groups which emphasize the spiritual rather than the physical *jihad* (such as Sufism and Ahmadiyyah). The Sufi teaching explains that "The warrior (*mujahid*) is one who battles with his own self (*nafs*) and is thus on the path of God." Others suggested that *da'wah* (calling to spread Islam through preaching and persuasion) is the major form of *jihad* for a Muslim. See Javad Nurbakhsh, *Tradition of the Prophet: aHadith*, vol. 2, New York: Khaniqahi-Nimatullahi Publications, 1983, p. 76.

60 Sahih al-Bukhari, vol. 3, bk. 49, no. 857. Translation is based on Muhammad Muhsin Khan, *supra* n. 37.

61 'Abd al-Malik Ibn Hisham, *al-Sirah al Nabawiyah*, Bayrut: Dar al-Fikr lil-Tiba'ah wa-al-Nashr wa-al-Tawzi, 1992, p. 192.

62 Arbitration in Islam was also explored by other researchers, such as Khadduri in Majid Khadduri, *War and Peace in the Law of Islam*, London: Oxford University Press, 1955. He

identified several occasions in which the Prophet acted as arbitrator and mediator before and after prophethood. For example, in the incident of the Aws and Khazraj tribes of Medina, the Prophet acted as mediator according to the Arab tradition and ended their enmity; in arbitration between the Prophet and Banu Qurayza (a Jewish tribe) both agreed to submit their dispute to a person chosen by them. Khadduri concludes that the third party intervention was an acceptable option to end fighting. The third party is binding if their relatives are not affected by their decision. He also adds the arbitration case between Ali and Mu'awiya, which was initiated to end the civil war. For full details of these events in the life of the Prophet see Ibn Hisham, *supra* n. 61, at p. 288.

63 James Laue and Gerald Cormick, "The Ethics of Intervention in Community Disputes," in *Ethics of Social Intervention*, Gordon Bermant, Herbert Kelman and Donald Warwick (eds), New York: Halsted Press, 1978; Burgess and Burgess, *supra* n. 35.

64 Sahih al-Bukhari, vol. 5, bk. 59, no. 603. Another saying that supports such forgiving attitude when the Prophet entered Mecca is: "There is no censure from me today on you (for what has happened is done with), may God, who is the greatest amongst forgivers, forgive you." Muhammad Ibn Sa'd, *al-Tabaqat al-Kubra*, vol. 2, Beirut: Dar al-Fikr, 1957, p. 142.

65 Muhammad Ibn Is'haq, *Kitab al-Siyar wa-al-Maghazi*, Beirut: Dar al-Fikr, 1978, p. 184. Translation is based on Alfred Guillaume, Muhammad Ibn Ishak, *The Life of Muhammad*, Lahore: Oxford University Press, 1955.

66 Sahih al-Bukhari, vol. 4, p. 175; vol. 9, p. 141. Javad Nurbakhsh, *supra* n. 59, at p. 81.

67 Ibid.

68 In fact, since 1990, an important development in the field of peace and conflict resolution has been the emerging focus on the role of forgiveness and healing in the process of reconciliation in the post-war phase.

69 See other verses emphasizing the same principle of individual choice and responsibility: Qur'an 5:8; 9:6; 16:125; and 42:48.

70 Individual responsibility, choice, and God's arbitration on the Judgment Day are also reflected in the verses in the Qur'an 18:29; 109:6; 88:21, 22; and 34:28.

71 Al-Tarmidhi, *supra* n. 33, cited by Muhammad Ali, *supra* n. 55, at p. 384.

72 The ethical axioms in Islam are:

   1) Unity (*tawhid*);

   2) Equilibrium in regards to justice and doing good (*al-adl wa-al-ihsan*) refers to the desirability of an equitable distribution of income and wealth, the need for helping the poor and the needy, the necessity for making adjustment in the entire spectrum of consumption, production and distribution relations, and others. All these instructions are aimed to prevent or correct the *zulm*;

   3) Free Will (*ikhtiyar*), a person is capable of choosing the right if he/she follows the correct path of God. But humans are also capable of making the wrong choice. Humans are free to make the choice, but their freedom is not absolute;

   4) Responsibility (*fard*), the responsibility toward oneself, God, and others. By doing good things and observing faith, humans can insure their correct path. The person is an integral part of a society, which he/she ought to treat well, doing good. The person will not be responsible for what others have done, will not be questioned about the deeds of others.

   Based on Syed Nawab Haider Naqvi, *Islam, Economics and Society*, New York: Kegan Paul Intl, 1994, p. 25.

73 Based on Abdullah Yusuf Ali interpretations of *sabr* in the Qur'an, *supra* n. 14, at p. 28.

74 Some of those verses are: 10:109; 11:115; 16:126–127; 20:130–132; 40:55, 77; 46:35; 50:39; 70:5; 73:10–11.

75 Sahih al-Bukhari, vol. 8, bk. 73, no. 135.
76 Ibid., vol. 3, bk. 43, no. 18.
77 Abdullah Yusuf Ali, *supra* n. 14, at p. 670.
78 Sahih al-Bukhari, vol. 3, bk. 43, no. 623.
79 Ibid., vol. 1, bk. 2, no. 12.
80 Islam attempted to abolish such value of tribal solidarity; however it remains a strong norm among many Arab and non-Arab Muslims.
81 Farid Esack, *Qur'an Liberation and Pluralism: An Islamic Perspective of Interreligious Solidarity Against Oppression*, Oxford: Oneworld Publications, 1997. In *Qur'an Liberation and Pluralism*, Farid Esack has completed a pioneer study on the Islamic theology of liberation based on the experience of Muslims in South Africa in fighting against Apartheid. Esack describes an astonishing account of the utilization of Islamic beliefs and values in mobilizing Muslims to resist and fight the South African system, particularly by building community coalitions with non-Muslims. Such experience affirms the great potential to construct coalitions across religious boundaries and identities in resisting war, violence, and injustice.
82 Akbar Ahmed, *supra* n. 13, also supports this notion of the *Ummah* being diverse religious and individual community, particularly in the Medinan period in which the Qur'an mentions it 47 times, and only nine times in the Meccan period. See Farid Esack, "Religion and Cultural Diversity: For What and With Whom?" in *Cultural Diversity and Islam*, Abdul Aziz Said and Meena Sharify-Funk (eds), Lanham, MD: University Press of America, 2003, pp. 165–185.
83 Sahih al-Bukhari, vol. 3, bk. 43, no. 626.
84 See Wahid, *supra* n. 25.
85 Tawfiq al-Shawi, *Fiqh al-shura wa-al-istisharah* (the Jurisprudence of Consultation and Shura), al-Mansurah: Dar al-Wafa', 1992, p. 293, cited in Howeidy, *supra* n. 47, at p. 117. Azizah al-Hibri establishes the principle for Islamic governing systems – the will of the people shall be the basis of the authority of the government. She identifies the *bay'ah*: "the act of accepting and declaring allegiance to a potential ruler." This process of contracting with the people is recognized as a participatory and democratic principle in Islam. Azizah al-Hibri, "Islamic Constitutionalism and the Concept of Democracy," *Journal of International Law*, vol. 1, n. 12, 1992, p. 24.
86 There are other verses in the Qur'an that support this notion, for example see verse 3:159. Also Abu Bakr established an early example for other Muslim leaders by deriving his governing legitimacy from the people: "I have been given authority over you, but I am not the best of you. If I do well help me, and if I do ill, then put me right." Muhammad Salim Awwa, *On the Political System of Islamic State*, 1980, p. 115, cited in al-Hibri, *supra* n. 85, at p. 21 and p. 24.
87 The Battle of Uhud is a good example for such consultation, in which the Prophet, contrary to what he thought, agreed to meet with Quraysh's army outside of Medina. See Abd Al-Malik Ibn Hisham, *Al-Sirah Al-Nabawiyah*, 9th Century, reprint, M. Sirjani (ed.), Cairo: al-Maktabah al-Tawfiqiyah, 1978, pp. 192–193, cited in al-Hibri, *supra* n. 85, at p. 20.
88 Muhammad Musa, *Nizam al-Hukum fi al-Islam* (Governing System in Islam), Cairo: Dar Al-Ma'rifa, 1967. Some of the verses in the Qur'an in this matter are 88:21, 22.
89 Muhammad ibn Yazid ibn Majah, *Sunan*, vol. 2, bk. 3950, p. 1303, Beirut: Dar al-Kutub al-Ilmiyah n.d., cited in al-Hibri, *supra* n. 4, at p. 506.
90 Al-Ghazali, *Ihiya'Ulum al-Din* (Revival of Religious Studies), vol. 2, Leon Zolondek (trans.), Leiden: E.J. Brill, 1963, p. 306, cited in Howeidy, *supra* n. 47, at p. 106.
91 Freedom and choice are supported in the Qur'an through 2:256; 18:29; 17:107; 10:99. Cited in Howeidy, *supra* n. 47, p. 107.
92 Muhammad Salim Awwa, *Fi al-Nizam al-Siyasi li-l-Dawlah al-Islamiyyah* (The Political System of the Islamic State), Cairo: al-Maktab al-Masri al-Hadith, 1983, p. 215, cited in Howeidy, *supra* n. 47, at p. 108.

172   *Mohammed Abu-Nimer*

93 See discussion of the principle of equality in Islam in text accompanying notes 48–49, *supra*.
94 Sahih al-Bukhari, vol. 2, bk. 23, no. 399. In addition, the Qur'an stresses the legitimacy of differences in various verses such as: 49:13; 30:22; 11:118, 119.
95 See verses 46:12; 42:42; 4:148.
96 Howeidy, *supra* n. 47, at p. 112.
97 There are many Qur'anic verses that support this notion of appreciation of differences. See 2:213; 10:19; 7:38; 13:30; 16:63; 29:18; 35:42; 41:42; 64:18.
98 Farid Esack, [*Religion and Cultural Diversity*].
99 Ibid.
100 Ibn Hisham, *supra* n. 61, at pp. 501–504.
101 Howeidy, *supra* n. 47, at p. 202.
102 Wadad al-Qadi, "The Conceptual Foundation of Cultural Diversity in Pre-modern Islamic Civilization," in *Cultural Diversity and Islam*, Abdul Aziz Said and Meena Sharify-Funk (eds), Lanham MD: University Press of America, 2003, pp. 85–106.
103 Esack, *supra* n. 98 at p. 15.
104 Satha-Anand, *supra* n. 25.
105 See Satha-Anand, *supra* n. 25, at pp. 7–12, for discussion of three case studies in which Muslim communities in South East Asia have used the religious practices of fasting and praying as nonviolent resistance methods.
106 Ibid.; Abu-Nimer, *supra* n. 25.

10 The Missing Logic in Discourses of Violence and Peace in Islam

The Necessities of a Middle View after the 11th of September 2001

Nadia Mahmoud Mostafa

Introduction

The concern with Islam's position on issues of peace and violence, peace and war, peace and *jihad*, peace and terrorism is an old (as well as a new) continuous and lasting concern, which has never departed from the focus of Muslim jurisprudents, political thinkers or Orientalists. Throughout Islamic history, studies in Islamic *fiqh* (jurisprudence), Orientalist studies, studies of modern social sciences and political science have all shown various degrees and types of concern over these issues.

In the last hundred years, this concern was reflected in the impact of some main events and developments that helped shape together the characteristics of the contemporary Muslim world and its position in the world order, such as: colonialism, two world wars, independence and liberation wars, Islamic revival, the end of the Cold War and 9/11 events and their aftermath. In this respect a number of ontological, methodological and policy-oriented remarks can be made.

First Introductory Remark

The concern with these issues has always taken the form of "dichotomies" with peace being a constant at one end with variables such as *jihad*, war, terrorism or violence being placed on the other end. However, now there is a serious necessity to distinguish between these various dichotomies simply because the different variants do not carry the same connotations. For example, one can mention that *jihad* is not necessarily the antonym of peaceful means; at the same time it is not necessarily the synonym of war or violence. Another example is the term "terrorism" which is but one form of armed violence and is not by any means an all-inclusive concept covering all forms of violence. It can also be said that terrorism is not only an activity exercised by individuals in the name of religion, for it is sometimes practiced by states and groups in the name of religion as well as under many other different labels. In addition, the Qur'anic concept and the Arabic linguistic meaning for the term terrorism (*erhab*) does not coincide with any of the ongoing definitions adopted by political or legal institutions.

The same goes for regular warfare, liberation war or independence (resistance) war. Even violence as a concept does not necessarily imply armed violence alone (nor all degrees of armed violence) for there are still other forms of violence, such as structural violence. The frequent usage of these variants leads to the negligence of other concepts derived from the Islamic *fiqh* (jurisprudence) that can better describe the cases referred to by the more frequently used concepts such as *"odwan," "baghyh," "fetnah"* and *"hirabah"* which indicate the use of military force both at the internal level (i.e. the Islamic world level) as well as the external level (i.e. *vis-à-vis* other nations). This is why dealing with the theoretical aspect of Islam's position on violence or with its position on violence as reflected by historical experience or by its present reality requires the disentanglement of these intertwined concepts not only at the level of *fiqh* (jurisprudence) but also at the level of political thought.

Second Introductory Remark

The issue at hand has been tackled from an Islamic as well as a Western perspective, therefore special attention should be paid to the differences between these two worldviews within the content of the positions of each group in the global hierarchy of power. No doubt these differences affect both the methods and the goals suggested by the two kinds of propositions.

The Western perspectives rely on the previously mentioned dichotomies in order to achieve certain goals and to address issues and problems affecting Western interests. For example, Islam and the Muslim world are considered by some trends in the West as sources of threat to the international order and as the main source of terrorism and violence in the name of religion. Therefore, the Muslim world is the main addressee of initiatives either calling for dialogues of peace and tolerance on one hand or calling for the use of all kinds of violence to defeat Islamic terrorism on the other.

At the same time, the Muslim world suffers – both in theory and in practice – from *fiqh* and political disagreements on the subject where everybody seeks to prove that violence has nothing to do with the original Muslim preachings and to defend the right to use force as long as it is used to do justice. That is why it is highly important when speaking about Islam and violence to determine what exactly is our starting point. Is it an attempt to reevaluate our own position as Muslims and our internal dialogue on the subject in order to decide how to best serve the interests of the *Ummah* and how to resist and confront the challenges facing these interests. Or is our departing point just another attempt to prepare more defensive and apologetic answers to be directed towards the West, which makes this conference at the Library of Alexandria just another reminder of the serious pressures under which the Muslim world suffers in a world full of submission and humiliation, or is our goal to revise and deconstruct Western discourses in order to unmask their prejudice as well as the revision of our own discourses and their deconstruction to unmask its prejudices?

One of the major prejudices that the Islamic discourse carries is reflected in the use of these pre-set dichotomies "Islam" and "war, violence or terrorism" or "Islam" and "non-violence, peace or tolerance," as if we are necessarily talking about opposites or as if Islam was either about war or about peace. Much more meaningful would be to ask about the conditions or the rules for peace, war, violence or terrorism in Islam.

In other words, why should talking about Islam and war, terrorism or violence be the dominant feature of an offensive Western discourse when addressing Islam? On the other hand why should peace and non-violence be the dominant feature of our defensive discourse, a discourse specially designed to face charges of terrorism, as if we (the Muslims) are all guilty and in need of defending ourselves? Is it really enough to reiterate juristic rulings that emerged within totally different temporal contexts? Shouldn't we also try to understand and contemplate the political and social reasons – internal and external – that lead to the description of any use of military force by Muslims regardless of its degree as terrorism, illegitimate violence, unholy war in the name of Islam, etc.?

Why don't we start by talking about Islam and "power" in general? Strength and weakness are original conditions while war and peace are nothing but two variations of the balance of power. Armed conflict (which doesn't necessarily always bring along negative consequences) is only one way of managing political conflict. Why don't we revisit *"jihad"* as an Islamic value that has its rules whether in peace or wartime instead of being dragged into a discussion about peace alone or war alone? Won't this avoid a distortion of the Islamic meaning of "power" and *"jihad,"* two concepts linked both in theory and in practice?

Why don't we recall the concept of *jihad* and clear the mystery surrounding it so as to revive its comprehensive nature and to stress that *jihad* is much more than a mere offensive war (in a way that confuses it with the common concept of terrorism and aggressive war) or merely a defensive war (in a way that makes it rather equivalent to the concepts of submission and surrender)? Why don't we concentrate on understanding the present reality so as to comprehend the justifications and motives behind armed *jihad* and armed resistance? Why don't we take into consideration the features of the present state of the Muslim *Ummah* instead of judging the political and juristic legitimacy of the resort to violence by calling upon the rulings and experiences of past historical eras?

In other words in international relations theory terms: why don't we distinguish between the requirements that must be met in order to have and sustain peace and between the arguments on war and violence. These are two different issues, different in their points of departure and in their final aims.

Third Introductory Remark

Talking about "contemporary Islamic synthesis" means admitting that there are present debates about this old-new subject.

This requires the following. A good understanding of all the aspects of the present context; global, regional and domestic, especially after 9/11 in order to grasp the kind of changes that this context introduced into the debate. This should be done in light of the map of different types of violence in the Muslim world that cannot be equally treated, neither juristically nor politically, such as:

a)   Armed resistance seeking national independence (also called secession move-
     ments such as in Kashmir, Chechnya, East Turkistan, the Philippines and the
     Balkans).

b)   Armed resistance with the aim of putting an end to foreign occupation (such as
     the Palestinian case [especially since the beginning of the second Intifada in
     September 2000] and the Iraqi case since the American invasion).

c)   Armed opposition employed against present ruling regimes (such as the
     violence that took place in Egypt or Algeria and that is currently taking place
     in Saudi Arabia, Kuwait, Turkey, Morocco and Indonesia against Western,
     Jewish or national targets following 9/11 in general and the occupation of Iraq
     in particular).

d)   Finally, the new type of armed violence exercised against the U.S. on 9/11,
     which has been dominantly described as "terrorism" and "blessed" by Bin Laden
     as *jihad*. This new type has activated an American retaliation called "the war
     against terrorism" whose main target is the Muslim world under which
     different types of American violence is being committed against Muslims. It is
     this last type of violence that has opened the stage for a new phase of debate
     about the types of armed violence and their relationship with terrorism and
     jihad in the Muslim world.

In addition, one should wonder about the new elements introduced in these contemporary debates. Can the debate about the bombings in Bali (Indonesia), Saudi
Arabia, Casablanca or in Turkey and the debates initiated by the armed violence
incidents that took place in Egypt in the 90s and later in Taba (2004) and Sharm El-
Sheikh (2005) as well as the debates initiated by the Intifada incidents be treated as
equals?

These debates are not only limited to the sphere of *fiqh* for they exist in theoretical, political and societal spheres as well. For political disagreements exist as much
as *fiqh* disagreements. It can even be said that the latter are being nourished by the
former. Thus both types of debate should be given equal attention.

In the light of the previously stated remarks, this study is based on the following
assumption: *Not all sorts of armed violence are necessarily evil and not all sorts of peace are
necessarily good.* Hence, focusing on the *fiqh* disagreements (about the Islamic legitimacy or non-legitimacy of each type of violence) although essential is not enough by
itself; it should be accompanied by a renewal of political thought on the issue under
study. Therefore, the understanding of "reality" and its features is a basic requirement for formulating a balanced view after 9/11. Thus the need for revising a
number of basic attitudes (juristic and political) emerged as a result of international
changes that had their impact on the Islamic regional and national context.

In other words, the principal determinants of contemporary Muslim reality
stress the need for studying and analyzing reality as much as the need for studying
and analyzing the "Islamic *fiqh* ." Consequently, this study is not a study of Islamic
fiqh (jurisprudence) on violence and peace; rather it is a study that heads from
Islamic *fiqh* towards reality and from reality towards Islamic jurisprudence. It is
mainly a political study of a theoretical nature that explores the reality of the

Ummah and the impact of this reality on the established methodology of *"fiqh"* and *"iftaa."*

This study seeks to discover the requirements for a juristic, theoretical and cultural renewal on the issue of "violence." It claims that this renewal could base itself on the revival of a comprehensive concept of *jihad*, a revival needed to introduce an Islamic perspective on how to clear up the confusion between the concept of terrorism and other types of violence. This study will also attempt to answer the following questions:

1) Does violence in the name of religion mean that religion is a main source of conflict? Are there religious/cultural justifications for violence? Or is religion just a pretext used to disguise conflict of interests that are the true reasons behind violence?

   In light of these questions, a reference should be made to the theoretical propositions about the relationship between religion and the study of international relations.[1] This kind of theorizing is regaining importance after a period of "secularization" as witnessed in the study of international relations and as reflected in the renewal of cultural aspects and their importance in international relations theory.[2] It is that kind of theorizing that pays attention to the religious dimensions as related to the material dimensions when exploring the sources of international conflicts.

2) If the *fiqh* (juristic) and *"fatawa"* rulings concerning specific acts of violence is the product of certain temporal contexts and if the juristic disagreements have always been present across time and space, then what is new in the end of the twentieth century and the beginnings of the twenty-first century? What are the new features of reality that need to be considered if jurisprudents want to do more than just recall previously outdated rulings concerning acts of violence? In other words, what are the new features of reality that need to be thoroughly investigated before we can decide whether one type of armed violence is legitimate or not? How has the relationship between the types of violence (domestic, regional and international) been altered as a result of the interrelation between the internal and the external – or as a result of the penetration of the domestic by the foreign during the intensive globalization process?

3) What are the methodological and ontological areas in need of reformulation in order to rid them of their embedded prejudices – whether in Western or Islamic propositions? A reformulation would be highly valuable because many of the suggested propositions cause a lot of confusion. For example, when we talk about the sources of threat to global peace, it should be clear that we don't mean western peace alone, for global peace is an indivisible concept.

Many questions emerge: Is Islam and the Muslim world the real source of threat for the entire global peace and in what sense? What kind of threat do other religious fundamentalist movements constitute (if we accept a western claim that Islamic revival does really constitute a threat to peace)? In other words, what is the amount of violence present in the Muslim world and the amount of violence it initiates in comparison with the amount, scope, intensity and nature of violence in the Western world or committed by Western powers (during the twentieth century and throughout world history)? Four years have passed since the events of 9/11, during which violence against Muslims has enormously increased; is it still acceptable to limit the discussion to the relationship between violence and Islam only? Isn't it more practical to ask about violence initiated by the West in the globalization era and after 9/11, especially against Muslims?

Still more questions can be asked: What does "defense" (against aggression) imply when the tools and types of aggression have changed, when "aggression" – as a consequence of globalization and the mixing of hard power and soft power mechanisms – is no longer limited to the violation of borders and military occupation of land but a violation of religion, values and culture? What are the available means left for individuals and groups – who have been acknowledged as international actors in our globalized world – to defend their material and moral interests or to express their feelings of injustice? Don't they have a right to resort to armed violence at a time in which the nation-state system in the Muslim world has stopped employing force as a tool of foreign policy not even in retaliation to the aggression directed towards the Muslim *Ummah*? In other words, has the time come in which we can no longer talk about force as a tool to protect the interests of countries of the South, to threaten aggressors or even to express a rejection of injustice?

These questions raise even more questions: Is violence a goal in its own? Does it always imply a rejection of democracy, tolerance and peace or can it be – in some cases – a way or a means of establishing these systems and of protecting these values? Is violence in the name of Islam the only kind of violence clashing with democracy, justice, freedom and peace as perceived by Westerners? What about the "secular violence" that has accompanied the revolutions in France, the United States, China and Russia? Why should the principles of these revolutions be a reference to justify the resort to violence in protection of these principles, i.e. in the name of freedom, justice, equality and civilization? Why are people holding on to "Islamic principles," such as justice, identity and independence, being accused of terrorism when they use "armed violence" to protect these principles and as a retaliation to the injustice that is falling upon them? Is the present "Islamic" violence a dependent or independent variable? Is it structural, i.e. embedded in the nature of Islam – as claimed by some – or is it just a reaction or a response to threats made by others? Is Islam a threat to world order or rather, is it, subject to an ever-increasing global threat? Is the non-use of force becoming a virtue, privilege enforced, only on the South?

In the light of these preliminary remarks and in an attempt to answer the questions at hand with the aim of reaching a middle perspective that can effectively address the new international and domestic changes, this study can be divided into four main parts. First, the juristic position on the types of armed violence. Second, the development of the *jihad* discourses in Muslim international relations and the types of contemporary armed violence in the Muslim world. Third, the events of 9/11 and its aftermath (the features of the new global context and its impact on the debates about Islam's position on violence both internally and externally and the obstacles facing the need to compose a new middle view revolving around the concept of *jihad*). Fourth, the features of a *"wasatya"* – middle Islamic discourse – needed to create global peace, and do not sacrifice the need to activate the *jihad* concept.

The Juristic Position on Armed Violence

The Internal Level

As previously mentioned, armed violence – which is one way of managing political conflicts – does not have a single type, not only because its targets vary from one case to the other but also because the amount of military force and the nature of actors involved in violence vary as well. Islamic *fiqh* made a thorough distinction between the various types of armed violence. Many arguments strongly prohibit and object to the use of any of these types at the domestic level. This goes for *hirabah*, *fetnah*, and *baghyh*.[3]

Without going into details it might be useful to make the following general remarks. First, the prohibited types of violence are all related to the "inside" whether they are related to the political system and the ruling authority or the relations between individuals and groups on the inside. Prohibiting these types of violence indicates that the use of "armed violence" as a way of managing inter-Muslim relations is totally rejected – whether concerning relations between Muslim countries and each other, between opposition groups and ruling authorities or between extremist groups and the rest of the Muslim *Ummah*.

Second, although the divine wisdom – behind the strict prohibition of *hirabah* and the invitation to confront *fetnah* and *baghyh* is quite obvious, this should not undermine the importance of understanding and analyzing the temporal and special contexts that produced throughout Muslim history this thought and stimulated the actions of groups such as *Elkhawareg*. This would be highly useful in understanding the conditions of equivalent contemporary movements.

By the same token, although it is – religiously speaking – strongly prohibited to disobey the ruler except under extreme conditions (like in cases of proclaimed paganism), this prohibition does not imply by any means that Islam encourages passivity in the face of the ruler's injustice. Islam strongly calls for the rejection of injustice but without resorting to armed violence and with extreme prohibition of fighting between Muslims. This specific aspect in the *fiqh* (Islamic jurisprudence) has been frequently referred to when accusing Islam of being anti-pluralistic and pro-tyrannical. A comparative study of Muslim history would help understand the present stage of Islamic militant opposition as well as the juristic disagreements about the legitimacy of this opposition.

Third, the *fiqh* rules concerning cases of violence – although related to the internal level – face a number of challenges resulting from the fact that major transformations are affecting this internal level. These transformations actually necessitate (according to some) a reconsideration of what used to be described as *hirabah* or *fetnah*.

One of these transformations, for example, is that Muslims inside are no longer separated from the outside: a major indicator of this fact is the strong alliance characterizing the relationship between ruling systems and major foreign powers, these same powers that happen to constitute a major threat to the *Ummah*'s interests. So ruling systems equate "national security" with their own security, not necessarily security against foreign aggression. This induces a vital question: To what extent do foreign factors need to be taken into consideration when deciding on the issue of whether armed violence can be legitimately used as a means of domestic opposition against foreign intervention. This question is important because external penetration achieved through the mechanisms of globalization is no less dangerous than direct external military aggression on the homeland, let alone semi-direct military occupation disguised under claims of "maintaining security."[4]

This situation created a conviction by militant groups before and after 9/11 (as will be shown in more detail) that these ruling systems should be resisted not because they are pagan but because they are allied with the enemies of Islam. They are not considered enemies because they are non-Muslims but due to their unjust policies towards Muslims.

The External Level

The rulings of armed *jihad* – whether offensive or defensive – are derived from "the *fiqh* on the basis of the relationship between Muslims and non-Muslims: Is it peace or war?"[5] Throughout Muslim world history, *jihad* was considered as a core concept in Islamic perspective towards the relation between Islam and the world. This concept stimulated different interpretations on the level of classical and contemporary Islamic *fiqh*, as well as on the level of Orientalist writings. On other hand, the term *jihad* was used to specify different types of external Islamic relations.

The changing circumstances surrounding the Muslim world have affected deeply the interpretations of *jihad* as well as the justifications for its use. The concept of *jihad* during the era of Islamic power had revealed positive meanings and had been the motive for achieving enormous ends and objectives. Unfortunately, during the contemporary period of Islamic decadence, *jihad* gained a very bad reputation since it became intertwined in the Western minds with terrorism that emanated from the backward Muslim world.

In other words, *jihad* as a historical concept and process should be comprehended in the light of its historical significance. This memory reveals the dilemma of interaction between the doctrine and the real facts. Literally, *jihad* means that Muslims should fulfill their duties to promote the cause of Islam. It is not only an outward act, it is also an inward one to strengthen oneself and correct one's own mistakes. Clearly, the assertion of the self in all directions, in every effort and act, personal and collective, internal and external, is the essence of *jihad* in the Islamic sense. This rule illustrates that *jihad* does not necessarily involve waging a war (offensive or defensive).

Jihad, from this perspective, is supposed to run through all phases of a Muslim's life: as it is their duty in every possible way to do good in the world and prevent harm. This can, of course, include war, but to equate *jihad* exclusively with waging aggressive war is to be found only in some limited phases in the experience of the classical period of Islamic history.

It was understandable for the classical jurists to think of Muslims as a powerful established society able to wage war against the sources of threat and denial. But in the contemporary world the jurists and scholars are in a different situation. Seeking to narrow the Islamic position to become purely defensive, peaceful and tolerant, the modernists found the methodology of abrogation unhelpful, a methodology which was used intensively by classical jurists to prove their interpretations.

However, some Orientalists, either classical or modern, had only highlighted the interpretation of *jihad* that equated it with offensive destructive war. They were overly selective in their use of interpretations of some *faqihs* while neglecting others. Thus it is noticed that the Western prevailing use of the term *jihad* only refers to waging aggressive war. This limited type of *jihad* is sometimes equated with holy war (either offensive or defensive) and at other times called the classical or modern theory of *jihad*.

In Muslim thought and jurisprudence, interpretations of *jihad* interfere with and are related to other terms such as *Dar El-Islam* and *Dar El-Harb*. These terms are pertaining in the Islamic Vision concerning the base of external relations. The Islamic schools of interpretations on *jihad*, as offensive or defensive war, differed according to their divergence (between traditionalists and modernists schools) on the base of Muslim external relations: whether it is war or peace with non-Muslims. This divergence could be explained in terms of differences of methodology (applying the abrogation rule or not) and historical experiences (periods of Muslim strength or power).

Aside the details of the divergences between traditionalists and modernists, a third trend of interpretations could be traced as a middle course. This middle course is based on the following six points. First, *jihad* is the Muslim's ability to strive and to fulfill his responsibilities and to serve the Islamic practice and principle in a manner that is consistent with the Islamic framework. Thus, it does not mean warfare alone. *Jihad*, in this sense, is the active expression of the Islamic commit-ment to human responsibility and a sense of duty wherever it is required in practical life. So, to interpret *jihad* only as an offensive or defensive war is to misunderstand the meaning of the word and the philosophy behind it. It is equally wrong to assume that *jihad* is a holy war in its Western meaning. Second, to interpret the base of Muslim external relations as war or peace is to misunderstand the meaning of Islam which is truly based on the *"daawa"* (Islamic mission) that needs *jihad* to reach it. Third, *jihad*, as a basic Islamic principle either excludes the possibility of armed conflict, or imposes peace, as a sole needed alternative in all situations. So it is necessary to pay attention to the variety of its meanings and applications in any specific situation. Only then, will a better understanding of the motives and conse-quences of any specific course of Muslim external relations be possible.

Therefore the inquiry concerning when, why and how the use of force or peaceful orientations should be used must be carefully addressed and answered in light of the Islamic rules on waging a war, and taking into consideration the realities of the contemporary world and the challenges that it imposes on Muslims. In other words: the third trend of interpretation does not drop either war or peace for the absolute sake of the other. It stands for a comprehensive meaning of Islam in terms of its principles, rules, values message and experiences which are valid whenever they are applied in the light of changing circumstances in broad human life and experience. Thus, the use of a dynamic Qur'anic outlook is always needed.

Fourth, *jihad* is the intellectual instrument and a key value pertaining to *daawa* which is the main foundation for Muslim and non-Muslim relations. Hence, war or peace is considered not as a base of external relations but as instruments for *daawa* through a *jihad* process. Fifth, according to this third trend of interpretation, classical jurists were criticized of being influenced by the adversaries of non-Muslim major powers. It was also criticized of giving absolute weight to the abrogation methodology, regardless of the total meaning, basic objectives and value system of Islam.

This middle trend of thought gives more weight to the integrity of the Islamic values system, and to the nature of its constructive message. So, stressing the aggressive nature of *jihad* (i.e. fighting others just because they are non-Muslims and to force them to convert to Islam) could only be done by applying the abrogation rule to a wide category of Qur'anic verses, instead of being concerned with reviving human consciousness for erecting an egalitarian human society. This aggressive attitude is seen as reducing the Islamic mission to a kind of spiritual totalitarianism.

Sixth, this middle trend also criticizes contemporary jurists that have interpreted *jihad* in a purely defensive way to the extent that they based Muslim external relations on peace only. They were criticized of dropping the abrogation rule and underestimating the negative consequences of the unjust and aggressive Western policies toward the Muslim world that justify the use of force. Finally, I think that this middle trend of thought presents a broad and realistic understanding:

1)   it gives place to the different situations and contexts that could surround the *Ummah*;
2)   it makes the *jihad* movement a necessary one aiming to correct (military or peacefully) unjust relationships;
3)   it doesn't give place to either accusation nor for exaggerated claims against or for Islam; and
4)   it refuses the Muslim objection that adaptation to new circumstances might result in loss of identity.

At last, according to this middle trend of thought, the spread of Islam and the *daawa* took several forms. This *daawa* is crucial for Muslim external relations while peace and war are present in an extreme state of relations that contradict with the nature of Islam's mission. Thus, this trend differentiates between *jihad* and war it refuses to equate *jihad* with holy war or to qualify *jihad* as legal *jihad* or holy *jihad*; rather, it argues that the term *jihad* should not legitimate a war until this war fulfills the legal conditions for launching it. As long as these conditions are not fulfilled, launched war should not be called *jihad*.

Many questions can now be raised: What are the conditions of launching a war? Who is responsible for launching *jihad* (defensive or offensive war)? What is the relevance of the different Islamic historical experiences? Which experiences illustrated the defensive or offensive *jihad*? Does the actual situation of Muslims in the world justify a defensive or offensive war? What is a defensive war and what is an offensive one?

The Events of 9/11 and its Aftermath: the Need for a New Middle View

Almost a decade before the events of 9/11 the relationship between religion and international relations gained renewed attention in social sciences. This renewed attention reflects a major shift in the paradigms of the study of social phenomena in general and political phenomena in particular. It involves a renewed importance of normative studies.[6] All of this renewed attention paved the way to the elaboration of an Islamic paradigm for studying international relations.[7]

This renewed attention paid to the role of religion and cultural aspects had been stimulated during the last quarter of the twentieth century by events accompanying the Islamic revival and the end of the Cold War that opened the way for increasing domestic and regional conflicts of religious and cultural nature. It has also been stimulated by an expanding discussion about "the Islamic threat to the West" and "conflict between civilizations."[8]

Now it can be said that the events of the 11th of September 2001 and its consequences came to prove that paying attention to the role of religion is no longer a mere theoretical or ontological requirement and that religion is indeed a variable that cannot be skipped either from global political calculations or from scientific researches and studies.

Indeed, after the 11th of September the real role and weight of the Zionist Christian/Conservative Right alliance in the U.S. was unmasked.[9] Consequently, the attention paid to that alliance enlarged its scope, after a long period of being restricted to professional circles and studies. Also the impact of this alliance on the Muslim world's interests became gradually quite apparent. Now the Muslim world has been bluntly indicated as the source of evil that needs to be confronted under the claim that acts of violence exercised by Muslims reflect the inherent violent nature of Islam. Gradually the attack against terrorists who hid behind religious labels was replaced by an attack on Islam for being a violent religion. Additionally, the Islamic movements use of armed violence has entered a new stage of its development, a stage that can be described as "the foreign extension or the global dimension" stage.

We can say that the phenomena of Islamic movements has acquired a new dimension: *jihad* international, that not only declares *jihad* against governments in the Muslim world and attacks western representatives and institutions in the region, but now makes America and the West a primary target in an unholy war of terrorism. Al-Qaeda represents a new form of terrorism, born of transnationalism and globalization. It is transnational in its identity and recruitment and global in its ideology, strategy, and targets. So after the involvement of western power in local and regional conflict, the 9/11 events have empowered "political Islam" to become internationalized.

This is why increasing attention has been paid by Islamic and western circles to the role of religion as a source of conflict and not just as an indicator of its presence and to the reason behind religious revival (usually called fundamentalism without distinction between the western and Islamic connotations of the word) as well as to the routes through which religion can become a driving force towards peace and ethics.

If we drop the theoretical aspects involved in this increasing attention and try to concentrate on the consequences and the significance of these previously indicated features, characterizing the juristic and political debates about Islam's position on violence after 9/11, we can come up with a number of conclusions. The same *fikh* (juristic) rulings and political analyses have been applied to incompatible cases because the present realities were not given enough attention. For instance, can we really equate the operations planned by the Islamic groups and Al-Jihad group (which took place in Egypt in the 90s) with those operations that took place in Saudi Arabia, Casablanca, Bali, Turkey or Kuwait during the year 2003? Or with operations executed by Palestinians against Israeli targets? Can these actions be simply regarded as equals so that in each case we can talk about Muslims or non-Muslim civilians who should not be targeted and warn against the consequences of these actions on the stability and security of existing ruling systems and on the image of Islam or on the peace process in the Middle East? Why don't we equate between the victims of American aggression in Afghanistan, Iraq and Palestine (also Chechnya and Kashmir) and the victims of aggression in New York and Washington when we condemn acts of violence exercised against civilians?

Actually a lot of similar questions about other cases – directly or indirectly related to violence – need to be addressed. Perhaps this is the reason why we find a number of political analyses[10] (although condemning the attack on civilians on the 11th of September) showing conviction that the act was the product of the American unjust policies towards the Muslim world. From this perspective, American violence is not a reaction to the attacks of the 11th of September but rather a continuation of the old American policies of violence and aggression against Muslims. Others explain why some Muslim groups (since the end of the Cold War) have recoursed to violence, especially against non-Muslims.[11] They explain this violence by referring to the suppression (exercised by the governments in Muslim countries with the support of the United States) of moderate Islamic forces that reject the resort to violence.

The logic of this trend of analysis can be summarized as follows:

1)   Many Islamists are now prepared to embrace democratic means to achieve their goals within their own countries. So the Islamists will certainly emerge as politically significant actors in almost any free democratic Muslim state;

2)   The Islamists call for democratic change instead of revolutionary transformation of violent *jihad* – a fundamental shift in their strategy. Moreover, violent *jihad* has popular support only when it is perceived as war of liberation, or it is understood as self-defense. *Jihad* to take over Muslim countries or kill western civilians is out of popular favor;

3) As long as autocratic Muslim governments are terribly threatened by even the possibility of democracy in their countries, and as long as the attacks of 9/11 have fed the popular perception that all Islamists (and perhaps even all Muslims) are fanatics whom one would not dare trust to govern themselves by democratic means.

The American war on terrorism has pushed the U.S. to rely on its Muslim allies that are mostly autocrats. Since 9/11, it has become easier for those autocrats themselves to label every Islamically inspired opposition group a terrorist threat, and it seems unwise in the current American political climate to stick up for any Islamist group that might turn out to be less democratic than it appears on the surface.

Conclusion

To conclude this chapter I want to stress the need to understand and contemplate Muslim reality and its main determinants more thoroughly in order to issue sound legalistic rulings; especially since *fatawa* are capable of crossing national borders. We as Muslims need to understand what is meant by *"fiqh."* As pointed out by Dr. Seif el-Din Abdel-Fattah,[12] what level of *fiqh* are we talking about: Is it of the nation-state reality, of international relations, of globalization and Muslim minorities in non-Muslim societies?

According to Abdel-Fattah, such talking about "the *fiqh* of reality" doesn't mean ignoring the original rulings or accepting reality as it is. This is one way of avoiding the shortcomings characterizing the rulings and *"fatawa"* concerning cases of violence in the Muslim world and these shortcomings are indeed many. Abdel-Fattah mentions some of these shortcomings, such as the lack of evidence or its misinterpretation, the negligence of its full context, as well as the interference of internal or external authority through direct or indirect pressures in order to create a public opinion supportive of the outside even if it is an enemy or adversary.

In addition to the "reality of *fiqh*" arguments, I would also like to mention that the national policies in Muslim states (not only the unjust Western policies) are mainly responsible for producing the various types of violence. Many national policies that failed to achieve independence and development, to get rid of dependence, to reach Islamic unity and to provide freedom and justice for Muslim societies have paved the way for the uncommitted and unbalanced interpretations of many Qur'anic verses (as well as the *Sunnah*). Some interpretations accept the use of violence as a tool for opposition (regardless of the juristic distinction between the inside and the outside) while others, under pressure from national and external authorities, totally reject violence and judge it as illegitimate. Both types of interpretations simply ignore the basic principles and values of Islam. Ignoring these values and principles is the mistake that leads to clashing and contradicting discourses.

Things are made even more complicated by the fact that there is a "gap" at the level of scholarship. This is because under pressures of reality, scholars either serve the interests of authority or totally withdraw from reality and become attached to the history of *fiqh* alone and, hence, offer the *Ummah* no real answers to its present state of confusion and pain. This is also why we find uncommitted and unbalanced *fatawa*.

The whole of this analysis indicates the desperate need for a renewed *fiqh*, a *fiqh* that represents the middle way (*wasateya*) of Islam and calls upon Islam's basic principles and tenets when dealing with those challenges imposed by a changing world. At the forefront of these challenges comes the relationship between Islamic movements and ruling systems. Also among these challenges are the global pressures bluntly seeking to redraw the map of the region and to totally destroy the remaining ties that keep the Muslim nations together. That renewed *fiqh* should take over the task not only of stopping violence against the ruling systems and the American or foreign targets, but also of making it clear for all rulers that the nation's security is not equivalent to the regime's security. In other words, the *fiqh* needed is the one that reflects an Islamic middle way as it addresses both rulers and ruled, both opposition and ruling systems and elites.

It is a *fiqh* that doesn't kneel down under the pressures of reality, by taking this reality for granted, but one that seeks to correct the wrongs and to renew the *Ummah*'s awareness of the means of change, including *jihad*; a *fiqh* that teaches the true meanings of "acquaintance" and diversity and that teaches that the protection of Islam and of the interests of Muslims are indeed coequals. Hence, the formulation of a discourse that explicitly states that *jihad* is not about rejecting the other, be they Christian or Jew, but about rejecting injustice is of great necessity.

Finally, I would like to also suggest that an American long-term strategy for relations with the Muslim world must be developed; one that will serve American interests and American values and one that will build on Muslim capacities for shaping their own future in a peaceful and democratic way. Such a strategy would see the role of religion and culture as means for the advancement of world peace. To narrow the gap between the American worldview and challenges facing Muslim societies, Americans should not hesitate to elaborate on how concepts rooted in values and morality can be applied to address the world's many injustices and intolerances.

Notes

1   See, for example, George Weigel, "Religion and Peace: An Argument Complexified," in *Order and Disorder After the Cold War*, Brad Roberts (ed.), Cambridge, MA: MIT Press, 1996; Barry Rubin, "Religion and International Affairs," *The Washington Quarterly*, Spring 1990; "Special Issue: Religion and World Politics," *Orbis*, vol. 42, no. 2, 1998; Jeff Haynes, *Religion in Third World Politics*, Boulder, CO: Lynne Rienner, 1994, pp. 122–145; Pablos Hatzopoulos and Fabio Petito (eds), *Religion in International Relations: The Return from Exile*, Basingstoke: Palgrave Macmillan, 2003; Jeff Haynes, "Religion," in *Issues in World Politics*, Brian White, Richard Little and Michael Smith (eds), Basingstoke: Palgrave Macmillan, 2001, pp. 153–170.

2   See Martin W. Sampson, "Cultural Influences on Foreign Policy," in *New Directions in the Study of Foreign Policy*, Charles F. Hermann, Charles W. Kegley and James N. Roseneau (eds), London: Routledge, 1987; Valerie M. Hudson (ed.), *Culture and Foreign Policy*, Boulder, CO: Lynne Rienner, 1997; Simon Murden, "Culture and World Politics," in *Globalization and World Politics*, S. Smith and K. Booth (eds), Oxford: Oxford University Press, 1997; Youssef Lapid (ed.), *The Return of Culture and Identity in International Relations*

Theory, Boulder, CO: Lynne Rienner, 1996; Fred Halliday, "Culture and International Relations: a New Reductionalism?," in *Confronting the Political in International Relations*, Michi Ebata and Beverly Neufeld (eds), New York: Millennium Press Ltd., 2000; Marysia Zalewski and Cynthia Enloe, "Questions about Identity in International Relations," in *International Relations Theory Today*, K. Booth and S. Smith (eds), Pennsylvania: Pennsylvania State University Press, 1995, pp. 279–305; Lawrence E. Harrison and Samuel P. Huntington (eds), *Culture Matters*, New York: Basic Books, 2000.

3   On the distinction between these three types of violence and on the Islamic juristic arguments explaining their non-legitimacy see Ahmed Abdel Rahman, *Islam and Combat*, Cairo: Middle East Publishers, 1990, pp. 43–72 (in Arabic); Mohamed Bahgat Oteba, *Lectures of Islamic Criminal Jurisprudence*, Cairo: Higher Institute on Islamic Studies, 2001, pp. 190–244 (in Arabic); Abdel Nasser Herez, *Political Terrorism: an Analytical Study*, Cairo: Madboly Library, 1996, pp. 205–217 (in Arabic). See also an historical-political study based on the *Serah* of the Prophet Mohammed (*pbuh*) which argues for the illegitimacy of violence between Muslims: Abdel Hamid Abu Sulayman, *Violence and the Administration of Political Conflict in the Islamic Thought: Between the Principle and Choice, an Islamic Perspective*, Cairo: Dar El Salam Publishers, 2002 (in Arabic).

4   For more details on the challenges of globalization in the the Muslim world see Nadia M. Mostafa, "The External Political Challenges on Muslim World: The Emergence of Cultural Aspects," in Nadia M. Mostafa and S. E. Abdel Fattah (eds), *The Ummah in a Century: Challenges, Responses and Future Volumes*, Cairo: Civilization Center for Political Studies, El Sherouk International Publishers, 2003, vol. 6, pp. 87–155 (in Arabic).

5   See Abdul Hamid Abu Sulayman, *The Islamic Theory of International Relations*, Virginia, VA: International Institute of Islamic Thought, 1987; Nadia. M. Mostafa, "How to Comprehend Jihad? Problematic of the Concept and the Practices," on www.islamonline.net. For more details on theoretical, epistemological, methodological, and historical aspects for studying international relations in Islam from an Islamic perspective see Nadia Mostafa, *et al.*, *The Project of International Relations in Islam*, 12 vols, Cairo: The International Institute of Islamic Thought, 1996 (in Arabic).

6   On the renewed importance of values, ethics, and norms in the study of international Relations, see Charles R. Beitz, "Recent International Thought," *International Journal*, Spring 1988; P. Viotti and M. V. Kauppi, *International Relations Theory: Realism, Pluralism, Globalism and Beyond*, New York: Prentice Hall, 1993; K. Booth, "Security in Anarchy: Utopian Realism in Theory and Practice," *International Affairs*, vol. 67, 1991, pp. 527–545; Martha Finnemore, "Norms, Culture and World Politics: Insights from Sociology's Institutionalism," *International Organization*, vol. 50, no. 2, Spring 1996, pp. 325–345.

7   On the motives, justifications, objectives, aspects and critiques of the process of developing an Islamic paradigm for studying international relations, see Nadia M. Mostafa, "Process of Developing an Islamic Paradigm for Studying International Relations: Problematiques of Research and Teaching Experiences," in N. M. Mostafa and S. E. Abdel Fattah (eds), *The Islamic Methodology in Social Sciences: the Case of Political Science Field*, Cairo: Civilization Center for Political Studies, International Institute of Islamic Thought, 2002, pp. 187–260 (in Arabic).

8   For example see a comparative critical survey of literatures in Nadia M. Mostafa, "Dialogue of Civilizations on the Light of the Contemporary International Relations," in A. Gamei, *et al.*, *Lectures on the Dialogue of Civilizations*, Damascus: Center of Arab-Iranian Relations, 2001, pp. 145–205 (in Arabic).

9   See Samir Mourcos, "The Religious American Right," in Nadia M. Mostafa (ed.), *American Policy towards Islam and Muslims*, Cairo: Program for the Dialogue of Civilizations, Faculty of Economics and Political Science, Cairo University, 2002, pp. 145–173 (in Arabic); Samir Mourcos, "Christianized Zionism and Religion Discrimination in Israel," in Nadia Mostafa and Heba Raouf Ezzat, *Israel from Within*, Cairo: Center for Political Research and Studies, 2003, pp. 421–437 (in Arabic).

10 See Nadia Mostafa, *My Ummah in the World: An Annual of Muslim Affairs*, Cairo: The Civilization Center for Political Studies, Fifth issue, 2003: This issue treats thoroughly the events of 9/11 and after, their interpretations, consequences and significance for the Muslim world (in Arabic).
11 Noah Feldman, *After Jihad: America and the Struggle for Islamic Democracy*, New York: Farrar, Straus and Giroux, 2003.
12 See S. E. Abdel Fattah, op.cit., pp. 535–585.

11 Transforming Terrorism with Muslims' Nonviolent Alternatives?

Chaiwat Satha-Anand (Qader Muheideen)

Before he left the village that night, 24-year-old Nabil sorted out a few things. At four in the afternoon he went to see his cousin Abdullah Halabiyeh, who lived next door, and paid him back the $15 he had owed him for a year and a half. Then he cleaned his new car for nearly two hours. At 6 p.m., he handed over a petition he had been gathering to get the local council to tar the road outside the family home and told Abdullah to keep bothering them until the job was done. And then at 9.30 p.m. he went to his bare room to pray.

He was crying and reciting the Qur'an. After 10 minutes or nearly 15 he finished the prayer. And Abdullah then asked him why he was taking such a long time to pray and he said nothing and smiled.

Abdullah watched him drive off around 10 p.m. Nabil's final destination was only 10 minutes away so he must have stopped somewhere to pick up his companion and fellow villager Osam Bahar, and the explosives they would wrap round their waists. At about 11.30 p.m. they walked into Jerusalem's crowded Ben Yehuda pedestrian shopping mall and, in the midst of the bright lights and chatting teenagers, pulled the detonators. Nails and shrapnel, mixed in with the explosives, mutilated anyone within 20 feet of these two exploding human bombs. Eleven Israelis were killed and 37 injured. There was little of the bombers left to pick up. . . . [1]

On September 7, 2003, Ariel Sharon gave the final order to an Israeli F-16 fighter plane to fire a laser-guided bomb at an apartment in Gaza in an effort to assassinate Sheikh Ahmed Yasin, the revered leader of Hamas. The sheikh managed to escape with a minor injury and Hamas threatened unprecedented revenge, declaring that any Israeli who occupies their land is a potential target and that this assassination attempt has "opened the gates of hell." [2]

AFP recently reported that on the second anniversary of the September 11th attack, the Muhajiroun, a British Islamic group, was planning a London rally dedicated to the terrorists/hijackers whom they called the "magnificent 19." The group spokesperson told BBC radio that "I believe the Muslim community around the world believes those 19 were magnificent." [3] Meanwhile, Abdul Hadi Awang, President of the opposition Pan-Malaysian Islamic Party, speaking to 2,000 supporters at his party annual meeting in Kuala Lumpur on September 12, 2003, denounced the US as an enemy of Islam and voiced support for Palestinian suicide bombers.[4]

These newspaper clippings indicate at least three points. First, violence related to Muslims will continue, some carried out with Muslims as targets, while others will be committed in the name of Islam. Second, terrorism, especially the 9/11 incident where some 3,000 people were killed with 19 suicide killers, can be seen by some Muslims as justified, and in fact celebrated. Third, given the above two conditions and the fact that there is a high percentage of Muslims who express support for the use of suicide bombing as a method to "defend Islam" in several countries – 73 percent in Lebanon and 27 percent in Indonesia[5] – I don't think it would be difficult to find another "Nabil," an ordinary young Muslim, who would sacrifice his/her life for the cause he/she believes in.

This chapter is an attempt to suggest that terrorism, seen as a form of political violence, grounded in its own reasons yet producing destructive results to all concerned, needs to be transformed into more productive/creative conflicts with Muslims' nonviolent alternatives. I would argue that this radical transformation is possible precisely because of the similarities, not differences, between terrorism used by some Muslims and "principled nonviolence." I will begin with an attempt to understand terrorism as a form of political violence and ask not what it is, but how does it work. Then the religious edicts condemning and justifying terrorism by traditional religious scholars as against/supporting the tenets of Islam will be critically examined by drawing attention to three philosophic issues: questioning the supremacy of instrumental rationality, the absence of innocents, and the reduction of humans to objects. Then, examples of Muslims' nonviolent actions as a creative form of resistance aimed and engaged to move conflicts in the world towards "truth and justice" will be explored as an alternative to terrorism, highlighting not only the obvious differences, but more importantly the similarities between principled non-violence and religious-based terrorism.

Understanding Terrorism: Rationality and Dynamics

In the past five years from 1998–2002, there have been 1,649 incidents which the US Department of State has termed "international terrorist attacks." Contrary to conventional understanding, most of these occurred in Latin America with 676 incidents compared to 387 in Asia and 135 in the Middle East. Business targets have been attacked 1,462 times which accounts for more than 66 percent compared to all other targets: diplomatic, governmental, military and other. It goes without saying that civilians have been the primary victims while the military accounted for only 1.7 percent of all targets. The highest number of casualties in the past five years excluding the 9/11 incident, however, was in Asia with 4,161 compared with 283 in Latin America and 1,462 in the Middle East. The September 11th, 2001 attack clearly contributed most significantly to the number of casualties in North America with 4,091.[6]

Focusing only on suicide terrorism, a researcher found that from 1980 to 2001, there have been 188 separate suicide terrorist attacks, where 179 or 95 percent were parts of organized campaigns with the non-religious Marxist-Leninist Tamil Tigers of

Sri Lanka becoming the world leader of this type of terrorism. More importantly, this phenomenon has been steadily on the rise since those who committed them have learned that "it pays." As a result of terrorism, American and French military forces were compelled to leave Lebanon in 1983, Israeli forces to quit Gaza Strip and the West Bank in 1994 and 1995, and the Sri Lankan government to work towards an independent Tamil state from 1990 on, among other cases.[7] In addition, according to B'tselem, the Israeli Information Center for Human Rights in the Occupied Territories, between 29 September 2000 and 30 November 2002, the number of Israelis killed by Palestinians was 640; among them were 440 civilians and 82 under the age of eighteen. The number of Palestinians killed by Israelis was 1,597, while 300 were minors. From the signing of the Oslo agreement in 1993 until the beginning of August 2002, there have been 198 suicide-bombing missions; 136 of these ended with the attackers blowing up themselves and others.[8]

Terrorism as a phenomenon is therefore important to any analysis of the present global trends and politics because it is increasingly prevalent. In addition, the American reaction to the 9/11 tragedy with the use of force to correct the wrong of terrorism has plunged the world deeper into deadly conflicts. President George W. Bush spoke on the second anniversary of September 11th that

> The memories of Sept. 11 will never leave us. We will not forget the burning towers. . . . We will not wait for further attacks on innocent Americans. The best way to protect the American people is to stay on the offensive, to stay on the offensive at home and to stay on the offensive overseas.[9]

In the past two years after the September 11th incident, the US has started two wars, in Afghanistan and Iraq. With reports of casualties from these deadly conflict sites coming in almost daily while George W. Bush and his Vice-President had been advised not to be present at Ground Zero memorial services this year, it seems the President was right when he said that his "war on terror" was not over. In fact, this war has in some ways transformed the world into a more dangerous place plagued with the specter of violence – where ordinary people are trapped between the deadly force of terrorism carried out by both state and non-state actors on the one hand, and the hardened arms of the state drowning the call for rights and liberties on the other.[10]

If the effects of terrorism are to be mitigated in the long run, the phenomenon needs to be critically construed. It is important to first underscore the fact that the term terrorism itself is extremely political. For example, the US government's policy in dealing with terrorism clearly states that while concession to terrorists will not be made, it will apply pressure on states that sponsor terrorism and enhance international collaboration against it. More importantly, it will try to bring terrorists "to justice for their crimes."[11] According to Richard Falk, terrorism in the US and Israeli political discourse has been associated with anti-state forms of violence that were so criminal that "any method of enforcement and retaliation was viewed as acceptable, and not subject to criticism."[12] However, those who use terror tactics normally avoid the term and claim they are resisting oppression and fighting for

justice.[13] But then most governments also exclude "state terrorism" and thereby rele-
gate a major source of violence and fear suffered by civilians around the world to
silence.[14] To better understand terrorism, therefore, it might be instructive to hear
the voices of a perpetrator and a victim.

In the morning of December 23, 1929, Lord Irwin, the British Viceroy, had just
returned from a tour of South India. As he had approached Delhi, a bomb had
exploded under his train. Lord Irwin escaped injury and Gandhi congratulated him
on his miraculous escape.[15] Gandhi also delivered a speech to a meeting of the Indian
Congress party and drafted a resolution denouncing terrorism. He wrote that he
would despair for nonviolence if he were not certain that bomb throwing was nothing
but "froth coming to the surface in an agitated liquid." The danger of terrorism lies
in its internal consequences: from violence committed against the foreign ruler there
was only an "easy, natural step to violence to our own people whom we may consider
to be obstructing the country's progress."[16] He seems to think of terrorism as a kind of
delusional, irrational act. As a matter of fact, in January 1930, a small left-wing
Indian terrorist group founded in 1928, the Hindustan Socialist Revolutionary Army
(HSRA), published a manifesto titled: "The Philosophy of the Bomb," attacking both
Gandhi's policy of nonviolence and his criticism of terrorism which was due to, "sheer
ignorance, misrepresent(ation), and misunderstand(ing)," and that those who
committed them are "delusional" and "past reason."[17]

Most of the HSRA members had earlier been members of Gandhi's nonviolent
movement, but they turned to the use of violence when their goals could not be realized. It claims that the terrorists do not ask for mercy nor compromise, that their
war is a war to the end, and that the mission of the youth of India is to conduct not
just "propaganda by deed" but "propaganda by death." It argued that a revolution
cannot be completed without terrorism and that it was not an imported European
product but homegrown. Most importantly, a terrorist does not sacrifice his/her life
out of the psychological need for appreciation or any other form of irrationality/
insanity. Instead, the document emphatically stated that "It is to reason and reason
alone that he (a terrorist) bows."[18] Because of British domination, an Indian was
forced by reason and dictated by conscience to go into violence by accepting
terrorism. This is because:

> Terrorism instills fear in the hearts of the oppressors, it brings hope of revenge
> and redemption to the oppressed masses. It gives courage and self-confidence to
> the wavering, it shatters the spell of the subject race in the eyes of the world,
> because it is the most convincing proof of a nation's hunger for freedom.[19]

According to Laura Blumenfeld, terrorism is "not so much about killing people as
about dehumanizing them to make a political point." She should know because her
father, a New York rabbi, was shot and wounded by a Palestinian in Jerusalem's old
city in 1986. Twelve years later, she confronted Omar Khatib, the Arab gunman, in
an Israeli courtroom and after several meetings, Omar wrote her father a letter
stating that "Laura was the mirror that made me see your face as a human person
[who] deserved to be admired and respected."[20]

From the perspectives suggested above, terrorism can be seen as a threat or an act of violence against civilians. Construed as a form of political violence, it can also be seen as a reaction to oppression and injustice, and hence, rational from the perspective of perpetrators. More importantly, the act of terror becomes possible when the victim has been dehumanized and no longer recognized as a human being. But apart from specific conditions, such as organizational/technical skills or financial support for terrorists, it is also important to emphasize three other ways that terrorism works.[21]

First, it works by severing the link between the targets of violence and the reason for violence. This is perhaps the most glaring reason why it is often seen as irrational since there seems to be no reason why the civilian victims, directly unrelated to the conflicts, are attacked. The point, however, is when that logical link is cut off; the question of innocent lives becomes irrelevant to the terrorists. The "enemy" society, already dehumanized, can be effectively turned into a monolith devoid of complexities that exist in reality, and thus anyone can be attacked.

Second, since terrorism can attack anyone at any time or place, it successfully robs a society of that precious sense of certainty that allows members to continue their lives in normality. I would argue that in the Hobbesian sense, terrorism retrogresses a political society to a "state of nature" when fear for one's own life replaces a sense of certainty grounded in a confidence that the state can protect its own citizens. When its ability to protect is compromised, if not altogether lost, its legitimacy to exist will be seriously called into question since this protection of its citizens' lives is seen as the absolute minimum of the normal functioning of the state. This is one of the reasons why some scholars believe that the September 11th attack which discloses a structural modification in the character of power and security, hence a different approach to terrorism, guided perhaps by the framework of war and a reformulation of the limits of the use of force, is required.[22]

Third, with the absence of normality amidst the hegemony of fear, it transforms the society that mourns the tragic fate of its victims into a society of possible victimizers bent on using violence against others. The purpose of terrorism as political violence is not exactly to create material nor human destruction, though a case can be made for symbolic attack as in the September 11th incident, but to transform the very existence of the "enemy" society itself into an alienated collective self facing internal contradictions at the moral, cultural and political levels that might eventually tear it apart.[23]

Treating Terrorism: Muslims' Condemnations and Justifications

A most curious little booklet circulated among Muslims which I have recently come across has two titles: *Clarification of the Truth In Light of Terrorism, Hijackings & Suicide Bombings* and *An Advice To Usaamah Ibn Laaden from Shaykhul Islam Ibn Baaz.*[24] As the former Mufti of the Kingdom of Saudi Arabia, Abdul Azeez Ibn Baaz (d. 1999 or 1420 AH) was considered by many a great scholar of "traditionalist" Islam and *Sunnah* (traditions of the Prophet). The booklet has two parts. The first is a religious-based argument in favor of obedience to the rulers. The second is a collection of various Islamic scholars' opinions on hijackings and suicide bombings.

Ibn Baaz called bin Laden a "*khaarijee*," a member of the *Khawaarij* which was a sect that appeared in the early history of Islam and was said to be responsible for the killings of many of the Prophet's companions.[25] They committed three major crimes: rebelling against Muslim rulers, declaring Muslims to be unbelievers due to sins, and making permissible the taking of human life unlawfully. Ibn Baaz cited a Hadith related by Ahmad and Tirmidhi that the Prophet said: "There are three things towards which the heart of a Muslim never shows hatred or rancour: Making one's actions sincerely for Allaah; giving obedience to the rulers (*wulaatul-umur*); and sticking to the *Jamaa'at* (united body)."[26] It is interesting to note that in an interview with the *Nida'ul Islam* (no. 15) bin Laden charged some of the Muslim leaders as well as the scholars especially "in the country of the two sacred mosques" as engaging in the major *Kufr* (falling outside of the faith). This is another reason, if not a more important one, why Ibn Baaz regarded bin Laden as a *khaarijee* because his statement was seen as a blanket *takfeer* (declaring Muslims to be unbelievers and therefore make allowable the spilling of their blood).[27]

In an interview with *Al-Jazeerah* at the end of 1998, Osama bin Laden said:

> I look with great veneration and respect at those great men in that they lifted the humiliation from the forehead of our *Ummah* (community of believers), whether it was those who bombed in Riyaadh or those in Khobar or in East Africa, and whatever resembles these acts.

Ibn Baaz gave his *fatwa* (religious ruling) on "the terrorist attack in Riyadh" by stating:

> And there is no doubt that this act can only be undertaken by one who does not believe in Allah or the Last Day. . . . Only vile souls which are filled with enmity, jealousy, evil, corruption and absence of faith in Allah and His Messenger can perform the likes of these acts.

Then he added his judgment that, "And those who perform the likes of this are more deserving of being killed and being restrained on account of what they have committed of great sin."[28]

Citing a Hadith compiled by Imam Muslim, Ibn Baaz made a point that a Muslim has to "hear and obey" his/her ruler even if "he flogs your back and takes your wealth," even if these leaders have "hearts of devils in the bodies of humans." He also cited the teaching of Imam al-Barbahaaree (d. 329 AH) who taught that:

> If you find a man making supplication (*du'a*) against the ruler, know that he is a person of innovation (*bid'ah*). If you find a person making supplication for the ruler to be upright, know that he is a person of the *Sunnah* (traditions of the Prophet), if Allah wills.[29]

Based on early Islamic history when Uthman Ibn Affaan (the third noble caliph) was killed as a result of discord (*fitnah*) among the elites of the time, especially between

Ali and Mu'aawiya (the fourth and fifth caliphs after the Prophet), Ibn Baaz was extremely antagonistic to the idea of challenging or disobeying the rulers. In other words, Ibn Baaz claimed that discord and open rebellion resulted from "open proclamation of the faults of the rulers." Armed with hatred for the rulers, the people will kill them.[30]

Ibn Baaz's concern could be illustrated by the Sadat assassination. Muhammad 'Abd al-Salam Faraj, who was tried and executed in 1982 for the October 6, 1981 assassination of President Sadat, wrote in his *Al-Farida Al-Gha'eba* (The Neglected Duty), a most important repository of his group's thought, that:

> Fighting the near enemy is more important than fighting the distant enemy. . . . The cause of the existence of imperialism in the lands of Islam lies in these self-same rulers. To begin the struggle against imperialism would be . . . a waste of time. . . . There can be no doubt that the first battlefield of the *jihad* is the extirpation of these infidel leaderships . . . .[31]

When asked to explain his motive, Khalid al-Islambouli, an officer who was the instigator and executor of the Sadat assassination, stated in the Egyptian investigation file record that: "I did what I did, because the *Shari'ah* was not applied, because of the peace treaty with the Jews and because of the arrest of Muslim *Ulama* without justification."[32] It could be said that the killing of President Sadat was perceived as a necessity by the assassins because he was a heretic (*Kufr*) since he did not rule in accordance with traditions of the Prophet (*Shari'ah*); a traitor because he made peace with the enemy; and an unjust ruler because he arrested Islamic scholars (*Ulama*) unjustly.[33]

In other words, Ibn Baaz's argument for obedience to rulers is based on the idea that disobedience, even criticism of the leaders, will eventually undermine their authority, create disunity among the Muslim community, and then lead to deadly conflicts, which in history appeared in the form of rightful rulers killed. This, in turn, would result in the weakening and disunity, if not disintegration, among the Muslim *Ummah* (community). The theoretical question of limit to obedience, *a la* Aristotle's rights to revolt, was responded with the words of Imam ash-Shawkaanee (d. 1250 AH) who wrote that a believer can disobey the ruler if the latter disobeys God. Yet, "it is not permissible to revolt against the leaders even if they reach excessive levels of oppressions, as long as they establish the Prayer and no manifest disbelief appears from them."[34] This formulation of the ruler's disobedience to God, and therefore a justified pretext for disobeying him/her, is quite problematic for at least two reasons. First, it is a highly constricted notion of disobedience since only the sacred religious duty, prayer, is specified while other duties – for example, treating the scholars and citizens justly, are excluded as the basis for obedience among Muslims. Second, it seems that only "manifested" disobedience or glaring disbelief of God would justify Muslims' disobedience. This condition seems to establish the primacy of appearance over other types of "reality," easily concealed in the present times. Both conditions, including the fact that criticisms of the Muslim rulers are discouraged, effectively result in a contracted space of politics. It is therefore not surprising that in the eyes of some Muslims who claim to kill in the name of Islam, the most dangerous enemies of Islam are those within and that killing becomes a wedge driven into the texture of society to create a necessary space for desirable socio-political changes. In this sense, it could be argued that even with global-reach organizations such as Al-Qaeda, terrorism begins and exists in distinct contexts where local grievances are voiced. The interplay between local conditions such as the erosion of distributive capabilities of the states, perceptions of corrupt rulers and the power of universal messages such as the Islamic call for social equity and moral piety would contribute significantly to the rise of violent alternative in a constricted political space. I would therefore suggest that to treat terrorism as a purely "outside" or "international" phenomenon is insufficient for a critical understanding of the subject.[35]

The last part of the booklet entitled "The Verdicts of the Major Scholars Regarding Hijackings & Suicide Bombings" mainly comprises the words of two religious scholars: Ibn Baaz and Ibn Al-Uthaymeen (d. 2000/1421 AH), but a short section by Ibn Taymiyyah (d. 728 AH) on the "Seceders" or those who go out of the faith (*khawaarij*) is included. It is divided into sections condemning "suicide bombings," "attacking the enemy by blowing oneself up in the car," "hijacking planes and kidnapping" and "those who partake in bombings, hijackings." Importantly, the document claims that the verdicts reflect "the true position of Islam and the people of *Sunnah* (traditions of the Prophet) towards the evils of those who hold permissible the shedding of blood without just cause."[36] But it is the reasons given for these condemnations that shed light on the problematic nature of how terrorism is treated by Islamic scholars.

According to the booklet, there are three reasons why terrorists' actions such as suicide bombings and hijackings are wrong judging from "the true position of Islam." First, suicide bombing is wrong because suicide itself is unacceptable in Islam. Citing the Holy Qur'an and a Hadith on the authorities of Bukhari and Muslim, Ibn Uthaymeen categorically states that one who commits *jihad* by means of suicide such as attaching explosives to a car and storming the enemy, knowing full well that he/she who carries out the act will die, is regarded as "one who has killed himself, and as a result he shall be punished in Hell."[37] Suicide is a major sin because it is born out of desperation. In such a state, a Muslim calls for help from God and with patience, God would assist him. To commit suicide then means a suspension of faith in God's infinite Mercy. In condemning suicide as a major sin, Ibn Uthaymeen quoted another verse from the Qur'an which reads: "And whoever kills a believer intentionally, his recompense is Hell to abide therein, and the Wrath and the Curse of Allah are upon him, and a great punishment is prepared for him." (IV: 93) It is interesting to note that the content of this verse has very little to do with suicide but everything to do with homicide, unless one chooses to assume that the suicidal bomber is schizophrenic. Splitting the self into two, the self that was intentionally killed in "suicide" is seen as that of the believer, killed by another part of the self that has fallen from the faith. Hence suicide in this sense is seen as taking the life of the believer and he/she who commits it will be punished with a life in hell.

Second, Ibn Uthaymeen suggests that suicide bombings will be acceptable if, according to Ibn Taymiyyah, it is a *jihad* in Allah's cause, "which caused a whole nation to truly believe (and become Muslims), and he did not really lose anything, since although he died he would have to die anyway, sooner or later."[38] Death for a Muslim is not a negative state but a return to the Origin (*Al-Qur'an*, II: 156).[39] But these acts of tying explosives to themselves and then "approaching unbelievers and detonating them amongst them" is a clear case of suicide and those who commit it will certainly be in Hell because "this person has killed himself and has not benefited Islam."[40] The Shaykh advises against terrorism of this kind because if the terrorist kills himself along with a large number of other people,

> then Islam will not benefit by that, since the people will not accept Islam, . . .
> Rather it will probably just make the enemy more determined, and this action
> will provoke malice and bitterness in his heart to such an extent that he may
> seek to wreak havoc upon the Muslims.

In other words, suicide bombing is condemned on the grounds that it would engender a stronger negative reaction from Muslims' opponents and would then adversely benefit their plight, as is the case in Palestine. Would this then mean that, had it furthered the Islamic cause, defined by practical, and at times quantitative consequences to the Muslims, it would have been acceptable "to the true position of Islam"?

Third, Ibn Baaz maintains that hijacking planes and kidnapping children, which are now encompassing the whole world, are "extremely great crimes." Governments and scholars must try to end "this evil" which has caused "great harm and inconvenience" to "the innocent." Those who partake in these acts of terror

> are not to be co-operated with, nor are they to be given salaams to. Rather, they
> are to be cut off from, and the people are to be warned against their evil. Since
> they are a *fitnah* (tribulation/trial) and are harmful to the Muslims, and they are
> the brothers of the Devil (*Shaytaan*).[41]

It seems that Ibn Baaz here condemns terrorism because of its harmful effects on *the innocents*. But then he instructs the Muslims to dissociate themselves from those who "partake in these acts" because of its harmful effects on *the Muslims*. A question can therefore be raised if the violent effects on the innocents, and not necessarily Muslims who are innocents, constitutes a sufficient ground for the believers to dissociate themselves from the perpetrators of these acts? This instruction of cutting off the tie that binds Muslims in a community of faith because of the acts of terror committed is substantiated by the teaching of Ibn Taymiyyah (d. 728 AH), who said that: Muslims must fight against those who strive to kill *every Muslim* who did not agree with their view, declaring the blood of the Muslims, their wealth, and the slaying of their children to be lawful, while making *takfeer* (declaring Muslims to be unbelievers) of them. This is because "they are more harmful to the Muslims than others, for there are none which are more harmful to the Muslims than them, neither the Jews and nor the Christians."[42]

In the eyes of these scholars who condemn terrorism, the terrorists are the enemies most harmful to Muslims because they are born from inside the bosom of Muslim communities. They were made into the "harmful" others, fallen from the ties of mercy that bind members together, and deserve to be destroyed. This last reason is strikingly similar to the argument made by those who are committed to the acts of terror themselves, notably by some of those responsible for the 1981 Sadat assassination discussed above. In the final chapter of *Al-Farida Al-Gha'eba*, Faraj writes that the situation of Muslims resembled the time when they were under "the yoke of the Mongols." He then concluded that:

> Governments in the Islamic world today are in a state of apostasy. . . . Our *Sunna* has determined that the apostate be punished more severely than he who had always been an infidel. The apostate must be killed even if he is in no posi-tion to fight, while an infidel does not merit death in such a case.[43]

More important, perhaps, is to see how those Muslims who support and played their parts in committing violent acts against civilians justify their terror.

Mahmoud Abouhalima, convicted for the 1993 World Trade Center bombing, explains that the act of terror was committed for "a very specific reason" aiming at a "specific achievement." Commenting on the Oklahoma City federal building bombing, he said it was an attempt to "reach the government with the message that we are not tolerating the way that you are dealing with our citizens." Following Shaykh Abdul Rahman's teaching, Abouhalima condemns the US because it helped to create the state of Israel, supported secular Egyptian govern-ment, and sent its troops to Kuwait during the Gulf war. But in his view, he is against the US and its abhorring policies not because he is anti-Christian, but because of the American ideology of secularism which is hostile towards religion, especially Islam. When asked if the US would be better off with a Christian govern-ment, he replied: "Yes, at least it would have morals."[44] He also said that secular America did not understand him and people like him because "the soul of religion, that is what is missing." He compared a life without the soul of religion to a pen without ink, even if that pen is worth "two thousand dollars, gold and everything in it, it's useless if there's no ink in it." Religion as the soul revived the whole life while secularism has none and therefore secular people "are just moving like dead bodies."[45]

The feeling by the terrorists that others would not understand them is quite common. What is not, are the explanations for this lack of understanding. While Abouhalima attributed this absence of understanding to the presence of secularism, others pointed to a lack of shared experience of suffering. Eyad Sarraj, a recipient of the Physicians for Human Rights Award, is a Palestinian psychiatrist who was detained three times by Arafat's forces during 1996. He expressed his shock when a BBC interviewer appeared to understand his comment that the struggle of the Palestinians is about how *not* to become a bomb and that the amazing thing is not the occurrence of suicide bombing, but its rarity. He believed that suicide bombings by Palestinians are acts of desperation, a serious stage of "the seemingly perpetual conflict" after "we have tried everything." He explained what it means to live under Israeli occupation. Among other things, it means:

> identity number and permit to live as a resident which will be lost if one leaves the country for more than three months;
> a traveling document which specifies that the holder is of an undefined nationality;
> being called twice a year by the intelligence for routine investigation and persuasion to work as an informer on "your brothers and sisters;"
> leaving your home in the refugee camp in Gaza at 3 a.m., going through roadblocks and checkpoints to do the work that others won't and returning home in the evening to collapse in bed for a few hours before getting up for the following day;
> losing respect from one's own children when they see their father spat at and beaten before their eyes;
> seeing the (name of the) Prophet being spat on and called a pig by Israeli settlers in Hebron.

Sarraj concluded that these are why the Palestinian children have been throwing stones, and as a result killed almost daily. When arrested, they were tortured and made to confess. Consequently, everyone in the community suspected one another of being spies. "We were exhausted, tormented and brutalized." He ends his account with a question: "I've told you a few things. Now do you understand why we have turned into suicide killers?"[46] But killing oneself out of utterly exhausted and brutalized existence is one thing; killing others who are women and children, who have nothing to do with the brutal life one has to endure is quite another. How then could these acts of terror which destroy the lives of innocents be justified?

Dr. Abdul Aziz Rantisi, one of the founders of Hamas, answers this question in an interview by saying: "We are at war." It was a war not only with the Israeli government but with the whole of Israeli society. He then clarified that it was not against Jewish culture or religion. He said, "We're not against Jews just because they're Jews," but especially because of Israel's stance towards the Hamas concept of an Islamic Palestine. It was "Islamic nationalism" which Israel wants to destroy. It is interesting to note the shift from Hamas' military operations aiming at military targets to the use of terror aiming at anyone anytime. Rantisi clearly stated that this shift took place when Palestinian demonstrators were attacked by Israeli police in front of the Al-Aqsa mosque in 1990 and the massacre of Muslims in Hebron by Dr. Baruch Goldstein during the month of Ramadan in 1994 while the Israeli soldiers were standing nearby. Rantisi concluded that these were "attacks on Islam as a religion as well as on Palestinians as a people." For this reason, the question posed about innocent lives lost was irrelevant because this war between Hamas and Israel was one with no innocent victims.[47] He added that the fact most misunderstood by others is that the Palestinians were seen as aggressors. Based on the reality of the occupation and the accompanying violence, he categorically stated that "we are not (the aggressors): we are the victims." In this sense, Rantisi thought of the bombings as a "necessary" moral lesson intended to make innocent Israelis feel the pain that innocent Palestinians had felt so that they can actually experience the violence before they could understand what the Palestinians had gone through.[48]

In *Rehearsals for a Happy Death*, Anne Marie Oliver and Paul Steinberg recounted the statements of young volunteers for suicide-bombing missions in Gaza using some of the data from videotapes. In one case, a smiling lad, no more than eighteen years old, who would carry out the mission of suicide bombing with plastic explosives attached to his body, stated that his act of terror would be committed

> for the sake of God, out of love for this homeland and for the sake of the freedom and honor of this people, in order that Palestine remain Islamic, and in order that Hamas remains a torch lighting the roads of all the perplexed and all the tormented and oppressed [and] that Palestine might be liberated.

Another young man said that "what a difference there is between one death and another. . . . Truly there is only one death, so let it be on the path of God."[49] Seen from the perspective of these perpetrators, their acts are not irrational or aimless wanton violence. Those who condemn it and even call it "suicide bombings" are wrong since it conveys the meaning of an impulsive act by a deranged individual. These acts should instead be called, according to Rantisi, "self-chosen martyrdom" (*istishhadi*) because those who undertake them deliberately choose to carry them out as part of their religious obligation. Rantisi claims that Hamas does not order them to do it but "gives permission for them to do it at certain times."[50]

It goes without saying that terrorists grow out of and operate in their specific contexts. But the accounts of those related to terrorism discussed above suggests some common threads which indicate that terrorism often grows out of a context of extreme injustice and carried out to communicate those grievances in situations where other channels are absent or inadequate. People who committed "suicide bombing," for example, are young ordinary men (and women) who made their choices based on their sets of political and religious justifications. What is important, however, is that these deliberate decisions to kill or be killed in the name of Islam are made in a redefined world as a world at war without innocents. As a result, the logic of exclusivity assumes paramount significance. In the notebooks of some Uzbek students belonging to the Islamic Movement of Uzbekistan led by Soviet Army veteran Juma Namangani, who attended training courses on terrorism in the Fergana Valley during 1994–1996, *jihad* is considered "a cleansing act" where one of the aims is to raise popular awareness that the enemies are among them. A student writes:

> . . . unbelievers and the government are oppressors; that they are connected with Russians, Americans and Jews, to whose music they are dancing; and that they don't think about their people. . . . We speak of the fate of faith betrayers, according to Islamic law and about how people should distance themselves from those who breach the faith and should side with the *mujahideen*. . . . it has to be announced that jihad is a necessary religious requirement, for all social groups

of people, And in life, everyone must either be a Muslim or a non-Muslim, that is, no one can remain in the middle.[51]

Four groups of religious people were identified as targets for killing. They are:

> Those who try to gain converts to Christianity on Muslim soil. Spies who work as Christian clerics. . . . Christians and Jews who speak against the *mujahideen* and those who propagate against Islam. Those Christians who collect money for the struggle against Muslims, and those who speak against Muslims.[52]

Reviewing these accounts of Muslims who chose the ways of terror as well as those who condemn them, I am struck not by the differences between these two groups but similarities. What is definitely at work is a drawing of the line between the Muslims and the others which make violence/injustice against them readily possible. Among the scholars working for the state, Muslims who disobey the rulers and become terrorists have fallen from the faith and therefore deserve to be punished, killed in this life and will go to hell in the Hereafter. The world they live in, born out of their concrete experiences, is a world at war where killing and violence can be justified. Yet this war is different because it is not a war between two armies or combatants (a place for non-combatants do exist). This is a war between two societies, Palestinian/Israeli or Muslim/non-Muslim, and therefore there are no innocents. The Muslims who use terror claim that they are the victims and the terror is intended to communicate their grievances so that their significant others will experience what they have been through. These people who commit and are committed to terror were deliberate in sacrificing their lives for the cause of something greater which they believe in.

If terrorism is construed as a form of political violence born out of structural causes such as the absence of democracy and unjust distribution of national wealth, and legitimized by religious convictions, among others, trying to put an end to it by military might is futile.[53] If terrorism poses a profound threat to the world, especially in the ways that different people connect to one another with some degrees of certainty, then there is a need to deal with it. I would argue that violence is powerless against terrorism and condemnations are futile because their proponents ask the wrong question. Perhaps, a question which does not ask how to end terrorism but to transform it will provide a more promising alternative.

Transforming Terrorism: Muslims' Nonviolent Alternatives?

Among my collection of newspaper clippings about violence in the Middle East, there is a picture of a man comforting another injured man in a road accident. The rescuer was gently patting the other's face with water. It would not be remarkable but for the fact that the injured man was an Israeli police officer on the way to the scene of clashes in Jerusalem, the place of accident was near a cliff in the Jaber-al-Mukaber, Palestine and the one who comforted him was a local Palestinian. In fact, local Palestinians came out to help all four Israeli officers.[54] This picture shows two things. First, a line drawn to divide humans into enemy camps that deserve only to be killed is not impervious to crossing. Second, given the degree to which different groups of people have to stay together, it is possible to imagine that there are more crossings of such lines than what has been recorded in the press.[55]

In surveying 18 cases of unarmed insurrections against authoritarian governments in the Third World from 1978 to 1994, both successful and failed, a researcher found some which took place in Muslim societies, which naturally involved Muslim participation.[56] There are also cases of Muslims' unarmed resistance in the Middle East, North Africa,[57] as well as the use of communal nonviolent actions among Muslim minorities in Thailand.[58] Some years ago, there was a study on *sulha* (mediation/arbitration/reconciliation), the Palestinian ceremony which is a positive symbol of reconciliation necessary for an alternative kind of cultural analysis highly important for Peace Studies.[59] Recently, a Palestinian academic has written a most comprehensive study which identifies principles and values grounded in Islamic traditional sources for nonviolence based on an indigenous Islamic context which could be guiding principles needed as a framework for the application of peacebuilding/nonviolence in the Islamic context.[60] The discussion of these studies is obviously beyond the scope of this chapter. But suffice it to suggest here that at a minimum, these studies show that Muslims' nonviolent actions do exist in contemporary societies. Moreover, Muslims' nonviolence is by no means inaction nor passive but has evidently been part of spirited struggle against injustices where Islamic scriptural sources continue to serve as fountains of justifications for them. The question here, however, is in what ways could Muslims' nonviolent actions become alternatives in transforming terrorism?

Based on a specific understanding of terrorism as a rational form of political violence and justifications of terror given by perpetrators themselves discussed above, I would argue that similarities between terrorism and Muslims' nonviolent actions do exist especially on two important issues: fighting injustice and death. However, two other important issues which characterize terrorism pose a hindrance to such transformation: the absence of the innocents and the instrumental logic governing terrorism. By overcoming these important obstacles, given existing similarities, transforming terrorism becomes a distinctive possibility.

Existing Injustice

Understood as a form of political violence, terrorism is a response to perceived injustice, shaped by a fusion of local and global conditions. This is not that much different from the conditions faced by nonviolent movements around the world, especially a Muslim nonviolent movement fighting against British occupation in India from 1930 to 1947. In mobilizing support from the Pathans in the Northwest subcontinent to fight against the British with nonviolence, Abdul Ghaffar Khan (1890–1988), known to his people as *Badshah Khan* (emperor or king of kings) and to Indians as "the Frontier Gandhi," said:

Fifty per cent of the children in our country are ill. The hospitals are meant for the English. The country is ours, the money is ours, everything belongs to us, but we are hungry and naked in it. We have not got anything to eat, no houses. He has made *pukka* roads because he needs them for himself. These roads were built with our money. Their roads are in London. These are our roads but we are not allowed to walk on them . . . He excites the Hindus to fight the Muslims and the . . . Sikhs to fight the Muslims. Today these three are the sufferers. Who is the oppressor and who has been sucking our blood? The English.[61]

The 95-year-old Gurfaraz Khan who had listened to Badshah Khan's speech before joining him, said:

> . . . He told us that it was wrong that this land was ours but rule was in British hands . . . he pointed out that injustice of our children running barefoot and they being in their suits . . . they could even afford to kick bread and we did not have enough to eat.[62]

Listening to Khan's speeches, many of those who later joined his nonviolent movement admitted that they did not know that the British were ruling India at the time.

> He explained to us about the British and said how they had come from 80,000 miles away and were occupying our land that was not theirs. They were here to colonize us. He said that we must demand our independence and fight for it.

Another said,

> The mullahs (local Islamic religious leaders) and the *khans* were in the pay of the British so they never told people the truth. No one in the whole Frontier had the spirit or the guts to speak against the British other than Badshah Khan.[63]

Not only did the British occupy and exploit India, they dealt with those who fought nonviolently for independence with imprisonment, forced labor and sometimes direct killings. One example of direct killings was the Amritsar massacre at the order of General Dyer on April 13, 1919 when British troops fired into a nonviolent crowd killing 379 and injuring more than a thousand notwithstanding,[64] in Kohat, 1932, following the arrest of Badshah Khan. British detachments opened fire at the people, killing some 300 Red Shirts (the *Khudai Khidmatgar*: the Pathan nonviolent movement in their uniforms) and injuring a thousand more.[65] The fact that these nonviolent Muslims could face the force of violence with nonviolence could be attributed to their organization, strict discipline not unlike a military organization,[66] and the strong commitment to nonviolence. This last quality is related to a specific understanding of death.

Death

The terrorists, especially suicide bombers or "self-chosen martyrs," committed their acts of terror for much larger causes, such as the liberation of their people. They are willing to sacrifice their lives because of their specific appreciation of "meaningful" death as a religious obligation in the Path of God. According to Gandhi, humans are advised to

> learn to love death as well as life, if not more so. . . . Life becomes livable only to the extent that death is treated as a friend, never as an enemy. To conquer life's temptations, summon death to your aid. In order to postpone death a coward surrenders honor, wife, daughter and all.[67]

For the Pathans, when Badshah Khan invited volunteers to join his nonviolent movement, he made it quite clear that given the authorities' brutality, death was a real possibility. Emphasizing the singularity and inevitability of death, he said, "As death will come only once therefore it is much better to die for the sake of one's nation and country." Then in a speech at a mosque on December 16, 1931, he added that

> A man is sure to die whether he is brave or not. But there is a difference between every sort of death. Do not forget your object – your object is to liberate your country. The best death is that when one dies the way of God and Holy Prophet.[68]

One of the reasons why *jihad* is so problematic is not only because of different understandings between physical and spiritual *jihad* as often indicated,[69] but also its relationship with death. *Jihad* as a phenomenon has at times been reified and dehistoricized. As a result, contradictions and ambivalence that have characterized its complex history have been erased; and the changing understandings of death as political action that have in part been revealed by history, effaced. Seery argues that this situation is a result of how "Westerners" view non-Western cases of political suicide as "culturally pathological" where terrorists, guerrilla fighters, *sati* (Hindu women who followed their husbands to their deaths) and *satyagraha* (Gandhi's principled nonviolence) are lumped together as "crazed fanatics."[70] In a curious way, a Pathan's choice of using nonviolence against the British is remarkably similar to a suicide bomber's choice because by renouncing violence while confronting the possibility of death, the death of a nonviolent Pathan would draw "the poison of violence" that was destroying the Frontier to himself literally and symbolically. Following Rene Girard's influential *Violence and the Sacred*, his death would become an act that "trick(s)" violence into spending itself on the victim whose death will provoke no reprisals and save others.[71] But unlike Girard's notion, the nonviolent Pathan is not a ritualized scapegoat but a "self-chosen martyr" who chose to take up this burden with full awareness of the price he might have to pay in the name of purification and renewal. Far from pathological, death for a Muslim, especially a good death, is a return to the Origin and hence taken as a next step closer to the End of Time and the Almighty (Qur'an, XLV: 24–26).

The Innocents

When a terrorist decides to blow up an airplane or a crowded bazaar, it is understood that the tie between the targets and the reasons for hurting the targets has been severed. But more important, perhaps, is the terrorists' conception of the world on the other side, on the "enemy's side." Rantisi, a Hamas founder, answered the question about justification for killing innocent victims by redefining the situation as a war situation. But even in war, not unlike just war theory, there are Islamic injunctions which stipulate that non-combatants, or innocent members of that society such as women, children and the old, are not to be harmed. In fact, this is one of my basic arguments for the affirmation of nonviolent actions in Islam because modern warfare with its destructive technology has blurred the line separating "the enemies" from "innocent victims."[72] However, the world of terrorism is different. To justify such an indiscriminate act of terror, a redefined "world at war" is seen as a warring world without any innocents on the "enemy's side." This negative monolithic, and in a sense "essentialized" understanding of the others, renders violence against them easily justified and therefore highly probable.

My question is what does Islam say when one looks at the world and sees no innocents, especially on the other side? Would this inability to see innocents among "the others" be reflective of an impaired faith in God as all Merciful? In his sadness and anger because his people went astray, Moses prayed to God asking to be forgiven and: "Admit us to Thy mercy! For Thou art the Most Merciful. Of those who show mercy" (Qur'an, VII: 151). When Jacob's sons came to ask his permission to bring his youngest son, Benjamin, with them to collect grain, Jacob was sad and afraid the same fate might await Benjamin because he had lost his beloved son, Joseph, once before. Then he said: "But God is the best. To take care (of him), and He is the Most Merciful of those who show mercy!" (Qur'an, XII: 64). What these verses reflect, among other things, is the connection between God's Infinite Mercy and human's faith in it. Both Moses and Jacob could go on because they have faith in God's Mercy. If God's Mercy is Infinite, will it be possible to imagine a world where there is an absence of the innocents on the "other side" who would not, and will never receive God's Mercy? What would be the consequences of such a perspective on a Muslim's faith?

Here is perhaps where nonviolent action is most different from terrorism. In the oath taken by recruits to be a member of Badshah Khan's Khudai Khidmatgars (Servants of God), the Pathans have to pledge to refrain from violence and revenge; forgive those who oppress them or treat them with cruelty; refrain from taking part in feuds and quarrels, antisocial customs and practices; live a simple life; practice good manners; devote at least two hours a day to social work; and be fearless and prepare for any sacrifice. But most relevant to the present discussion is the very first pledge which says: "I am a Servant of God, and as God needs no service, but serving his creation is serving him, I promise to serve humanity in the name of God."[73]

There are three important issues significant to Muslim nonviolent action within this pledge. First, it reaffirms God's Omnipotence and therefore needs no human service to Him. Second, it celebrates God's Mercy by the way in which serving humanity becomes a surrogate to serving Him. Third, it underscores God's universal magnanimity by identifying the target of service as the "humanity," an inclusive category. This very last point is significant both theologically and historically. True, Qur'anic verses can be cited to support exclusivity and thereby used to justify violence against the others who have fallen outside the faith as evident from the opinions of those who condemn and justify terrorism discussed above. But the theological ground for Muslim nonviolent action rests on Words of God that are inclusive. God says in the Qur'an that killing a person, who does not kill others or cause mischief, is like killing the whole people, while "if any one saved a life, it would be as if he saved the life of the whole people" (V: 35).[74] The choice of action by Muslims, inspired or justified by the sacred text, is profoundly conducive both to the kinds of Muslim one wishes to become, and by extension the kinds of world Muslims seek to help create. Historically, Badshah Khan's Khudai Khidmatgars was different from the Maududi's *Jama'at-I-Islami* and Muhammad Ilyas' *Tablighi-Jama'at*. The Muslim nonviolent movement was non-sectarian since there were Hindus and Sikhs as members. It did not invite people to join the movement to improve themselves as good Muslims primarily but to fight the British colonizer. And it did not seek to recreate the local community on the basis of early Islamic example.[75] In this sense, I would argue that this Muslim nonviolent movement fought against the colonizer with nonviolence without impairing their faith in God's Omnipotence, Infinite Mercy and Universality.

Instrumental Logic as Dehumanization

On August 16, 1946, declared "direct action day" by Muhammad Ali Jinnah, communal violence erupted in India. In Calcutta, more than 6,000 Muslims and Hindus were killed while some 20,000 women and children were raped and maimed. Abdul Ghaffar Khan remarked: "I fail to understand how Islam can be served by setting fire to religious places and killing and looting innocent people."[76] I would argue that Islam cannot be served because the use of violence, in communal violence and especially in terrorism, is governed not only by the motives and desires of the perpetrators, but more importantly, by a specific kind of logic. The political theorist Hannah Arendt suggested some four decades ago that the very substance of violence is ruled by the "means-end category" where the end is always in danger of being overwhelmed by the means that it justifies. She clearly stated that "Violence, finally . . . is distinguished by its instrumental character."[77] This instrumental character means that violence in general, and terrorism in particular, is but a tool. Its instrumental character is best described by Mahmud al-Zahar, a Hamas leader in Gaza. Following the cessation of suicide attacks in October 1995, he announced that: "We must calculate the benefit and cost of continued armed operations. If we can fulfill our goals without violence, we will do so. Violence is a means, not a goal."[78] As a tool, it is governed by an instrumental logic. This instrumental logic depends more on the specific character of the tool than on the intention of users. For example, if one decides to use terror against the others, the nature of terrorism itself will dictate the way in which the act is to be carried out. Secrecy becomes part of the tool that would govern the user. Small and closed organization is another part of the tool that would make it possible to acquire the necessary C-4, for example. In other words, I would argue that it is the logic of the instrument that governs the users and the ways in which they perceive their targets. Although targets of terror can be conceptualized differently,[79] all share one thing in common: they have been turned into objects, at times through a complex dehumanization process which would make killing them easier.

This logic is markedly different from Muslim nonviolent action where the opponents remain distinctively humans. In fighting against injustice, the logic of nonviolence dictates that the user is willing to sacrifice oneself without harming the others who are the opponents precisely because they are humans.

A Khudai Khidmatgar nonviolent soldier, Khalam Khan from Nowshera, said in an interview:

> We were hit on several occasions but never hit back. I had sworn against violence. Badshah Khan had explained to us that we are waging a war against the British with non-violence and patience . . . and we believed in him and followed him. Once a British police officer asked me why we followed Badshah Khan. He said: 'Are you paid to do this?' I said, 'No, we even have to take dry bread from our own houses to sustain us, and then go with Badshah Khan to oust you from our country.' The officer patted me on the back.[80]

Turning humans into objects under the governing instrumental logic is also problematic from an Islamic point of view. Partaking in the most important article of faith, a Muslim believes that he/she is created by God, the Creator. God, the Creator, created humans with a purpose (Qur'an, II: 30), while mankind "can have nothing but what he strives for" and most importantly, "thy Lord is the final Goal" (Qur'an, LIII: 39–42). If God has His purpose, created humans for a purpose and they in turn have to strive by themselves with God Himself as the final goal, then to turn humans into objects is to rob them of their natures as the created with purpose. It also cuts the tie between humans and the pursuit of their final goal, which is God. In this sense, terrorism, and violence in general, which turns humans into objects, effectively creates a world where the created has no purpose and the purposeful tie to the Divine cut off. Instrumental logic governing the use of violence, therefore, profoundly contradicts the Islamic cosmos governed by Purpose of the Divine.

Conclusion: Transforming Terrorism?

Terrorism, as a form of political violence happens, because injustice exists at the local and sometimes global levels. In addition to addressing the structural causes that give rise to terrorism, it is important to transform it. I have argued that Muslim nonviolent action could serve as a platform for such transformation because of two important similarities: the imperative to fight injustice in the world and the willingness to die for a good cause. However, two profound differences do exist: the negation of the possibility of the innocents among the opponent and instrumental logic governing terror. From a Muslim's point of view, both the negation of the innocents on the other side and turning humans into objects cannot be supported by a profound philosophic understanding of Islam where God's Mercy is Infinite and the creation of the universe, especially mankind, is done with a Divine Purpose. Muslim nonviolent action as evident from the examples of the Khudai Khidmatgar, a case of Muslim nonviolent soldiers who fought valiantly against the British colonizer with nonviolence, provide a possible alternative where injustice can be corrected, self-sacrifice honored, and beliefs in God's Mercy and Divine Purpose not compromised. In this chapter, I have tried to understand terrorism as a rational phenomenon, discussed the ways in which it was both condemned and justified by those most directly involved with the act in order to suggest that transforming terrorism with Muslim nonviolent action is not merely wishful thinking. The possibility that Muslim nonviolent action could present itself as an alternative to terrorism is distinctive because profound similarities do exist and important differences could be overcome so that the Muslims' struggle for justice, based on critical Islamic understanding of the world, could continue.

Notes

1 Kevin Toolis, "Where suicide is a Cult," *The Observer*, December 16, 2001, quoted in Jonathan Barker, *The No-Nonsense Guide to Terrorism*, Oxford: New International and Verso, n.d., p. 11. Given the dates of some of the citations used in this highly useful book, I would say that it was published either in late 2002 or early 2003.
2 *Bangkok Post*, September 8, 2003.
3 *Bangkok Post*, September 9, 2003.
4 *Bangkok Post*, September 13, 2003.
5 The Pew Global Attitudes Project, *What the World Thinks in 2002: How Global Politics View their Lives, their Countries, their World, America*, Washington DC, 2002.
6 *Patterns of Global Terrorism 2002*, Washington DC: US Department of State, 2003.
7 Robert A. Pape, "The Strategic Logic of Suicide Terrorism,"*American Political Science Review*, vol. 97, no. 3, August 2003, pp. 343–361. The quote is on p. 344.
8 Avishai Margalit, "The Suicide Bombers,"*The New York Review of Books*, vol.I, no.1, January 16, 2003, p. 36.
9 *Bangkok Post*, September 12, 2003.
10 International Council on Human Rights Policy (ICHRP), *Human Rights After September 11*, Versoix, Switzerland: International Council on Human Rights Policy, 2002.
11 *Patterns of Global Terrorism 2000*, Washington DC: US Department of State, 2001, p. iii.
12 Richard Falk, *The Great Terror War*, New York: Olive Branch Press, 2003, p. xviii.
13 Barker, *The No-Nonsense Guide to Terrorism*, p. 23.
14 See for example the data on governments' killings of their own civilians in William Eckhardt, "Death by Courtesy of Governments, 1945–1990," *Peace Research*, vol. 24, no. 2, May 1992, pp. 51–56.
15 B.R. Nanda, *Mahatma Gandhi: A Biography*, Delhi: Oxford University Press, 1997, p. 284.
16 M.K. Gandhi, *Young India*, January 2, 1930.
17 Bhagwat Charan, "The Philosophy of the Bomb," in Walter Laqueur, *The Terrorism Reader: A Historical Anthology*, London: Wildwood House, 1979, pp. 137 and 139.
18 Ibid., p. 139.
19 Ibid.

20 Susan Sachs, "Punishing a Terrorist by Showing Him His Victim's Humanity," *New York Times.com*, April 6, 2002. Laura Blumenfeld's exploration of the many faces of vengeance is in her *Revenge: A Story of Hope*, New York: Simon & Schuster, 2002.
21 See Chaiwat Satha-Anand, "Understanding the Success of Terrorism," *Inter-Asia Cultural Studies*, vol. 3, no. 1, April 2002, pp. 157–159.
22 See, for example, Richard Falk, *The Great Terror War.*
23 It is interesting to note the militarized transformation of advanced democracies which are increasingly undertaking prolonged military operations that include counter-terrorism and peacekeeping. See an insightful study on the repositioning of the Israeli military in the policymaking process which resulted from its engagement in warfare and other forms of military operations against the Palestinians in Yoram Peri, *The Israeli Military and Israel's Palestinian Policy: From Oslo to the Al Aqsa Intifada*, Washington DC: United States Institute of Peace, 2002.
24 *Clarification of the Truth In Light of Terrorism, Hijackings & Suicide Bombings* and *An Advice To Usaamah Ibn Laaden from Shaykhul Islaam Ibn Baaz (died 1420 AH/1999 CE)*, Birmingham: Salafi Publications, October 2001. The inside cover indicated that it is translated into English by www.Fatwa-online.com, among others.
25 Called the "seceders" because they regarded the succession of caliphs after the Prophet's death as unlawful. They later became disillusioned with Ali, the Prophet's son-in-law who was the closest male relative and the fourth caliph, for his compromise that one of them, Ibn Muljam, assassinated Ali. See a brief description of *khawarij* in Malise Ruthven, *Islam: A Very Short Introduction*, Oxford and New York: Oxford University Press, 1997, p. 53; p. 59.
26 Ibid., pp. 2–3.
27 Ibid., n. 8, pp. 7–8.
28 Ibid., p. 4.
29 Ibid., pp. 12–13.
30 Ibid., pp. 14–15. It could certainly be argued that the ardent support many Islamic scholars have given to the rulers in the Saudi Arabia is a result of the specific historical context of symbiotic relationship between the state and religious establishment, beginning in the mid-eighteenth century between Muhammad ibn' Abd-al-Wahhab (1703–1781), a puritan reformer and Muhammad al-Sa'ud, a local ruler who ruled the area from 1745 to 1765. A useful, though brief, account of contesting sacred authority in Saudi Arabia is in Dale F. Eickelman and James Piscatori, *Muslim Politics*, Princeton, NJ: Princeton University Press, 1996, pp. 60–63. But here I am concentrated on the rationality of justifications for obedience given by the religious scholars.
31 Quoted in Bernard Lewis, *What Went Wrong?: The Clash Between Islam and Modernity in the Middle East*, New York: Perennial, 2002, pp. 107–108.
32 Cited in Nemat Guenena, *The 'Jihad': An 'Islamic Alternative' in Egypt* [Cairo Papers in Social Science, vol. 9, monograph 2, Summer 1986] Cairo: The American University in Cairo Press, 1986, p. 44.
33 Ibid.
34 Ibn Baaz, *Clarification of the Truth In Light of Terrorism, Hijackings & Suicide Bombings*, p. 17.
35 This is a modification of Barker's conclusion that "all terrorism is local." See Barker, *The No-Nonsense Guide to Terrorism*, p. 120. See also a report on the rise of "religious extremism" in South Asia and the Middle East which are consequences of the absence of democracy, the failure of governments to address social changes, and external support and the breakdown of *ijtihad* (independent interpretations of Islam under changing circumstances) within Islam itself, in Judy Barsalou, *Islamic Extremists: How Do They Mobilize Support?*, United States Institute of Peace Special Report 89, July 2003.
36 Ibn Baaz, *Clarification of the Truth In Light of Terrorism, Hijackings & Suicide Bombings*, p. 19.
37 Ibid., pp. 23–24. Al-Qur'an cited is from "An-Nisaa": "And do not kill yourselves. Surely, Allah is Most Merciful to you." (IV: 29). The Hadith cited from both Bukhari and

Muslim is the saying of the Prophet that "Indeed, whoever (intentionally) kills himself, then certainly he will be punished in the Fire of Hell, wherein he shall dwell forever."

38 Ibid., p. 20.
39 *The Glorious Qur'an*, translation and commentary by A. Yusuf Ali, n.p.: The Muslim Students' Association of the United States & Canada, 1977, p. 62.
40 Ibn Baaz, *Clarification of the Truth In Light of Terrorism, Hijackings & Suicide Bombings*, p. 21.
41 Ibid., p. 22, pp. 26–27.
42 Ibid., p. 26.
43 Quoted in Emmanuel Sivan, *Radical Islam: Medieval Theology and Modern Politics*, New Haven and London: Yale University Press, 1985, p. 128.
44 Mark Juergensmeyer, *Terror in the Mind of God: the Global Rise of Religious Violence*, Berkeley: University of California Press, 2000, pp. 67–68.
45 Ibid., p. 69.
46 Eyad Sarraj, "Why We have Turned into Suicide Bombers: Understanding Palestinian Terror," *Just Commentary*, no. 3, September 1997, pp. 1–2.
47 Juergensmeyer, *Terror in the Mind of God*, p. 73.
48 Ibid., p. 74.
49 Quoted in ibid., pp. 70–71.
50 Ibid., pp. 72–73.
51 Martha Brill Olcott and Bakhtiyar Babajanov, "The Terrorist Notebooks," in *Foreign Policy*, March/April 2003, p. 36. It is interesting to note the subtitle of this article which provocatively states: "During the mid-1990s, a group of young Uzbeks went to school to learn how to kill you. Here is what they were taught." (p. 30).
52 Ibid., p. 38. See also what some Evangelicals are trying to do in Muslim lands at present in David Van Biema, "Missionaries Under Cover: Growing numbers of Evangelicals are trying to spread Christianity in Muslim lands. But is this what the world needs now?," *Time*, June 30, 2003, pp. 51–58. It is interesting to note some of these missionaries' prayers. One prays that "the weapon of mass destruction, Islam, be torn down" (p. 52), while the other prays every early morning when he hears the muezzin's call the Muslims to prayer that "I pray against that call – that it would not affect their souls" (p. 53).
53 Barker, *The No-Nonsense Guide to Terrorism*, pp. 138–140. See also Jason Burke, *Al-Queda: Casting a Shadow of Terror*, London: I.B. Tauris, 2003, who argues that the basis for support of terrorism among some Muslims is the sympathy felt for the cause worldwide and therefore fighting against terrorism by killing individual leaders or stopping their financial activities is "ludicrous" and will do nothing to solve the problem.
54 Reuters' photograph in *Bangkok Post*, September 30, 1996.
55 I have discussed this issue in Chaiwat Satha-Anand, "Crossing the Enemy's Line: Helping the Others in Violent Situations Through Nonviolent Action," *Peace Research*, vol. 33, no. 2, November 2001.
56 Stephen Zunes, "Unarmed Insurrections against Authoritarian Governments in the Third World: a New Kind of Revolution,"*Third World Quarterly*, vol. 15, no. 3, 1994, pp. 403–426.
57 See Stephen Zunes, "Unarmed Resistance in the Middle East and North Africa," and Souad Dajani, "Nonviolent Resistance in the Occupied Territories: a Critical Reevaluation," in Stephen Zunes, Lester R. Kurtz and Sarah Beth Asher (eds), *Nonviolent Social Movements: a Geographical Perspective*, Malden, MA: Blackwell Publishers, 1999, pp. 39–74.
58 Chaiwat Satha-Anand, "Muslim Communal Nonviolent Actions: Minority Coexistence in a Non-Muslim Society," in Abdul Aziz Said and Meena Sharify-Funk, *Cultural Diversity and Islam*, Lanham, New York and Oxford: University Press of America, 2003, pp. 195–207.
59 Daniel L. Smith, "The Rewards of Allah,"*Journal of Peace Research*, vol. 26, no. 4, November 1989, pp. 385–398.
60 Mohammed Abu-Nimer, "A Framework for Nonviolence and Peacebuilding in Islam," *Journal of Law and Religion*, vol. XV, no. 1–2, 2000–2001, pp. 217–265. See also a highly

promising book on the subject: Mohammed Abu-Nimer, *Nonviolence and Peace Building in Islam: Theory and Practice*, Gainesville, FL: University of Florida Press, 2003.

61 Quoted in Mukulika Banerjee, *The Pathan Unarmed*, Karachi, New Delhi and Oxford: Oxford University Press, 2000, p. 60.

62 Ibid., p. 63.

63 Ibid., p. 62.

64 Geoffrey Ashe, *Gandhi*, New York: Stein and Day, 1969, p. 194.

65 Ibid., p. 114.

66 Ibid., pp. 84–91.

67 M. K. Gandhi, *Non-Violence in Peace & War*, vol. II, Ahmedabad: Navajivan Publishing House, 1949, p. 338.

68 Banerjee, *The Pathan Unarmed*, p. 151.

69 Ibid., p. 148.

70 John E. Seery, *Political Theory for Mortals: Shades of Justice, Images of Death*, Ithaca: Cornell University Press, 1996, p. 7 as quoted in Roxanne L. Euben, "Killing (for) Politics: Jihad, Martyrdom and Political Action," *Political Theory*, vol. 30, no. 1, February 2002, p. 8.

71 Rene Girard, *Violence and the Sacred*, by Patrick Gregory (trans.), Baltimore and London: The Johns Hopkins University Press, 1979, p. 36.

72 See Chaiwat Satha-Anand, "The Nonviolent Crescent: Eight Theses on Muslim Nonviolent Action," in Abdul Aziz Said, Nathan C. Funk and Ayse S. Kadayifci (eds), *Peace and Conflict Resolution in Islam: Precept and Practice*, Lanham, New York and Oxford: University Press of America, 2001, pp. 195–211.

73 Robert C. Johansen, "Radical Islam and Nonviolence: A Case Study of Religious Empowerment and Constraint Among Pashtuns,"*Journal of Peace Research*, vol. 34, no. 1, 1997, p. 59. It is interesting to note that there are different versions of these oaths. See a different version by the 86–year-old Sarfaraz Nazim, a member of the Khudai Khidmatgars, in Banerjee, *The Pathan Unarmed*, p. 74.

74 *The Glorious Qur'an*, translation and commentary by A. Yusuf Ali, p. 252. It should be noted that in other translations, this text appears in verse 32 and not 35. See, for example, *The Koran*, N.J. Dawood (trans.), London: Penguin Books, 1985, pp. 390–391.

75 Banerjee, *The Pathan Unarmed*, pp. 161–162.

76 N. Radhakrishnan, *Khan Abdul Ghaffar Khan: The Apostle of Nonviolence*, New Delhi: Gandhi Smriti and Darshan Samiti, 1998, pp. 31–35. The quote appears on p. 34.

77 Hannah Arendt, *On Violence*, New York: Harcourt, Brace & World, Inc., 1970, p. 46.

78 Quoted in Robert A. Pape, "The Strategic Logic of Suicide Terrorism," *American Political Science Review*, vol. 97, no. 3, August 2003, p. 348.

79 See for example Alex Schmid, "The Strategy of Terrorism: The Role of Identification." A report of a seminar in *Transforming Struggle: Strategy and the Global Experience of Nonviolent Direct Action*, Cambridge, MA: Program on Nonviolent Sanctions in Conflict and Defense, Center for International Affairs, Harvard University, 1992, p. 65.

80 Banerjee, *The Pathan Unarmed*, p. 122.

Part IV

Coexistence and Reconciliation

An Enduring Responsibility of the
Muslim *Ummah*

12 Within the Limits of Western Historical Boundaries

Mohammed Arkoun

Before I start to tackle the subject of Islamic synthesis, coexistence, reconciliation and the enduring responsibility of the Muslim *Ummah*, I feel the necessity to make the following statements.

First, we are going to use a vocabulary, a frame of thinking, understanding and interpreting, ways of arguing and demonstrating, as well as a historical space and time of knowledge mainly related to the European-American frame of thinking and conceptualizing values. Even when we consider other cultures and historical experiences, we still refer and rely on Western scholarship. This fact cannot be disputed. Muslim scholarship for Muslims might be the subject of a scholarly work, but it will never be quoted in a scientific work as a reliable source worthy of debate, praise or refutation, unless it is admitted by the academic authorities as satisfactory in its formal presentation and content. If I produce a piece of scholarship on any field or subject related to Arabic and Islamic studies, I must respect all the conditions of academic research fixed and controlled by the Western scientific community.

Second, there is no competing model for scholarship to be opposed to the established model for thought and knowledge since the eighteenth and nineteenth centuries in Europe and America. And we do not see any possibility for any model to be set and opposed successfully to what is being done in Islamic studies found in the West.

Third, it is a historical fact that the intellectual revolution achieved in Europe – since the first emergence of modernity in the sixteenth century up to our present day – has no equivalent in any other culture or tradition of thought in the world. I am not saying that this revolution is intrinsically good and intellectually indisputable; on the contrary, by its own founding principles, it requires a continuous critical debate. But the fact remains that no refutation from other cultures and systems of thought has succeeded in dismissing the operative value of the intellectual and epistemological shift achieved in Europe through substituting the supremacy of philosophical and scientific reason for the Medieval supremacy of religious theological reason.

Fourth, Islam as a tradition of thinking is ignored totally and a large majority of Muslims are still rejecting the building process and the main intellectual and scientific revolutions carried on by modernity. The intellectual field represented by Greek philosophy in the classical Islam has been eliminated and deleted from the programs of research and teaching since the death of Ibn Rushd (1198). It is not the place here to elaborate a clear distinction between the *Ishraqi* "philosophy" developed in Iran after Ibn Rushd and the philosophical attitude developed in Europe since the thirteenth century.

Fifth, for these reasons, we need to locate our epistemological posture in order to attempt any kind of Islamic synthesis. Presenting an Islamic synthesis without regard for the scientific results achieved by Western scholarship in this field might please traditional Muslims who are unaware of scientific debates on criteria of valid and invalid scholarship. If, however, we intend to maintain standards of scientific inquiry, the search for a genuinely new Islamic synthesis will remain at most a subject of research on the use of scientific criteria by contemporary Muslims.

Approaches to Islamic Synthesis

The general title of this conference as well as the subtitle proposed to me raise several questions that need to be clarified from the start.[1] Every title introduces implicitly and/or explicitly assumptions, postulates, goals to be reached and tasks to be achieved. The expression "Islamic synthesis" is not currently used; it is the first time I face the necessity to react to. Similarly, the words coexistence and reconciliation refer us clearly to the ongoing dramatic conflicts between what I refuse to call, as every one does Islam and the West. Is it really a matter for coexistence and reconciliation, or rather a historical necessity to change the grounds of all our discourses and to search for an intellectual paradigm more appropriate, more efficient to undertake the real work imposed on the present generation by the breakdown of all systems of thought and values, all the inherited cultural codes and political institutions, including the most advanced democratic regimes? The intellectual and cultural upheaval generated by the most significant events in the world since 1945 is not yet fully taken into consideration by those disciplines – social, political, human sciences – on which we put all our hopes, confidence, and expectations in order to interpret the world as well as enlighten the ways we follow which produce our historical existence.

Before we come to the problems related to coexistence and reconciliation, let us discuss the conditions of possibility to produce an Islamic synthesis. We shall start with two statements by the French archbishop Georges Gilson who declared the following about the famous *Concilium* Vatican II:

> Ce sont les événements du monde qui ont bousculé l'itinéraire tracé entre 1961–65 ... Une meilleure intelligence des textes et un meilleur travail des documents nous auraient mieux aidés à assumer les provocations des temps modernes.
>
> It is the world events that hustled the itinerary traced from 1961–65 ... A better understanding of the [holy] texts and a better working out of the documents would have helped us much better to assume the provocations of the modern times.

The situation thus described for Catholicism in the sixties shows how even that strong branch of Christianity remained reluctant, resistant to any serious integration of the most indisputable intellectual conquests of Modern Thought. The new synthesis elaborated, defended and applied since Vatican II (1965) has not yet totally delivered orthodox theology from its cautious use – if not rejection – of modern reason to resolve problems of knowledge, especially when religious truth is at stake. Surely, the historicity of holy texts is more or less accepted thanks to major progress made by great historians in the religious field. But still, religious personalities like G. Gilson have to constantly call for a "better" understanding, which means a more audacious acceptance of the epistemological principles taught by discourse analysis.

We need to keep this example in mind when we want to consider the ambitious task of a contemporary Islamic synthesis (CIS). More generally, it is vital for the case of Islam, to draw all the consequences of the undeniable fact we are witnessing in everyday life: namely, the radical transformation, disintegration, and recomposition process affecting every living religion since 1945. The previous impacts of global history on the itinerary of each religion are much less radical than those we are experiencing with terrorism in the name of God combined with nationalist ideologies, struggles for local identities, and the totalitarian domination of a large number of postcolonial states.

These remarks are not sufficient to protect us from the illusion that we can offer today an Islamic synthesis without looking to the *dialectical tensions* between *historicity* and all religions (not only since the intervention of modernity, but as soon as the founders of religions started to announce their teachings). This means that for Islam, we have to follow the development of such tensions from the first articulation of the first verses of what became the Qur'an during the life of Muhammad and what I call the Official Closed corpus after his death. If we examine further the expression CIS we discover that it suggests several interpretations.

It can mean a global vision stemming from the contemporary context on Islam as an important historical force commanding the evolution of many societies and nations-states through the present world. Or it can also mean the historical shift from what I call the *Qur'anic phenomenon* to the *Islamic fact*. I shall come back later to these two important concepts to illustrate what I have in mind when I refer to historical shift. Before this we have to decide if we want to reproduce the traditional version of Islam as the "true religion" (*din al-haqq*) as bequeathed and developed by the "Pious Ancestors" (*al-salaf al-salih*), or integrate the methodologies, the problematizations and all the positive conclusions of modern scholarship currently discussed, revised, and revisited to reach a consensus among the scientific community. However, the option is not between one or several cognitive postures against others. We know that modern attitude considers carefully all the positions, schools, interpretations, and productions coming from the tradition: the reverse is still far from being the rule. Actually, we are not facing an optional situation, but rather the existing pressing necessity to move ahead with modern critical approaches to give to the tradition all its rights to express itself; especially without giving up any rights towards free thinking and criticism.

The modern cognitive posture does not oppose any more mythological knowledge to positive, critical historical, anthropological, linguistic knowledge. Myth and mythologies are totally integrated as fields of historical display, manifestations and productions. They are and should be studied as historical forces contributing to the shaping process of global history. Insofar as religious discourses and texts have a strong mythical dimension, they cannot be insulated from the debates on their cognitive status compared to other forms and levels of discourse and writing. In other words, the status of religious truth and even more of the "true religion" cannot be left to the exclusive control and protection of the jurist-theologian with his traditional claim to infallibility.

On these understandings, if we are asked to attempt to define CIS, we need to enlarge our vision and consider Islam as:

1) a religion with a system of beliefs and non-beliefs that has a strict ritual expression of these beliefs and non-beliefs;

2) an intellectual cultural frame of perception, interpretation and scientific building process of knowledge;

3) a number of sociological fractions (*firaq*), called heterodox sects opposed to the only one Community linked to the orthodox understanding and practice of every canonical obligation (*fard*);

4) a common cultural frame interacting with a large number of local, regional, national, ethnic, linguistic cultures existing through the world for a long time before the intervention of the Islamic impact;

5) a historical process diversified according to the determinant factors commanding the evolution of each group, society, and nation;

6) a common collective memory covering, interacting with, giving and receiving from a great number of less expanding, but very alive local, limited collective memories; and

7) a strong common social, political imaginary encompassing, mobilizing, and comprising several local social imaginaries as we have witnessed since the Iranian so-called Islamic revolution.

One who would be able to cover in one work such a synthesis would be simultaneously both a *scholar* (*chercheur* in French) and a few critical *thinker* (*penseur* in French). I link the two concepts with a dash, *chercheur-penseur*, for each concept he chooses to elaborate, each expression or statement he articulates, and, *a fortiori*, each attempt to propose a theoretical approach to any domain of reality. In other words, there are two ways to achieve a CIS: the way of a Muslim intellectual using his traditional knowledge to reactivate, revivify the "orthodox," original, authentic faith bequeathed by the Qur'an, the prophet and various imams presented as the founders of classical schools; or the way of the *chercheur-penseur* aiming a radical critical rethinking not only of the religious spiritual legacy of Islamic tradition, but also the reassessment of the cognitive status and the functions of the religious phenomenon as a whole in the historical emancipation of the human condition. The first option is well represented by the works of two major Muslim thinkers: al-Ghazali (d. 1111) in his *Revivification of Religious Sciences* (*Ihya' 'ulum al-din*) and Muhammad Baqir Majlisi (d. 1700) in his encyclopedia, *The Seas of Flowers* (*Bihar al-anwar*). The second option is just beginning to emerge with some innovative *chercheurs-penseurs*. So far, I do not know of any one essay in Arabic or Persian considering the study of the religious phenomenon on the basis of a comparative historical and anthropological exploration of several religions. The theological definition of Islam as the true religion (*din al-haqq*) agreed by God for all mankind is always maintained as the ultimate frame of reference when other religions are considered. The comparative approach would give priority to the concepts and practices shared by all religions such as the building process of the living tradition, the ritual expressions of the canonical beliefs and non-beliefs, the sacred and sacralization, the sainthood and the sanctification, the mythical narratives and mythologization, the transcendence and transcendentalization, the eschatological hope, the attitudes before life, death, love, justice, polity, sexuality, male and female, human person, cosmos, nature and so on. No concession should be allowed to apologetic statements, or dogmatic theological definitions used as indisputable divine statements superseding historical, anthropological, psychological, linguistic or sociological facts.

I do not minimize the importance of the ongoing debates about the relevance, the objections, and the difficulties of the second option applied to religious matters. But the more the debates are repeated, intensively and meticulously, the more the results are encouraging and reliable. There are some significant contributions of religious thinkers to these approaches and debates in Catholic and Protestant communities recently converted to modern scientific methodologies and epistemological postures of mind. This does not mean that they are totally liberated from the impact of theological "orthodox" principles and beliefs. Nevertheless, apart from those that share a common fundamentalist attitude, everyone can notice an intellectual and scientific gap between Muslims, Jews and Christians, not to speak of Hindus and Buddhists, in every international conference or seminar on inter-religious dialogue. The gap is historical more than doctrinal, because Western European Christians had to cope since the sixteenth century with the philological historicist reading of the Bible and other Greek and Latin ancient texts referring to non-monotheist systems of thought and beliefs. Islam ignored and still rejects such intellectual and cultural experiences; for various reasons, the majority of Muslims remain cut off from the Western modern scholarship even in Islamic studies. This attitude points to the necessity to introduce a contemporary Islamic synthesis with a long chapter on the continuous regressive historical process of the intellectual field in Islamic Thought and culture since the thirteenth and fourteenth centuries. This regression is even more visible and damaging since contemporary nationalist movements and postcolonial states have confiscated the symbolic functions of religion for their ideological vision of so-called national identities, programs for liberation and relation to modernity. The research on as well as the writing and the teaching of this intellectual history to serve the position I am defending is not yet on the agenda of scholars, teachers, not to speak of the *ulama* who are all too often devoted to the service of the official Islam and/or the new imaginary expressions of populist Islam.

Since the sequence of events *"from Manhattan to Baghdad,"*[2] one feels more compelled to undertake the tasks required for a contemporary Islamic synthesis. The tragic events of 9/11 and the conquest of Iraq have blurred – if not dismantled – all

220   *Mohammed Arkoun*

discourses on legitimacy, the religious ones as well as the modern democratic attempts to legitimize a *"just war"* for the protection of insuperable "Western" values. Highly praised intellectuals in the US took part in the debate and defended the legitimacy and the vital necessity to fight a *just war* against terrorist nihilism. Muslims who are the objects of this debate have chosen either to remain silent, or to reaffirm the superiority of Islam as a religion and a civilization, or to extend the terrorist "solution" to several Muslim societies. On both sides (Western and Muslim), a discourse remains terribly absent while the conquering legitimizing discourse and subsequent action (terrorism vs. just war) are daily confirmed by the political decision-makers and their supporters in civil societies.

This missing discourse could be articulated by a *charismatic*[3] political voice on either side of the ongoing conflict. Such a discourse is present in the minds of many citizens who are concerned by the urgent necessity for hope, truth and solidarity to a world polity; however, there are two conditions which allow such a discourse not to be heard, read, and debated. The first condition refers to the fact that currently no one political regime in the present geopolitical map is eligible to be a charismatic voice for his people as well as for the contemporary world consciousness. This means that we all suffer from a deep crisis of political thought itself generated by a crisis of reason (for the historical genesis of this crisis in Europe see J. W. Burrow's *The Crisis of Reason: European Thought, 1848–1914*).[4] Philosophers have identified the positive and negative contributions of that crisis to what they call the superseding effectiveness of the *teletechnoscientific reason* over the critical philosophical reason. The experimental, empirical, and instrumental applied sciences in the domains of telecommunications, technology and biology are confiscated by the *will to power* of some hegemonic political regimes described as the unique defenders of democratic values. This is indeed the supreme debate opened for the whole world in new political terms after the fall of the Berlin wall and the building of a new wall in the Holy Land to which Jews, Christians and Muslims have been referring with a violent, mimetic rivalry for more than 2000 years.

If the semantic disorder expanding all over the world is not reversed, there will be no way for any kind of religious or modern secularized (*laic*) synthesis. Reason will remain trapped in the service of the double criteria discourse used since Machiavelli and Ibn Khaldun converged in recognizing that *Realpolitik* always gives priority to *Machtpolitik*, to the "will to power." Meanwhile the quest for meaning will be relegated to the "managers of the sacred," the intellectuals, the artists and the academic authorities. Since 9/11, this realistic "philosophy" has been elevated to the level of orthodoxy for the sake of mankind's protection and ultimate Salvation. Is there any place, any chance left for coexistence and reconciliation between cultures, civilizations, religions in such a mythohistorical context?

Changing the Historical Paradigm?

It is clear after these introductive observations on CIS that we cannot just call people to coexistence and reconciliation. We need to examine the concrete conditions in which peaceful coexistence is not only possible, but is also open to a dynamic creative exchange and sense of solidarity in order to build a common future. Similarly, asking for or dreaming of reconciliation after a devastating event appears to be an impossible initiative. For who would be the partners of such reconciliation and what would be the themes and the perspectives of the reconciliation? Is it possible to reconcile fundamentalist Muslims with the principles of a secular democracy? Can one argue intellectually, spiritually, historically, politically that the "true," "authentic," "original" Islam has nothing in common with the Islam defended by fundamentalist movements? All this vocabulary belongs to the traditional religious and ethical sermons. I know that this rhetoric is still alive not only in synagogues, churches and mosques, but also in the political discourse of the most powerful decision-makers. This is what Robert Kagan, a vibrant republican militant, calls the discourse of double criteria: the definite option for *Real* and *Machtpolitik* is and has to be veiled with a warm, convincing "humanist" discourse using either spiritual religious references, or secular democratic values, or a skilful mixture of both. Bringing democracy to Iraqi people, delivering millions of oppressed people from a monstrous dictator is undeniably a noble and desired goal; but the human price to be paid for this action cannot be evaluated just by a brain trust of political and military leaders more or less enlightened by some "elected" political scientists. We cannot deny that the present world is dangerous: rogue states have multiplied since 1945 and terrorism is a threat to every person in our small and closed planet. We also have to add to these absolute horrors that the answers, the options, and the so-called solutions given so far add even more threats, horrors, despair, uncertainty, rage, rejection, revolt, and structural violence – not just for the internal policy of a nation, but for the human condition as a whole.

I have mentioned the crisis of reason in its European-American trajectory. I have never used this expression to oppose it by insisting, as millions of Muslims obsessively do, that Islamic reason remains healthy, well rooted in the divine Law, and ready to offer a unique reliable alternative to the failure of Western reason. I describe this discourse as a *mythoideology*. I used this concept to philosophically critique reason in its Western historical itinerary in my book, *Critique of Islamic Reason* (Paris, 1984); therefore, I shall not repeat here a long and complex inquiry.[5] However, I shall defend the following vision of a new historical paradigm.[6]

The most striking phenomenon after 9/11 is the resurgence of the medieval vocabulary as articulated through the mouth of G. W. Bush. Undoubtedly, this discourse reached the American imaginary about values, good and evil, just war and the right to self-protection, just punishment of aggressors, innocent and guilty persons, communities, peoples, etc. Although several sociologists have stated that it expresses the return of religion, I would like to argue that it translates rather into the persistence of the traditional frame of perception, interpretation and representation, despite the scientific knowledge accumulated and taught in the West since the eighteenth and nineteenth centuries. A culture of disbelief is also very prevalent in dominant media, at schools, and in daily life. With tragic events like 9/11, the traditional "values" can easily be reactivated and mixed with this culture of disbelief. Outside the West, cultures remain under the semantic and symbolic impact of a religious system of representation, interpretation, expression and judgement. Even intellectually trained "elites" share this loose, spontaneous, simplistic instrumentalization of religiosity and fragmented secularized culture. Just like humans use disposable material objects in their daily life, so too are societies being more or less converted to disposable ideas, impressions, images, interpretations, values, and thoughts. Such structural forces are constraining not only for individual behaviour, but also for human thinking and engaged citizenship (i.e., political and ethical responsibilities).

Contemporary societies in the West as well as in the rest of the world do not need more than empirical, pragmatic reasoning to solve the immediate daily problems. This is to say that modern culture and thought limit their expression to the entertaining form imposed by TV mass culture. The critical posture of mind, theoretical debates on events like 9/11, or the conquest of Iraq, the Palestinian-Israeli conflict, the Algerian civil war, the history of Indonesia or China, the relation between Qur'anic and Biblical discourse, the philosophical, theological, anthropological, sociological, political regimes of truth – the rational procedures, the methodologies, the epistemological postulates used to articulate a discourse on truth – all these essential matters of enlightening knowledge are just put aside, neglected, or simplified in such a way that they lose all intellectual significance and philosophical impact.

These are the actual conditions in which societies produce their history; the teaching of that history does necessarily and clearly unveil to the successive generations the true effective roles of all the actors, the real motivations of the most important events, the concrete stakes assigned to a war, the limits and the eventual subversive substance of a literary, artistic, philosophical work or school, and so on. For centuries, historians have selected some heroes, saints, leaders, events, "representative" works, schools of thought or artistic creativity to build a glorifying picture and a rich, sumptuous memory of the national or religious community. Programs of historical teaching at school, sometimes for some subjects in universities, are, in fact, reduced to a mythohistorical presentation officially called "history." Religious collective memories are then also built with the same selective, expanding, glorifying, symbolizing, mythologizing, literarizing tools and styles. The modern study of all historiographical traditions shows that all cultures share the same model of historical action and translation of *lived history* into represented, amplified, mythologized, and overvalued as well as glorified past. Historians started in the 1930s only to write the archaeological history of that historiography encapsulated in a political-theological or metaphysical frame of thinking. Classical Islamic historiography started to be explored with philological and historicist method by Orientalists in the nineteenth century; but it is only recently that it has submitted to the new multidisciplinary approaches and the genealogical archaeological methodologies. Still, we notice how several obstacles and political religious forces are preventing the Western production in this important field from being spread, read, taught and debated in many Muslim contexts.

It will take a long time to get out from this common traditional, deeply rooted model of historical action preserved and approved by the institutions of research and learning itself. I call this phenomenon *institutionalized ignorance*. Professors, teachers, religious authorities teach and transmit ignorance under the cover of scientific disciplines. I say this out of my experience as a professor who received at the Sorbonne and in many other universities worldwide, generations of students coming from several Muslim and European countries. The levels of Westerners and Muslims are of course different; but their fields and aspects of ignorance are shared by all.

How do we shift in these conditions to what I call the new historical paradigm? Like the persistent described model, the new paradigm will be the product of an historical building process. The context of globalization should foster the process and facilitate the intellectual, cultural and scholarly programs of research and teaching. In particular, the focus would be on the fault lines, the differences, the discrepancies, the frontal oppositions, the systems of truth, beliefs and non-beliefs identified as the key points, the crucial themes, the permanent sources of the recurrent conflicts between nations and communities, smaller groups and collective memories inside each society. Well-trained and strongly motivated actors selected from all over the word by an international *ad hoc* institution would be committed to initiate a new historical process to build up a worldwide-oriented history in a common effort based on an intangible solidarity between states, civil societies and peoples, regardless of their demographic, economic and political dimension, and of their religious, philosophical, cultural and political belonging. This project would require, of course, international negotiations and the contributions of NGOs, official organizations like UNESCO, the European Union, great American foundations, as well as private and public universities. I know there are several initiatives working in the line I am tracing; but the intellectual conditions and philosophical vision attached to the new paradigm are not yet clearly defended and efficiently promoted.

Before I end this chapter, I would like to comment briefly, as I promised, on the two mentioned concepts: Qur'anic phenomenon and Islamic fact. If we keep thinking, assessing, evaluating, and interpreting in the "orthodox" Islamic frame of dogmatic beliefs and non-beliefs, we shall equate the Qur'an with Islam and contend that Islam is ideally the full implementation of the Qur'anic teachings. We observe an interesting example of this postulated equivalence in the contemporary fundamentalist discourse: the word Islam has practically usurped the status, the place and the functions of Allah in the Qur'an. For instance, while "Allah" is mentioned 2,697 times in the Qur'an (fulfilling all the grammatical functions which will become theological substantive actions and attributes), "Islam" is used only seven times.[7] This contrast is very striking when we read the contemporary Muslim literature reflected also in the Western studies on Islam. Why? "Islam" is everywhere in the same grammatical functions of "Allah" in the Qur'an and is received and interiorized as the accurate transposition of Allah's actions. Consequently, one can say that Allah is reified and made immanent, reachable by anyone under the name of Islam. This shift has of course enormous theological consequences not yet evaluated in Contemporary Islamic Thought.

With the expression the "Qur'anic phenomenon," I am aiming at the necessity to develop for the first time in Islamic Thought a strict phenomenological reading of the whole discourse. This means as I have shown in my *Lectures du Coran* (first published in 1982) that we must start from a linguistic, semiotic discourse analysis of the whole text and continue with a historical anthropology of what I call the prophetic discourse.[8] It is only after these explorations that an attempt of theological interpretation becomes methodologically and epistemologically legitimate. Unfortunately, the whole tradition has done the exact reverse since the first instrumentalization by theologians and jurists of the normative texts finally received as the *uncreated* Word of God.

The Islamic fact has a totally different status. I say *fact* not phenomenon because Islam is the result of a continuous historical and social construction of human actors; it is a series of political, intellectual, cultural, economic, and juridical *faits accomplis* given to be perceived, interpreted, lived, as well as interiorized by the believers as the accurate, authentic, indisputable translation for all ritual, ethical, juridical rules and institutions, not to forget the divine commandments and prohibitions (*awamir wa nawahi*), or, as the Qur'an puts it, the *"limits traced by Allah"* (*hudud Allah*). Islam then as a strictly human product is entirely subjected to historicity and, like any other religious fact, it belongs to the field of study of social and human sciences.

There is an objection to this clear-cut distinction: the Qur'anic phenomenon is also the subject of social and human sciences in its material manifestations as an oral discourse enunciated by Muhammad, written down and collected afterwards in an Official Closed Corpus, read liturgically and interpreted by the interpreting communities, and so on. The irreducible difference between the Qur'anic phenomenon and the Islamic fact is that the Qur'anic discourse raises by its grammatical and semiotic structure, problems the social sciences describe yet cannot interpret as theologians and jurists followed by millions of believers currently do. A difficulty remains for social sciences: how to interpret the link between Qur'anic, Biblical, and Gospel *phenomena* and the Jewish, Christian, and Islamic *facts*? What I call the link is named "faith," or "believing" by theologians. Research on the cognitive status and functions of "faith" and believing as anthropological categories are left mainly to theologians who are then dismissed as non-scientists by academic secular "authorities." This is a pending issue for both theologians and modern academic thought.

This short survey on two key concepts shows the pending difficulties neglected and left to the orthodox answers of religious authorities or to the anarchic, irresponsible manipulations by all types of social actors. This situation confirms the urgent necessity to mobilize all available human resources to get out from the illusionary historical models followed during centuries and inaugurate a more emancipating historical paradigm. Just after 9/11, I developed at the Library of Congress the idea to transform the revelatory dimensions of a tragic *event* into the *advent* of a politics of hope for billions of peoples struggling desperately for their survival.

Postscript: After the Conference

To comply with the will of the organizers, I wrote this text before meeting with the other authors in Alexandria. I knew that I would not just read it as it is formulated; I had not only to improvise my presentation, but also to delete practically all the reasoning and the posture of mind proposed in the written text. This happens systematically in all the international conferences, the seminars, and the think-tanks I have kept attending throughout the world for almost forty years. I started during the Algerian war of liberation (1954–1962) when I was a student in Paris to develop a personal critical approach to Islam, as a religion and frame of thinking, and as an Arabic logosphere and culture. I refused already to mix the ideological militant discourse of colonial victimization with the scientific analytical critical elaboration of a reliable operative knowledge on the vast Islamic and Arabic logosphere field of reality. I coined the concepts of "discourse of victimization" and "ideology of struggle" to recognize the historical legitimacy of ways that colonized countries use these tools for political liberation. At the same time I have refused to neglect the intellectual obligation to control the limits of these tools. I have focused on their danger for the freedom of expression and for scholarly search and criticism on a wide variety of matters concerning the building process of the nation-state in Islamic contexts. In particular, I have concentrated on issues related to Islam as a system of beliefs and non-beliefs. In doing so, I look at a variety of factors: the dogmatic and mythohistorical construction by social actors of what is called with uncritical vener-ation faith (*iman*), the canonically founding Islamic Tradition, the divine Law (*shari'ah*), the pious ancestors (*al-salaf al-salih*), and the orthodox observance. All of these factors have led up to today's Islamic fundamentalist ritualistic dogma and identity.

Forty years later, I discovered in Alexandria the intellectual struggle between ideological militancy and the intellectual commitment to freedom of thought, of religion, of expression, of critical knowledge applied to religion and politics in all contemporary Islamic contexts. My attempt to problematize several decisive concepts used in the title of the conference – Islamic synthesis, coexistence and reconciliation, enduring responsibility, Muslim *Ummah* – generated more misunder-standings, resistance, and intellectual reluctance than the immediate sharing of an engaging program of research and thinking with fully shared historical solidarity. We need not only to reach a more relevant and updated knowledge of the deepening historical gaps between the so-called West and the rest of the world – including the so-called Muslim world – but also to examine together with Western scholars, thinkers, and political and religious decision-makers, the conditions required from each citizen of the new coming worldwide space of citizenship, to contribute to the building process of a new common thinking aiming at the elaboration of a new international law based on a more emancipating ethical philosophy. This program is defended by some isolated forerunners in several disciplines and domains of emanci-pation; but regressive forces, wills to power, uncertain economy, and fragile weakened states are generating more obstacles on the way towards building histor-ical solidarity and binding responsibilities. As a result, we witness deepening gaps between peoples, civil societies and polities.

We witnessed in Alexandria one of the most recurrent obstacles that break any momentum towards a more effective intellectual and epistemological communica-tion in the practice of human and social sciences. What I called the unthinkable and the unthought in contemporary Islamic thought affects also the use made of Western thought by scholars who are supposed to master the historical differences between archaic, premodern, modern, post-modern, meta-modern postures of reason and types of rationality. There are scholars who cannot grasp the difference between discourse analysis according to the most recent linguistic, semiotic and literary criticism and the medieval exegesis based on what was called *fiqh al-lugha*, a science between lexicography and philology. Another confusion that breaks relevant communication is the confusion between the positivist historicism and philologism dominant in historical writing and interpretation during the nineteenth century up to 1950, versus positive historicity as a historical and philosophical concept. During the discussions following the presentations, we had several illustrations of these epistemological and methodological ruptures between what I call classical modernity (1680–1940) and the emerging reason after a short-lived post-modernity. After 9/11, the gaps became clear-cut ideological frontiers not only between the two constructed poles "Islam" and the "West," but also inside each one of the two conflicting blocks. We all entered into regressive, imaginary systems of mutual exclusion.

Notes

1   I was asked by the organizers of the conference at the Library of Alexandria to address the following questions: How can an Islamic synthesis for today be derived from the diversity of Islamic interpretations and cultures? Can this synthesis establish common ground between Islam and the West without compromising core Islamic principles? How can the conception of Muslims as a "Middle People" be applied to efforts to resolve cultural and ideological conflicts within Islamic societies?

2   This is the title of a book I have published with Joseph Maïla in French (Paris: Desclée de Brouwer, 2003). The subtitle of the book *Beyond Good and Evil* is as challenging intellectually as the main title.

3   The concept of charisma (from Greek grace, favour, has been worked out by Max Weber with reference to the Christian theological status of exceptional persons gifted with supernatural qualities and powerful impact on other people.

4   J. W. Burrow, *The Crisis of Reason: European Thought, 1848–1914*, New Haven, CT: Yale University Press, 2000.

5   If interested in a prolonged conversation of this topic see my recent and even more radically critical book, *The Unthought in Contemporary Islamic Thought*, London: Saqi Books, 2002.

6   I use the term "paradigm" not in the sense of a rigid, dogmatic model, but in its Greek etymological meaning: to show an outstandingly clear and typical example.

7   See my article on "Islam" in the *Encyclopaedia of the Qur'an*, J. D. McAuliffe (ed.), Leiden, Netherlands: Brill Publishers, 2005.

8   See chapter 2 in my latest book, *The Unthought in Contemporary Islamic Thought*.

13 Pluralism, Coexistence and Religious Harmony in Southeast Asia

Indonesian Experience in the "Middle Path"

Azyumardi Azra

> *Ummatan wasatan* [middle people, by extension middle path] has been the paradigm adopted to establish a new image of Islam and the Muslim world . . . This trend of searching for a moderate and quality oriented ummah has been implemented by Southeast Asian Muslims for decades . . . [1]

> And if your Lord had willed, whoever is in the earth would have believed, all of them, all together. Would you [O Muhammad] then constrain the people, until they are believers.
>
> (Qur'an, 10:99)

Islamic revelation presents a theology that resonates with the modern pluralistic belief that other faiths are not merely inferior manifestations of religiosity, but variant forms of individual and communal responses to the presence of the transcendence in human life. All persons are created in the divine nature (*fitrat Allah*), with a disposition that leads to the knowledge of God, the Creator, to whom worship is due simply because of the creation.[2]

The September 11th, 2001 tragedy in the United States has brought the world to seemingly endless conflicts. The American military operation in Afghanistan, followed by its war against terrorism, and later its military campaign in Iraq has cornered Islam and Muslims in particular into a dark place. Even though the "neo-con" regime in Washington, DC has tried to distinguish radical elements among Muslims from that of the moderate, tolerant and peaceful majority of the Muslim believers, many in the world (both Muslims and non-Muslims alike) feel that currently there is a significant increase of conflict between Islam and the West.

In light of this growing fact, there is an urgent need not only for a better mutual understanding among people in the world, but also for reconciliation among peoples and cultures. For that purpose there should be sincere efforts among concerned people of the world to create a synthesis that would be able to forge peace at a variety of social levels: international, regional, and national. One of the syntheses would be the recognition of social, cultural, and religious pluralism among peoples and nations.

According to Muslim traditions, there are many principles and practices within the religion of Islam that basically recognize pluralism among peoples and nations.

However, the search for authenticity among some Muslims has led to the rise of exclusivist religious literalism and radicalism. The proponents of such a narrow interpretation of Islam even believe that there is only "one" Islam, a monolithic Islam upholding the belief that different interpretations of Islam have corrupted Islam and weakened Muslims *vis-à-vis* the West.

From a Southeast Asian – and particularly Indonesian – perspective, Muslims have long adhered to the Islamic paradigm of a "middle path" (*Ummah wasat*). In the political field, this "middle path" has been translated into the adoption of the national ideology of the *Pancasila* ("five principles"). The Pancasila, adopted during the proclamation of Indonesian independence on August 17, 1945, has been (and still is) the common platform among peoples of different religious, social, and cultural backgrounds in Indonesia. This chapter attempts to discuss the subject of "pluralism" as it relates to basic Islamic precepts and to Indonesian Islamic experiences of the middle path.

Pluralism and Endless Religious Conflicts

The term "pluralism" is increasingly becoming one of the most important catchwords in the era of globalization. As Abdulaziz Sachedina argues, pluralism in our present world inspires both exhilaration as manifested in the endless creations of human expression and exhaustion as experienced through the seemingly irreconcilable conflicts amongst the followers of different religious traditions. The invocation of pluralism has become much as a summons as a celebration; an urgent exhortation to the citizens of the world to come to terms with their increasing diversity.[3]

It is unfortunate that in addition to endless political conflicts among nations, the world continues to see the seemingly endless conflicts between Christians and Muslims, Hindus and Sikhs, Tamils and Buddhists. Worse still, religious conflicts have taken place among followers of one single religious tradition; between Sunnis and Shias or even among Sunnis within Islam; between Catholics and Protestants; among Hindus, and the like.

All of these hard realities have imparted the urgent need for better recognition and management of religious pluralism. One of the main reasons for the recognition of religious pluralism among the followers of different religious traditions is the promise and attitude of inclusivity. Such an inclusiveness, not exclusiveness, would enhance accommodation, not conflict, amongst competing claims to religious truth in religiously and culturally heterogeneous societies. It also would lead to multiple and unique possibilities for enriching the human quest for spiritual and moral well-being.

As pointed out by Sachedina, recognition of religious pluralism appeals for an active engagement with the religious other not simply to tolerate, but to understand. Toleration does not require an active engagement with the other; it makes no inroads on mutual ignorance. In a world in which religious differences historically have been manipulated to burn bridges between communities, recognition and understanding of religious differences require all the believers to enter into knowledgeable dialogue with one another, even in the face of major disagreements. A morally and spiritually earnest search for common undertakings within any particular religious tradition can lead to transforming societal identities from ethnocentric interests to ethnorelative understandings. Religious pluralism then can function as a working paradigm for a democratic, social pluralism in which people of diverse religious backgrounds are willing to form a community of global citizens.[4]

With respect to Sachedina's argument above, Khalil Masud is right when he states that pluralism is a part of the project of modernity that favors the freedom of individual.[5] According to Masud, pluralism does not stress multiplicity *per se* as much as it is concerned with questioning the traditional monopoly of certain persons, groups, or institutions on prescribing ethical values authoritatively. In this sense, pluralism is not against the idea of unity and universalism on the basis of rationalism and humanism. This does not, however, mean that pluralism should ignore religious or local values. In fact, pluralism derives its legitimacy and acceptance by justifying universal values in local contexts.

Islamic Roots of Pluralism

Historically and sociologically speaking, Islam can be viewed from many different perspectives. Theologically and doctrinally, there are many factors responsible for this; however, one predominant reason is the multiple, sometimes conflicting, interpretations of sacred Islamic texts (the Qur'an and Hadith). These texts have been interpreted in many ways and at various levels and from different perspectives. For instance, the interpretations of the Qur'an include the exterior (*zahir*, or *shari'ah*, more legalistic) and the interior (*batin*, or *tasawwuf*, more mystical), the real and the metaphorical, the certain (*qat'i*) and the uncertain (*zanni*). As Moussalli argues, around the sacred text of the Qur'an, many sciences and schools of thought were shaped, developed, legitimized, and delegitimized, including tradition (*hadith*), exegesis (*tafsir*), jurisprudence (*fiqh*), theology (*kalam*), Sufism (*tasawwuf*) and ethics (*akhlaq*).[6] Thus, the contextual interpretations of many verses of the Qur'an are multiple, but in contemporary Muslim discussion and debate, the point of departure is increasingly the Qur'an itself and not the many layers of scholarly interpretations that have accumulated over the centuries. It would be wrong to assume that there is a single, monolithic view among Muslims concerning religious pluralism and other issues.

With this in mind, it is important to note that while the text of the Qur'an is a source for different interpretations among Muslim scholars, it also is the source for justifying differences, diversity and pluralism. In other words, the Qur'an is the main factor that establishes the legitimacy of differences, diversity, and pluralism. Indeed, in the Qur'an there are only a limited number of verses that speak of political disunity whereas there are many verses which point out the need for diversity of tribes, sects, nations, and peoples as well as races and languages. These "positive" verses of the Qur'an also acknowledge the natural differences in the intellectual and physical capabilities of human beings and view the different ways of living as a natural and even as a divine aspect of creation.

There is no forcible unification called for by the Qur'an; rather there are a number of verses of the Qur'an which offer a distinctly modern perspective on tolerance, pluralism and mutual recognition in a multiethnic, multicultural and multicommunity world. Some verses which illustrate these points are:

> To each among you, We have ordained a law and assigned a path. Had God pleased, He could have made you one nation, but His will is to test you by what He has given you; so compete in goodness.
>
> (Qur'an, 5:48)

> Had your Lord willed, He would have made mankind one nation; but they will not cease differing.
>
> (Qur'an, 11:118)

> O mankind, We created you from a male and a female and made you into nations and tribe, that you may know one another.
>
> (Qur'an, 49:13)

Pluralism among Muslims is of course also related to the different historical, social, cultural, political, and economic conditions of Muslims. In fact, I would argue, there are now at least eight cultural realms among Muslims that reflect the very pluralism of the Muslim world. The eight cultural realms are: Arab, Persian, Turkic, Sudanic (Black Africa), the Indian sub-continent, Malay-Indonesian, Sino-Islamic, and the Western hemisphere. Each of the cultural realms, to a certain degree, represents the distinctive cultural expression of its own Muslim population. Therefore, it is wrong to assume that Muslims are a monolithic phenomenon; in contrast, pluralism is a fact of life among Muslims.

Islamic doctrinal, theological and sociological roots of pluralism, however, have been contested by truth claims among Muslims themselves, by putting forward certain verses of the Qur'an that emphasize the truth of Islam above any other religion. One of the most often-cited verses states: "Whoever desires another religion (*din*) than Islam, it shall not be accepted of Him; in the next world he shall be among the losers" (Qur'an, 3:85). As Sachedina observes, a number of Muslim commentators have used this verse to argue for the finality of Islam over all other religions, thereby pressing the case for intolerance. Thus, this verse has been interpreted, in both historical and modern commentaries, as restricting salvation to Islam only. This kind of interpretation and self-understanding has led to intolerance, even to the exclusion of the other from the divine-human relationship. Such an exclusivist theology can envision a global human community only under Islamic hegemony. Islamic tradition, so interpreted, then becomes an instrument for furthering Muslim political and social power over other nations.[7]

The apparent contradiction between some passages of the Qur'an that recognized the existence and validity of other religions, and other passages that declared Islam as the sole source of salvation, has to be resolved in order to establish a stable system of peaceful coexistence with these religions. This tension between the pluralist and exclusivist strains of Islam can be resolved only through the reexamination of the specific contexts of traditional rulings and the ways in which they were conditioned by the beliefs, desires, hopes, and fears of the classical age. Such reexamination would allow us to compare traditional rulings with contemporary issues and reapply them with a refreshed historical perspective. Furthermore, Muslim scholars should disentangle Qur'anic perspective on pluralism from medieval interpretation in order to elaborate and formulate new Muslim participation in a plural global society.

Southeast Asian Pluralism

Pluralism and diversity have been and are a prevalent reality in Southeast Asia. As Robert W. Hefner argues, few areas of the non-Western world illustrate the legacy and challenge of cultural pluralism in a manner more striking than in the Southeast Asian countries of Malaysia, Singapore, and Indonesia.[8] J. S. Furnivall, a British administrator and political writer before World War II, also identified the countries known today as Indonesia, Malaysia, and Singapore as "striking" examples for plural society to exist and flourish.

According to Furnivall, a plural society is a society that comprises "two or more elements of social orders which live side by side, yet without mingling, in one political unit." He further maintained that such a situation is accompanied by a caste-like division of labor, in which ethno-religious groups play different economic roles. This social segregation in turn gives rise to what Furnivall regarded as these societies' most unsettling political trait: their lack of "common social will." Facing this unfortunate situation, Furnivall asserted that unless some kind of formula for pluralist federation could be devised, Southeast Asian pluralism seemed doomed to a nightmarish anarchy.[9]

Furnivall's "doomed scenario" by and large fortunately failed to materialize itself. In contrast, post-war Southeast Asia saw the establishment of independent Indonesia, and Malaysia Federation in which Singapore was a part. But this national independence has been assumed to stimulate the rise of ethno-religious sentiment in the struggle for control and power of the new states.

As a result the region has been marked by horrible ethno-religious conflict and violence. Malaysia was swept by fierce communal violence in the years following World War II and again in much larger scale in 1969. Chinese–dominated Singapore witnessed ethnic riots in 1964, and in 1965 pulled itself out of a two-year federation with Malaysia after a dispute over the rights of Malay and Chinese citizens. Indonesia saw outbreaks of communal violence in the late 1950s and 1965; more shocking yet, Indonesia was shaken by bitter, though intermittent, ethno-religious violence since 1996 – the final years of President Soeharto's regime – up until today.

The Indonesian Islamic Roots of Pluralism

Indonesia is indeed one of the most pluralistic societies in terms of ethnic, linguistic, cultural, and religious differences. The Indonesian archipelago – the largest one in the world, which consists of more than 17,800 islands, isles, and islets – and its history make Indonesians an extremely pluralistic society. Reflecting the diverse ethnic groups living in the country, Indonesians speak over 525 languages and dialects.

As far as religious life is concerned, according to some latest estimates, the total population of Indonesia is about 206 million people of which 87.21 percent Muslims, 6.04 percent Protestants, 3.58 percent Catholics, 1.83 percent Hindus, 1.03 percent Buddhists, and 0.31 percent other religions and spiritual groups. Up until today the Indonesian government officially recognizes the five world religions of Islam, Protestantism, Catholicism, Buddhism, and Hinduism. Even though there are attempts in the post-President Soeharto period from among followers of other religious traditions, such as Confucianism, to get similar recognition, there has been no change made by the government to recognize religions other than the five mentioned above.

Despite its religious diversity, Indonesia has until recently been generally known as a country where a number of great world religions meet and develop in peaceful coexistence. The early history of the spread of Islam and Christianity in the archipelago had been largely peaceful, though bitter contests and struggles took place in certain areas. Consolidation of Islam and Christianity in much of the period between the twelfth and seventeenth centuries had in fact produced clear boundaries among the adherents of these religions.[10]

It is important to point out that although the population of the archipelago converted mostly to Islam, the region is known as the one of the least Arabicized areas throughout the Muslim world. Geographically it is also the farthest from the Arabian Peninsula, or more precisely Mecca and Medina, where Islam was originally revealed and developed. Therefore, Islam in the archipelago was regarded by many outsiders as "marginal" or "peripheral" Islam, as "impure" or "syncretic" Islam. Furthermore, Islam in the archipelago was regarded by many outsiders as "marginal" and "peripheral" Islam, as impure or "syncretic" Islam.

The most important proponent of this perception is, no doubt, the American anthropologist Clifford Geertz. Having a great reluctance to recognize the deep influence of Islam in the Java in particular, he called his work "religion of Java" rather than, for instance, "religion of Islam in Java."[11] In this seminal work, he proposed that there are three variants of Islam in Java particularly and, by extension, in the archipelago generally. The three variants were: *priyayi* (aristocrat Muslims); *santri* (strict and practicing Muslims); and *abangan* (nominal or ID card Muslims). According to Geertz, the *priyayi* variant was heavily influenced by Indic-Sanskrit culture, whereas the *abangan* variant was the most indigenous, syncretic, and even animistic. Therefore, in his judgment, it is only the *santri* variant, with its heavy orientation to Middle Eastern Islam, that is the real Islam of Java; although the members of this variant are seen as the minority within the general population. With that said, Geertz implies that the majority of Javanese (as well as Indonesians) are not real Muslims, and Islam is adhered to only by a small fraction of the population.

One of Geertz's fiercest critics was Marshall G. S. Hodgson, a prominent expert of Islamic civilizations from the University of Chicago. In his celebrated work *The Venture of Islam* (vol. 2, 1974) he admits the importance of Geertz's *Religion of Java*. However, after his praise comes sharp criticism:

... [Geertz's study] deals with the twentieth century, and with inner Java in particular, but much in it throws light on what happened earlier and is relevant to other parts of the archipelago. Unfortunately, its general high excellence is marred by a major systematic error: influenced by the polemics of a certain school of modern Shari'ah-minded Muslims, Geertz identifies 'Islam' only with what that school of modernists happens to approve, and ascribes everything else to an aboriginal or a Hindu-Buddhist background, gratuitously labeling much of the Muslim religious life in Java 'Hindu'. He identifies a long series of phenomena, virtually universal to Islam and sometimes found even in the Qur'an itself as un-Islamic; and hence his interpretation of the Islamic past as well as of some recent anti-Islamic reactions is highly misleading. His error has at least three roots. When he refers to the archipelago having long been cut off from 'the centers of orthodoxy at Mecca and Cairo', the irrelevant inclusion of Cairo betrays a modern source of Geertz' bias. We must suspect also the urge of many colonialists to minimize their subjects' ties with a disturbingly worldwide Islam (a tendency found also among the French colonialists in the Maghrib); and finally his anthropological techniques of investigation, looking to functional analysis of a culture in momentary cross-section without serious regard to the historical dimension. Other writers have recognized better the Islamic character even in inner-Javanese religion: CAO van Nieuwenhuijze, *Aspects of Islam in Post-Colonial Indonesia* (The Hague, 1958); W. F. Wertheim, *Indonesian Society in Transition* (2nd ed., The Hague, 1959), but Geertz stands out in the field. For one who knows Islam, his comprehensive data – despite his intention – show how very little has survived from the Hindu past even in inner Java and raise the question why the triumph of Islam so complete.[12]

Recent studies have further refuted much of Geertz's assertion. As shown by Azra[13] for the period between the seventeenth and eighteenth centuries and beyond, and by Laffan,[14] Islam in the archipelago has never been "cut off" from the Islam in the Middle East. In fact there is a great deal of intense connections, networks and religio-cultural exchanges among Muslims in the two regions. All these in turn have influenced the course of Islam in the archipelago, including in Java. These thoughts are also shared by such scholars as Hefner,[15] Woodward,[16] Ricklefs,[17] Riddell[18] and many others. All of them basically are arguing that Islam in fact forms an obvious layer of Javanese and, by extension, Indonesian cultures.

Even though Indonesia is increasingly known as the largest Muslim nation in the world, it is not an Islamic state. Politically and ideologically, Indonesia is a state based on *Pancasila* (five principles): (1) Belief in One Supreme God; (2) Just and Civilized Humanism; (3) the Unity of Indonesia; (4) Democracy; and (5) Social Justice. Proposed initially by Soekarno, the First President of the Republic of Indonesia, *Pancasila* was (and still is) a compromise between secular nationalists who advocated a secular state and Muslim leaders who demanded an "Islamic state." After a series of "Islamization" of all the five principles – that was also accepted tacitly by non-Muslim groups — Muslim leaders lastly accepted *Pancasila* and regarded it as having no incompatibility with Islamic teaching.[19]

Therefore, Muslims' acceptance of *Pancasila* is no doubt one of the most important Indonesian Islamic roots of pluralism. For the bulk majority of Indonesian Muslims, *Pancasila* is, in line with a verse of the Quran, a "*kalimah sawa*," a common platform, among different religious followers. Addressing the Prophet Muhammad, the Qur'an has this to say:

> Say: O the people of the Book [*ahl al-kitab*, who are the Jews and Christians]; come to common terms between us and you; that we worship none but God, that we associate partners with him, that we erect not, from ourselves, lords and patrons, other than God . . . .

(Qur'an, 3:64)

As Nurcholish Madjid rightly argues, the *Pancasila* thus becomes a firm basis for development of religious tolerance and pluralism in Indonesia. Adam Malik, who was once Vice President during the Soeharto period, maintained that Pancasila, in Islamic perspective, is in a similar spirit to the *modus vivendi* that was created by the Prophet Muhammad in Medina after having migrated (*hijrah*) from Mecca. The Prophet laid down the *modus vivendi* in a famous document called the "Constitution of Medina" (*mithaq al-madinah*). The document includes a provision which states that all Medinan factions, including Jews, were one nation (*ummah*) together with Muslims, and that they have the same rights and duties as Muslims. Adam Malik interprets the "Constitution of Medina" as a formula for a state based on the idea of social and religious pluralism.[20]

Similarly, for Robert N. Bellah, the American sociologist of religion, the Medinan state was a root of Islamic modernity and pluralism. He argues that Islam in its seventh-century origins was for its time and place "remarkably modern . . . in the high degree of commitment, involvement, and participation expected from the rank-and-file members of the community."[21] Despite that, the Prophet Muhammad's experiment eventually failed because of the lack of necessary sociocultural prerequisites among the Arab Muslims. In other words, the *modus vivendi* failed because it was "too modern" for the Medinan society. Looking to Indonesian experience with *Pancasila* as a common platform, it is a part of what Bellah believes as an effort of modern Indonesian Muslims to depict the early community as the very type of equalitarian participant nationalism, which is by no means entirely an unhistorical ideological participation.

As a basis of Indonesia pluralism, *Pancasila* unfortunately had been used by the Soeharto regime as a tool for repression. The forced implementation in 1985 of *Pancasila* as the sole ideological basis for all organizations in the country was resented by many Indonesians. Through special training, the *Pancasila* then was indoctrinated to Indonesians, which in the end gave the *Pancasila* a bad name. It is clear that for most Indonesians nothing is wrong with the *Pancasila* as such, but when it was abused and manipulated for the benefit of President Soeharto's political status quo, then people rapidly lost their belief in the *Pancasila* as an integrating factor within plural Indonesia.

Contemporary Religious Conflict in Indonesia

Despite the continued *Pancasila* indoctrination by the Soeharto regime, Indonesia in the second half of the 1990s was marked by social unrest and violence in various parts of the country. Soeharto had increasingly lost support from many elements of Indonesian society in the midst of increased economic injustices and deprivation. Consequently, much of the violence has been caused by political and economic factors. But the unrest has also often been associated with religion or at least seems to have strong religious overtones. An example that is often put forward in this respect is the religious-communal violence in Ambon and other parts of the Maluku archipelago in post-Soeharto Indonesia, which involves Muslim groups on the one hand and Christian groups on the other.[22] Religious aspects seem to be also apparent in the Poso (Central Sulawesi) violent conflict that erupted among Muslim and Christian groups not long after the Maluku violence. However, it is important to note that these so-called "ethno-religious" conflicts in Indonesia are very complex phenomena consisting of many root causes: political, economic, demographic as well as religious. Therefore, it is simplistic to regard that religious and theological differences are the primary cause of the communal riots and violence.[23]

The Ambon communal violence, which erupted in January 1999 and spread to other parts of the Maluku province, is perhaps the most often quoted case of religious conflict in Indonesia in recent years. This observation, on the surface, perhaps to some extent is true. Communal conflict and violence in Ambon and other places in Maluku such as Halmahera and Ternate involved the Muslim community on the one hand and the Protestant community on the other. The large-scale violence between the two religious groups resulted not only in the killing of a large number of people (both Muslims and Christians), but also in the burning of mosques, churches, houses, markets, and other public buildings and facilities.[24]

It is no secret of course that Muslims and Christians in Maluku had long been involved in a sort of race to gain the upper hand in religion, economics and politics of the region.[25] According to more reliable sources, Islam came to Maluku in the fifteenth century, and by the end of that century, the Ternate Sultanate had been established. The Portuguese came to Maluku in 1513 not only to trade, but also to spread Christianity. As a result, they also came to challenge the Sultanate of Ternate. However, the Portuguese surrendered in 1575 after a long siege in Ternate by Sultan Baabullah. Before long though, the European forces were arriving at Maluku. This time it was the Dutch who initially came in 1599 and began to take control of one area of Maluku after another and Dutch missionaries gained a strong position to spread Christianity in Maluku.

After Indonesia gained independence on August 17th, 1945, groups of Moluccan Christians, who used to possess political, military and economic privileges during colonial times, proclaimed the independence of the South Moluccan Republic (in April 1950). This separatism, despite the fact that it created prolonged political problems for both the Republic of Indonesia and the Netherlands, failed to realize its political ambitions. But deep suspicions, particularly among the Muslims about their fellow Christian neighbors, remain as reflected in the recent violent events and the growing separatist movement.

This brief historical account seems to justify the argument that communal riots and violence in Ambon and elsewhere in Maluku are religious in nature. I would argue that religion indeed plays a certain role in this communal conflict and violence; however, there are other important factors that have also created hostilities between the two religious communities. One suggestion that I would like to put forward is that the Ambon or Maluku communal riots have their root-causes in the contest for economic resources and the increasingly disproportionate distribution of political power in the local bureaucracy between Muslims. Over the last two decades, this local bureaucracy consists of indigenous Maluku and migrants better known as the BBM [Buginese, Butonese and Makasarese], as well as indigenous Christian. The New Order government of Soeharto failed to address these latent problems. Instead, the regime tried to hide the problems under the carpet mainly through the all-too-familiar security approach. In the framework of this approach, no one had been allowed to discuss the problems openly and thus find feasible and viable solutions for these problems, since all issues involved here were of SARA (Suku, Agama, Ras, Antar golongan, or ethnicity, religion, race, inter-group) issues, which were considered by the regime to be very sensitive and divisive.

Furthermore, during the Soeharto era, the demographic composition of the Maluku province changed rapidly. According to some reports, up until 1970, the indigenous Christians constituted the slim majority of the total population. Since the early 1980s, however, with the improved economy and better means of trans-portation, the BBM people came steadily in large numbers and settled in various areas of Maluku, particularly in Ambon. With their coming, the Muslims in Maluku increasingly outnumbered the Christians. This development did not only affect the demographic composition, but also resulted in increasing changes in the fields of economics and politics. Before long, BBM migrants dominated the Maluku economy as economic opportunities became opened for them due to the fact that native Christians were more interested in being civil servants than being traders. As a result, the resentment of the native Christian population was doubled since almost all the BBM migrants were Muslims.

Communal relations rapidly worsened when the Muslims became increasingly politically mobile. To take one obvious example, the last two governors of Maluku province have been Muslims. This seemingly unstoppable Muslim political mobility challenged the Christians who used to dominate the local bureaucracy, and undoubt-edly was an important factor in the rapid growth of ethnic and religious hostilities. All these demographic, economic, and political changes strained the already fragile fabric of Maluku society, waiting only for the right time to explode.

Therefore, the sudden fall of Soeharto and the shaky authority of President Habibie soon rekindled the embers of the conflict and tension within the Ambon/ Maluku society as a whole. Triggered by a quarrel between a Christian youth and Muslims over the fare of a city public bus, large-scale riots erupted in Ambon on the 19th of January 1999, the very night before the Muslims celebrate 'Id al-Fitr, the celebration which marks the end of the fasting month of Ramadan. Since that time, intermittent clashes and violence between Christian and Muslim groups have continued, leaving large numbers of people dead and countless homes, markets, and other buildings completely destroyed. Clashes and riots, which initially erupted in Ambon, the capital city of Maluku province, spread to some other parts of the Maluku province, giving the strong impression that communal riots are far from being resolved by the central government.

One of the most important factors also responsible for the prolonged communal riots has been the indecisiveness of the police and military failing to put an end to the continuing violent conflicts. At the same time, there is a lot of evidence that Indonesian security forces are also entangled in the violence. Some members are even taking positions to defend either Christians or Muslims. Worse still, they use their armaments to confront groups of people who do not belong to their religion. This is why the military commander in Jakarta has replaced most of the security forces in Maluku with those recruited from other places in Indonesia. Unfortunately, again, this policy by and large has also failed.

The election of Abdurrahman Wahid brought new hopes for a peaceful settlement of the Ambon case. President Wahid, a few days after his instalment, assigned Vice President Megawati Soekarnoputri to resolve the conflict through dialogue and other peaceful means. But the situation in Ambon remained unsettled. Outbursts of violence continued to take place. Vice President Megawati was very indecisive; she kept quiet and did not implement any specific policy that could put an end to the conflict. Only later, an initiative was taken in 2002 by Coordinating Minister of Social Welfare, Jusuf Kalla, that succeeded in bringing all conflicting parties to the negotiating table to sign a peace agreement called "Malino I" (for Ambon and Maluku) and "Malino II" (for Poso, Central Sulawesi). The agreements have been able to bring peace to the troubled areas. And now, under the period of President Susilo Bambang Yudhoyono and Vice-President Jusuf Kalla, the reconciliation between the two communities has continued to strengthen.

Religious Pluralism and Democracy

Looking at the conflict and violence between Muslim and Christian groups in Indonesia, one should be aware that this case in Andon is far from reflecting Indonesia as a whole. This prolonged conflict had spread at most to Poso, Central Sulawesi, not to anywhere else in Indonesia. There are of course conflicts and riots in other places in Indonesia such as in West Kalimantan, Central Kalimantan, and Aceh. But all of these have nothing to do with religion; rather, most of these conflicts deal with economic and political grievances. Therefore, one might conclude that due to religious pluralism and peaceful coexistence among the followers of different religions, Indonesia has overall remained intact.

Given the fact that Islam is the single largest religion in Indonesia, it also is reasonable to expect that Islam and Muslims play a greater and more positive role in the development and enhancement of a democratic and multicultural Indonesia. Indonesian Islam possesses distinct traits and characters that to a large extent are different from the Islam in the Middle East. Indonesian Islam is essentially a tolerant, moderate, and "middle way" (*Ummah wasat*) Islam given the history of its early spread which was basically peaceful and had been integrated into diverse ethnic, cultural, and social realities of Indonesia. The bulk majority of Indonesian Muslims belong to a moderate mainstream organization such as the Nahdlatul Ulama, Muhammadiyah, and many other regional organizations throughout Indonesia. All of these Muslim organizations support modernity and democracy. They oppose the establishment of an Islamic state in Indonesia as well as the implementation of *shari'ah* in the current Indonesian nation-state.

All of these moderate and mainstream organizations are basically civil society organizations, which play a crucial role in the development and enhancement of democracy as a means for peaceful resolution to conflict. These organizations are very active in the dissemination of ideas concerning democracy, human rights, justice, and gender equality; all of which are crucial for modern Indonesian society.

Not least important, mainstream Muslim organizations have been very active in conducting religious dialogues with Christian and other non-Muslim organizations at local, national, and international levels. Through cooperation, they put a lot of pressure on the government to find ways to resolve communal conflicts that in the end would affect national life as a whole. Through these kinds of efforts, they are able to anticipate possible communal violence and play a part in putting an end to certain current communal conflicts.

There is a number of small and fringe groups of radical Muslims which have captured a lot of media imagination such as the Islamic Defense Front (FPI), the Jihad Troops (Lasykar Jihad), the Council of Jihad Fighters (Majelis Mujahidin Indonesia), and the Muslim Brotherhood of Indonesia (Jama'ah Ikhwan a-Muslimin Indonesia). As reflected in the media, these groups have the potential to create tension not only among Muslims, but also with non-Muslims. However, with the leadership mostly in the hands of non-native Indonesian Muslims, or more precisely figures of Yemeni origin, these groups have in fact very limited influence over Indonesians as a whole. One should not exaggerate their influence and have some sort of exaggerated fear against them. Moreover, following the bombing in Bali on October 12, 2002, most of these radical groups have either disbanded themselves or been forced to lay low.

In the end, I believe that one of the most important keys to address the tendency of radicalism among Indonesian Muslims is the strengthening of democracy, the enforcement of law and order, and economic recovery. Indonesia has been able to conduct peaceful general elections in 2004. These general elections have been very historic, since this was the first direct presidential and vice-presidential election. With the success of the 2004 general election, Indonesia, the largest Muslim country in the world, has shown the compatibility between Islam and democracy.

There are, of course, a great deal of urgent agendas for the President Susilo Bambang Yudhoyono to keep the nation united in order not to be threatened by religious-communal conflict. Among the most important agendas, no doubt, are the creation of good governance, the acceleration of economic recovery, and the strengthening of law and order.

Notes

1 Tarmizi Taher, *Aspiring for the Middle Path: Religious Harmony in Indonesia*, Jakarta: Center for the Study of Islam and Society (Censis), IAIN Jakarta, 1997, p. 85.

2 Abdulaziz Sachedina, *The Islamic Roots of Democratic Pluralism*, Oxford: Oxford University Press, 2001, p. 14.

3 Ibid., p. 22.

4 Ibid., p. 35.

5 Muhammad Khalil Masud, "The Scope of Pluralism in Islamic Moral Tradition," in *Islamic Political Ethics: Civil Society, Pluralism, and Conflict*, Sohail H. Hashmi (ed.), Princeton: Princeton University Press, 2002, pp. 135–136.

6 Ahmad S. Moussali, *The Islamic Quest for Democracy, Pluralism, and Human Rights*, Gainsville: University Press of Florida, 2001, p. 85.

7 Abdulaziz Sachedina, *The Islamic Roots of Democratic Pluralism*, p. 39 and p. 44.

8 Robert W. Hefner (ed.), *The Politics of Multiculturalism: Pluralism and Citizenship in Malaysia, Singapore and Indonesia*, Honolulu: University of Hawaii Press, 2001, p. 4.

9 Ibid., pp. 4–6. See also J. S. Furnivall, *Netherlands India: A Study of Plural Economy*, New York: Macmillan, 1944 [orig. 1939], p. 46 and pp. 468–469.

10 Anthony Reid, *Southeast Asia in the Age Commerce 1450–1680: Volume Two, Expansion and Crisis*, New Haven: Yale University Press, 1993. See also Azyumardi Azra, "The Race between Islam and Christianity Theory Revisited: Islamization and Christianization in the Malay-Indonesian Archipelago 1530–1670," *Documentatieblad voor de Geschiedenis van Nederlandse Zending en Overzeese Kerken*, vol. 7, no. 2, 2000, pp. 26–37.

11 Clifford Geertz, *Religion of Java*, Glencoe: Free Press, 1960.

12 Marshall G. S. Hodgson, *The Venture of Islam*, vol. 2. Chicago: University of Chicago Press, 1974, p. 551.

13 Azyumardi Azra, *The Origins of Islamic Reformism in Southeast Asia*, Crows Nest: ASAA & Allen-Unwin; Honolulu: University of Hawai'i Press; Leiden: KITLV Press, 2004.

14 Michael F. Laffan, *Islamic Nationhood and Colonial Indonesia: The Umma below the Winds*, London and New York: RoutledgeCurzon, 2003.

15 Robert W. Hefner, *Hindu Javanese, Tengger Tradition and Islam*, Princeton: Princeton University Press, 1985.

16 Mark R. Woodward, "The Shari'ah and the Secret Doctrine: Muslim Law and Mystical Doctrine in Central Java," PhD diss., University of Illinois, Urbana-Champaign, 1985.

17 M. C. Ricklefs, *The Seen and Unseen Worlds in Java, 1726–1749: History, Literature, and Islam in the Court of Pakubuwana II*, St. Leonards, Aust. and Honolulu: ASAA, Allen & Unwin, and University of Hawaii Press, 1998.

18 P. G. Riddell, *Islam and the Malay-Indonesian World: Transmission and Responses*, London and Singapore: C. Hurst & Horizon Books, 2001.

19 Nurcholish Madjid, "Islamic Roots of Modern Pluralism: Indonesian Experience," *Studia Islamika: Indonesian Journal for Islamic Studies*, 1, I, 1994, pp. 57–58.

20 Ibid., p. 64.

21 Robert N. Bellah, "Islamic Tradition and the Problems of Modernization," in his *Beyond Belief: Essays on Religion in the Post-Traditional World*, New York: Harper & Row, 1970, pp. 150–151.

22 Azyumardi Azra, "Communal Riots in Indonesia: The Decline of Indonesian Nationalism and the Rise of Separatism," in Chaider S. Bamualim *et al.* (eds), *Communal Conflicts in Contemporary Indonesia*, Jakarta: Center for Languages & Cultures, State Islamic University (UIN) and Konrad Adenauer Stiftung, 2002, pp. 77–100. See also Azyumardi Azra, "Islam and Christianity in Indonesia: The Roots of Conflict and Hostility," in Joseph A. Camilleri (ed.), *Religion and Culture in Asia Pacific: Violence or Healing?*, Melbourne: Pax Christi & Vista Publications, 2001, pp. 84–92.

23 Recently, the eruption of communal violence in Indonesia can be viewed as the culmination of political and social discontentment stewing since the mid-1990s – not only

among the lower classes of the population, but also among the middle classes. Even though Indonesia in the 1990s continued to enjoy an "economic boom," it seems that this discontentment had its roots, at least in its initial phases, in the widespread economic injustices and deprivation. At a later phase this economic discontentment amalgamated with political injustices that had been suffered by most Indonesians since the 1970s. Finally, the crisis stripped Soeharto from his long-held power of more than three decades. Unfortunately, the unusual succession of the presidency from Soeharto to Habibie following the monetary, economic and political crises in May 1998 had shaken and threatened not only Indonesian political unity, but also produced further conflict and violence in Indonesian societies.

24 Azyumardi Azra, "Communal Riots in Indonesia," pp. 87–91.
25 Azyumardi Azra, "The Race between Islam and Christianity Theory Revisited," 2000.

Other Sources Used as References:

Abu Khalil, Shawqi, *Tasamuh al-Islam wa Ta'asub Khusumih*, Beirut: Manshurat Mu'assasat May, 1990.

Azra, Azyumardi, *Konteks Berteologi di Indonesia: Pengalaman Islam* [Contextual Theology in Indonesia: Islamic Experience], Jakarta: Paramadina, 1999.

—— "The Islamic Factor in Post-Soeharto Indonesia," in Chris Manning and Peter van Diermen (eds), *Indonesia in Transition: Social Aspects of Reformasi and Crisis*, Singapore: RSPAS ANU & ISEAS, 2000.

Eickelman, Dale F., "Islam and Ethical Pluralism," in Sohail H. Hashmi (ed.), *Islamic Political Ethics: Civil Society, Pluralism, and Conflict*, Princeton: Princeton University Press, 2002.

Esack, Farid, *Qur'an, Liberation and Pluralism: An Islamic Perspective of Interreligious Solidarity against Oppression*, Oxford: Oneworld Publications, 1996.

Hanafi, Hassan, *al-Turath wa al-Tajdid: Mawqifuna min al-Thawrah*, Cairo: al-Markaz li al-Bahth wa al-Dirasat, 1980.

—— *al-Yamin wa al-Yasar fi al-Fikr al-Dini*, Cairo: Dar al-Thaqafah al-Jadidah, 1996.

Hashmi, Sohail H., *Islamic Political Ethics: Civil Society, Pluralism, and Conflict*, Princeton: Princeton University Press, 2002.

Hefner, Robert W., "Religion: Evolving Pluralism," in Donald K. Emmerson (ed.), *Indonesia beyond Suharto: Polity, Economy, Society, Transition*, Armonk, NY and London. ME Sharpe, 1999.

Moussali, Ahmad S., "Modern Islamic Fundamentalist Discourses on Civil Society, Pluralism and Democracy," in A. R. Norton (ed.), *Civil Society in the Middle East*, vol. 1, Leiden: E.J. Brill, 1995.

—— "Discourses on Human Rights and Pluralistic Democracy," in Anders Jerichow and J. B. Simonsen, *Islam in a Changing World*, London: Curzon, 1997.

Nakamura, Mitsuo, Sharon Siddique and Omar Farouk Bajunid (eds), *Islam & Civil Society in Southeast Asia*, Singapore: ISEAS, 2001.

an-Na'im, Abdullah Ahmad, *Toward an Islamic Reformation: Civil Liberties, Human Rights, and International Law*, Syracuse: Syracuse University Press, 1990.

Roff, William R., "Islamic Movements: One or Many," in his (ed.), *Islam and the Political Economy of Meaning*, London and Berkeley: Croom Helm and University of California Press, 1987.

Tibi, Bassam, *The Challenge of Fundamentalism: Political Islam and the New World Disorder*, Berkeley and Los Angeles: University of California Press, 1998.

—— *Islam between Culture and Politics*, New York: Palgrave and The Weatherhead Center for International Affairs, Harvard University, 2001.

14 Reviving Islamic Universalism

East/s, West/s, and Coexistence[1]

Asma Barlas

For this chapter I was asked to reflect on the proposition that Islam transcends exclusive identifications with either East or West and that Muslims, as a middle people, can play a unique role in bringing about cultural reconciliation. Several questions were also sent to us to help frame our discussions and I have focused on those pertaining to the concepts of synthesis, reconciliation between Islam and the West, and peace/dialogue.

In keeping with this wide thematic focus, the first part of this chapter explores the relationship between synthesis and method; the second interrogates the Islam/West binary and its implications for cross-cultural understanding, and the third dwells on some aspects of Islamic thinking that can become a basis for inter- and intra-religious dialogue, hence reconciliation. By way of a conclusion, I draw out some lessons suggested by my engagement with these themes. At the outset, however, I must clarify that this is very much a work in progress and that I make many arguments only preliminarily.

Synthesis and Method

The conference description refers to the process by which Muslims seek to transform our understanding of the Qur'an into a lived reality as a synthesis, but I wonder if we can have a synthesis in the absence of ethically sound and contextually legitimate readings of the Qur'an, especially with respect to women's rights. In particular, I am concerned that traditional methods of knowledge creation have failed to generate such readings as is obvious from the numbers of Muslims who believe that the Qur'an "itself" discriminates against women without pausing to consider how such misogynistic readings of the text are generated, or what they say about our conceptions of God.

What I am referring to as traditional methods involve the practice of "reading backward" through the work of past generations and they rest on two highly objectionable epistemic claims. First, that "expertise in the use of interpretive reasoning, more than knowledge of the revelation itself is integral to the definition of practice," and, second, that "the authority of the practice defined by later generations [is equivalent to] the authority of revelation."[2] As I have argued elsewhere,[3] these claims violate the specificity and sanctity of divine discourse inasmuch as they nullify the distinction between the Qur'an and its (male-authored) exegesis and allow (male) interpretive communities to displace divine writ by extending "authority from a posited canonical text [i.e., the Qur'an]"[4] to themselves instead. As an alternative, I have proposed a method that draws on some criteria that the Qur'an itself specifies, including reading it for its best meanings. This injunction confirms that while we can have more than one reading of the Qur'an, we are obligated to accept only the best. By leaving it up to us to define what we mean by best, the Qur'an indirectly confirms our right to live in open, tolerant, and pluralistic societies where we can make interpretive choices freely and in a reasoned and deliberative manner.

I also contend that in order to arrive at the best readings of the Qur'an, we must base our interpretation of it in a sound theological understanding of God since there is a close relationship between God and God's speech. For instance, if we believe that God is just and never transgresses against the rights of humans (never does *zulm* to them), then we also should not read the Qur'an as allowing men to transgress against women's rights by discriminating against them. Similarly, if we believe that God is unlike anything created, hence beyond sex/gender, we should not read the Qur'an as teaching that God has a special affinity with males or that, being made in God's image, men are ontologically superior to women. This is, of course, a more nuanced argument and in summarizing it here, my intent is simply to emphasize the need to find new methods for reading the Qur'an if we are to interpret it in more egalitarian modes and if we are to evolve a truly Islamic synthesis.

"Islam and the West"

One of the questions before our panel at the Library of Alexandria in October 2003 is whether Muslims can arrive at a synthesis capable of establishing "common ground between Islam and the West without compromising core Islamic principles." To appreciate the concerns that impel this question is not, however, to approve of the manner of its framing, and not only because we also are being asked to free Islam from parochial associations with East or West. Counterposing Islam and the West is problematic for other reasons as well. Firstly, Islam is a religion and the West is a geographic space/identity; the two are thus not really comparable. Moreover, Islam exists within the West while the West "is now everywhere, within the West and outside; in structures and in minds."[5] More crucially, representing religious and cultural diversity in terms of oppositions already presumes irreducible difference, making talk of reconciliation moot. Finally, it makes no sense for Muslims to associate Islam with East or West given the Qur'an's teachings and our own history. I will address each of these issues in turn.

East/West as the Epistemology of Othering

There is by now a sizeable literature on the representational division of the world into East/West, but Edward Said's *Orientalism* remains the paradigmatic critique of this "imagined geography" a quarter of a century after its writing, notwithstanding its many critics and flaws. Here I want to recall Said's central argument, that the East/West binary grows out of, and also sustains, an asymmetric relationship in which one half of the dyad (the West) enjoys *"positional* superiority"[6] over the other (the East), both because of political and economic dominance and because of the normalization of the idea of radical difference. For Muslims, it is especially troubling that for nearly a thousand years "Arabs and Islam . . . together [have] stood for the [East, or] Orient."[7] Indeed, it was in "the Arab Near East, where Islam was supposed to define cultural and racial characteristics, that the British and the French encountered . . . 'the Orient' with the greatest intensity, familiarity, and complexity."[8] It was in the course of this encounter that they came to articulate "a political vision of reality whose structure promoted the difference between the familiar (Europe, the West, 'us') and the strange (the Orient, the East, 'them')." The East/West binary, then, not only naturalizes Otherness, but also the idea that "European identity [is] superior in comparison with all the non-European peoples and cultures."[9] For precisely this reason, pitting Islam against the West buys into an Orientalist view of religious and cultural difference as ontological and as signifying an absence of mutual recognition, thus foreclosing the possibilities for inter-religious dialogue and reconciliation.

Having said that, however, I will admit that the East/West binary is useful for denoting an unequal configuration of power that cannot just be wished away or, worse, obscured by fudging language. The challenge, then, is not to let the Islam/West binary contain or define our understanding of Islam and also to recognize that in the absence of a just and humane global division of labor, people also will find it hard to find common ideological ground.

East/West from a Muslim and Qur'anic Perspective

In the original version of my paper which I presented at the Library of Alexandria, I refer to the history of the Crusades as a way of reminding ourselves that before Orientalist discourses normalized the Islam/West binary, it was customary to speak of Eastern and Western Islam and Eastern and Western Christianity. As the rulers of Spain, Muslims already were in the West, and Christianity too was defined doctrinairely in terms of a Latin Christianity and a Western Christianity. Even the Crusades did not originate in notions of geographical particularism or exclusion and, indeed, can be viewed as conflicts between two universalisms laying equal claims to both East and West rather than to one or the other.

If our history unsettles Orientalist associations of Islam with the East, so does the Qur'an which also discourages us from defining Islam in terms of imagined geographies. For instance, when it specified a direction, or *qibla,* for Muslims to face while praying, the Qur'an clarified that:

> It is not righteousness
> That ye turn your faces
> Towards East or West;
> but it is righteousness –
> To believe in God.[10]

After the Muslims migrated from Mecca to Medina and their *qibla* was changed from Jerusalem to the Ka'ba, the Qur'an observed that:

> The Fools among the people
> Will say: "What hath turned
> Them from the *Qibla* to which
> They were used?" Say:
> To God belong both East and West:
> [God] guideth whom [God] will
> To a Way that is straight.[11]

The Qur'an's teaching that God is the Cherisher of the two Easts and the two Wests and all that is in between should, in truth, free us from the need to link "pious expression and geographical space"[12] and also to delink Islam from identifications with East or West.

Islamic Universalism

By Islamic universalism I mean those scriptural, theological, philosophical, and mystical traditions that allow Muslims to cultivate mutual regard, reconciliation, and dialogue based on respect for diversity. Here, I will consider the Qur'an's standpoint on religious difference as well as that of two of Islam's most influential thinkers, one a theologian (al-Ghazali), and the other a sufi (Ibn al-Arabi), the former from the lands of Eastern Islam (Persia) and the latter from those of Western Islam (Spain). Specifically, I will focus on al-Ghazali's position on theological tolerance and Ibn al-Arabi's on religious diversity with the intent of showing the pluralistic, democratic, and rational elements inherent in Muslim tradition and history.

The Qur'an, Differences, and Mutual Recognition

The Qur'anic approach to diversity contrasts sharply to Orientalist thought in that the Qur'an does not use difference to make ontological and epistemological distinctions between "nations or tribes" or between women and men.[13] Nor does it treat difference itself as degenerative.[14] On the contrary, it locates difference in the same source and tells us that differences exist by divine will and enable us to recognize a universal humanity:

> O Humanity [*Insan*]! We created
> You from a single (pair)
> Of a male and a female,
> And made you into
> Nations and tribes, that
> Ye may know each other
> (Not that ye may despise
> Each other). Verily

The most honoured of you
In the sight of God
Is ([the one] who is) the most
Virtuous of you.[15]

In terms of Qur'anic teachings, then, differences rather than identicalness/sameness enable mutual recognition and inasmuch as they do, the absence of difference (the Other) renders self-knowledge incomplete or unattainable. However, even though we need Others in order to understand ourselves, this does not mean that the Other serves as a mere foil for the Self against which it must construct itself oppositionally, as in Orientalist thought. Rather, the "knowing one another" the Qur'an speaks of indicates mutuality and dialogue. As such, it may be argued that difference in the Qur'an serves an essentially moral function by providing the framework for mutual regard.[16]

The Qur'an's position on religious diversity also is fundamentally and astonishingly egalitarian. Thus, while the Qur'an defines Islam as the culmination and perfection of religion, it is only within the context of the teaching that "Revelation [itself] is a universal phenomenon." We are told that God sent each nation and people its own messenger who brought essentially the same message even if its details were unique, establishing "the universality of religious truth . . . [as] an article of Islamic faith."[17] In other words, Islam's special status is not dependent on denying that religious diversity exists by God's grace and as a means for God to test the virtue of communities that have received God's law. This Qur'anic teaching calls into question the intolerance and bigotry of those Muslims who believe that Islam has a divinely sanctioned enmity with Judaism and Christianity even though the Qur'an calls Jews and Christians, "People of the Book."

Al-Ghazali and Theological Tolerance

Muhammad al-Ghazali was born in the middle of the eleventh century in Persia and is considered "the most famous Muslim intellectual in the history of Islam." Indeed, his influence on "the Islamic world" is said to have been so pervasive as to have left much of it lingering in "a Ghazalian twilight."[18] However, judging by the absence of tolerance and reasoned discourse in many Muslim societies, one is forced to conclude that it is a rapidly waning twilight. To appreciate how profound a loss this represents for Muslims, one has but to recall his *Faysal al-Tafriqa Bayna al-Islam wa al-Zandaqa*, regarded as "one of the most thoughtful and illuminating theological essays"[19] ever to have been written.

Basically, *Faysal*'s objective is "to define the boundaries within which competing theologies can coexist in mutual recognition of each other."[20] Al-Ghazali undertook to clarify these boundaries at a time (much like our own) of "intolerance, mutual suspicion, and psychological intimidation engendered by narrow and under-inclusive definitions of orthodoxy manufactured and brandished with reckless abandon" by different schools that had taken to dubbing their critics *kuffar*, or Unbelievers. According to Sherman Jackson, al-Ghazali was troubled as much by this "theological intolerance" as by the "theological *laissez-faire*" of the neo-Platonists, both of whom are the targets of *Faysal*. However, what interests me most are some of the arguments that al-Ghazali advances against extremists.

First, he maintains that "the domain of acceptable theological interpretation is much broader than they allow,"[21] even arguing that "not everyone who embraces senseless hallucinations must be branded an Unbeliever, even if his doctrines are clearly absurd." This argument flows in part from his conviction that no school can claim "a monopoly over the truth to the exclusion of the other."[22] Those who do claim such a monopoly, he argues, are conflating their own "interpretation with revelation," failing "to recognize that their doctrines are grounded in interpretive presuppositions that are historically determined." Only by denying their "historical situatedness" can they represent their knowledge as universal. It is thus "the very invisibility of the theologian's history that makes both him and his theology so powerful."[23]

Second, al-Ghazali believes that the only way for theologians to decide between the legitimacy of different readings of the Qur'an is methodologically, by establishing "among themselves a mutually agreed-upon criterion for determining the validity of logical proofs that enjoys the recognition of them all." As he says, "if they do not agree on the scale by which a thing is to be measured, they will not be able to terminate disputes over its weight."[24] Thus, in spite of his attack on philosophy (or, rather, on neo-Platonism and Aristotelian rationalism), al-Ghazali continues "to appeal to reason as the only means of avoiding intolerance and fanaticism."[25] Third, he questions the extremists' tendency to naturalize tradition and to cast differences and disagreements as unsanctioned innovations. To al-Ghazali, it is clear that the past cannot pass into the present "unprocessed and unmediated." He thus views tradition as a "synthetic rather than a 'natural' product, bearing clear signs of selective endorsement."[26] Tradition, he points out, is not mere imitativeness – as he says, he is thankful not to have been "afflicted by that blindness that condemns people to being led around by others (*taqlid*)"[27] – but an active process of constructing meaning in, and through, the present.

Even this cursory review illustrates the remarkable lessons of *Faysal*, of which I have highlighted only three: first, that religious knowledge is not sacred or universal but historically grounded and open to a critique; a critique, in turn, can open up the possibility of reaching consensus through dialogue. Second, no interpretive school can claim a monopoly over the truth which can only be apprehended through reason, not assertions of privilege. Finally, tradition is not an inert historical legacy but a process of selective reconstruction that involves both agency and freedom of choice. Thus, from within Muslim tradition, al-Ghazali provides a compelling defense of the centrality of intellectual freedom, reason, and dialogue to the construction of religious meaning. Whatever one's stance on the criteria he advances, his work also establishes the importance of a sound methodology for reading the Qur'an.

Ibn Al-Arabi: Religious Diversity and the Other

In contrast to al-Ghazali's work, which offers a theological and philosophical critique of Muslim intolerance and a prescription for intra-religious dialogue, Ibn al-Arabi's serves as a guide for accommodating religious differences and thus as a call for inter-religious reconciliation. Born a hundred years after al-Ghazali in the mid-twelfth century in Islamic Spain, Ibn al-Arabi is viewed as "the most influential thinker of the second half of Islamic history" whose impact "has been felt throughout western Islam down to the present day." His work, which is situated within the sapiential[28] tradition, testifies "to the possibilities of preserving rationality while simultaneously transcending it."[29] Of immediate relevance to this chapter are his views on religious diversity.

As William Chittick argues, Muslim approaches to "religions other than Islam" tend to represent two extremes. At one end are "those who focus almost exclusively on the *shari'ah* [law] and the divine rigor. They tend to condemn non-Muslims as unbelievers, sometimes including in the category of non-Muslims any Muslims who do not agree with them." As we have seen, this is the tendency that al-Ghazali criticizes. At the opposite end are "those who see the human relationship with God almost completely in terms of love" and who therefore "like to give all those who follow a religion the benefit of the doubt." Ibn al-Arabi, however, situates himself between these two positions; while advocating the "absolute necessity of observing the Shariah," he also defends the need to respect diversity on the grounds that "All things are intimately interrelated through their common roots in the Divine Reality;"[30] "multiplicity is almost as real as unity, since it also has its roots in God;" "diversity has been established by God's wisdom and compassion."[31] He (therefore) affirms the Qur'an's particular excellence or the Prophet's superiority "over all other prophets is not to deny the universal validity of revelation nor the necessity of revelation's appearing in particularized expressions."[32] I will examine these claims briefly so as to clarify the relationship between them.

At the heart of Ibn al-Arabi's understanding of divine and human reality, and the conceptual lens through which he analyzes it, is the concept of *Tawhid*, or divine unity. In his formulation, however, the "Oneness of Being or Unity of Existence" does not rule out the "manyness of reality" since unity embraces, but also transcends, polarity. This view of oneness and "manyness" derives from his interpretation of the tradition that God created humans because God wanted to be known. To Ibn al-Arabi this suggests that divine reality is itself polarized "into subject and object, knower and known," though not in the sense of implying "real otherness, since it is a case of divine self-consciousness for which the principle of otherness is simply for self-realization." Moreover, since the "origin of the divine longing to be known is love," the Other comes into being as an expression of this love.[33] Alterity, or otherness/difference, then, has its roots in divine reality and is a necessary condition for expressing our humanity and our ability to express love.

A corollary of Ibn al-Arabi's view of oneness and "manyness" is his belief that the natural order also is like "[many] forms reflected in a single mirror or as a single form reflected in many mirrors."[34] To illustrate that this does not signal a conflict between the forms, he likens them to the limbs of a man, Zaid, noting that

> Zaid is a single personal reality, and that his hand does not look like his foot, head, eye, or eyebrow. In other words he is multiple and single, multiple in form and single in essence, just as man is, without doubt, one in his essence.[35]

In the same way, revealed religion also is one in its essence in spite of its different forms; each "is a path that takes to God, and these paths are diverse." For Ibn al-Arabi, the diversity of paths to God suggests that God's "self-disclosures must be diverse, just as divine gifts are diverse."[36] Thus, by the Qur'anic affirmation "that God has sent a great number of prophets and established many ways to return to Him," he understands that Being "never repeats itself in cosmic self-disclosure, so also it never repeats itself when it sets down ways of guidance." That being so, "revealed religions are diverse because they cannot possibly not be diverse." However, they all denote a single Being, or *wujud*, even though "each is a providential specification of that *wujud* with a view towards human felicity."[37] Another way to put this would be to say that since all of God's self-disclosures reflect the same reality, all our beliefs about this reality have to be equally true.[38] The perfect human being therefore seeks to "worship God in a way that harmonizes with the teachings of every religion" since every religion carries the imprint of God's self-disclosure, albeit in a unique way.

This view of diversity does not, however, keep Ibn al-Arabi from arguing that "all beliefs do not have the same effect on human becoming, and this provides an important criterion for discerning among them." For reasons that it is difficult to summarize here, he argues that Islam is the most conducive to the process of human becoming thus reconciling his belief in the distinctive status of Islam with respect for other religions. However, even as he privileges Islam, Ibn al-Arabi argues that God's mercy (which takes precedence over God's wrath), "demands both religious diversity and human felicity through that diversity."[39] It then follows that "The Reality is more evident in one whose awareness is universal than in one who lacks such universality."[40]

By connecting divine mercy, religious diversity, and universal awareness, Ibn al-Arabi's work provides Islamic universalism its most profoundly spiritual dimensions. In addition, it gives us powerful reasons as Muslims to cultivate a universal consciousness based in respect for difference whatever forms – religious, cultural, racial – it may take.

Conclusion: Contemporary Challenges to Synthesis

Although the preceding discussion has been illustrative rather than exhaustive, it suggests certain lessons that I would like to draw out as a way to address some challenges facing Muslims today.

I have argued that we cannot have a viable synthesis in the absence of better readings of the Qur'an and that, to arrive at such readings, we need different methods of knowledge creation than those we consider "Islamic." As al-Ghazali's work shows, Muslim thinkers have been struggling with this issue for over a millennium but their efforts have borne little fruit largely because the nature and structure of religious (and secular) power and authority in Muslim societies discourage a critique of religious knowledge. For this reason, efforts by many Muslims today to propose new methodologies or new readings of the Qur'an are also likely to remain marginal unless there is a restructuring of Muslim religious and sexual politics and, indeed, a broad-based democratization of Muslim societies. Given the structure of global power, this will depend partly on the policies the US chooses to pursue; its present course of invading Muslim countries is, of course, unlikely to be productive.

I also argued that if we are to promote mutual understanding between "Islam and the West," we will need to reject the Islam/West binary that legitimizes the idea of radical difference and lends credence to the apocryphal view, shared by many Muslim extremists and US secularists, that Islam and the West are fated to clash with one another. This reductive thesis not only demonizes Islam, but also deprives people of agency for, if something is destined to happen, there is nothing we can do about it. As a way partly to contest this radical fatalism, which both overshadows and undermines attempts at mutual coexistence, I drew on the history of the Crusades in order to demonstrate that religious identities as well as views of religious differences were more complex and fluid during medieval times than they seem to be now. In this context, it appears to me – though I have not pursued this point – that the current rigidity towards Islam may have something to do with the rise of secularism in the West and the desire to "fix" identities in the absence of religious certainties. This may sound counterintuitive given that we have been taught to conceive of secular identities as adaptable and of religious as immutable, but I believe this idea merits study.

Ultimately, of course, the onus is on Muslims to evolve a synthesis that embodies the best aspects of our religious and historical traditions which is why I focused on the different sources of Islamic universalism, taking a scriptural and historical approach to the subject. I feel such an exercise is essential for reviving our communal memories in which the most universalistic aspects of Islam's teachings and history seem to have been forgotten or repressed. While many people see this as a failure of Islam itself, as I like to say, religions don't interpret themselves, people do, and it is therefore important to ask who is doing the interpreting, how, and in what particular contexts.

My own view is that misogynistic and violent interpretations of Islam rely on "the tendency of public discourse to make some forms of experience readily available to consciousness while ignoring or suppressing others."[41] This is the Gramscian definition of hegemony though it begs the question of why only certain understandings of Islam have been foregrounded in our consciousnesses while others have been suppressed. We need to address this question not only at an ideological level, but also at the political and economic. I say this both because political and economic conditions in Muslim societies have a great deal to do with how Muslims think and also because I believe that ideology is always "grounded in the forms of our social life"[42] and is, in fact, "a response to certain specific problems posed by reality."[43] It cannot, therefore, be considered in isolation from this reality.

However, in seeking to understand contemporary realities, we ought not to forget the most egalitarian aspects of our history and traditions. Even if certain ideals are no longer manifest in our lived realities, and perhaps never fully were for much of our history, they are nonetheless part of the teachings of our religion and intellectual heritage and can inspire us to develop a better theory and practice of Islam. After all, the task is not only to reconcile practice with theory, but also to create a theory that can inspire the best possible praxis through a process of critical reasoning, or *ijtihad*.

I want now to take a moment to reflect upon the significance of the venue in which the conference on Islamic synthesis is being held. As we know, the Alexandria Library was built by the Ptolemaic pharaohs and was "the center of gravity for the knowledge seekers of the world for many centuries . . . before it was destroyed." To Suroosh Irfani, a lifelong searcher after the truth and one of Pakistan's foremost cultural critics, our presence in this library opens up the question of whether there is a link between the rule of "foreign-origin dynasties" and

> openness to knowledge. After all [he says], if the Ptolemaic dynasty was Greek in origin . . . the Mughal dynasty [in India] and its House of Knowledge for interfaith dialogue under Akbar had Central Asian Turkic origins. And then of course there was Spain with its knowledge friendly Muslim rulers, which made it possible [f]or all those luminaries like Ibn Rushd and Ibn al-Arabi to flourish.

Even the British raj "made India the cradle of a new Islamic religious thinking with Syed Ahmed Khan."

I read Irfani's comments as a defense not of imperialist ventures, but of the "synthesizing impulse running through the ages and blending with historical experience," which is what the noted Muslim philosopher and poet, Muhammad Iqbal, seems to have had in mind when he described "life as a 'forward assimilative movement' full of creative possibilities. Might it not be, then," asks Irfani, that what is "holding back the creative efflorescence of an Islamic synthesis today has something to do with the foreswearing of such an 'assimilative' impulse by a Muslim mindset that has 'barricaded itself in the past to overthrow the future'?"[44]

I ended my original paper for the conference on this note. However, after having written it, I became aware of a silence in it which I want to break now, and this has to do with the fact that we are talking about contemporary Islamic synthesis within the constraints of a closed conference. I wonder if we can derive a real synthesis in such circumstances. I say this knowing that it might well be the closed nature of this space that is allowing my own voice, as a woman, to be heard. Nonetheless, I find it unsettling that my freedom to speak should have had to be so carefully crafted; I feel this especially keenly knowing that millions of Egyptians are having to listen to the same Friday *khutba*[45] in the country's 88,000 mosques. To me, then, the best place to end my intervention on contemporary Islamic synthesis is by pointing to this simultaneous opening up and shutting down of conversations, knowledge, and freedoms.

Notes

1 This is an abridged and revised version of a much longer paper that I submitted before the conference at the Library of Alexandria and it includes some comments from my presentation at the conference itself on October 5, 2003.

2   Brannon Wheeler, *Applying the Canon in Islam: The Authorization and Maintenance of Interpretive Reasoning in Hanafi Scholarship*, Albany, NY: SUNY, 1996, p. 68 and p. 88.

3   Asma Barlas, *"Believing Women" in Islam: Unreading Patriarchal Interpretations of the Qur'an*, Texas: University of Texas Press, 2002.

4   Wheeler, *Applying the Canon in Islam*, p. 237 and p. 226.

5   Ashis Nandy, *The Intimate Enemy*, Delhi: Oxford University Press, 1991, p. xi.

6   Edward Said, *Orientalism*, New York: Vintage, 1979, p. 7; his emphasis.

7   Ibid., p. 17.

8   Ibid., pp. 74–75 and p. 41.

9   Ibid., p. 43 and p. 7.

10   Verse 2:177 in Abdullah Yusuf Ali, *The Holy Qur'an*, New York: Tehrike Tarsile Qur'an, 1988, p. 69.

11   Verses 2:142–143 in Yusuf Ali, *The Qur'an*, p. 57.

12   Jonathan Riley-Smith (ed.), *Oxford Illustrated History of the Crusades*, Oxford: Oxford University Press, 1997, p. 27.

13   See Asma Barlas, *"Believing Women" in Islam: Unreading Patriarchal Interpretations of the Qur'an*, 2002.

14   On Western views of diversity as degenerate, see Naeem Inayatullah and David Blaney, *The Problem of Difference in International Relations*, New York: Routledge, 2003.

15   Verse 49: 13; in Yusuf Ali, *The Qur'an*, 1407.

16   Asma Barlas, *"Believing Women" in Islam* 2002, p. 145.

17   William Chittick, *Imaginal Worlds: Ibn al- 'Arabi and the Problem of Religious Diversity*, Albany, NY: SUNY, 1994, p. 35 and p. 24. However, as Chittick notes, Muslims don't universally hold this view.

18   Nomanul Haq quoted in Sherman Jackson, *On the Boundaries of Theological Tolerance in Islam*, Karachi: Oxford University Press, 2002, p. xi and p. ix.

19   Ibid., p. 4 and p. 5.

20   Ibid., p. xiv.

21   Ibid., p. 32, p. 5 and p. 44.

22   Ibid., p. 85 and p. 89.

23   Ibid., p. 6 and p. 67.

24   Ibid., p. 106.

25   Ibid., p. 59.

26   Ibid., p. 20 and p. 24.

27   Ibid., p. 88.

28   Sufism. See the introduction by R. W. J. Austin, *Ibn Al'Arabi: The Bezels of Wisdom*, Austin, NJ: Paulist Press, 1980.

29   William Chittick, *Imaginal Worlds*, p. 1 and p. 2.

30   Ibid., p. 3, p. 39 and p. 123.

31   Ibid., p. 16, p. 3 and p. 4.

32   Ibid., pp. 125–126.

33   See R. W. J. Austin's commentary in *Ibn Al'Arabi: The Bezels of Wisdom*, p. 27 and pp. 28–29.

34   R. W. J. Austin, *Ibn Al'Arabi: The Bezels of Wisdom*, (trans.) p. 87; brackets in original.

35   Ibid., p. 232.

36   William Chittick, *Imaginal Worlds*, p. 160.

37   Ibid., p. 156.

38   Ibid., p. 165.

39   Ibid., p. 165 and p. 156.

40   Ibid., p. 191.

41   T. J. Jackson Lears, "The Concept of Cultural Hegemony: Problems and Possibilities," *American History Review*, pp. 90:3 (1985) (567–593), p. 577.

42   J. Mepham, quoted in Asma Barlas, *Democracy, Nationalism, and Communalism: the Colonial Legacy in South Asia*, Boulder: Westview Press, 1995, p. 33.

43 Antonio Gramsci, *Selections from the Prison Notebooks*, New York: International Publishers, 1971, p. 324.
44 Suroosh Irfani, private correspondence, September 14, 2003. Irfani attributes the last quote to Mohammed Arkoun.
45 The address delivered by the imam at the end of the Friday prayer.

Index

Universalistic School of Law in Islam 25, 28;
arguments from Qur'an and the Hadith
39; category of *adamiyyah* and 37; disbelief will be punished by God 38;
expanded beyond Hanafi School 35; inviolability to humanity 34–9;
non-Muslims who accept authority of
Islamic state (the *dhimmis*) 40
universalist position, characterized by two
features 29
universalists, coalition of may establish inviolability of the Other 46; constitute a
single group, share same universalistic
values to the Other 25; not only member
of Muslim *Ummah* but also humanity 40;
"value rationality" from different societies, respect for the Other's inviolability
28; we/they line inconsequential as far as
basic human rights concerned 29
Universalist School, arguments from Qur'an
and the Hadith 30

"Verdicts of the Major Scholars Regarding
Hijackings & Suicide Bombings" 196
Vico, Giambattista, *aequum bonum* of 97;
alternative modernity and channeled into
concerns by Asad 96; *Diritto universale*
("Universal law") 91; meaning of asylum
as civic institution antecedent of the
"city" 94; need to situate himself in the
sensus communis (common sense) of
commoners 92, 100n13; only dealing
with otherness can vindicate public
reasoning 93, 100n19; reconstruction of
natural law requires genealogical method
92–3; Roman law and 94; *Scienza nuova*
("new Science") 89–91, 93, 100n10
Victoria, Francisco de 92
violence 173–4; armed is one way of
managing political conflicts 179; distinguished by its instrumental character
206, 208, 211n77; secular in France,
United States, China and Russia 178
virgin sacrifice to the Nile (Egypt), not
allowed under Islamic law 42
Voegelin, Eric, reciprocally schismatic
formations of modern nation-states 87

waaf (institution which handles assistance to
the poor) 144
Wadud, Amina, talk on Islam, Qur'an and
the Female Voice 113
Wahhabi movement (Saudi Arabia) 69, 120

Wahid, Abdurrahman (President of
Indonesia) 237
Wal-mart 123
waqf, contributing to a voluntary charity
144
war between two societies, Palestinian/Israeli
or Muslim/non-Muslim 201
"war and peace" group of scholars, does not
associate Islam with violence or expansion 137–8
wasatya (middle Islamic discourse), needed
to created global peace 179, 186
Washington DC 9/11 1
Wasiyah (will) 144
Weber, Max 54, 62n13
Wertheim, W.F. *Indonesian Society in
Transition* 233
West, believes East should imitate West in
everything 21; contemporary societies
limit expression to TV mass culture 222;
the Other and 24; pressures on Muslim
World and 174; rigidity towards Islam,
desire to "fix" identities in absence of
religious certainties 250; universalists in
cannot succeed if Muslim extremists
continue attacking their societies 28
Western culture, represented in "conventional" equations 66
Westerners, view non-Western cases of political suicide "culturally pathological" 204
Westerners and Muslims, levels different but
ignorance shared by all 223
Western Europe, colonialism the main agent
of the view of Islam as a "culture" in need
95
Western legal thought, universalism and
communalism coexist as two rivals 33
Western media reports, violent and aggressive images of Islam 131, 166n4
Western peacebuilding, forgiveness and
reconciliation central values and practices
153, 170n68
Western political practices, detrimental to
Islamic values and interests 13
Western scholars, apply "reformist" label to
Islam 65–6; peace defined as "absence" of
particular conditions 7; simplistic "good
Muslim"/"bad Muslim" 5; use term *jihad*
referring to waging aggressive war 181
"we/they" line 26, 29; separates the Self from
the Other 29, 45
"white man's burden", task of civilizing non-
Europe 87
Woodward, Mark R. 233, 239n16